SCIENCE in the MARKETPLACE

Florence G. Korchin

Tiger Publications, Inc.
32 Friendship Court
Red Bank, NJ   07701
908-747-9042

LIBRARY OF CONGRESS CATALOG
CARD NUMBER 83-071013

Copyright © **1995**, 1992, 1987, 1986, 1983, F. G. Korchin

5th Edition 1995   ISBN 0-9611318-5-3
4th Edition 1992   ISBN 0-9611318-3-7

Published by Tiger Publications, Inc.
Printed in USA

To my parents

PREFACE

Much of our everyday world revolves around the marketplace. Among the items we purchase are food, medicines, transportation, and housing. When we are not purchasing or using products, we are being assaulted by advertisements for them.

In **SCIENCE IN THE MARKETPLACE,** consumer items are evaluated and consumer concerns discussed. However the emphasis is not on actual product selection, rather it stresses basic knowledge for informed spending. This requires simple mathematics and leads to a strengthening of evaluative skills. A variety of hands-on experiences are provided. Some require laboratory apparatus which would be readily available wherever science courses are taught.

Therefore, **SCIENCE IN THE MARKETPLACE** is a text and laboratory manual for a one year course in physical science, consumer chemistry, practical chemistry or contemporary science, depending on which topics are chosen. It presumes no science or mathematics background on the part of the reader. But readers with science backgrounds will also find the text informative.

A teacher's manual is available. It contains a suggested course outline, a list of lab materials, and answers to the questions in the book.

It is the hope of the author that this book will awaken an interest in science, provide an understanding of its methods, and be of value to the consumer.

ACKNOWLEDGEMENTS

I wish to thank my colleagues at Middlesex County College for their enthusiastic support of the course and the text.

My thanks go to Dr. Bernard Kauderer for his encouragement. My admiration to Dr. Stephen Kowalski for having led the way. My appreciation to my editor, Robert Woolf, for his tact and technical skill. The illustrations drawn by Virginia Asman and Denise Satter enliven the text. My great esteem for the abilities of the typists, Joan Utrecht and Darlene Barnes.

The suggestions made by Ellen Wallen, Clayton High School; Evelyn P. Russo, Christ the King Regional High School; Cynthia Page, Palmyra Adult Education School; Donald Kruck and James Cimmino, Bergen County Vocational and Technical High School; Peter Guastella, Great Neck North Senior High School; Leonard Koupiaris, Bound Brook High School; Anthony J. Tabeek, New Milford High School; Dan Ajerman, Tottenville High School, NY.; and Robert Pursley, Vancleave High School, MS. are greatly appreciated.

My eternal gratitude to Herb and my family for their confidence and assistance.

F. G. Korchin

CONTENTS

LAB EXPERIENCES

FIGURES

TABLES

APPENDICES

PROLOGUE

SCIENTIFIC METHOD

Scientists in every country use a system of five steps to guide them in understanding our world. This system is called the scientific method. The steps require observation and experimentation which are carried out under controlled conditions. The steps are:

1. Observation
2. Statement of Problem
3. Hypothesis
4. Experiment
5. Verification

1. OBSERVATION: The scientist sees an event which needs an explanation.

2. STATEMENT OF PROBLEM: This should be a clear statement of the event which has been observed and the conditions under which the observation has been made. This is important since the events which follow depend on a precise understanding of the problem.

3. HYPOTHESIS: This is an educated guess. It includes all known facts and describes a possible answer to the problem. The hypothesis, like the statement of the problem, must be clear and testable. That is, it must be possible to find a way to test the truth of the hypothesis using known methods.

4. EXPERIMENT: This is the test of the hypothesis. Experiments are performed and data collected. The experiment should include a control and a variable. The control acts as a standard for comparison while the variable is what is being tested. Since the control and variable are being tested at the same time and under the same conditions, it is possible to come to some conclusion about the truth of the hypothesis.

5. VERIFICATION: Other scientists must be able to repeat the experiment with the same results under the same conditions. This makes it possible to check the accuracy of the experiment and the truth of the conclusions. Scientists practice the scientific method as they work. We all unconsciously apply some, or even all, of the five steps as we make everyday decisions.

SAFETY PRECAUTIONS

Safety in the science class is all important. It is essential that you think, exercise caution, avoid fooling around, and follow directions.

Here are 8 rules to follow when you are in the science lab:

1. Read each assigned activity carefully before beginning. Note each CAUTION.

2. Wear safety glasses whenever a lab experience involving chemicals or special equipment is being performed.

3. Use care in handling glassware.

4. Do not point a test tube that is being heated at yourself or at any other person. Do not look directly into a test tube in which a reaction is occurring.

5. Whenever an activity involves chemicals that give off fumes, make sure the room is well ventilated.

6. If any chemical solution should splash into your eyes or on your skin, wash the affected area with plenty of water. Report the accident to your teacher immediately.

7. Report any accident or injury to the teacher immediately.

8. Do not perform any unauthorized activities.

SAFETY GLASSES

UNIT 1

MATHEMATICS

THE METRIC SYSTEM

Through the ages man has learned to communicate with his neighbors by developing a common language. The language of measurement was first imposed regionally by the reigning monarch, and then internationally by far-sighted men like Napoleon. He decreed that the metric system was to be used in all of the lands under French control. The metric system was applied to all sorts of measurements, i.e., money, land measure, dry measure, and liquid measure. We use the metric system in physics, chemistry, and biology and because these sciences are described by a common language called mathematics. It too uses the metric system.

We have all handled money and we know that 10 pennies make up a dime and 10 dimes make up a dollar. That's the metric system. It's a decimal system based on tens and hundreds. We've used it all our lives but didn't know to call it "metric".

We will proceed to explain area, volume, weight, mass, and density. Then we will do a lab experiment where we will draw a scale floor plan of the classroom and three lab experiments to determine the mass, volume, and density of both regular and irregularly shaped objects.

We will discuss the Universal Product Code and unit pricing. After some practice in unit pricing, there is a laboratory experience comparing commercial foods with regular foods using unit price and cost per serving.

Let us begin.

AREA

It is possible to describe an object by determining several things about it. Now suppose we want to carpet a room from wall to wall. The room measures 10 feet long and 12 feet wide. Since carpeting is sold in square yards (yds²) or square meters (m²), we must do some conversions and calculations to know how much carpeting to buy. Notice we can use the symbols (' and " respectively) as a mathematical shorthand for feet and inches. The room dimension are:

Length: $10' = 120''$
Width: $12' = 144''$

We know that:
1 ft = 12 inches ($1' = 12''$)
$1'' = 2.54$ centimeters (cm). For our purposes we will use 2.5 cm.
1 meter (m) = 100 cm

LENGTH

There are 12 inches in 1 foot. How many inches are there in 10 feet?

1. $\dfrac{12''}{1'} = \dfrac{X''}{10'}$

$$X = (10)(12); \quad X = 120''$$

Further, if there are 2.5 cm in 1 inch, then how many centimeters are there in 120 inches?

2. $\dfrac{2.5 \text{ cm}}{1''} = \dfrac{X \text{ cm}}{120''}$

$$X = (120)(2.5)$$
$$X = 300 \text{ cm}$$

Since there are 100 cm in 1 meter, then,

3. $\dfrac{100 \text{ cm}}{1 \text{ m}} = \dfrac{300 \text{ cm}}{X \text{ m}}$

$$(300)(1) = 100(X)$$

$$\dfrac{300}{100} = X \text{ m}$$

then X $= 3$ m

WIDTH

How many inches are there in 12'? See 1. for method.

$$X = 144''$$

How many centimeters are there in 144"? See 2. for method.

$$X = 360 \text{ cm}$$

How many meters are there in 360 cm? See 3. for method.

$$X = 3.6 \text{ m}$$

Now we know that 10 ft is equal to 300 cm which is equal to 3 m, and 12 ft is equal to 360 cm which is equal to 3.6 m.

Wall to wall carpeting means covering the entire floor, or the area of the room. The area is length times width. (A = 1 × w). If the length is 3 m and the width is 3.6 m, then the area is 10.8 m². Note that meters times meters equals meters squared (m²).

If the carpeting comes in four meter widths, we could buy a three meter length of the carpeting. A three meter length times a four meter width is equal to 12 square meters and we would accomplish what we set out to do. We would even have a nice piece of carpet left over which could be bound with tape and used as a carpet runner somewhere else in the house.

VOLUME

Now that we have the floor carpeted, how about filling the room from floor to ceiling and from wall to wall with cartons? This wouldn't mean anything except that we could then determine the amount of space, or the volume, these cartons would take up. Assume that the room is 8' high. Use Figure 1.1 to refresh your memory and do the calculations for converting the depth of 8 feet to meters.

DEPTH

Depth is the third dimension of volume. We have already calculated the length as

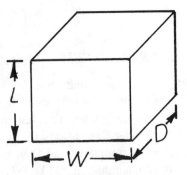

Figure 1.1 *Definition of Volume*

being 3 m, and the width as being 3.6 m. All that remains to be calculated is depth.

$$\frac{12''}{1 \text{ ft.}} = \frac{X''}{8'}$$

$$X = (12)(8); \quad X = 96''$$

$$\frac{1''}{2.5 \text{ cm}} = \frac{96''}{X \text{ cm}}$$

$$X = (96)(2.5); \quad X = 240 \text{ cm}$$

$$\frac{1 \text{ m}}{100 \text{ cm}} = \frac{X \text{ m}}{240 \text{ cm}}$$

$$100X = 240; \quad X = 2.4 \text{ m}$$

Depth: 8' = 96" = 240 cm = 2.4 m

Well, volume is the product of length, width, and depth (or height). The answer comes out in cubic units such as cubic meters (m³). Note that meters × meters × meters equals meters cubed (m³).

Assume that the volume of each carton is 1 m³. How many cartons are needed to fill the room? A carton measuring 1 m³ means that its dimensions are 1 m long, 1 m wide, and 1 m high. We might have to cut one of the cartons down a bit.

In another example, assume that we have a quart container of milk and want to drink a glass of it. A single serving of milk would be 8 ounces. Take a measuring cup that is marked, or calibrated, in ounces and pour 8 ounces of the milk. That's liquid volume read in ounces (English system of measurement), but there are measuring cups and graduated cylinders calibrated in milliliters and liters (metric system). Keep in mind that 1 liter = 1000 milliliters. If we poured the 8 fluid ounces of milk into a metric measuring cup it would read close to 250 ml.

Suppose we had to find the volume of an irregularly-shaped object. That is, one that didn't have regular sides and couldn't be measured with a ruler. Remember that volume is the amount of space an object takes up. To find this object's volume, carefully place it into a calibrated container filled with water, and see how much space the object takes up when it pushes the water out of its way. The water displaced would be exactly equal to the volume of the object and the amount could be measured in milliliters. When measuring a liquid with a graduated cylinder or graduated beaker keep in mind that water, as with most liquids, will tend to creep up the sides of the container and dip slightly in the center of the liquid surface. This condition is referred to as the meniscus of the liquid. To correctly read the liquid level in the graduated container, it is necessary to stand directly in front of the container and with the eye at the level of the liquid, read the lowest point of the level.

Methods for measuring the volume of irregularly shaped objects are shown in Figure 1.2.

WEIGHT vs MASS

Here on earth we say that weight and mass are describing the same thing, but the scientist knows that there is a difference between the two terms.

WEIGHT

Weight is described in pounds (English system) or in newtons (metric system). Weight is entirely dependent upon the pull of gravity. When you hop on the bathroom scale in the morning to "weigh yourself", you are really ascertaining the effect, or the pull, of gravity upon you. Now you may or may not be happy by what the scale reads, but that is a topic to be discussed later on.

Should you weigh yourself on the very same scale while on the moon or even in outer space, you would get an entirely different reading. The pull of the moon's gravity is only 1/6 that of earth, and you'd find that your weight on the moon would be only

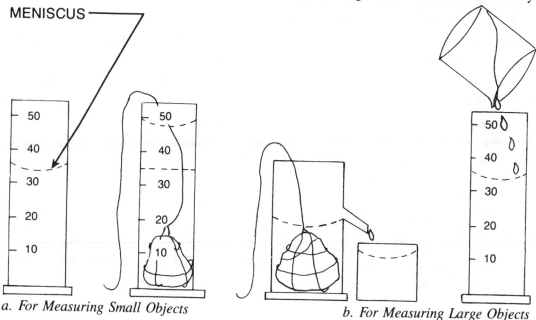

MENISCUS

a. For Measuring Small Objects

b. For Measuring Large Objects

Figure 1.2   Water Displacement

17% of what you weighed on earth. In outer space, you would be virtually weightless. Of course it wouldn't be convenient to get yourself weighed regularly on the moon or in outer space, so I guess you'll just have to go along with your earth weight. Ah, me . . . .

MASS

Mass, described in kilograms or grams, gives the amount of matter contained in an object. This quantity remains constant regardless of where we are located, whether here on earth or in outer space. Keep in mind that 1 kilogram is equal to 1000 grams.

The scientist must include the effect of gravity on an object's mass, and in his work always states that weight is equal to mass times gravity. However, since all our experience will take place here on earth, let us assume that gravity remains constant. For our purposes weight and mass will be used interchangeably, and we will use the gram or the kilogram to describe what we are talking about.

DENSITY

The density of a large object can be determined by taking a small sample from the large object. Since density is the ratio of mass to volume, then this relationship between the mass and the volume will be the same for the large object as well as for the small sample.

$$\text{Density (g/cm}^3) = \frac{\text{mass (g)}}{\text{volume (cm}^3)}$$

Note: Measurement units must be consistent. Mass units of grams (g) go with volume units of cubic centimeters (cm³) or cubic millimeters (mm³) or the milliliter (ml); while kilograms (kg) go with cubic meters (m³) or the liter (l). Remember 1 g = 1 cm³ = 1 ml, and 1 kg = 1 m³ = 1 l.

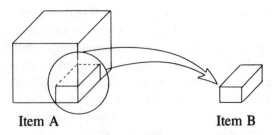

Item A   Item B

Figure 1.3   *Two Blocks, Same Density*

Item A weighs 50g and is regular in shape. If we multiply length × width × depth we find:

$$\text{Volume} = 2.5\text{cm} \times 2.5\text{cm} \times 2.5\text{cm}$$
$$= 15.625\text{cm}^3$$

Note that 2.5cm = 25mm
$$= 15,625\text{mm}^3$$

$$\text{Density} = \frac{\text{Mass}}{\text{Volume}}$$

$$= \frac{50 \text{ g}}{15.625 \text{ cm}^3}$$

$$= 3.198\text{g/cm}^3$$

or 3.2g/cm³ (rounded off)

Also: $\text{Density} = \dfrac{50 \text{ g}}{15,624 \text{ mm}^3}$
$$= 0.0032\text{g/mm}^3$$

Item B weighs 0.21 g, and it is a sample from Item A. If we multiply length × width × depth, we find:

$$\text{Volume} = 4\text{mm} \times 4\text{mm} \times 4\text{mm}$$
$$= 64\text{mm}^3$$

$$\text{Density} = \frac{\text{Mass}}{\text{Volume}}$$

$$= \frac{0.21\text{g}}{64\text{mm}^3}$$

$$= 0.0032\text{g/mm}^3$$

The density is the same for both the large object and the small sample. This physical property called density can thereby be used as an identification test.

LAB EXPERIENCE 1.1

MEASUREMENTS — LINEAR

Purpose: To make a floor plan using a meter stick.

Materials:

Metric ruler
Meter stick
8.5" x 11" Graph paper
Pencil

Procedure:

1. Measure the size of the classroom.

2. Use a scale of 1 meter = 4 cm.

3. Lay out classroom on paper using the metric ruler.

4. On bottom of sheet, write the scale you are using.

5. Draw the exact location of windows, doors, wall mounted closets, cabinets, sinks, etc.

6. Draw the location and size of moveable furniture (desks, chairs, cabinets, etc.)

7. Measure the size of each item in Steps 5 and 6 and be sure to draw them to scale on your floor plan. Drawing to scale means representing an item by a reduced measurement of size.

8. Show location of electric switches and wall sockets.

9. When completed the plan should represent the room.

Questions:

1. What is the largest unit on a meter stick?

2. What is the smallest unit on a meter stick?

3. What is the relationship between the largest and the smallest units?

LAB EXPERIENCE 1.1 (Continued)
MEASUREMENTS — LINEAR

4. If 4 cm = 1 m, what is the proportion or ratio of the plan to the room?

5. From wall to wall, how many square meters are there in the room?

6. If carpeting comes in rolls 3 m wide, how long must the roll of carpeting be to cover the floor of your room?

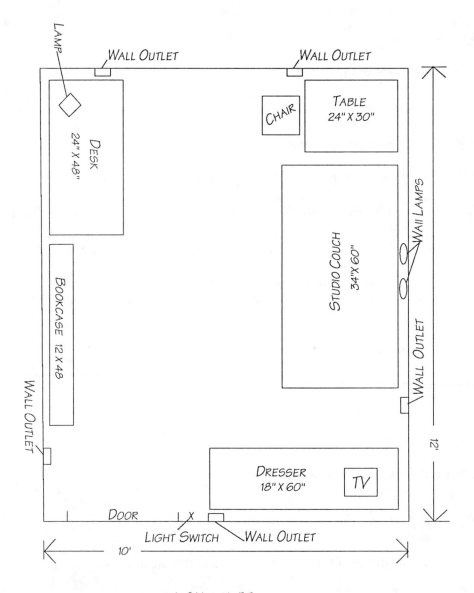

1 CM = 1 FT.

LAB EXPERIENCE 1.2

MEASUREMENT — MASS

Purpose: To learn how to use a balance.

Materials:

Double pan balance
Set of weights
250 ml Beaker
50 ml Graduated cylinder

General Directions:

1. The double pan balance is an instrument for determining weight. (Remember our discussion about weight and mass.)

2. The instrument sits on knife edges that are not visible to you. Therefore, it is important not to drop any heavy objects on the balance pans since this might knock the instrument off balance.

3. The object to be weighed is placed on the left pan. The weights are added to the right pan until the pointer swings freely.

4. Slowly move the slide until the pointer swings an equal distance on either side of the center point. The slide reading is taken on the left side of the slide. It is not necessary for the pointer to completely stop swinging before taking the reading.

5. A beam balance is an instrument used to weigh materials. The material to be weighed is placed in the left pan and is compared to a sum of masses which are placed on the right pan plus the mass indicated by the slide of the balance. Since the balance, masses, and object being weighed are all under the same influence of gravity, we may correctly refer to this process as the weighing of the object.

Procedure:

1. Place the beaker on the left pan. Add sufficient masses and adjust the slide to determine the weight of the empty beaker. Enter on data chart below.

2. Measure 20 ml of tap water in the graduated cylinder. Remember to read the meniscus level. Carefully add the water to the beaker. Adjust the weights and enter the reading on the chart.

3. Repeat Step 2 adding 20 ml of water each time until a total of 100 ml of water have been added to the beaker. Enter the reading on the chart each time you add water.

LAB EXPERIENCE 1.2 (Continued)

MEASUREMENT — MASS

	Mass Beaker (g)	Mass Beaker with Water (g)	Mass Water (ml)
50-ml Beaker + 20 ml			
+ 40 ml			
+ 60 ml			
+ 80 ml			
+100 ml			

Questions:

1. What is the weight of 1 ml of water?

2. What is the weight of 1 liter of water?

Suggested Activities:

1. Invite a representative of the State's Bureau of Weights and Measures to talk to the class.

2. Compare the accuracy of weighing devices such as a digital scale, a balance beam scale, and a spring scale.

3. Have students bring in household scales and determine accuracy.

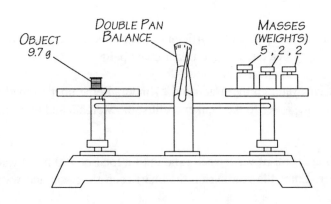

LAB EXPERIENCE 1.3
MEASUREMENT — POPCORN

Purpose: To determine the mass of popcorn before and after heating.

Materials:

Hot plate
Hot mitts
Balance
Safety glasses
500 ml Erlenmeyer flask with cotton plug
200 g popcorn
100 ml cooking oil

Procedure:

1. Weigh the flask empty.

2. Weigh and count the number of kernels in 15 g of popcorn.

3. Determine the average mass of a single kernel of corn. Record on data chart below.

4. Put sufficient cooking oil in the Erlenmeyer flask to just cover the bottom of the container. Weigh the flask and oil, and record on chart below.

5. Add the popcorn, and loosely close the flask with the cotton plug. Weigh the flask with the oil and popcorn, and record on chart below.

6. Place the flask and contents on the hot plate which is maintained at medium high heat.

7. Using a hot mitt, shake the flask every 5 minutes when the popping begins and continue until it ceases. Weigh the flask and contents.

8. Determine the mass of the total "popped" corn and find the average mass of a single piece of "popped" corn. Record on data chart.

9. Before eating the popcorn, answer the questions below.

10. After eating all the popcorn, weigh flask and any unpopped kernels.

LAB EXPERIENCE 1.3 (Continued)

MEASUREMENT — POPCORN

Material	Mass (g)
Flask	
Flask + oil	
Flask + oil + corn	
Unpopped corn	
Single kernel (average)	
"Popped" corn	
Single kernel "popped" corn	
Flask + unpopped corn	

Questions:

1. How does the mass of the corn compare before and after popping?

2. How does the volume compare before and after popping?

3. Is there any similarity in the ratio of the mass of a single corn kernel before and after popping to the total masses?

4. What causes corn to "pop"?

5. Why do you add oil to flask or frying pan but not to a hot-air popper?

Suggested Activities:

1. Library research on calorie count of popcorn and the healthiest way to prepare popcorn. List references.

2. Research on the way that the hot-air popper works to make popcorn.

LAB EXPERIENCE 1.4

MASS, VOLUME, DENSITY

Purpose: To determine the mass, volume and density for both regular and irregularly-shaped objects.

Materials:

Balance   2 Wooden blocks
Metric ruler   3 Stone fragments
Graduated beaker   Water supply

Procedure: Use the following methods to determine each aspect of the experiment.

Mass: This is the amount of matter that goes to make up an object. Recall that on earth, this is found by weighing the object. The answer is given in grams or kilograms.

Volume: This is the amount of space the object takes up. If found directly by measuring with a metric ruler, the answer is in cubic millimeters (mm^3), cubic centimeters (cm^3), or cubic meters (m^3).   Since volume is three-dimensional, then volume = length x width x height, and the answer must reflect these three dimensions. If volume is found indirectly, by using the displacement of water method, then the answer is given in milliliters or liters. The object is pushing the water out of its way and you are reading the amount of water displaced. The answer is in milliliters or liters.

Density: This is the ratio of mass to volume. The answer will be in grams/ cubic centimeter (g/cm^3), kilograms/cubic meter (kg/m^3) or grams/ milliliter (g/ml), kilograms/liter (**kg/L**).   Since one cubic centimeter is equal to one milliliter, this relationship is possible.

MASS, VOLUME AND DENSITY DATA CHART

Sample	Weight (g)	Volume (cm^3 or ml)	Density (g/cm^3 or g/ml)
Block 1			
Block 2			
Stone 1			
Stone 2			
Stone 3			

LAB EXPERIENCE 1.5

PROBLEMS IN MASS, VOLUME, DENSITY

Purpose: To solve problems in mass, volume, and density.

1. Find the density of a piece of metal whose mass in 4200 grams and whose volume is 750 cm^3. (Answer: 5.60 g/cm^3).

2. A block of material has been sold as pure aluminum. It weighs 6250 g and measures 40 cm long, 10 cm wide, and 5 cm high. What is its density in g/cm^3? The density of pure aluminum is 2.7g/cm^3. Is this pure aluminum?

3. Find the unknown in each line:

Density	Mass	Volume
5g/cm^3	_____	30 cm^3
8g/cm^3	15 g	_____
_____	3 kg	2 L

4. How would you measure the volume of a potato?

5. If the stone fragments from the lab experiment were from a statue weighing 100 kg, what would be the volume of this statue?

Suggested Activity

1. Measure areas for carpeting.

2. Measure windows for shutters, drapes or curtains.

3. FILM: The Metric Film.

REVIEW OF DEFINITIONS

In summation, it is possible to evaluate an object in terms of size by determining several facts about it.

1. This may be accomplished by finding the *area*. Area is an object's length times its width (A = 1 × w). Answers are given in m², cm², mm².

2. It may be accomplished by finding the *volume*. The volume of an object is its length times it width times its height or depth (V = 1 × w × h). Volume is the amount of space an object takes up. Answers are given in m³, cm³, mm³.

3. To find the area or volume of a regularly-shaped object, you would use a meter stick or ruler.

4. To find liquid volume, you would use a graduated cylinder or measuring cup. Answers given in milliters (ml) or liters (L).

5. To find the volume of an irregularly-shaped object, you would carefully lower the object into a container filled with water to see how much water the object pushes out of its way, or displaces. The object must be completely submerged. The displaced water would be equal to the volume of the object. Answers given in milliliter (ml) or liter (l). 1 liter = 1000 ml.

6. It is possible to determine an object's size in terms of its *weight*. Weight depends on the mass of the object, but also depends on the gravitational force acting upon the object.

7. It is possible to determine an object's size by finding its *mass*. Mass describes the amount of matter that goes to make up the object. The mass of an object is a constant property which does not depend on its location. Answers are given in kilograms or grams. 1 kg = 1000 g.

8. to find the weight or the mass of an object, you would weigh it, or mass it, on a scale or balance.

9. The *density* of an object is the relationship of its mass to its volume.

$$\text{DENSITY} = \frac{\text{Mass}}{\text{Volume}}$$

Answers given in $\frac{\text{kg}}{\text{m}^3}$

or $\frac{\text{g}}{\text{cm}^3}$ or $\frac{\text{kg}}{\text{L}}$ or $\frac{\text{g}}{\text{ml}}$

METRIC MEASUREMENTS

The metric system is based on the decimal system of numbers which involves multiples of 10. Therefore, it is very easy to go from small units to large units, or vice versa, by simply moving a decimal point.

The basic metric units that the consumer will see on nutrition labels are grams (units of mass or weight) and liters (units of volume). Once the basic unit is determined, whether it is grams or liters, other multiples are built onto it with suitable prefixes. Whenever the prefix "kilo" precedes a unit, it is 1000 times that unit. One kilogram is equal to 1000 grams. The prefix "milli" indicates one-thousandth and "micro" one-millionth of the basic unit. A milligram is one-thousandth of one gram. A microgram is one-millionth of one gram.

It may help to memorize these approximate equivalencies:

One ounce = approximately 28 grams
Three and one-half ounces = 100 grams
Eight ounces = 227 grams
One pound = 454 grams

To convert the metric system into the system to which we Americans are more accustomed, the English system:

1 kilogram = 2.2 pounds
1 pound = 454 grams
1 ounce = approximately 28 grams
1 liter = 1,000 milliliters
A liter is a little larger than a quart.
1 kiloliter = 1,000 liters

To translate the system we currently use into the metric:

1 gallon = 3.79 liters
1 quart = 0.95 liters
   or 950 milliliters or approximately
   1 liter
1 pint = 0.48 liters
   or 480 milliliters or approximately
   500 ml
1 cup (8 fluid ounces) = 0.24 liters
   or 240 milliliters or approximately
   250 ml
1 tablespoon = 15 milliliters
1 teaspoon = 5 milliliters

METRIC MEASURES ON NUTRITION LABELS

One of the first things to be noticed on the new nutrition information food labels shown in Figure 1.4 is that metric units are used throughout. These are the measuring units used in most of the world.

The U.S. Food and Drug Administration prescribed the metric system for nutrition labels because the unit we are most accustomed to, the ounce, is too large to conveniently describe the amounts of nutrients in foods. For instance, 1 gram is about equal to the weight of a paper clip. If a food contains 9 grams of protein, then expressing this in our customary terms, it would be 9/28 ounce. This is just an example of how customary measurements used for food composition would not only be very small but appear as confusing fractions, and we cer-

```
XXXXX Very Young & Tender Sweet Peas
Net Wt:  17 oz. (1 lb. 1 oz); 482 grams
Weight of Peas:  10¼ oz.

Ingredients:  Peas, water, sugar, syrup and salt

            Nutrition Information Per Serving

Serving Size:  1 cup
Servings per Container:    Approx. 2
Calories:  120              Carbohydrate:  23 grams
Protein:  7 grams           Fat:  1 gram

        Percentage of Recommended Daily Allowance (U.S. RDA)

Protein  . . . . . .   10      Riboflavin . . . . . .  10
Vitamin A . . . . .    20      Niacin . . . . . . . .   8
Vitamin C . . . . .    30      Calcium  . . . . . . .   2
Thiamine . . . . . .   15      Iron . . . . . . . . .  10

XXXX, YYYYY, & ZZZZ Inc.
Chicago, IL  60604 Distr.
Made in U.S.A.
```

Figure 1.4 *A Typical Label Showing Nutrition Information*

tainly don't want to be confused at this point.

Metric units of volume may appear in the serving size for liquid foods as well as in the container's net volume. The upper portion of the label will use weight metric units as grams for protein, carbohydrate, and fat in a single serving of food.

The lower portion of the nutrition information panel gives the percentage of the U.S. Recommended Daily Allowance (U.S. RDA) for protein, vitamins, and minerals in a single serving. It does not require any understanding of the metric system.

UNIVERSAL PRODUCT CODE

The *Universal Product Code (UPC)* shown in Figure 1.5 is a series of closely spaced lines, bars and numbers which is scanned and read by a laser beam. The message is sent to the store's computer which identifies the item and "rings" it up on the computer terminal at the checkout counter. It also prints a description of the item and the price on the customer's receipt.

The UPC symbol contains information about the name, the manufacturer, and the size of the product. The UPC can provide information for the store's computer in the areas of inventory, which products are moving fastest, how much money should be in the cash register at any time, and the amount of sales handled by each clerk.

Supermarkets claim that universal prod-

uct codes will eliminate the need for each item in the store to be individually marked with a price, and would thereby result in lower prices and savings for the customer. However, customers will find it more difficult to do price comparisons. Often shelf prices do not correspond to the items above them. Therefore, without the price on the item, it is not possible to know how much it cost without a register receipt. Many organizations, including the Consumer Federations of America have been fighting to continue item pricing. For the moment they have been successful.

Figure 1.5 *Universal Product Code*

UNIT PRICING

Unit pricing is the cost per unit of the item. For example, for an item weighing 50 grams and costing 25¢, the unit price would be 25¢/50g or 0.5¢/g. Unit pricing enables you to compare the cost per quantity, and make a decision as to what size or package is the best buy. Complete the following chart. Note the given example.

LAB EXPERIENCE 1.6

UNIT PRICE COMPARISON

Purpose: To calculate the unit price of groceries.

Item	Ounces	Grams	List Price	Unit Price Per Pound	Unit Price Per Gram
Corn Flakes	18 oz.		$ 2.39		
	12 oz.		$ 1.49	$ 1.99	
	8 oz.		0.45		
	6 oz. (8 indiv. pkg., 3/4 oz. each)		0.83		
Canned Tomatoes	8 oz.		$ 0.35		
	17 oz.		0.55		
	16 oz.		0.59		
	28 oz.		0.65		
	35 oz.		0.79		

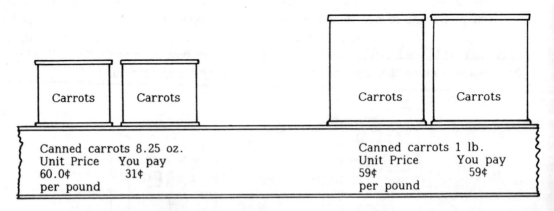

Figure 1.6 *Typical Unit Price Labels*

LAB. EXPERIENCE 1.7

UNIT PRICING PROBLEMS

Complete the following exercises:

UNIT PRICING is the ratio of cost to quantity. Another way to say this is that unit pricing is the cost of one of something.

1. A cook buys 10 pounds of potatoes for 95 cents. What is the cost in cents per pound?

2. A customer bought a 15 oz box of raisin bran for $1.47. What is the unit price in cents per ounce?

3. A customer bought a 12 oz package of oat flakes for $1.27. What is the unit price in cents per ounce? Round to the nearest hundreth of a cent.

4. Which has the lower unit price? A 14 oz can of baked beans selling for 39 cents or a 1 pound, 15 oz can for 63 cents?

5. Which has the lower unit price? A 12 fluid oz can of apple juice for 36 cents or a 1 qt, 14 fluid oz for $1.40? Note: 1 qt = 32 fluid ounces.

6. The fabric for a dress costs $33.25 for 3.5 yds. What is the cost per yard?

7. A 13 oz can of coffee costs $2.79. What is the unit price in cents per oz?

8. A 1 1/4 lb container of cottage cheese costs $1.35. Find the unit price in dollars per pound.

9. Which has the lower unit price: Brand A Chili Sauce, 12 oz for 59 cents or Brand B, 16 oz for 81 cents?

10. A 6 lb bottle of glue costs $4.38. Find the unit price.

11. A 6-bottle carton of 12 fluid oz bottles of soda pop costs $2.49. What is the unit price in cents per fluid ounce? Round to the nearest hundreth of a cent.

12. A 2/3 pound package of cheese costs $1.69. Find the unit price in dollars per pound. Round to the nearest hundreth of a dollar.

Complete the following exercises on unit pricing. What are the unit prices? Which has the lower unit price per category?

13.   Napkins
    Brand A: 140 napkins for 61 cents
    Brand B: 125 napkins for 44 cents

LAB EXPERIENCE 1.7 (Continued)

UNIT PRICING PROBLEMS

14. Tomato Juice
   Brand A: 89 cents for 1 qt, 14 fluid oz
   Brand B: 25 cents for 18 oz

15. Soap
   Brand A: $1.00 for 3 bars
   Brand B: $1.29 for 4 bars

16. Fancy Tuna
   Brand A: $1.29 for 7 oz
   Brand B: $3.96 for 1 lb, 8 oz

17. Soda Pop
   Box A: Six 16 fluid oz bottles for $3.49
   Box B: Eight 16 oz bottles for $4.49

18. Evaporated Milk
   Brand A: 46 cents for 13 oz
   Brand B: $1.10 for 1 qt, 8 oz

19. Vegetable Soup
   Brand A: 14 oz for 39 cents
   Brand B: 11 oz for 37 cents

20. Flour
   Brand A: $1.25 for 3 lb, 2 oz
   Brand B: $0.99 for 28 oz

21. Preserves
   Jar A: $2.48 for 1 kilogram
   Jar B: $3.49 for 1.5 kilograms

22. An 8 pound shankless ham contains 36 servings of meat. How many servings per pound?

23. A 12 pound boneless rib roast contains 30 servings of meat. How many servings per pound?

LAB EXPERIENCE 1.8

COST vs CONVENIENCE

Purpose: To determine the high price of convenience foods.

Procedures:

1. Examine several convenience foods, such as packaged sauces, cake mixes, and puddings.

Product	Brand & Product	Cost Per Serving
Convenience Food		
Regular Food		
Convenience Food		
Regular Food		

2. Compare the cost per serving of the convenience food to the same food product made from "scratch".

Questions:

1. What is the relationship between convenience and price?

2. What factors will influence a consumer's decision to use regular food rather than convenience food?

LAB EXPERIENCE 1.9

COMPARISON OF BULK PRICE vs SERVING PRICE

Purpose: To calculate cost per serving as compared to cost of total package.

Procedure: Compare several potato products.   Calculate price per serving (4 servings per pound or 1/2 cup cooked vegetables).

Product	Price Per Market Quantity	Price Per Serving
Idaho Baking		
Regular Potatoes		
Canned Potatoes		
Dehydrated Potato Flakes		
Frozen French Fries		
Packaged Hash Browned Potatoes		

Questions:

1.   What three (3) factors would influence your choice of product for dinner tonight?

2.   How would the season of the year affect the prices?

LAB EXPERIENCE 1.10

COMPARISON OF MILK PRODUCTS

Purpose: To calculate cost per serving as compared to cost of total package.

Procedure: Compare the following milk products.

Product	Market Quantity	Cost Per Market Quantity	Cost Per 8 oz. Cup
Nonfat Dry Milk: National Brand	Bulk		
Nonfat Dry Milk: Store Brand	Bulk		
Nonfat Dry Milk	Quart Pkg.		
Evaporated Milk	1 Can (13 oz.)		
Evaporated Skimmed Milk	1 Can (13 oz.)		
Fresh Skim Milk	1 Quart		
Fresh 1-2% Lowfat Milk	1 Quart		
Fresh Whole Milk	1 Quart		
Fresh Whole Milk	1/2 Gallon Pack		

Questions:

1. What is meant by the term "store" brand?

2. How do brands differ as to price?

3. What factors would account for these differences in price?

LAB EXPERIENCE 1.11

MATHEMATICAL CONVERSION PROBLEMS

Purpose: To practice mathematical conversion.

Procedure:

Diet Soda: 6 pack/$1.69; 12 fl. oz./can

1. What is the cost per can?

2. Convert ounces to milliliters (ml).

3. What is the unit price in ml?

Wheat Crackers: 37¢/box; 57g

1. When opened, you find 43 crackers in box. What is the cost per cracker?

2. What is the explanation if, when opening box, you find it only 3/4 filled?

3. What is the unit price in grams?

Corn Niblets: 29¢/can; net. wt.: 12 oz.,
                             wt. of corn : 10.5 oz.

1. Calculate the weight of the corn in grams.

2. What percentage of the contents is actually corn niblets?

3. What is the unit price of the corn in grams?

Tomato Juice: 6 pack/$1.19; 6 fl. oz./can

1. What is the cost per can?

2. Convert ounces to ml.

3. What is the unit price of the juice in ml?

45¢

$2.49

GRAPHING

A picture is worth a thousand words and sometimes the picture can represent what would take long paragraphs or long columns of numbers to show. A graph can be used to present such information. There are many kinds of graphs but the most common are the bar graph, circle graph, and line graphs.

BAR GRAPHS

The bar graph has a vertical axis and a horizontal axis. The vertical axis is read from bottom to top while the horizontal axis is read from left to right. The vertical axis gives a range or spread of values and is called a "scale". The horizontal axis or scale represents the items or time. Each bar represents the amount or quantity of each item.

To interpret a bar graph, read directly across from the top of a bar to the value on the vertical axis. If the top of the bar is not precisely even with a unit of value on the vertical, the value may be estimated.

For example, the following bar graph shows the noontime temperature for the first five days in August.

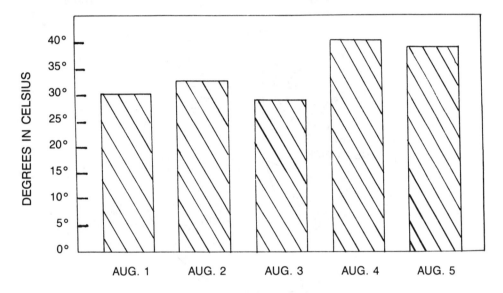

Figure 1.7 Bar Graph—Noon Temperature for August

The bar graph above together with the following questions and answers illustrate how to use the information displayed in the graph:

1. What does the horizontal axis represent? The first 5 days in August.
2. What does the vertical axis represent? Degrees in Celsius.
3. What is the value of one unit on the vertical axis? 5 degrees C.
4. Which day was the hottest? August 4.
5. What was the temperature on the hottest day? 40 degrees C.
6. Which day was the coolest? August 3.
7. What was the temperature? 29 degrees C.
8. Estimate the temperature for August 2. 33 degrees C.
9. Estimate the temperature for August 5. 38 degrees C.

CIRCLE GRAPHS

Information can also be displayed in a circle graph. The circle is divided into parts called sectors. The entire circle equals 100%.

A circle graph is constructed as follows:

1. Draw a circle with a compass and locate the center of the circle.
2. Using a protractor, divide the circle into 10 equal parts. Each part of 36 degrees represents 10% of the whole circle. Mark off each part on the edge of the circle.
3. Draw a line from the center of the circle to each point marked on the edge of the circle.
4. Label each sector of the circle with the name of the item and its percentage, and give a title to the graph. For example, the following data table represents the budget of the Jones family on a monthly basis.

Jones Family Monthly Budget

Item	Percent
Food	30%
Rent	25%
Savings	5%
Utilities	15%
Insurance	15%
Clothing	10%
	100%

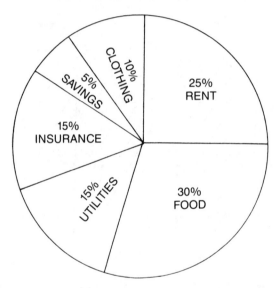

Figure 1.8 Circle Graph—Jones Family Monthly Budget

BROKEN-LINE GRAPHS

Another way to represent information is by using a broken-line graph. Broken-line graphs are used to show changes in information such as math scores, stock prices, and the consumer price index.

Draw a broken-line graph as follows:

1. Draw the vertical and horizontal axis. Mark the divisions on each axis using the given data. The units on each axis should be equally spaced.
2. Mark or plot the data points in the correct location on the graph.
3. Using a ruler, connect the points moving from left to right.
4. Label the axis and give a title to the graph. For example, here are T. Smith's math test scores:

Test Number	Score
1	60
2	95
3	70
4	100
5	88

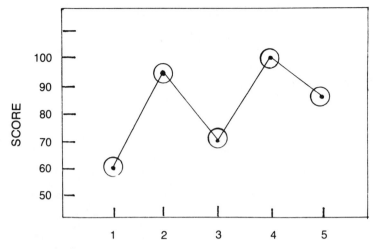

Figure 1.9 Broken-line Graph—T. Smith's Math Test Scores

Interpret a broken-line graph by reading directly across and down from each point to the number on each axis. If the point is not exactly even with a unit on the vertical scale, then estimate the value.

The broken-line graph above together with the following questions and answers illustrate how to use the information displayed in the graph:

1. What does the vertical axis represent? Test scores.
2. What does the horizontal axis represent? Tests.
3. What was T. Smith's average test score? 82.6 The answer was arrived at by adding all the test scores and dividing by the number of tests.

$$\frac{60 + 95 + 70 + 100 + 88}{5}$$

The following lab experiences will give you an opportunity to practice what you have learned about graphs.

LAB EXPERIENCE 1.12

BAR GRAPHS

Purpose: To draw a bar graph.

Materials:

Graph paper
Pencil
Ruler

Procedure:

1. Using the following data table, draw a bar graph representing Students' Favorite Sport.

2. Label the vertical axis "Number of Students", and label the horizontal axis "Sport".

3. Data Table: Students' Favorite Sport

Sport	Number of Students
Baseball	8
Tennis	15
Basketball	5
Track	3
Swimming	7
Skiing	8
Jogging	11

Questions:

1. Which sport is the most popular?

2. Which sport is the least popular?

3. How many students prefer tennis over basketball?

LAB EXPERIENCE 1.13

CIRCLE OR PIE GRAPHS

Purpose: To construct a circle graph and analyze how it represents data.

Materials:

Paper
Compass
Pencil
Ruler

Procedure:

1. Using the following data table, construct a circle graph to show how an individual's monthly income and budget may be represented pictorially.

2. Data Table: Monthly Budget for $2400

Item	Percent
Food	35%
Clothing	10%
Rent	25%
Recreation	7%
Savings	13%
Miscellaneous	10%

3. Show the percent values in the circle graph.

Questions:

1. On which item does the individual spend the most money?

2. On which item does the individual spend the least amount of money?

3. What percent is spent per month on rent?

4. What percent is put into savings per month?

5. Why is a circle graph the best to use for this type of data?

LAB EXPERIENCE 1.14

BROKEN-LINE GRAPHS

Purpose: To construct a broken-line graph that represents changes in information.

Materials:

Graph paper
Pencil
Ruler

Procedure:

1. Using the following data table, draw a broken-line graph to show changes in temperature in a 24 hour period.

2. Data Table

Temperature (degrees F)	Time
70	12 AM
69	2 "
68	4 "
70	6 "
72	8 "
76	10 "
80	12 PM
84	2 "
85	4 "
82	6 "
78	8 "
74	10 "

Questions:

1a. At what hour was the temperature highest?

 b. What was the temperature?

2a. At what hour was the temperature lowest?

 b. What was the temperature?

LAB EXPERIENCE 1.14 (Continued)

BROKEN-LINE GRAPHS

3. What was the difference in the temperature between 12 PM and 10 PM?

4. What was the difference in temperature between 12 AM and 4 AM?

5. Between the hours of 12 AM and 12 PM, at what hours was the temperature the same?

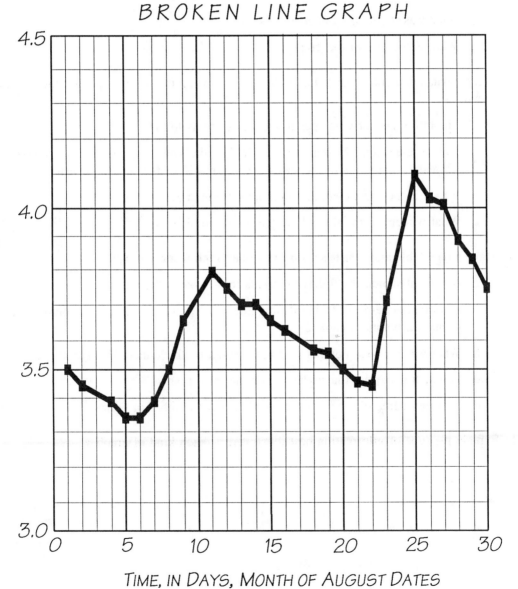

LAB EXPERIENCE 1.15

GRAPHING EXERCISES

Additional exercises in drawing graphs.

1. Make a data table and construct a bar graph using the following data:

    Four auto salesman were in a sales contest to see which one sold the most cars for the month of August. Jim J. sold 5, Sally T. sold 6, Ed L. sold 3, and Hazel W. sold 9.

    a. Which salesperson sold the most cars? How many?

    b. Which salesperson sold the least number of cars? How many?

    c. What was the total number of cars sold?

    d. What is the title of the graph?

2. Make a data table and construct a circle graph showing the driving ages for the states or provinces.

    a. The mimimum driving ages in the states are as follows:

    10% of the states, 15 years of age; 76% of the states, 16 years; 8% of the states, 17 years of age; 4% of the states, 18 years; 2% of the states, 21 years .

    b. Which is the most common minimum driving age?

    c. What percent of the states have the minimum driving age?

3. Make a data table and construct a broken-line graph using the data:

    a. A student scored the following points in 5 basketball games:

    10 points in game 1, 18 points in game 2, 12 points in game 3, 6 points in game 4, and 22 points in game 5.

    b. What was the total number of points scored by the student in the 5 games?

    c. In which game did the student score the most points?

    d. In which game did the student score the least number of points?

4. Explain the type of information best illustrated by each kind of graph

SCIENTIFIC METHOD QUESTIONS

1. Which of these five steps is not part of the scientific method: a) observation, b) statement of problem, c) hypothesis, d) experiment, e) patent.

2. Which of these is incorrect: a) a guess, b) a needle, c) clear, d) testable.

3. An experiment: a) tests a hypothesis, b) tells the law, c) is used for injection, d) all of the above.

4. Verification means that: a) an experiment may be repeated, b) that the conclusions are true, c) that the conclusions are false.

SAFETY QUESTIONS

1. Before beginning a lab activity: a) read the directions, b) learn the magic words, c) make sure it shows you are right, d) all of the above.

2. Wear safety glasses: a) only if you can't see, b) whenever you work with chemicals, c) when the teacher is watching, d) all of the above.

3. Which of the following is a safety consideration in the laboratory: a) looking into the top of a test tube, b) room ventilation, c) all the above, d) none of the above.

4. If chemicals splash in your eye(s): a) wash the eye(s) thoroughly, b) wipe your eyes with your lab coat, c) wipe your eyes with your clean handkerchief, d) all the above.

5. If you think of a new lab activity: a) try it out, b) discuss it with your teacher, c) invite classmates to try it with you, d) all the above.

HANDLE CAREFULLY!

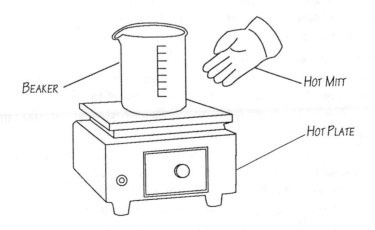

BEAKER   HOT MITT   HOT PLATE

UNIT 1

MATHEMATICS QUESTIONS

1. To calculate the area of a room, the equation is: a) length × width × height, b) length × width × depth, c) length × width, d) mass × volume.

2. If a room is 10 feet long, 12 feet wide, and 8 feet high, the area is: a) 120 cubic feet, b) 120 square feet, c) 960 cubic feet, d) 960 square feet, e) none of the above.

3. A 9′ × 12′ carpet at $6.99 per square yard would cost: a) $167.76, b) $83.88, c) $251.64, d) $194.25.

4. You wish to tile the floor of your workshop. You find the room measures 96″ × 96″. The tiles you like are each 1 ft. sq. How many tiles would you require? a) 46, b) 64, c) 56.

5. Similar tiles are available which measure 16″ × 16″. If you purchase these, you will need: a) 36, b) 48, c) 42.

6. Ceramic tiles for the same workshop are available on spaced-backing sheets, measuring 24″ × 24″. How many sheets will you need to buy a) 16, b) 12, c) 14?

7. You have also seen some attractive tiles which were imported from France. However, they are marked as being 10 cm × 10 cm. For the same workshop you will need: a) 48, b) 240, c) 576, d) 595.

8. A map shows a scale of 5km = 1 cm. Two points are 4.5cm apart on the map. How many kilometers (km) apart are these points? a) 44km, b) 22.5km, c) 2.25km, d) 4.4, e) none of the above.

9. A chart shows a scale of 1m = 5cm. How large would a 50cm long object appear on the chart? a) 2.5cm, b) 6cm, c) 1.2cm, d) none of the above.

10. While in Paris on your summer vacation, you stopped at a fruit stall and purchased 1 kilogram of apples. If each apple weighs 1/5 of a pound, you would expect to receive: a) 5 apples, b) 11 apples, c) 2 apples.

11. To find liquid volume, you would use a container called a _____.

12. You can measure an irregularly-shaped object by a method called _____.

13. The prefix "centi" indicates: a) one thousand times less than the unit, b) one hundred times more than the unit, c) one hundredth of the unit.

14. The volume of a block measuring 10 cm on each side is: a) 100 cm³, b) 100 cm², c) 100 cm, d) 1000 cm, e) none of the above.

15. Volume: a) is the measure of the space occupied by a 3-dimensional object, b) cannot be reasonably determined if the item under observation is damaged or irregular, c) does not apply to anything other than solid objects.

16. For an object whose length is 5 cm, width is 5.5 cm, and whose height is 5 cm, its volume is: a) 15.5 cm², b) 137.5 cm³, c) 55 cm³, d) none of the above.

17. A packing crate measures 4 ft. in length, 4 ft. in width, and 4 ft. in depth on its inside. How many packages measuring 12 in. × 12 in. × 12 in. can you ship in this crate? a) 16, b) 64, c) 48, d) none of the above.

18. Weight is: a) the amount of matter contained in an object, b) ratio of mass to volume, c) dependent on pull of gravity, d) none of the above.

19. Mass is described in: a) kilogram, b) grams, c) milligrams, d) both a and b, e) all of the above.

20. The mass of an object whose density is 4 g/cm³ and volume is 8 cm³ is: a) 0.32 g, b) 2.0 g, c) 0.2g, d) 32 g.

21. We bring an object from earth to the moon. It now weighs: a) the same, b) more, c) less, d) none of the above.

22. The same object from the previous question now will have a mass which is: a) the same, b) more, c) less, d) none of the above.

23. If we first determine the mass of an item on a pan balance located on earth and then on the moon, its mass on the moon would be: a) the same, b) more, c) less, d) none of the above.

24. If we weigh an item on a spring scale on the moon, it will weigh: a) the same, b) more, c) less, than on earth.

25. In Lab Experience 1.2, we weigh the empty beaker: a) for practice, b) so we can tell if it can be lifted, c) so we can subtract this from the total including the added water, d) all the above.

26. If a one kilogram object reads 1.002kg on a scale, this scale is accurate: a) to 0.02%, b) to 20%, c) not at all.

27. In the popcorn experiment we wear safety glasses because: a) we have to see better, b) we are cautioned to so whenever we use chemicals, c) scientists wear glasses, d) it makes us look professional.

28. The popped corn weighs less because: a) it is fluffier, b) it is softer, c) it has lost moisture, d) all the above.

29. The density of a 30 cm³ block of wood compared to a 90 cm³ block of the same wood is: a) the 30 cm³ block has a larger density, b) the 30 cm³ block has a smaller density, c) they both have the same density.

30. If a piece of metal has a mass of 3500 g and its volume is 650 cm³, then the density is: a) 5.38 g/cm³, b) 1.85 g/cm³, c) 1.86 g/cm³, d) none of the above.

31. The density of an object whose mass is 260 g and whose volume is twenty-five cm³ is equal to: a) 10.4 g/cm³, b) 0.10 g/cm³, c) 0.25 g/cm³, d) none of the above.

32. If you have an item that weighs 20 g and has a density of 5 g/cm³, its volume will be: a) 4cm³, b) 0.4 ml, c) 0.4 cm³.

33. The density of an object whose volume is 40 cm³ and which weighs 200 g is: a) 0.2 g/cm³, b) 2 g/cm³, c) 5 g/cm³, d) 0.5 g/cm³.

34. A bar of bath soap weighs 4.5 oz. and measures 2″ × 4″ × 1″. The density of the soap is: a) 6.3 g/cm³, b) 1.008 g/cm³, c) 0.563 g/cm³, d) 0.961 g/cm³.

35. If the bar of soap is cut into identical quarters, one of the quarters alone would have a density of: a) 1.008 g/cm³, b) 2.52 g/cm³, c) 6.3 g/cm³, d) 0.961 g/cm³.

36. If another brand of soap has a density of 3.5 g/cm³ and is of the same dimensions as in Question 24, then that bar would: a) weigh more, b) weigh less, c) weigh the same.

37. If both brands of bath soap were on sale and the 4.5 oz. bar cost 50¢ each, and the bar

with a density of 3.5 g/cm³ was 5 bars for $1.00, the best buy would be: a) the first at 50¢, b) the second at 5 for $1.00, c) they would be equal.

38. The volume of an object whose density is 10 g/cm³ and whose mass is 20 g is: a) 2 cm³, b) 0.2 cm³, c) 0.5 cm³, d) 5 cm³, e) none of the above.

39. 50 cm are equal to: a) 20 inches, b) 5 inches, c) 10 inches, d) none of the above.

40. Ten inches are equal to: a) 2.5 cm, b) 30 cm, c) 25 cm, d) 250 cm, e) none of the above.

41. Two tablespoons are equal to: a) 15 ml, b) 10 ml, c) 20 ml, d) none of the above.

42. A liter is: a) smaller than a quart, b) larger than a quart, c) equal to a quart.

43. The basic metric units that the consumer will see on nutrition labels are _____.

44. Whenever the prefix _____ precedes a unit, it is 1000 times that unit.

45. A microgram is _____ of one gram.

46. The U.S. Food & Drug Administration prescribes the use of the metric system for nutrition labels because: a) it is the best way to teach metrics to the public, b) cooks and dieticians insist upon it, c) it avoids confusing and complicated fractions.

47. The RDA on a nutrition label tells you: a) the weight in grams of the vitamin or mineral, b) the calorie content of the vitamin or mineral, c) the percentage of minimum allowance contained per serving.

48. The UPC symbol contains information about: a) the manufacturer, b) the size of the product, c) the name of the product, d) all of the above, e) none of the above.

49. The Universal Product Code: a) allows the consumer to figure the cost(s) of his purchase before getting to the checkout register, b) can provide inventory information for the market manager, c) is required by the Federal Government.

50. The _____ is a series of closely spaced lines, bars, and numbers which is scanned and read by a laser beam.

51. Unit pricing enables you to compare the _____ per _____.

52. The unit price of a 32 oz. bottle of cola whose price is $1.39 is: a) $0.043 per ounce, b) $0.023 per ounce, c) $0.040 per ounce, d) none of the above.

53. If the unit price per ounce of a 8 oz. box of cereal is $0.174, the cereal would cost you: a) $1.40, b) $1.59, c) $1.39, d) $1.29.

54. If a sirloin steak is priced at $2.70 per pound, how much would 18 ounces cost you: a) $2.48, b) $4.19, c) $3.14, d) $3.35, e) $3.04.

55. Unit pricing is important because: a) you know the cost of an item before you get to the checkout register, b) the supermarket can determine which goods are moving well, c) it helps the customer decide which brand or size is most economical.

56. If a box of laundry detergent weighs 2 lb. 10 oz. and costs 99¢, the unit price will be: a) 38¢ per pound, b) 47¢ per pound, c) 99¢ per pound.

57. If the detergent in the preceding question is next to another brand weighing 3 lb. 1 oz. and costs $1.59, the best buy is: a) the box costing 99¢, b) the box costing $1.59, c) neither brand.

58. If a regular size (1 lb.) jar of applesauce costs 39¢ and the large size (2 lb. 3oz.) jar costs 89¢, then: a) the regular size is a better buy, b) the large size is a better buy, c) no saving difference.

59. The density of a bar of soap can be determined as the density of one piece of the soap. How would this compare to the density of the whole bar   a) twice as dense,   b) 20% more dense,   c) same density,   d) none of these?

60. If a block of wood weighs 11340 g and measures 10 cm on each side, then the density of a statue made of the same wood would be: a) equal to that of the block,   b) twice the density,   c) half of the density,   d) insufficient data given.

Which type of graph would you use to show the following:

61. The number of cars sold by five major producers?   a) bar,   b) circle,   c) broken-line.

62. The percent of a budget spent on various items?   a) bar,   b) circle,   c) broken-line.

63. The improvement in sales per month?   a) bar,   b) circle,   c) broken-line.

UNIT 2

BIOLOGY

The purchaser of food should understand nutritional requirements and know how to evaluate food products to best fulfill the body's biological needs. It is necessary to understand the function of protein, fat, and carbohydrates as a balance of prime nutrients and the quantities in which they are needed. Calorie requirements and food values must be considered. The consumer should be familiar with how foods are labeled and the laws relating to labeling and advertising.

Let us examine these topics in addition to looking at vitamins, minerals, and the effects of a well balanced diet.

NUTRITION

The body requires food for three distinct purposes:

1. Obtain energy
2. Build and maintain tissue
3. Regulate body processes

Within the body, the food must undergo three processes before it can be utilized. It must be:

1. Digested
2. Absorbed
3. Assimilated

The food requirements are selected from the six food groups. They are:

1. Bread, cereal, rice, pasta
2. Vegetables
3. Fruits
4. Milk, yogurt, cheese
5. Meat, poultry, fish, dried beans, eggs, nuts
6. Fats, oils, sweets

NUTRIENTS

Nutrients are necessary for energy, growth, and maintenance of the body. Nutrients include proteins, carbohydrates and fats and are to be found in the food we eat.

PROTEINS

Proteins are responsible for the tough fibrous nature of hair, nails, and ligaments, and for the structure of muscles. They are a part of hemoglobin, which transports oxygen in the blood; of insulin, which regulates blood sugar; and of the enzymes necessary for the digestion of food.

Amino acids, which contain the nitrogen essential to animal life are the building blocks of proteins. In protein molecules, hundreds of amino acids are linked into long chains. It is the variations in the composition and the arrangement of amino acids in the protein molecule that give protein its remarkable versatility. About 20 amino acids are commonly found in proteins, allowing for an almost infinite number of combinations and sequences in the amino acid chain. Thus, a wide variety of proteins occur in plant and animal tissues.

Amino acids are required by the body for building and maintaining body tissues. The greatest amounts of protein are needed when the body is building new tissue rapidly, such as during infancy, pregnancy, or when a mother is nursing a child. Extra protein also is needed when excess destruction or loss of body protein occurs from such causes as hemorrhage, burns, surgery, or infections.

Proteins are needed for building the thousands of enzymes which control the speed of chemical reactions in the body, and for making hormones such as insulin and thyroxine, which regulate metabolism. Proteins are also needed for forming antibodies. These antibodies combine with foreign proteins which enter the body, producing an immunity response that helps ward off harmful infections. They also help regulate the water balance and the acid-base balance in the body.

Protein is found in meat, fish, poultry, eggs, and most varieties of cheese. Some additional good sources of protein are dried peas and beans, nuts, and enriched breads and cereals. Protein is a constituent of all body cells and is needed for growth and maintenance of blood, bone, and body tissue.

Protein, like carbohydrates and fats, can be burned to supply energy, and when the diet does not supply enough calories from the other two nutrients, proteins are used for energy, even at the expense of building body protein. If more protein is eaten than is required for the nitrogen needs of the body, the extra protein is used for calories or is converted to body fat. In developed countries, most of us eat more protein than our bodies need.

CARBOHYDRATES

The major function of carbohydrates in the diet is to provide energy for the work of the body. They also allow the body to manufacture some of the B-complex vitamins, and form part of the structure of many biological compounds.

Carbohydrates are made of the chemical elements carbon, hydrogen, and oxygen. The hydrogen and oxygen are in the same proportion as they occur in water — H_2O — two parts of hydrogen to one part of oxygen.

The carbohydrates which provide nourishment in our foods are the various starches and sugars. The simple sugars: glucose, fructose, and galactose are the foundation of most common carbohydrates. The disaccharides or double sugars: sucrose, maltose, and lactose all contain two simple sugars. The polysaccharides, such as starch, are formed by the union of many simple sugars. All carbohydrates must be broken down by digestion into simple sugars before the body can use them. Some complex carbohydrates, for example cellulose, cannot be digested by man but do supply the roughage needed for proper elimination of solid wastes from the body. In addition, carbohydrates add flavor to our food.

The cereal grains such as wheat, rice, corn, oats, pasta and noodles, many fruits and vegetables, such as potatoes, peas, beans, taro, sugar cane, and sugar beets are the world's major carbohydrate sources. Many processed foods are rich in carbohydrates. These include breads and other baked goods, jams and jellies, molasses, noodles, spaghetti and dried fruits.

STARCH

Starch is the most important carbohydrate food source since it is the form in which plants store energy for future use. The seeds of plants such as the cereal grains, legumes, and the roots or tubers, such as potatoes, are the richest sources of starch. Cereals contain principally starch, but important vitamins and minerals are present in the outer layer and in the germ of the grain called the kernel. Refinement, as in the milling of white flour, removes much of the outer layer and the germ. The enrichment of white bread and flour restores three of the B vitamins that are lost in processing, and also adds iron.

Starchy foods are not very flavorful if eaten raw. Cooking swells the starch granules, breaking them open, making them taste better, and allowing them to be more easily digested. In some vegetables, such as immature corn and peas, a sweet taste is present. This disappears as the plant ripens, and the sugar content changes to starch which has little flavor. In some fruit like bananas, the unripened fruit contains starch which changes to sugar on ripening.

Through digestion, the body changes the starch in foods to glucose, which can be used as a source of energy by all the tissues in the body. As a matter of fact, carbohydrates provide the bulk of the energy (calories) for the body's activities. If the body receives more glucose than it can use as energy, small amounts can be stored as glycogen in the liver and muscle tissues, but like all carbohydrates consumed in excess of the energy needs of the body they are rapidly converted to fat.

FIBER

The importance of fiber or roughage in our diet has been recognized through the ages. The fiber in our diet comes only from plant sources. It does not include the tough or "fibrous" portions of some meats.

Fiber is actually the indigestible residue of certain foods — fruits, vegetables, and whole grains. It is composed of complex carbohydrates — cellulose, lignin, hemicellulose, pectin and gums. These five components of fiber all resist the digestive enzymes in the stomach. The fiber from plants is important in the diet to stimulate the normal action of the intestinal tract in removing waste products. In addition to providing bulk, the fiber absorbs many times its weight in water, thus promoting softer stools. The greater bulk promotes regularity and more frequent elimination. Many diets for weight reduction encourage the consumption of raw vegetables and fruits. This is often helpful because these foods contain fair amounts of fiber and are generally low in calories. The increased bulk also contributes to satisfaction through a feeling of fullness.

Some recent studies have suggested that dietary fiber, in adequate quantity, may protect against many noninfectious diseases of the large intestine that are prevalent in our society. These conditions include cancer of the colon, hemorrhoids, appendicitis, colitis, and diverticulosis. The incidence of these diseases appears to be lower in less developed societies where the diets contain large amounts of dietary fiber. Some researchers have also associated increased dietary fiber with reduced blood cholesterol levels, suggesting that a relationship may exist between dietary fiber and freedom from atherosclerosis.

Some of the foods that are major contributors to fiber in our diet are whole grain flour and cereal, potatoes, fresh fruits and vegetables, dried beans and peas. As a general rule, unrefined foods contain more roughage than refined foods because some fiber is usually removed in processing. Raw apples or other fruits contain some roughage in the skins; fruits with seeds, such as strawberries, raspberries, and figs are high in fiber. Raw and cooked vegetables are excellent sources of fiber. Fiber, if added by the manufacturers of processed foods, would have to be added in quantities which would alter the appearance, taste, chewiness, and mouth-feel of many foods.

No minimum daily requirements for dietary fiber have been established. Nevertheless, nutritional guidelines issued by the government do recommend increasing consumption of fruits, vegetables and whole grain products and cutting down on fats and refined sugars.

Too much fiber can have some unpleasant and possibly harmful effects. An excess can lead to painful intestinal gas, nausea and vomiting. There is also some concern that it may interfere with the body's ability to absorb certain essential minerals.

SUCROSE

Sucrose, common table sugar, is mostly produced from sugar cane and sugar beets; the sugars from the two sources are chemically identical. Refined sugar is an unusual food in that it is pure carbohydrate. Therefore, it is only a source of calories because it contains no vitamins, minerals, protein, or fat.

FRUCTOSE

Fructose, or fruit sugar, occurs naturally in fruits, vegetables, and honey. It is somewhat sweeter than sucrose, ordinary table sugar, but has the same number of calories. High fructose corn sweetener is 55% fructose and the rest is water. High fructose corn sweetener is used in carbonated beverages because a lesser amount provides greater sweetness than sucrose. High fructose corn sweetener is also less expensive than ordinary table sugar.

The usefulness of fructose for diabetics has been under discussion for years. The body does not metabolize fructose the way it metabolizes glucose. In order for the body to utilize blood glucose, insulin, the hormone that regulates blood sugar, is needed. Fructose goes directly to the liver, and does not require insulin for metabolism. Theoretically, because there is no dramatic fluctuation in blood sugar, it is easier for diabetics to handle fructose.

A report released in May 1978 which was prepared for the FDA by the Federation of American Societies for Experimental Biology states "Leading authorities on the dietary management of diabetes mellitus affirm that the main emphasis in obese patients should be on control of caloric intake to achieve and maintain ideal body weight. Most authorities now recommend that dietary fat and sugar be reduced and that the proportion of calories as starch be increased in both of the main types of diabetes . . ." The report concludes that "There are insufficient data to determine if fructose, or any other carbohydrate, has beneficial properties for the long-term dietary management of diabetics."

There is some evidence that fructose converts more quickly to fat than other sugars. There is also some evidence that with the onset of diabetes in adults, it is accompanied by high triglyceride levels. Some scientists believe that an elevated triglyceride level is a risk factor in heart disease.

FATS

The fats in our food serve a variety of functions. Some fat is essential in the diet to provide linoleic acid, which is necessary for proper growth and a healthy skin. However, only a small amount of linoleic acid is required to meet this need — only about 1 to 2% of the total calories. Fats also carry fat-soluble vitamins A, D, E, and K into the body and aid in their absorption. Fats also serve as a concentrated source of energy and, because they slow digestion and the emptying of the stomach, they delay the onset of hunger.

Fats are essentially composed of glycerol with three fatty acid chains. Each fatty acid is made up of carbon atoms joined like links on a chain. The carbon chains vary in length, with most edible fats containing 4 to 20 carbons. Each carbon atom has hydrogen atoms attached to it. When a carbon atom in the chain has a minimum of two hydrogen atoms attached to it, it is called a saturated fatty acid. When a hydrogen atom is missing from two neighboring carbons, a double bond exists between the carbon atoms and the fatty acid is called unsaturated. A fatty acid which contains more than one such double bond in the chain is called polyunsaturated. The polyunsaturated fatty acid called linoleic acid is of particular nutritional importance since the body cannot manufacture it. Therefore, it is an "essential" fatty acid and must be supplied in the food you eat.

Fats made up of unsaturated fatty acids and the fatty acids composed of shorter chains have lower melting points, and are liquids (oils) at room temperature. All food fats, animal or vegetable, contain a mixture of saturated and unsaturated fatty acids, but generally, animal fats are more saturated than vegetable oils. Most vegetable oils, such as soy, safflower, corn, and sunflower, are liquid at room temperature and are highly unsaturated.

Safflower, corn, cottonseed, peanut and soybean oils, are especially rich in linoleic acid, and the labels on products made from these oils often state "high in polyunsaturates," or "high in polyunsaturated fatty acids." When oils have hydrogen added (hydrogenation), they become more solid. Margarine is an example of a food in which vegetable oils are hydrogenated to the consistency of a solid. In the process, the vegetable oil necessarily becomes less unsaturated. Animal fats such as lard, beef fat and poultry fat are highly saturated and are solid at room temperatures.

Fats provide more than twice the energy value than that of carbohydrates or proteins. This means that foods rich in fats add much to the calorie content of the diet. Some fat in the tissues helps cushion body organs and also helps to prevent heat loss through the body's surface. Fat is to be found in most foods, and is a major constituent of butter, margarine, lard, vegetable oil and salad dressings. Fats contribute to our enjoyment of foods because they add flavor and improve the texture of the food. A reduction in fat-rich foods is a sensible way to limit calories in the diet for the purpose of reducing or controlling weight. Table 2.1 gives some representative values:

TABLE 2.1

FAT CONTENT IN FOODS

Percent Fat	Food
100–90	Salad and cooking oils, fats, lard
90–80	Butter, margarine
80–70	Mayonnaise, pecans, macadamia nuts
70–50	Walnuts, dried unsweetened coconut meat, almonds, bacon, baking chocolate
50–30	Broiled choice T-bone, porterhouse steaks, spareribs, cheddar and cream cheese, potato chips, french dressing, chocolate candy, goose
30–20	Choice beef pot roast, broiled choice lamb chops, frankfurters, ground beef, chocolate chip cookies
20–10	Broiled choice round steak, broiled veal chop, roast turkey, eggs, avocado, olives, ice cream, chocolate cake with icing, french fried potatoes, apple pie
10–1	Pork and beans, broiled cod, haddock, halibut, broiled chicken, crab meat, cottage cheese, milk, beef liver, creamed soups, sherbet, most breakfast cereals
Less than 1	Baked potato, most fruits and vegetables, egg white, chicken consomme

In recent years, there has been great controversy over the relationship of dietary fats and cholesterol to atherosclerosis. This is a coronary heart disease in which cholesterol and other fatty substances are deposited on the inner walls of arteries. (Cholesterol is a fat-soluble substance which is contained in foods of animal origin. It is also manufactured by nearly all body tissues.) A high level of blood cholesterol has been identified as one of several risk factors in atherosclerosis. Some evidence has indicated that saturated fats in the diet tend to cause increased levels while polyunsaturated fats tend to result in decreased levels. However, many factors other than diet are also known to be associated with heart disease, including smoking, heredity, obesity, and the amount of exercise done.

The FDA permits manufacturers to show the percent of calories from fat, the grams of polyunsaturated and saturated fatty acids, and the cholesterol content of foods in nutrition labeling information. However, the FDA does not mandate that this information be given.

THE WELL BALANCED DIET

The normal well balanced diet consists of 10 to 15% protein, 20 to 30% fats, and 55 to 70% carbohydrates. To calculate the conversion of grams of the prime nutrients into calories, the following rule applies: One gram of protein yields 4 calories of energy, 1 gram of fat produces 9 calories, 1 gram of carbohydrate gives 4 calories of energy. Therefore,

100 grams of protein multiplied by 4 cal/g = 400 calories

100 grams of carbohydrate multiplied by 4 cal/g = 400 calories

100 grams of fat multiplied by 9 cal/g = 900 calories

100 grams is approximately 6½ tablespoons or a little more than 1/3 of a cup. So calories do count — and they do add up!!

Nutrition and obesity experts, who have examined the components of recent popular diets and the consequences suffered by those who follow them, have found that most are wanting in nutritional value and some are hazardous to health and life. Few diets can safely be followed for more than two weeks. Only rarely does a fad diet produce permanent weight loss.

All food enters the digestive tract as various combinations of proteins, fats and carbohydrates. Enzymes break down each food component to permit absorption. Carbohydrates are converted in the intestines to glucose; proteins to amino acids; fatty acids to triglycerides. Excess glucose can be stored in the liver in a form called glycogen. When glucose is needed to maintain normal blood glucose levels or to fuel muscle and brain cells, glycogen is converted back to glucose and released from the liver. If the glucose supply exceeds the body's immediate need and the liver has stored it's full capacity of glycogen, then glucose is converted to fat and is stored as fat tissue. To achieve a weight loss, fat tissue must release stored fat so that it can be burned as an energy source.

CALORIES

The number of calories you use in a particular exercise depends on how much you weigh, for how long, and how vigorously you exercise. A heavy person burns more calories than a lighter person. The longer you exercise, and the harder or faster you exercise, the more calories are burned or consumed.

In nutrition we need a large unit so the nutritionist uses the term kilocalorie (C) while in physics we use the term calorie (cal). A definition of the kilocalorie is the amount of heat needed to raise the temperature of one kilogram of water one degree Celsius. The definition of the calorie (cal) is the amount of heat needed to raise the temperature of one gram of water one degree Celsius.

The following reference table lists the minutes required at walking, bicycling, jogging, and swimming to consume the calories contained in certain foods.

TABLE 2.2

CALORIE/EXERCISE CHART

Food	Kcalories	Activity (minutes)			
		Walk	Bike	Jog	Swim
Apple, 1 medium	87	17	11	9	8
Banana, 1 medium	127	24	16	13	11
Beans, green, 1/2 c. cooked	15	3	2	2	1
Beer, 8-oz glass	115	22	14	12	10
Bread & butter, 1 slice	96	18	12	10	9
Cake, white layer, 1/16 of 9" layer	250	48	31	25	22
Carrot, raw, 1 large	42	8	5	4	4
Cereal, dry, 1 cup, with milk & sugar	212	41	26	21	19
Cheese, American, 1-oz slice	112	22	14	11	10
Cheese, cottage, 1 rounded teasp.	30	6	4	3	3
Chicken, fried, 1/2 breast	232	45	28	23	21
Chicken, TV dinner	542	104	66	54	48
Cola beverage, 8-oz glass	105	20	13	11	9
Cooky, chocolate-chip 1 average	50	10	6	5	5
Cooky, vanilla wafer, 1 average	15	3	2	2	1
Doughnut, 1 average	125	24	15	13	11
Egg, boiled or poached, 1 medium	78	15	10	8	7
Egg, fried or scrambled 1 medium	108	21	13	11	10
French dressing, 1 T.	57	11	7	6	5
Gelatin, with cream, 1 serving	117	23	14	12	10
Halibut, broiled, 1 serving	214	41	26	21	19
Ice cream, 2/3 cup	186	36	23	19	17

TABLE 2.2 (Continued)

CALORIE/EXERCISE CHART

Food	Kcalories	Activity (minutes)			
		Walk	Bike	Jog	Swim
Ice milk, 2/3 cup	137	26	17	14	12
Mayonnaise, 1 T.	100	19	12	10	9
Milk, skim, 8-oz glass	88	17	11	9	8
Milk, whole, 8-oz glass	160	36	20	16	14
Orange, 1 medium	73	14	9	7	7
Orange juice, 4-oz glass	54	10	7	5	5
Pancake, 1, with 2 T. syrup	204	39	25	20	18
Peach, 1 medium	38	7	5	4	3
Peas, green, 1/2 c. cooked	58	11	7	6	5
Pie, fruit, 1/6 of 9" pie	400	77	49	40	36
Pizza, cheese, 1/8 of 14" pie	185	36	23	19	17
Potato chips, 5 - 2" chips	54	10	7	5	5
Sandwiches: Hamburger	350	67	43	35	31
Roast beef with gravy	430	83	52	43	38
Tuna salad	278	54	34	28	25
Sherbet, orange, 2/3 cup	120	23	15	12	11
Spaghetti, meat sauce, 1 serving	396	76	48	40	35

Notes:

1. teasp = teaspoon;
   T. = tablespoon;
   c. = cup

2. Walking at 3.5 to 4 mph burns up about 5 calories per minute.

3. Bicycling consumes approximately 8 calories per minute.

4. Jogging alternated with walking (5 minutes for each alternately) uses approximately 10 calories per minute.

5. Average ability swimming consumes 11 calories per minute.

LAB EXPERIENCE 2.1

NUTRITIONAL VALUE OF PRODUCTS

Purpose: To evaluate the calorie, price, and nutrition difference among the regular and diet products of:

— canned fruit
— soups
— other foods

Procedure: Obtain the needed information from products at home or in the local supermarket and complete the chart.

	Brand & Product	Calories Per Serving	Nutrition Information	Cost Per Serving
Regular				
Diet				
Regular				
Diet				
Regular				
Diet				

Questions:

1. In your opinion, does the calorie difference justify the price difference?

2. Does the nutrient difference surprise you?

LAB EXPERIENCE 2.1 (Continued)
NUTRITIONAL VALUE OF PRODUCTS

3. How big a difference was there between the diet and regular product in terms of price and calories?

4. If you were on a long term diet, how important would these differences be to you?

5. How many of the diet products carried health warnings?

6. If you were on a long term diet, would you use diet products? Why or why not?

7. How nutritious were the diet products?

8. If you were dieting, which foods would you give up completely?

9. Which fresh, nutritious foods could you substitute for them?

10. What other changes could you make in your eating habits and daily routine to lose weight?

ARTIFICIAL SWEETENERS

Low calorie foods are probably the hottest items on the grocery shelves today and low calorie sweeteners are very important in this market. Although sugar has only 16 calories per teaspoon, saccharin has zero calories, and aspartame, the newest low calorie sweetener, has a few calories.

The artificial sweetener saccharin is 300 times sweeter than sugar and has little or no food value. For this reason it has been widely used in diabetic and reducing diets. However, it tends to break down chemically and lose its sweetness when used in cooking, and so it is used primarily as a table-top sweetener.

Aspartame is 180 times sweeter than sugar. The product sold under the name of Equal has 4 calories per packet and is equal to the sweetening ability of 2 teaspoons of sugar. However, since much less has to be used because of its inherent sweetness, the calories it contributes to food or drink are negligible. Aspartame was approved by the Food and Drug Administration for use in dry foods such as cereals in 1981, and in carbonated drinks in 1983. It is sold under the name of Equal for use as a table-top sweetener, and as NutraSweet for inclusion in a list of ingredients. Since it doesn't cause tooth decay and has little food value, it can be found in over 60 products including powdered beverages, chewing gum, desserts, and carbonated soft drinks.

Aspartame tends to break down if exposed to temperatures above 85 degrees F. so it presently has very limited use in cooking. At the time of this writing, although aspartame has been widely tested and found safe for consumption, its effect on human beings is still being investigated.

Other nonnutritive sweeteners, such as sorbitol, mannitol, and xylose, are used in sugar-free gums. They are not readily metabolized but still provide sweetness.

The following lab experience will give the student the opportunity to test the relative sweetness of artificial sweeteners as compared to sugar.

LAB EXPERIENCE 2.2

SUGARS and SWEETENERS

Purpose: To compare the relative sweetness of artificial sweeteners to sugar.

Materials:

Hot plate
Hot mitts
Safety glasses
Balance
Glass stirring rods
200-ml Graduated cylinder
3 200-ml Beakers
250-ml Paper cups
Distilled water
Granulated sugar
Saccharin
Aspartame* (Equal)

*Equal (the tradename for an artificial sweetener containing NutraSweet) is a product of the NutraSweet Company.

Procedure:

1. Take 3 paper cups and label one Sugar, one Saccharin, and one Aspartame. Label each of the three beakers the same way.

2. Weigh 5 g of each sweetener and place each in the appropriate beaker.

3. Add 200 ml of distilled water to each beaker and stir until the sweeteners dissolve. Clean the stirring rod before dipping into a beaker.

4. Pour 100 ml of each dissolved sweetener into respective paper cups.

5. Taste each sample, rinsing the mouth with water between each tasting.

6. Rate each product's sweetness on a scale of 1 to 3, with 1 being sweetest, 2 being medium sweet, and 3 being least sweet. Record on chart below.

7. Place the three beakers with remaining solutions on hot plate and heat for 1 hour at 90 degrees C.

8. Air cool beakers to room temperature.

LAB EXPERIENCE 2.2 (Continued)

SUGARS and SWEETENERS

9. Taste each sample, rinsing mouth with water between tastes, and rate each as in Step 6. Record on chart below.

10. Find the cost per pound or package of each sweetener.

11. Enter results on chart below.

Sweetness	Sugar	Saccharin	Aspartame "Equal"
Before heating			
After heating			
Cost/5 g			

Questions:

1. Which of the products was the sweetest?

2. Which was the least sweet?

3. Did any of the products carry warning labels? If so, what were they?

4. How does the calorie count compare for each of the products

   Sugar _____

   Saccharin _____

   Aspartame _____

5. How does the cost per 5 g compare? Five grams is about one teaspoon.

   Sugar _____

   Saccharin _____

   Aspartame _____

Suggested Activities:

1. Place a drop of sweetener on the tip of your tongue. Without disturbing it, can you taste it?

2. Place a drop of sweetener on back of tongue. Without disturbing it, can you taste it?

3. Heat a beaker of water and sweetener to a boil and smell the vapor. Can you taste the sweetener by just smelling the vapor?

4. Library research:

   a. The advantages of synthetic sweeteners in the instances of tooth decay and diabetes.

   b. Is brown sugar more nutritious than white sugar?

   c. What other "natural" sweeteners are available?

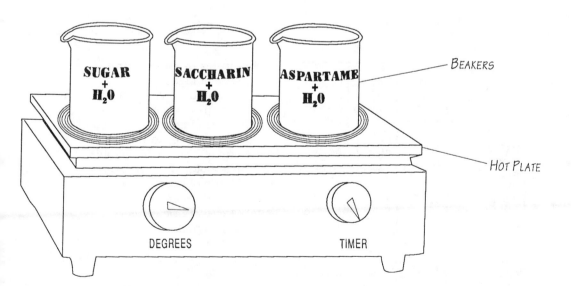

THE FOOD GUIDE PYRAMID

Courtesy of the US Department of Agriculture / US Department of Health & Human Services

SERVINGS PER DAY			
	women & some older aduls	children teen girls, active women, most men	teen boys & active men
CALORIE LEVEL	ABOUT 1,600	ABOUT 2,200	ABOUT 2,800
BREAD GROUP	6	9	11
VEGETABLE GROUP	3	4	5
FRUIT GROUP	2	3	4
MILK GROUP	**2-3	**2-3	**2-3
MEAT GROUP	2, for total of 5 oz.	2, for total of 6 oz.	3, for total of 7 oz.

*These are the calorie levels if you choose lowfat, lean foods, and use fats, oils & sweets sparingly
**Pregnant or breastfeeding women, and those under 24 need 3 servings

Examples of one serving:
 1 slice of bread
 1/2 cup of cooked rice or pasta
 1/2 cup of cooked cereal
 1 ounce of ready-to eat cereal
 1/2 cup chopped vegetables
 1 cup of leafy raw vegetables
 1 piece of fruit or melon wedge
 3/4 cup of juice
 1/2 cup of canned fruit
 1/4 cup of dried fruit
 1 cup of milk or yogurt
 1-1/2 to 2 ounces of cheese
 2-1/2 to 3 ounces of cooked lean meat
  poultry or fish
Count 1/2 cup of cooked beans or 1 egg, or two tablespoons of peanut butter as 1 ounce of lean meat. (about 1/3 serving)

LIMIT CALORIES FROM FATS, OILS, & SWEETS, especially if you have to lose weight.

LAB EXPERIENCE 2.3

THE FOOD GUIDE PYRAMID

Purpose: To evaluate the following menu according to the criteria of The Food Guide Pyramid:

Breakfast:
Grapefruit, 1/2
Cheese omelet ,
  2 eggs and 1 oz. cheese
Buttered toast, 1 slice

Lunch:
Yogurt, plain 8 oz.
Lettuce wedge with
  Russian dressing
Saltines (4)
Apple

Dinner:
Chicken Tetrazzini,
  3 oz. chicken, 1 oz. cheese
Cooked Spaghetti, 1/2 cup
Green Beans, 1/2 cup
Strawberry Jello, 1/2 cup
Whole Milk, 8 oz.

Snacks:
8 oz. Cola
Chocolate Chip Cookies, (4)
Sunflower Seeds, 1 oz.

Questions:

1. Construct a table as shown below, and fill in the values for the above menu.

2. Construct a similar table for the number of calories for the above menu.

3. How does this day's menu, and the recommended number of servings per day of The Food Guide Pyramid, provide for the nutritional requirements of a 20-year old student? Note that the amount of fat and sugar eaten is an approximation.

4. Construct a table as shown below, and fill in the values for your own food intake for the past two days. Evaluate with the criteria of The Food Guide Pyramid.

Food	Bread, Cereal, Rice & Pasta	Vegetabe Group	Fruit Group	Milk, Yogurt & Cheese Group	Meat, Fish, Poultry, Nuts, Eggs,etc.	Fats, Oils & Sweets
example: 1/2 grapefruit			1			

Suggested activity: Create a similar table showing the amount of carbohydrates, protein, fats, and calories for the above menu.

VEGETARIAN DIET

The word "vegetarian" was coined in 1842 in England by those who ate no meat. Formerly, the main incentives for giving up meat were religious beliefs, objections to killing animals for food, or just personal taste. Today, many people are becoming vegetarians because of inflation, the high cost of meat, and others believe that meat is harmful. There are several types of vegetarians. Some eat everything but "red" meat (beef, lamb, pork). Others also avoid poultry and fish. Most omit all meat but allow dairy products and eggs. Some allow dairy products but not eggs.

A few years ago in the United States, the National Research Council of the National Academy of Sciences studied vegetarian diets, and concluded that all but the most restricted are nutritionally safe.

A complete protein of animal origin has 22 amino acids. Our bodies cannot manufacture eight of these which are essential to health. They must be supplied by diet. The eight essential amino acids are valine, lysine, threonine, leucine, isoleucine, tryptophan, phenylalanine, and the sulfur-containing amino acids: methionine and cystine. These must be obtained from food preformed, ready to use, and in appropriate amounts. Further, for efficient utilization, the body requires that all eight essential amino acids be ingested at about the same time. The protein quality of a single food is judged by its capacity to provide the essential amino acids in appropriate amounts.

Plant proteins are an important part of a vegetarian diet. The key to using plant foods is mutual supplementation of the amino acids of various foods. Individual plant foods must be supplemented either by the use of a small amount of animal protein, or by combining them with other plant foods. Because animal foods generally have a complete amino acid pattern, they complement most plant foods. For example, a small amount of meat may be extended by combining it with grains or legumes, cereal and milk, macaroni and cheese, spaghetti and meat balls, peanut butter and milk are further examples of complementing plant foods with a small amount of animal food. Dairy foods are a particularly effective complement because they are a good source of lysine, one of the eight essential amino acids.

Combining two or more plant proteins to obtain high quality protein depends on matching the strength and weakness of individual foods. Nuts, seeds and grain are generally low in lysine and relatively good in tryptophan and sulfur-containing amino acids. In general, legumes are good sources of lysine and poor sources of tryptophan and sulfur-containing amino acids.

However, the evaluation of the total nutrient intake is required when extensive substitution of plant for animal foods is to be undertaken. Particular attention should be given to amounts of vitamin D, vitamin B_{12}, riboflavin and minerals provided in an all vegetable diet.

General advice to vegetarians is to incorporate a great variety of foods in their diet. This is good advice for all of us because then we are all more likely to be correctly nourished. The daily recommended allowance (U.S. RDA) of the necessary vitamins and minerals is tabularized in Table 2.2.

TABLE 2.3

U.S. RECOMMENDED DAILY ALLOWANCE (U.S. RDA)*

Vitamins Minerals and Protein	Unit of Measurement	Infants	Adults and Children 4 or More Years of Age	Children Under 4 Years of age	Pregnant or Nursing Women
Vitamin A	IU	1500	5000	2500	8000
Vitamin D	"	400	400[1]	400	400
Vitamin E	"	5.0	30	10	30
Vitamin C	mg	35	60	40	60
Folic Acid	"	0.1	0.4	0.2	0.8
Thiamine	"	0.5	1.5	0.7	1.7
Riboflavin	"	0.6	1.7	0.8	2.0
Niacin	"	8.0	20	9.0	20
Vitamin B_6	"	0.4	2.0	0.7	2.5
Vitamin B_{12}	mcg	2.0	6.0	3.0	8.0
Biotin	mg	0.5	0.3	0.15	0.3
Pantothenic Acid	"	3.0	10	5.0	10
Calcium	g	0.6	1.0	0.8	1.3
Phosphorus	"	0.5	1.0	0.8	1.3
Iodine	mcg	45	150	70	150
Iron	mg	15	18	10	18
Magnesium	"	70	400	200	450
Copper	"	0.6	2.0	1.0	2.0
Zinc	"	5.0	15	8.0	15
Protein	g	18[2]	45[2]	20[2]	

LEGEND:

IU = International Units
mg = milligrams
mcg = micrograms
g = grams

[1]Presence optional for adults and children 4 or more years of age in vitamin and mineral supplements.
[2]If protein efficiency ratio of protein is equal to or better than that of casein, U.S. RDA is 45 g. for adults, 18 g. for infants, and 20 g. for children under 4.

*U.S. DEPARTMENT OF HEALTH, EDUCATION, AND WELFARE, Public Health Service, Food and Drug Administration, Office of Public Affairs, 5600 Fishers Lane, Rockville, Maryland 20852, HEW Publication No. (FDA) 76-2042, Revised January 1976.

LAB EXPERIENCE 2.4

FOOD NUTRIENT ANALYSIS

Introduction:

In addition to the four food groupings, all foods contain nutrients which are classified as:

proteins
carbohydrates (starches and sugars)
lipids (fats and oils)
vitamins and minerals

The presence of these nutrients can be detected in our everyday foods by a few simple standard tests. The lab experience is divided into six parts as follows:

Part A - Test for simple sugars
Part B - Tests for starches
Part C - Tests for protein
Part D - Tests for lipids
Part E - Tests for minerals
Part F - Tests for all of the above nutrients

NOTE: Analysis for vitamin C will be done in a subsequent lab experience.

Materials

Safety goggles	Graduated cylinder, 10-ml	Triangle or wire
10% glucose solution	Biuret solution	gauze
1% starch solution	Hot plate	Cutting boards
Raw egg white	1 250-ml beaker per group	Porcelain crucible
Vegetable oil	2 test tubes, 1 holder & rack	Basin
Benedict's solution	per group	Detergent for glass-
Lugol's iodine solution	Foods to be tested	ware
Glass marking pencils	Distilled or deionized water	
Knife	Sudan 3 solution, freshly	
Hot mitts	prepared	
Test tube brushes	Rubber stoppers	

NOTE: Wash and dry test tubes thoroughly after each experiment so they may be used in the succeeding sections of the experiment. Wash hands thoroughly if chemicals spill on them. All solutions used in the experiment should be refrigerated between lab sessions.

LAB EXPERIENCE 2.4 (Continued)

FOOD NUTRIENT ANALYSIS

Part A.   Simple Sugar Test

Purpose: To perform a positive test for simple sugars, such as glucose or fructose.

Procedure: This test relies on a series of color changes that occur in the presence of the simple sugar.   A precipitate color of green to yellow to orange to rust indicates the presence of the simple sugar.   Sucrose and other complex sugars are not detected by this test.

1.   Put 200 ml of tap water into beaker and place it on hot plate until the water boils.   Mark 2 tubes--one "A", the other "B".
2.   Add 2 ml of distilled water to each tube.
3.   To test tube B add 2 ml of glucose solution.
4.   To both test tubes add 2 ml of Benedict's solution.
5.   Shake the tubes gently, and note the color of the solution in each of the tubes.
6.   Heat the mixtures by holding the test tubes with a test tube holder in a 250 ml beaker of boiling water.   Do not let the tubes rest on the bottom of the beaker.   At the end of 2 minutes remove from beaker.   Be careful of hot test tubes and boiling water.

Observations:

1.   Before heating, record solution color in test tube A: _____
     Before heating, record solution color in test tube B: _____
2.   After heating, record solution color in test tube A: _____
     After heating, record solution color in test tube B: _____

Question:

What is the purpose of test tube A?

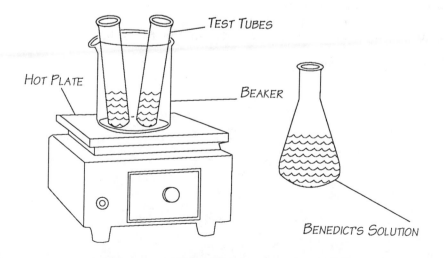

LAB EXPERIENCE 2.4 (Continued)

FOOD NUTRIENT ANALYSIS

Part B. Starch Test

Purpose: To perform a positive test for starch.

Procedure: This test uses Lugol's iodine test solution which turns blue or blue-black in the presence of starch.

1. Use 2 test tubes marked A and B respectively.
2. Add 2 ml of distilled water to each tube.
3. To tube B add 2 ml starch solution.
4. Add 4-5 drops of Lugol's iodine solution to each of the test tubes. Shake gently.

Observations:

1. What final color appears in tube A? _____
2. What final color appears in tube B? _____

Part C. Protein Test

Purpose: To perform a positive test for protein.

Procedure: This test relies upon the substance to turn purplish-violet or pink-violet in the presence of the Biuret solution.

1. Mark 2 clean test tubes one A and the other B.
2. Add 2 ml of distilled water to each tube.
3. Add 2 ml of raw egg white to test tube B. Shake gently to mix.
4. Add 2 ml of Biuret solution to each of the test tubes. Shake gently to mix.

Observations:

1. What color appears in tube A? _____
2. What color appears in tube B? _____
3. Is there any other difference between the two solutions?

   Yes _____   No _____

4. If so, describe.

LAB EXPERIENCE 2.4 (Continued)

FOOD NUTRIENT ANALYSIS

Part D. Lipid Test

Purpose: To perform a positive test for fat.

Procedure: In this test, the presence of fat causes the fat testing solution Sudan 3, to turn from orange to red. Cholesterol causes a less bright red color.

1. Mark 2 test tubes A and B respectively.
2. Add 2 ml of distilled water to each of the tubes.
3. Add 1 ml of vegetable oil to tube B.
4. Add 1 ml of fat testing solution to each tube. Place a rubber stopper in each tube and shake thoroughly. Allow to stand for 3 to 5 minutes. (A fat testing solution is a dye which is insoluble in water but soluble in lipids).

Observations:

1a. What color appeared in tube A? _____

 b. Where?

2a. What happened to the oil and water mixture in tube B?

 b. What color appeared?

 c. Where?

3. Is there a difference in color between the oil and the water?

Part E. Minerals Test

Purpose: To perform a positive test for minerals.

Procedure: In this test, a gray-white ash will result when the foods are exposed to flames.

1. Put the food in a porcelain crucible and place it on triangle or wire gauze over a flame. It will get hot!!

2. The substance may first turn to black ash and then gray-white. This gray-white ash shows the presence of minerals.

LAB EXPERIENCE 2.4 (Continued)

FOOD NUTRIENT ANALYSIS

Part F.   Testing Everyday Foods

Purpose: To detect simple sugar, starch, lipids, and minerals in everyday foods.

Procedure: In these experiments, substitute 6 different foods for the known food nutrients. Replace the glucose solution (sugar test) with a food; replace starch solution with food; replace egg white (protein test) with food; replace vegetable oil (lipid test) with food. Include a wide variety of foods for your tests.

In each of the tests, repeat the experiments exactly as you did them before except that now you are using real foods instead of known nutrients. Watch carefully, use clean dry test tubes, don't rush and only do one experiment at a time. Immediately after each test complete the following chart.

Data Chart: Indicate positive color reaction for each nutrient, draw a line where there is none.

	Food	Glucose	Starch	Protein	Fats	Minerals
1						
2						
3						
4						
5						
6						

Questions:

1.   Which of the foods show a positive test for more than one nutrient?

2.   Did any of the foods show negative results for all of the groups?

LAB EXPERIENCE 2.5

FOOD NUTRIENT ANALYSIS TABULATION

Purpose: To determine the nutritional value and calorie count of an average or typical breakfast or lunch.

Procedure: Determine the meal, and list the foods in the data chart. Then determine the remainder of required information to complete the chart.

Useful Information:

    Protein: 4 calories/g
    Carbohydrates: 4 calories/g
    Fat: 9 calories/g

List the foods and quantity of each item:

Food	Quantity	Protein	Carbohydrates	Fats	Calories

VITAMINS AND MINERALS

Vitamins are not intended as food replacements only as food supplements. They are a necessary part of the diet and should be eaten on a regular basis. The guidelines for vitamin supplements should be the age, weight, and activity of the individual. Vitamins are organic compounds. They are necessary in small amounts, in the diet, for the normal growth and maintenance in the life of every animal including man.

Vitamins do not provide energy nor do they construct or build any part of the body. They are needed for transforming foods into energy and for body maintenance. There are about 15 vitamins, and if any is missing, then a deficiency becomes apparent in the body.

Vitamins are alike because they are made of the same chemical elements: carbon, hydrogen, oxygen, and sometimes nitrogen. Vitamins are different because their chemical elements are arranged in different combinations, and each vitamin performs one or more exclusive functions in the body.

Vitamins are measured in extremely small amounts because it takes very little to generate the needed chemical reaction. Some vitamins are described in I.U. (international units) which simply means that a given amount of activity can be measured. Others are expressed by weight only (milligrams or micrograms).

Synthetic vitamins, manufactured in the laboratory, are identical to natural vitamins found in foods. The body cannot tell the difference and gets the same benefits from either source. Statements such as "Nature cannot be imitated" and "Natural vitamins have the essence of life" are without meaning. Vitamins will not provide extra pep or vitality beyond normal expectations, or an unusual level of well being. Vitamin sources are varied and abundant and have been for many centuries. Excess vitamins are a complete waste, both in money and effect. However, present food processing, stresses in our daily lives, and pollution in the environment all make for uncertainty as to individual vitamin requirements.

A brief "ABC" of vitamins is presented here and tabularized in Table 2.3.

1. *Vitamin A* — Vitamin A, a fat soluble vitamin, is stored principally in the liver. It occurs in significant amounts in fish liver oils, animal liver, eggs, whole milk, green and yellow vegetables, yellow fruits and fortified margarine. These green and yellow fruits and vegetables are the best sources of carotene which the body converts to vitamin A. When absent in significant amounts, night blindness and other eye disorders may occur, as well as dry and brittle hair and skin, and infections of the mucous membranes. Although this vitamin is necessary for new cell growth and healthy tissues, an excess of vitamin A may cause headaches, nausea, and irritability.

2. *Vitamin B_1* — Vitamin B_1, also known as thiamine, is a water soluble vitamin as are all of the vitamins in the B-complex group. Thiamine is required for normal digestion, and is necessary for growth, fertility, lactation, and the normal functioning of nerve tissue. It is needed on a daily basis because it aids in the efficient use of fats and carbohydrates by the body. Thiamine is found in lean pork, beans, dried peas and nuts, liver, milk, eggs, and enriched and whole grain breads and cereals. A severe deficiency of vitamin B_1 causes beriberi. Lesser deficiencies affect the efficiency of the central nervous system and brain, and cause

pains in the calf and thigh muscles.

3. *Vitamin B₂* — Vitamin B_2, also known as riboflavin, is water soluble. It is found in beef, chicken liver, salmon, nuts, beans, lean meat, milk, eggs, leafy vegetables, and in enriched and whole grain bread. It is needed for vision, growth, and the absorption of iron; it helps the body to obtain energy from carbohydrates and protein substances. A deficiency causes lip sores and cracks.

4. *Niacin* — Niacin, is water soluble. It is found in liver, fish, lean meats and poultry, peas, beans, potatoes, nuts, and whole grain products. Niacin is necessary for the healthy condition of all tissue cells, and for the efficient use of protein. A lack of niacin results in intestinal disorders, mental depression, skin rashes and rough skin. Niacin is one of the most stable of the vitamins, the most easily obtainable, and the cheapest.

5. *Vitamin B₆* — Vitamin B_6 known as pyridoxine, is water soluble. It is found abundantly in liver, whole grain cereals, potatoes, red meat, bananas, green vegetables, and yellow corn. Pyridoxine is essential in the metabolism of protein, for growth, and for maintenance of body functions. A deficiency may result in anemia, dizziness, nausea, weight loss, and sometimes severe nervous disturbances.

6. *Vitamin B₁₂* — Vitamin B_{12} is water soluble. It is only found in meat and other animal products. It is not present in any measurable amount in plants which is the reason that strict vegetarians should supplement their diets with this vitamin. Vitamin B_{12} is essential for the normal functioning of body cells and particularly for the normal development of red blood cells. A deficiency causes pernicious anemia, and if the deficiency is prolonged, a degeneration of the spinal cord occurs. There is some indication that the body's ability to absorb vitamin B_{12} may decrease with age.

7. *Biotin* — Biotin is water soluble. It is found in liver, oysters, eggs, beans, peanuts, and whole grains. It is important in the metabolism of fats, carbohydrates, and proteins. A mild deficiency may contribute to muscle pains, depression, lack of appetite, and sleeplessness.

8. *Folic Acid* — Folic acid, known as folacin, is water soluble. It is found in abundance in liver and dark green leafy vegetables. Folic acid helps in the manufacture of red blood cells and is essential in normal metabolism. When absent, the lack of it may cause gastrointestinal distress and lead to pernicious anemia.

9. *Pantothenic Acid* — Pantothenic acid is a water soluble B-complex vitamin. It is found abundantly in liver, eggs, white potatoes, sweet potatoes, peas and beans. Pantothenic acid is needed to support a variety of body functions, including proper growth and maintenance of the body. A deficiency causes headache, fatigue, poor muscle coordination, nausea, cramps, and some loss of antibody production in human beings.

10. *Vitamin C* — Vitamin C is a water soluble vitamin. It is found in oranges and other citrus fruits, tomatoes, raw potatoes, strawberries, currants and such green vegetables as lettuce, cabbage, broccoli, mustard and turnip greens, and raw green peppers. Vitamin C is essential in forming collagen which is the substance that holds the cells of the body together; it promotes growth and tissue repair, including the healing of wounds. It aids in tooth formation, bone formation, and repair. When used as a food additive, vitamin C acts as a preservative. A lack of this vitamin may cause bleeding, swollen joints, and scurvy. Vitamin C is easily destroyed by heat and air. It is the only vitamin which is not stored in body tissues; therefore the body must have some every day.

11. *Vitamin D* — Vitamin D is fat soluble. It is found abundantly in fish oils such as herring, salmon and tuna, in egg yolk, and vitamin D fortified milk. It is called the "sunshine" vitamin since it is formed in the skin by the sun's ultraviolet rays. It aids in the absorption of calcium and phosphorus for bone and tooth formation. A deficiency of vitamin D causes rickets which is a deformation of the skeleton. Too much vitamin D causes nausea, weight loss, hypertension, and calcification of soft tissues including the blood vessels and kidneys. The daily dietary requirement of vitamin D is small, and any excess is stored in the body.

12. *Vitamin E* — Vitamin E is a fat soluble vitamin. It is found in whole grain wheat products, vegetable oils, beans, eggs, and liver. Vitamin E is known as an antithrombin and an antioxidant. Thus, the vitamin helps to prevent oxygen from destroying other substances. It acts as a preservative and protects the efficiency of other compounds such as vitamin A. Its absence leads to reproductive failure in many animals. Vitamin E is not the most important vitamin, but it is one of the most talked about.

13. *Vitamin K* — Vitamin K is fat soluble. It is found in green, leafy vegetables, liver, and egg yolk. It is essential for the clotting of blood. One type is found naturally in food, another is made in the intestinal tract, and a third can be made synthetically.

TABLE 2.4

VITAMINS

Vitamins	Solubility	Adult Daily Requirements	Deficiency Symtoms	Good Sources
A	Fat	5000 IU	Night blindness, dry & brittle hair & skin, infections of mucous membranes	Green & yellow fruits & vegetables, whole milk, fish liver oils, liver, eggs
B₁ (Thiamine)	Water	1.5 mg	Retardation of growth, infertility, deficient functioning of nerve tissue, beriberi	Whole & enriched grains, dried peas, beans, nuts, lean pork, liver, eggs, milk
B₂ (Riboflavin)	Water	1.7 mg	Lip sores & cracks	Lean meat, leafy vegetables, liver, salmon, nuts, whole & enriched grains, milk, eggs
Niacin	Water	20 mg	Intestinal disorders, mental depression, skin rashes, rough skin	Meats, poultry, liver, fish, peas, beans, nuts, whole grains
B₆	Water	2 mg	Anemia, dizziness, nausea, nervous disturbances	Liver, red meat, whole grains, bananas, green vegetables, yellow corn
B₁₂	Water	6 micrograms	Pernicious anemia	Meat & other animal products
Biotin	Water	0.3 mg	Muscle pains, depression, lack of appetite, sleeplessness	Liver, oysters, eggs, whole grains, peanuts
Folic acid	Water	0.4 mg	Gastrointestinal upset, pernicious anemia	Liver, dark green leafy vegetables
Pantothenic acid	Water	10 mg	Headache, nausea, cramps, loss of antibody production, poor muscle coordination	Liver, eggs, potatoes, peas, beans
C	Water	60 mg	Bleeding & swollen gums & joints, scurvy	Citrus fruits, tomatoes, strawberries, green vegetables as peppers, cabbage, lettuce
D	Fat	400 IU	Soft bones and deformation of skeleton	Fish oils, egg yolk, Vit. D fortified milk
E	Fat	30 mg	Reproductive failure in laboratory animals	Whole grains, liver, eggs, vegetable oils
K	Fat	Not Known	Anemia	Green leafy vegetables, liver, egg yolk

VITAMIN C

Vitamin C is an essential food substance. Most animals are able to produce it from sugars within their own bodies. But humans must obtain it from food. Because the body has a limited ability to store vitamin C, adequate amounts must be ingested at frequent intervals.

The most important function of vitamin C, or ascorbic acid, is the control it has on the ability of the body cells to produce collagen. This is a substance that binds cells together and keeps them in proper relation to each other. The maintenance of the capillary blood vessels, the dentine of the teeth, the bones, and the connective tissues of the body are dependent on this function. A severe deficiency of vitamin C leads to a disease known as scurvy. The amount of vitamin C needed to prevent scurvy and to maintain good health was established by the Food and Nutrition Board of the National Academy of Sciences. Based on its recommendations, FDA has set the U.S. RDA of vitamin C at 45 to 60 mg daily for women and men, 40 to 55 mg for children, and 60 mg for women during pregnancy and nursing.

These amounts may be obtained from the many sources of vitamin C in the diet. Vegetables and fruits provide the greatest amounts. Foods with high vitamin C content, in descending order of concentration include: oranges, cantaloupes, fresh orange juice, grapefruits, fresh strawberries, broccoli, spinach and other "greens," sweet potatoes, and tomato juice. All of these foods provide more than 20 mg per serving. Among the foods that provide little or no ascorbic acid are dry beans, poultry, eggs, cheese, cereals, fats, oils, and sugar.

Actually, there is no way of knowing the exact ascorbic acid value of any particular food at the time it is eaten. Its content is affected by many factors, such as conditions under which the food was grown, the time and temperature involved in handling, the kind and amount of processing or cooking it has undergone, and the conditions of storage before use. However, anyone who eats a sufficient number of foods known to be high in vitamin C will have no trouble obtaining the recommended amount.

As has been the case with other vitamins, some people have assumed that "if a little is good, a lot will be better." In the case of vitamin C, this does not appear to be true. According to all studies documented at the present time, the body uses only the amount of ascorbic acid it needs and eliminates the rest through the kidneys. When body tissues are saturated with vitamin C, additional intake is excreted in the urine. When the body tissues are depleted of vitamin C, a high intake is absorbed and retained.

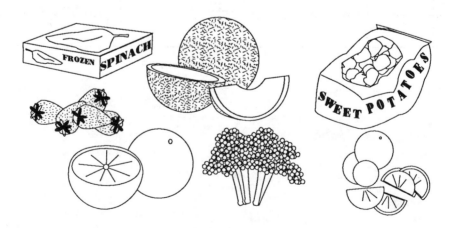

LAB EXPERIENCE 2.6

VITAMIN C DETERMINATION

Most measurements of vitamin C are based on its oxidation-reduction properties. When a substance loses hydrogen atoms or electrons, it is oxidized. The substance gaining the electrons is reduced. The second and third carbon atoms in the ascorbic acid chain easily lose their hydrogen atoms to appropriate substances, thereby forming dehydroascorbic acid.

You will be doing experiments using the dye 2,6-dichlorophenol indophenol. It is dark blue in oxidized form and changes to a light pink or becomes colorless when it is reduced. When solutions of ascorbic acid and the dye are mixed, the ascorbic acid gives up its hydrogen atoms to the dye. The ascorbic acid is oxidized and the dye is reduced.

The test, used with the suggested foods, gives a qualitative indication of the amount of vitamin C present in the foods. It also indicates the oxidation of vitamin C during processing. We will further check to see if there is any relationship between the Vitamin C content and the sugar content of the tested foods. You can obtain the necessary chemicals from a scientific supply company.

This lab experience is divided into the following five parts:

      Part A - Test for vitamin C in the cooking water of vegetables
      Part B - Test for vitamin C in fresh fruits and vegetables
      Part C - Test for vitamin C in the cooking water of vegetables which contains an additive
      Part D - Test for the effect of heat on sugar content of vegetables
      Part E - Test for sugar in cooked food solutions

The testing solutions are prepared as follows:

1. Prepare a stock solution of 2,6-dichlorophenol indophenol by dissolving 1 gram of 2,6-dichlorophenol indophenol in 100 ml of triple distilled water.

2. Prepare a 0.1% solution of 2,6-dichlorophenol indophenol by diluting the stock solution in a 1:10 ratio with triple distilled water and filter. May be kept under refrigeration for up to 5 days.

LAB EXPERIENCE 2.6 (Continued)

VITAMIN C DETERMINATION

Materials:

Knife
Glass marking pencils
Beakers, 2 50-ml, 2 100-ml, 1 250-ml
Low flat dishes (for storage)
Test tubes
Hot plates
Graduated cylinder, 50 ml
Test tube holder and rack

Strainers
0.1% dicholorophenol
   indophenol
Distilled water
Baking soda
Benedict's solution
Medicine dropper
Cutting board
Measuring spoon -
   1 tablespoon size

This test will indicate the presence of vitamin C in food and also indicate how rapidly vitamin C deteriorates under various conditions.

- Oranges
- Grapefruits
- Apples
- Green peppers
- Cabbage

Part A.

Purpose: To test for the presence of vitamin C in the cooking water of green peppers and cabbage

Procedure:

1. Place 2 tablespoons of chopped food in each of two 100 ml beakers. Add 30 ml of distilled water to each beaker. Place the beakers on a hot plate.

2. Heat one beaker for 7 minutes, the other for 25 minutes. Start timing when the mixture begins to boil.

   NOTE: Water will evaporate from the beakers. Add sufficient distilled water during heating to maintain a constant 30 ml volume, and to avoid burning.

3. When you have finished heating each sample, pour the liquid into a graduated cylinder. If 30 ml of liquid is not present, add sufficient water to make up to 30 ml volume. A constant volume is essential. Pour water into 50 ml beaker. Cool the cooking water. (Set it aside).

4. Remove and set aside 1 ml of each of the cooking waters for Part D (sugar test).

LAB EXPERIENCE 2.6 (Continued)

VITAMIN C DETERMINATION

Place 10 drops of 0.1% dichlorophenol indophenol in test tube. Add the reserved cooking water, drop by drop. Shake vigorously after each addition. Do not exceed 80 drops of the food solution.

If the dye solution turns pale pink or colorless, then vitamin C is present. Record the number of drops of cooking water needed to turn the dye colorless or light pink.

Repeat the experiment using the second vegetable.

NOTE: The more drops of food solution that is required to turn the dye colorless, the less vitamin C is present in the solution.

0-14 Drops	=	Most vitamin C
15-35 Drops	=	Goodly amount of vitamin C
36-55 Drops	=	Fair amount of vitamin C
56-75 Drops	=	Very little vitamin C
76 plus	=	Almost none or no vitamin C

Complete the following chart:

od	# Drops of Food Solution Used	Relative Amount of Vitamin C in Solution
een pepper solution		
7 minutes		
25 minutes		
bbage Solution		
7 minutes		
25 minutes		

estion:

at effect does cooking time have on loss of vitamin C?

LAB EXPERIENCE 2.6 (Continued)

VITAMIN C DETERMINATION

Part B.

Purpose: Test for the presence of vitamin C in fresh oranges, grapefruits, apples, green peppers, cabbage. Select two or three for testing purposes and prepare only one at a time.

Procedure:

1.   Peel the food, if necessary, and finely chop. Save as much of the juice as is possible.

2.   Measure 2 tablespoons of the chopped food and juice, and place it in a beaker containing 30 ml of distilled water.

3.   Allow to soak 15 minutes, then drain the vegetable, SAVE THE LIQUID. This is the testing solution. Reserve 1 ml for Part E (sugar test), the remainder is for this experiment.

4.   Place 10 drops of 0.1% dichlorophenol indophenol in a test tube. Initially the dye is a dark blue.

5.   Add the food testing solution, drop by drop to the dye in the test tube. Shake the tube vigorously after each addition of the food solution and observe color.

6.   If the dye solution turns light pink or colorless, then vitamin C is present. Record the number of drops of food solution that has been used to turn the dye light pink or colorless. Do not exceed 80 drops of the food solution.

7.   Record your findings on the chart.

Food	# Drops of Food Solution Used	Relative Amount of Vitamin C in Solution
Orange solution		
Grapefruit solution		
Apple solution		
Green pepper solution		
Cabbage solution		

Questions:

1.   Why was vitamin C detected in the soaking water?

2.   Why would there be a difference, if any, in the amount of vitamin C found in cooking water and soaking water of the same vegetable?

LAB EXPERIENCE 2.6 (Continued)

VITAMIN C DETERMINATION

Part C.

Purpose: Test for the presence of vitamin C in the cooking water of either green pepper or cabbage with the addition of an additive.

Procedure:

1. Place 2 tablespoons of the chopped food and a pinch of baking soda in 100 ml beaker. Add 30 ml of distilled water.

2. Place on hot plate and heat for 7 minutes. Start timing when mixture begins to boil.

    NOTE: Water will evaporate from the beaker. Add sufficient distilled water during heating to maintain a constant 30 ml volume, and to avoid burning.

3. When you have finished heating each sample, pour the liquid into a graduated beaker. If 30 ml of liquid are not present, add sufficient distilled water to make up the 30 ml volume. Cool the cooking liquid. Save the cooked vegetables.

4. Place 10 drops of dye in a test tube. Add the cooled cooking liquid, drop by drop. Shake vigorously after each drop. Observe the color.

5. If the dye (which starts out as dark blue) turns colorless or light pink, then vitamin C is present.

6. Record your findings on the chart.

Food	# Drops of Food Solution Used	Relative Amount of Vitamin C in Solution
Green Pepper Solution		
Cabbage Solution		

Questions:

1. What effect does the baking soda have on the color and texture of the vegetables?

2. What effect does the baking soda have on vitamin C?

LAB EXPERIENCE 2.6 (Continued)

VITAMIN C DETERMINATION

Part D.

Purpose: To test for the effect of heat on the sugar content of vegetables.

Procedure:

1. Use the reserved cooking solution (1 ml) from Part A, Step 4.

2. Place 1 ml of each of the green pepper solutions into test tubes, and add 1 ml of Benedict's Qualitative Solution to each tube.

3. Heat the mixtures by holding the tubes with a test tube holder in a 250-ml beaker of boiling water. Do not let the test tubes rest on the bottom of the beaker.

4. If the blue color of the Benedict's solution changes to green, orange, or reddish, or if a white precipitate forms, then a sugar is present.

5. Record results on the chart.

Food	First Test for Sugar		Second Test	
	Positive	Negative	Positive	Negative
Green pepper solution				
7 minutes				
25 minutes				
Cabbage solution				
7 minutes				
25 minutes				

6. Repeat the experiment using the reserved liquid from the second vegetable.

Questions:

1. What is the effect of heat on the loss of sugar during cooking?

2. Does the amount of sugar found in the cooking water correspond to vitamin C content?

3. What would be the best way to prepare and cook a vegetable so that the vitamin C content remains high?

LAB EXPERIENCE 2.6 (Continued)

VITAMIN C DETERMINATION

Part E.

Purpose: To test for the presence of sugar in fruits and vegetables.

Procedure:

1. Place in a test tube the 1 ml of reserved solution from Part B, Step 3 of the lab in vitamin C analysis of oranges, grapefruits, apples, green peppers and cabbage.

2. Add 1 ml of Benedict's Qualitative Solution.

3. Heat the solution by holding the test tube with a test tube holder in a 250 ml beaker of boiling water. Do not allow the test tube to rest on the bottom of the beaker.

4. If the blue color of the Benedict's solution changes to green, orange, reddish, or a white precipitate forms, then a sugar is present.

    Green color indicates the presence of sucrose;
    Orange or rust indicates the presence of glucose;
    Reddish color indicates the presence of fructose.

5. Record your observations on the following chart.

Food	Test for Sugar	
	Positive	Negative
Orange solution		
Grapefruit solution		
Apple solution		
Green pepper solution		
Cabbage solution		

Question:

What is the effect of soaking on loss of sugar?

LAB EXPERIENCE 2.7

VITAMIN C COMPARISONS

Purpose: To compare several fruit juice products for cost, vitamin C content, and the juice to water ratio.

Procedure: Using information from the labels on the following items complete the data chart. Use punch, ade, frozen juices, drinks.

Brand & Product	Cost Per Cup (8 oz.)	Vitamin C Per 8 oz. cup	% Fruit Juice Per Cup

Questions:

1. Considering the vitamin C content, which is the best buy in juice? Why?

2. Considering percent natural fruit juice in the beverages, which is the best buy? Why?

100% PURE ORANGE JUICE

1 LITER $1.75 PER LITER

ORANGE DRINK

25% FRUIT JUICE

1 LITER $1.67 PER LITER

MACROMINERALS

While vitamins usually take center stage in any discussion of dietary supplements, minerals too are essential for good health and for growth. Just the right amount of minerals in our diet is necessary.

Some minerals are needed in relatively large amounts in the diet: calcium, phosphorus, sodium, chlorine, potassium, magnesium, and sulfur. These "macrominerals" are needed in quantities from a few milligrams to one gram. Other minerals, called "trace minerals," are needed in small amounts. These are iron, manganese, copper, iodine, zinc, cobalt, fluorine, and selenium. Some minerals, such as lead, mercury and cadmium are considered to be harmful in any amount.

Even minerals the body requires for good health can be harmful in excess. Taking too much of one essential mineral may upset the balance and function of other minerals in the body. For example, an excess of calcium interferes with the functions of the essential elements iron and copper. An excess mineral intake may also reduce your ability to perform physical tasks, and can contribute to such health problems as anemia, neurological disease, and fetal abnormalities. The risks are greatest for the very young, pregnant or nursing women, the elderly, and those with inadequate diet or chronic disease.

Mineral elements have two general body functions: building and regulating. Their building functions affect the skeleton and all soft tissues. Their regulating functions include a wide variety of systems, such as heartbeat, blood clotting, maintenance of the internal pressure of body fluids, nerve responses, and the transport of oxygen from the lungs to the tissues.

A brief description of the macrominerals is presented here. The information is also tabularized in Table 2-4.

1. *Calcium* — Almost all of the 2 to 3 pounds of calcium present in the body are concentrated in the bones and teeth. Small amounts help to regulate certain body processes such as the normal behavior of nerves, muscle and blood clotting. All people need calcium in their diets throughout their lifetime. Milk and milk products are good sources of this mineral, as are green leafy vegetables, citrus fruits, dried peas and beans, salmon and sardines. Meat, grains and nuts do not provide significant amounts of calcium.

2. *Phosphorus* — This mineral is present with calcium, in almost equal amounts, in the bones and teeth of the body. Some good sources are meat, poultry, fish, eggs, and whole grain foods. Vegetables and fruits are generally low in this mineral.

3. *Sodium and Chlorine* — These two elements are combined in sodium chloride (table salt), but each has a separate function in the body. Sodium is found mainly in blood plasma and in the fluids outside the body cells. Sodium helps to maintain normal water balance inside and outside the cells. Sodium-rich foods come from animal sources such as meat, fish, poultry, eggs, and milk. Many processed foods, such as ham, bacon, bread, and crackers have a high sodium content because salt or sodium compounds are added in processing. Chlorine is part of hydrochloric acid, which is found in high concentrations in the gastric juice, and is very important for the digestion of food in the stomach.

Everyone needs some sodium in his diet (at least 230 mg/day) which is approximately 1/10 of 1 teaspoon of salt. By some estimates, Americans consume about twenty times that amount — about 2 teaspoons of salt per day. Fondness for salt is an acquired taste rather than a physiological need. Many people suffer no ill effects from a high salt intake, but about 20% of American adults tend to be affected by the amount of sodium in their diet. These people are suffering from high blood pressure, kidney disease, cirrhosis of the liver, and congestive heart disease. A decrease in sodium intake can reduce the retention of water in the body which is typically associated with these health problems. A discussion of high blood pressure is more fully covered in the paragraph on hypertension.

Today, about 55% of the food bought in developed countries is processed, and we eat about half of our meals outside the home. Other people therefore, have control over our salt intake. At the present time, all that a manufacturer must tell the consumer is that there is salt present as an ingredient. It is only optional for a manufacturer to list on the label the amount of sodium chloride present in the food. Sodium chloride is about 40% sodium. Other important sodium sources would be monosodium glutamate (MSG), sodium phosphate and sodium nitrate. Examples of the approximate sodium chloride content of some foods are:

   Corn Flakes — 1 oz.: 260 mg
   Cocktail Peanuts — 1 oz.:
      132 mg
   White Bread — 2 slices:
      234 mg
   Potato Chips — 1 oz. bag:
      191 mg

   Bologna — 3 slices/serving:
      672 mg
   Chocolate Flavor Instant Pudding — 1/2 cup: 404 mg
   Beans and Franks — 8 oz.
      serving: 958 mg
   Italian Dressing — 1 T.:
      315 mg
   Frozen Fried Chicken Dinner:
      1152 mg
   Dill Pickle — 1 large: 1137 mg
   Tomato Juice — per serving:
      292 mg
   Bacon — per serving: 302 mg
   Instant Beef Broth — per serving: 818 mg
   Chunk White Tuna — per serving: 628 mg
   Milk — per serving: 120 mg
   Beefaroni — per serving:
      1186 mg

4. *Potassium* — Potassium is found mainly in the fluid inside each of the body's cells. In conjunction with sodium, potassium helps to regulate the volume and balance of body fluids. A potassium deficiency is very rare in healthy people, but may result from prolonged diarrhea or from the use of diuretics. Potassium is abundant in bananas, milk, dates, citrus fruits, apricots and green leafy vegetables.

5. *Magnesium* — Magnesium is found in all body tissues, but principally in the bones. It is an essential part of many enzyme systems responsible for energy conversions in the body. A deficiency of magnesium in healthy humans eating a variety of foods is rare, but it has been observed in some postsurgical patients, and in alcoholics.

6. *Sulfur* — Sulfur is present in all body tissues and is essential to life. It is related to protein nutrition

because it is a component of several important amino acids. It is also part of two vitamins: thiamine and biotin.

TRACE ELEMENTS

These are present in extremely small amounts in the body, but as with the other essential nutrients, we could not live without them. Most of them do not occur in the body in their free form, but are bound to organic compounds on which they depend for transport, storage, and function. Our understanding of the importance of these elements comes primarily from studies in animals. A brief description of each mineral is presented here. The information is also tabularized in Table 2-5.

1. *Iron* — Iron is an important part of compounds necessary for transporting oxygen to the cells, and making use of the oxygen when it arrives. It is widely distributed in the body, mostly in the blood, with relatively large amounts in the liver, spleen, and bone marrow. Diets that provide enough iron must be carefully selected because only a few foods contain iron in useful amounts. Liver is an excellent source of iron. Other good sources are meat products, egg yolk, fish, green leafy vegetables, peas, beans, dried fruits, whole grain cereals, and foods prepared from iron enriched cereal products.

2. *Manganese* — Manganese is needed for normal tendon and bone structure, and is part of some enzymes. Manganese is abundant in many foods, especially bran, coffee, tea, nuts, peas and beans.

3. *Copper* — Copper is involved in regulating the storage of iron to form hemoglobin for red blood cells. The need for copper is particularly important in the early months of life and if the intake of the mother is sufficient, infants are born with a store of copper. Copper occurs in most unprocessed foods, organ meats, shellfish, nuts and dried legumes.

4. *Iodine* — Iodine is required in extremely small amounts, but the normal functioning of the thyroid gland depends on an adequate supply. When a deficiency of dietary iodine occurs, then thyroid enlargement (goiter) occurs. Foods from the sea are the richest natural sources of iodine.

5. *Zinc* — Zinc is an important part of the enzymes that (among other functions) move carbon dioxide via red blood cells from the tissues to the lungs where it can be exhaled. Zinc is usually associated with protein foods such as meats, fish, egg yolks, and milk. Whole grain cereals are also rich in zinc but because of the presence of other substances, such as phytin, the zinc may not be completely available for absorption.

6. *Cobalt* — Cobalt is an essential part of vitamin B_{12}. It is found in meat, eggs, and dairy products. Vegetarians who do not eat these foods can become deficient in cobalt since it occurs only in trace amounts in plants.

7. *Chromium* — Chromium acting in combination with insulin, is required for glucose utilization. A deficiency can produce a diabetes-like condition. Some good sources are dried brewer's yeast, whole grain cereals, and liver.

8. *Selenium* — Selenium appears to be a mineral necessary for growing animals. A variety of problems

occur in selenium and vitamin E deficient animals; it is reasonably certain that this mineral is also important for man.

9. *Fluorine* — Fluorine, like iodine, is found in small and varying amounts in water, soil, plants, and animals. Fluoride compounds contribute to solid tooth formation, which results in a decrease of dental caries, especially in children. There is also evidence that fluorides help retain calcium in the bones of older people. The acceptable level of this mineral in drinking water is only one part per million.

Cadmium, lead, and mercury are elements that are harmful to the body, and have no demonstrated essential function.

TABLE 2.5

MACROMINERALS

Macromineral	Adult Daily Requirements	Necessary For	Good Sources
Calcium	1 g	Normal behavior of nerves & muscles, blood clotting, strong bones and teeth	Milk & milk products, green leafy vegetables, fish, dried peas and beans
Phosphorus	1 g	Strong bones & teeth	Meat, poultry, fish, eggs, whole grains
Sodium	230 mg as sodium chloride	Normal water balance inside & outside body cells	Meat, fish, poultry, eggs, milk, processed foods, such as crackers bacon, bread, salami
Chlorine		Food Digestion	
Potassium	?	In conjunction with sodium to regulate the volume & balance of body fluids	Bananas, milk, dates, citrus fruits, green leafy vegetables
Magnesium	400 mg	Energy conversion in the body	Available in many foods
Sulfur	?	Protein nutrition	Readily available

LEGEND:

g	=	gram
mg	=	milligram
mcg	=	microgram
1g	=	1000 mg
1mg	=	1000 mcg
1g	=	approximately 1/5 of a teaspoon

TABLE 2.6

TRACE MINERALS

Trace Minerals	Adult Daily Requirements	Necessary For	Good Sources
Iron	18 mg	Red blood cells	Liver, red meats, dark green leafy vegetables, dried fruit, egg yolk, fish
Manganese	?	Muscle & bone structure	Bran, coffee, tea, nuts peas and beans
Copper	2 mg	Hemoglobin	Liver, tongue, shellfish, nuts, dried peas & beans
Iodine	150 mcg	Thyroid gland	Salt water foods
Zinc	15 mg	Respiration	Meat, fish, egg yolk, milk
Cobalt	?	Essential part of vitamin B_{12}	Meat products
Chromium	?	In combination with insulin, for glucose digestion	Dried brewer's yeast, whole grains, liver
Selenium	?	Growth	Readily available
Fluorine	?	Good tooth form-ation	Readily available

LAB EXPERIENCE 2.8

DRY CEREAL NUTRIENT ANALYSIS

Purpose: To compare the nutrients in dry cereals.

Procedure: Compare the labels of three dry cereals, and record the names and the indicated information of each.

Nutrients	Brands		
	1	2	3
Protein (g)			
Carbohydrate (g)			
Fat (g)			
Calories/oz.			
U.S. RDA:			
Protein			
Vitamin A			
Vitamin C			
Thiamine (B_1)			
Riboflavin (B_2)			
Calcium			
Iron			
Price/oz.			

Question:

Of the above cereals, which is the most nutritious? Why?

LAB EXPERIENCE 2.9

CEREAL ANALYSIS: WEIGHT vs VOLUME

Purpose: To compare four different cereals for weight vs volume, sugar and salt content, calories per serving. Also note the ingredients.

Procedure: From the label determine the six leading ingredients and the information from the label.

Ingredients	Brands of Cereals			
	1 _____	2 _____	3 _____	4 _____
1.				
2.				
3.				
4.				
5.				
6.				
Weight (oz) (from label)				
Volume of box (cm^3)				
Volume of contents (cm^3)				
Amount of sugar (g)				
Amount of salt (g)				
Calories (per serving)				

Questions:

1. Convert ounces to grams.

2. Convert grams to milligrams.

3. Calculate percentage of contents in box.

$$(\% \text{ Contents} = \frac{\text{Volume of contents}}{\text{Volume of box}} \times 100)$$

THE CHANGING AMERICAN DIET

The question often asked is: How nutritionally sound is fast food?

First, fast food is not synonymous with "junk" food. Junk foods provide few or no nutrients besides sugar and calories. Soft drinks, pastries, and candy are nutrient-deficient foods and are classic junk foods. Although a chocolate bar or doughnut may contain other ingredients that are more nourishing than sugar and fat, the amount of essential nutrients is disproportionately small as compared with the total number of calories it contains.

In terms of good nutrition, there is no room in your diet for junk foods unless you have fulfilled your day's requirements for essential nutrients and can afford to consume extra calories without gaining unwanted weight.

The main problem with most fast food meals is that they are not nutritionally balanced. Pizza, chicken or beef fast foods, usually contain more than enough protein for a child or adult for one meal. However, the number of calories they provide is more than a third of an adult's daily requirements. In addition, they generally oversupply you with fats and salt and undersupply you with vitamins A and C, several B vitamins and iron.

Pizza, one of the better balanced fast foods, supplies plenty of protein and less fat than other types of meals, but pizza's main drawback is its high salt content.

A good rule of thumb is to be sure you eat salad, vegetables and fruit at other meals on the days when you eat fast food. Also, finding a nutritious drink at a fast food restaurant is quite difficult. Milk or fruit juice (not fruit drink) is probably the best choice for youngsters. Regular soda provides no nutrients except for a hundred or more calories of sugar (which is why it is referred to as "empty" calories). Diet sodas contain saccharin and shakes are high in fat, sugar and calories.

HYPERTENSION

Hypertension is elevated blood pressure. Blood pressure is a measurement of the work the heart must do to pump blood through your body. The heart only pumps, or contracts, for about one-third of a second and then it rests, or dilates, for the remaining two-thirds of the second. The pressure inside the arteries when the heart is contracting is called the systolic rate. The pressure inside the arteries when the heart is at rest, dilating, is called the diastolic rate.

It is this pressure that causes the blood to circulate in our bodies. Although there is some disagreement, the general medical consensus is that a normal blood pressure reading for an adult between the ages of 18 and 45 is 120/80. These readings refer to the systolic or upper pressure, and the diastolic or lower pressure. These pressures are measured in millimeters of mercury because they are obtained by seeing how high the blood flow in an artery can push a column of mercury in a special glass tube.

The physician measures this arterial blood flow with an instrument called a sphygmomanometer (sfig mo mah *nom* a eter). The doctor wraps a cuff around the upper arm, then inflates it to stop the circulation. The doctor listens just below the cuff with a stethoscope as he gradually releases the air pressure. As the blood flow returns, the doctor hears the first beat sound. The pressure level at this point is called the systolic. As air continues to flow slowly out of the cuff, the beat fades out and this is the diastolic reading.

Everyone's blood pressure changes during the day. It goes down during relaxing times and goes up with meals or excitement. When your blood pressure remains elevated all the time, the condition is called hypertension or high blood pressure.

When the doctor gets consistently high blood pressure readings, he may want you to have a number of tests made to see if a specific disease is causing the high blood pressure. If this is the case, the doctor will treat the disease and the symptoms may be controlled.

When high blood pressure exists with no apparent cause, the condition is called essential hypertension. Essential hypertension is the most common type of high blood pressure.

CAUSES OF HIGH BLOOD PRESSURE

Although the specific cause of essential hypertension isn't clearly known, the following factors appear to have a role in its development:

1. A tendency toward hypertension runs in families, but frequently skips members or whole generations. It is therefore not necessarily inherited.
2. Although blood pressure, in general, rises with age, we are meeting more young people with elevated blood pressure readings. Stress that is prolonged and unresolved is more apt to bring on hypertension. This is especially true in people with family histories of high blood pressure.
3. At present, high blood pressure is the major disease suffered by this country's black population, as well as the most important factor in their shorter life expectancy. Developing earlier in their lives, it is frequently more severe than in the white population. It results in a greater number of deaths at a younger age from strokes rather than from coronary artery disease. Research is continuing, seeking answers to such questions as how much of the high blood pressure among the black population is due to environment, and how much can be ascribed to inherited susceptibility.

4. Generally speaking, people who are overweight tend to have a higher blood pressure than people of normal weight.
5. Nicotine is known to constrict blood vessels. This results in increased blood pressure and elevated pulse rate. Heavy cigarette smoking is very often implicated in hypertension.

If left untreated, the elevated blood pressure will get worse. Hypertension causes the heart to pump with extra force and subjects the blood vessels to ever-increasing pressure. The heart tends to enlarge when it must work harder than normal over a long period of time. The walls of the arterioles, the smallest arterial blood vessels, have the most influence on blood pressure. These walls are made of many muscle fibers, which, when contracted, shrink the arterioles. The resulting effect is to increase the resistance to blood flow which in turn tends to heighten pressure. It is comparable to narrowing the nozzle of a garden hose. The water pressure in the hose goes up.

The arterial blood vessels normally tend to harden as you grow older, but hypertension pushes the process along a little faster.

MODE OF TREATMENT

Since hypertension varies from patient to patient, so must the mode of treatment vary accordingly. Wherever possible, the patient should avoid undue emotional strain and tension. Although this is easier said than done, it will help the condition. Several relatively new methods have been devised to aid the condition without the use of drugs. Biofeedback, one of the newest modes of minimizing tension, anxiety and stress relies upon mental awareness of bodily functions.

Strenuous exercise should be avoided. Don't go out and play two hours of tennis singles if you are not in condition to do so. Simple exercises like walking or light jogging are good to start with. Walking, especially, requires no special equipment and can be done throughout your lifetime.

It is known that blood pressure goes down during sleep. Therefore a good night's sleep is important, and a short mid-afternoon nap is also a good idea. The doctor will decide whether drinking alcoholic beverages and smoking should be discontinued.

Some cases of hypertension can be handled strictly with diet. Those people who are overweight must usually lose weight because the extra pounds place an additional burden on the heart. In those cases it will be required to reduce the intake of salt and calories.

Where medication is called for, the doctor can choose from a large collection of antihypertension drugs. These drugs generally fall into three categories: those that relax blood vessels directly, those that block the nerves to blood vessels, and those that work by eliminating extra fluid from the body.

There is really no cure for high blood pressure. At best, it can be kept in check. What is certain is that when blood pressure is controlled, symptoms of heart failure often improve or vanish, kidney deterioration is arrested, and the threat of strokes is minimized. Early diagnosis and treatment ensures that most patients with high blood pressure can enjoy a normal, healthy productive life.

When the use of sodium chloride is not recommended, the use of spices and herbs in place of salt is suggested. Spices and herbs enhance the natural flavor of foods. Spices are defined as parts of plants, such as the dried seeds, buds, fruit or flower parts, bark or roots of plants, usually of tropical origin. Herbs are from the leafy parts of temperate zone plants. There is no general rule in the use of the correct amount of a spice or herb, as the pungency of each spice or herb differs, and its effect on different foods varies. The flavor of ground spices is imparted immediately so they may be added about 15 minutes before the end of the cooking period. Whole spices are added at the beginning of the cooking period so the long simmering, as in stews, can extract the full flavor and aroma.

Some suggested lab activities:

1. Check pulse rates, first sitting quietly then after some strenuous activity such as jumping rope or running.
2. Have the school nurse check the blood pressure of the students.

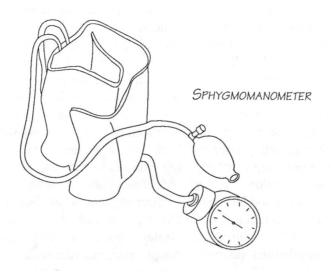

SPHYGMOMANOMETER

LAB EXPERIENCE 2.10

SALT SEARCH

Purpose: To determine your own daily intake of salt.

Procedure: Read the reference article and check all the foods you are likely
to eat in one day. Compute the amount of sodium you take in,
on average, every day.

Reference: "Salt Search", Consumer Reports magazine, March 1979

FOOD	SODIUM	FOOD	SODIUM
CEREALS		FAST FOOD MEALS	
Fruit Flavored (1 oz)	125 mg.	Hamburger, fries, shake	1800 mg.
Sugared Corn		Hot dog on bun	816 mg.
Flakes (1 oz)	185 mg.	Fried chicken, fries,	
Plain Corn Flakes		roll, shake	1860 mg.
(1 oz)	260 mg.	Pizza with works, cola	4170 mg.
FRUITS AND VEGETABLES		DRINKS	
Apple,	1 mg.	Milk, 1 cup	120 mg.
Celery, 1 large stalk	50 mg.	Cola 12 fl. oz	2 mg.
Carrots, 1 medium	34 mg.	Low-cal lemon 12 fl. oz	62 mg.
Potato, 1 medium	4 mg.		
Rice, 1/2 cup	2 mg.		
SANDWICH		SNACKS & DESSERTS	
Bologna, 3-1/2 oz.		Cookies, 4 assorted	292 mg.
with mustard on		Doughnut, 1 medium	568 mg.
white bread	1516 mg.	Potato Chips, 1 oz.	191 mg.
Tuna fish, 3-1/2 oz.		Pretzels, 4 oz.	1905 mg.
with mayonnaise on		Instant Chocolate	
white bread	1118 mg.	Pudding, 1/2 cup	404 mg.
Peanut butter			
and jelly on white	273 mg.		
bread			

TOTAL _____   TOTAL _____

TOTAL OF BOTH COLUMNS _____

LABELING

Nutrition labeling was developed by the Food and Drug Administration (FDA) and the food industry to provide consumers with nutrition information. Nutrition labeling is required on all foods to which a nutrient is added or for which a nutrition claim is made.

Some of the information shown on the label is required by the FDA. Some is included at the option of the manufacturer or processor. Some may be in the form of symbols or codes or dates.

Certain information is required on all food labels. These include:

1. The name of the product.
2. The net contents or net weight. The net weight on canned food includes the liquid in which the product is packed, such as water in canned vegetables, and syrup in canned fruit.
3. The name and place of business of the manufacturer, packer, or distributor.

The ingredients in most processed foods must be listed on the label. The ingredient present in the largest amount, by weight, must be listed first, followed in descending order of weight by the other ingredients. Any additives used in the product must be listed, but colors and flavors do not have to be given by name. The list of ingredients may simply say "natural flavor," "artificial color," or "artificial flavor." On the other hand, butter, cheese, and ice cream are not required to list the presence of artificial color.

The only foods not required to list all ingredients are so-called standardized foods. The FDA has set "standards of identity" for such foods. These standards require that all foods called by a particular name (such as catsup or mayonnaise) contain certain mandatory ingredients. Under the law, the mandatory ingredients in standardized foods need not be listed on the label. Manufacturers may add optional ingredients which are not now listed. However, the FDA is revising the food standards regulation to require that optional ingredients in standardized foods be listed on the product label.

Nutrient information is listed on the label of each processed product on the basis of a single serving. An example is shown in Figure 2.1.

The label tells the size of a serving, and the number of servings in the container. Listed directly below this are the number of calories and the amounts of protein, carbohydrates, and fat (the three major nutrients) in a single serving.

The lower portion of the nutrition label lists the percentages of the U.S. Recommended Daily Allowance (RDA) of protein, plus seven vitamins and minerals in one serving of the product. These are tabulated in Table 2.5. The RDAs are the amounts of protein, vitamins and minerals people need each day to stay healthy. These minimum allowances are set by the FDA, and are based on the body needs for most healthy adults. Add the percentage for each nutrient consumed through the day. When the daily total is 100 percent, an ample amount has been consumed.

Vitamins and minerals are described in percentages of the RDAs. On the foregoing label, vitamin A = 25 means that a serving of food contains 25% of the RDA for vitamin A.

The RDA for protein have also been established for nutrition labeling. They are based on the quality of total protein in a food product. When the protein is of high biological quality (meaning it contains a good balance of the essential amino acids), then less of it is needed to meet the needs of the body. In this case, the RDA is lower for protein of high quality. For labeling purposes, the quality of protein is determined by the protein efficiency ratio (PER), a measure of growth of young animals.

```
            Nutrition Information (per serving)
                 Serving Size = 1 cup
                 Servings per container = 2

        Calories  . . . . . . . . . . 110
        Protein   . . . . . . . . . .   1 gram
        Carbohydrates . . . . . . . .  25 grams
        Fat . . . . . . . . . . . . .   1 gram
        Sodium* (970 Mg/100g) . . . . 275 milligrams


        Percentage of U.S. R.D.A.

        Protein   . . . . . . . . .    2
        Vitamin A . . . . . . . . .   25
        Vitamin C . . . . . . . . .   25
        Thiamine (B₁).  . . . . . .   25
        Riboflavin (B₂) . . . . . .   25
        Niacin  . . . . . . . . . .   25
        Calcium . . . . . . . . . .    4
        Iron  . . . . . . . . . . .    4
```

*The label may show the amounts of cholesterol and sodium in 100 grams of food; and in a serving.

Figure 2.1 *Sample of Nutritional Label*

Since no single food can provide all the needed nutrients, we must eat a variety of foods each day. Nutrition labels tell what nutrients are to be found in each package of food, and how good the food is as a source of each particular vitamin or mineral.

Smart shoppers use nutrition labeling to serve better meals and to save money. The smart shopper compares labels to select foods that round out the nutrients needed on a daily basis, as well as to count calories. People on special diets use the label to help avoid restricted foods. The shopper uses labels to compare the cost per serving of similar foods. Also, to get the most for the food dollar, and to find substitutes for more expensive foods, by choosing canned and packaged products which have high amounts of protein at a reasonable price.

Today, many foods are manufactured into products that are different from traditional foods. Some classes of these foods include: frozen dinners, breakfast cereals, meal replacements, noncarbonated breakfast beverages fortified with vitamin C, and main dishes such as macaroni and cheese, pizzas, stews, and casseroles. The FDA is establishing voluntary nutritional guidelines for such foods, so consumers may be assured of getting a proper level and range of nutrients when using them. A product that complies with an FDA nutritional quality guideline may include on its label a statement that it meets the U.S. nutritional quality guidelines for that particular class of food.

Some foods are labeled as "imitations" of other foods. Under an FDA regulation, the word "imitation" must be used on the label when the product is not as nutritious as the product which it resembles and for which it is a substitute. If a product is similar to an existing one, and is just as nutritious, a new name can be given to it rather than calling it "imitation." For example, eggless products which are nutritionally equivalent to eggs have been given names such as Eggbeaters and Scramblers.

Judging from the label some foods may look as though they are one thing and may actually be another. To prevent deception of consumers, the FDA has ruled that such foods must have a "common or usual" name which gives the consumer accurate information about what is in the package or container. For example, a beverage that looks like orange juice but actually contains very little orange juice must use a name such as "dilute orange juice drink." The product also may be required to state on the label the percentage of the ingredient it contains. In this case, the common or usual name might be "diluted orange juice beverage, contains 10% orange juice."

A noncarbonated beverage that appears to contain a fruit or vegetable juice but does not contain any juice, must state on the label that it contains no fruit or vegetable juice.

Another special labeling requirement concerns packaged foods in which the main ingredient or component of a recipe is not included, as in the case of some "main dishes" or "dinners." On such foods, the common or usual name consists of the following:

1. The common name of each ingredient in descending order by weight; for example, "noodles and tomato sauce."

2. Identification of the food to be prepared from the package; for example, "for preparation of chicken casserole."

3. A statement of ingredients that must be added to complete the recipe for example, "you must add chicken to complete the recipe."

Some food products carry a grade on the label, such as "U.S. Grade A." Grades are set by the U.S. Department of Agriculture, based on the quality levels inherent in a product: its taste, texture, and appearance. U.S. Department of Agriculture grades are not based on nutritional content.

Milk and milk products in most states carry a "Grade A" label. This grade is based on FDA recommended sanitary standards for the production and processing of milk and milk products. The grade is not based on nutritional values. The FDA has established standards for milk which require certain levels of vitamins A and D when these vitamins are added to the milk.

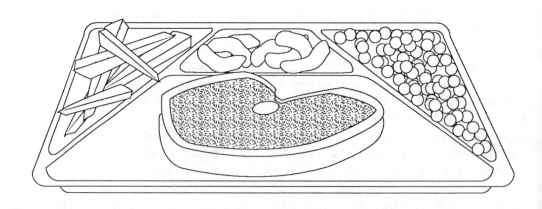

LAB EXPERIENCE 2.11

PRODUCT vs PRICE

Purpose: To determine differences of similar products by comparing contents and price.

Procedure: Compare labels of several brands on each of the following foods and record below.

- breads
- mayonnaise
- catsup

- pasta products
- jelly or jam products

Brand & Product	List of Ingredients	Quantity	Price	Unit Price

Question:

Why are some products permitted to omit a complete listing of ingredients?

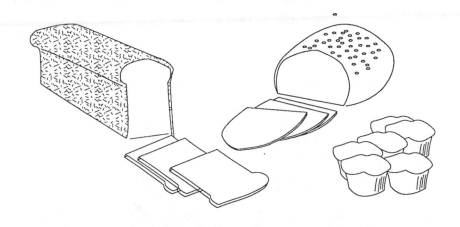

LAB EXPERIENCE 2.12

FROZEN FOOD vs PRICE

Purpose: To compare the differences between frozen food dinners.

Procedure: Study the labels of four frozen dinners and compare the information available to the consumer.

Brand & Product	Price Per Dinner	List of Ingredients	Nutrition Labeling

Questions:

1. What criteria would you use in selecting a frozen dinner?

2. How would nutrition labeling of frozen dinners assist the consumer in
selecting one?

FOOD DATING

To help consumers obtain food that is fresh and wholesome, many manufacturers date their product. Open dating, as this practice is called, is not regulated by FDA. Four kinds of open dating are commonly used. To benefit from this information, the consumer needs to know what kind of dating is used on the individual product and what it means.

1. The pack date: This is the date the food was manufactured, processed or packaged. This tells how old the food is when it is bought. Most canned and packaged foods have a long shelf life when stored under dry, cool conditions.

2. The pull or sell date: This is the last date the product should be sold, assuming it has been stored and handled properly. The pull date allows for some storage time in the home refrigerator. Cold cuts, ice cream, milk, and refrigerated fresh dough products are examples of foods with pull dates.

3. The expiration date: This is the last date the food should be eaten or used. Baby formula and yeast are examples of products that may carry expiration dates.

4. The freshness date: This is similar to the expiration date but may allow for normal home storage. Bakery products have a freshness date. Some are sold at a reduced price for a short time after the expiration date.

SPECIAL CODES

Many companies use code dating on products that have a long "shelf life." This is usually for the company's information rather than for the consumer's benefit. The code gives the manufacturer and the store precise information about where the product was packaged. If for any reason a recall should be required, the product can be identified quickly and withdrawn from the market.

Many food labels now include a small block of parallel lines of various widths with accompanying numbers. This is the Universal Product Code (UPC). The code on a label is unique to that product. Some stores are equipped with computerized checkout equipment that can read the code and automatically ring up the sale. In addition to making it possible for stores to automate part of their checkout work, the UPC, when used in conjunction with a computer, also can tell management how much of a specific item is on hand, how fast it is being sold, and when and how much to order.

The symbol which consists of the letter "U" inside a small circle is used for foods which comply with Jewish dietary laws. The symbol is copyright by the Union of Orthodox Jewish Congregations of America, more familiarly known as the Orthodox Union. It declares that the food is kosher.

The symbol which consists of the letter "K" inside a small circle is used to indicate that the food is "Kosher." That is, it complies with the Jewish dietary laws. The symbol is not copyright and is assigned by the manufacturer and not the official organization. Its processing may or may not have been under the direction of a rabbi.

The symbol "R" signifies that the trademark used on the label is registered with the U.S. Patent Office.

The symbol "C" indicates that the literary and artistic content of the label is protected against infringement under the copyright laws of the United States.

None of the symbols referred to above are required by, or are under the authority of, any of the Acts enforced by the Food and Drug Administration.

LAB EXPERIENCE 2.13

LABELING AND DIETARY NEEDS

Purpose: To determine how labeling can impact upon your dietary needs.

Procedure: This lab experience is to be done at home.   Record the answers below.

Read the article in the February 1979 issue of Consumer Reports on Labeling and "Margarine: The Better Butter?"

Questions:

1.   Do promotional health claims for margarine play on consumers' lack of knowledge about the relationship of fat consumption to heart disease?

2.   What are some reasons for the increase in margarine's popularity?

3.   Why are consumers concerned about the type of fat in margarine?

4.   Why is the type of fat in one's diet thought to be associated with an increased risk of heart disease?

5.   How do saturated fats and polyunsaturated fats affect levels of blood cholesterol?

6.   If polyunsaturated fats tend to reduce the level of cholesterol in the blood, why might consumers be misled by health claims for margarine?

7.   Which consumers would be concerned about the fat content listed on margarine labels?

8.   What other information on the label might be more important to consumers?

9.   What could consumers learn by checking the nutrition information?

10.   What could consumers learn by checking list of ingredients for their special dietary needs?

LAB EXPERIENCE 2.14

LABELING

Purpose: To determine how to improve the food label from a consumer's point of view.

Procedure: The following is a proposed list of changes in food labeling. Rank them from 1 to 9 in the order of importance to you with 1 being most important.

_____   Amount of salt in the food

_____   Amount of sugar in the food

_____   Which fats and oils are present in the food

_____   Amount of saturation of the fats

_____   Imitation foods or food ingredients

_____   Expiration date

_____   Quantity of each ingredient present in the food

_____   List of fortifiers as separate from the basic nutrients

_____   Any others

FOODS AND BACTERIA

Safe use of frozen foods begins in the store. When buying frozen foods, always check display cases to see that the foods are kept below the "frostline" or "load line" (the line marked on commercial freezer cabinets which indicates the safety level). In addition, only buy products that have been correctly stored below this line. Don't delay after shopping. Take frozen foods home and put them in the freezer immediately.

Bacterial contamination of foods can be reduced through either cooking or refrigeration. Both of these processes retard the growth of disease-producing bacteria. To grow and reproduce, bacteria need three things: moisture, warmth, and a source of food. If any of these elements is missing, the bacteria will not grow.

When food is refrigerated, one of the necessities, warmth, is lacking, and thus bacterial growth is retarded. Most bacteria are not killed by refrigeration, but refrigeration does stop them from multiplying. It also slows down the ability of bacteria to produce a toxin or poison.

If perishable food is to be kept for only three or four days, the temperature should be at 45 °F or below. If food is to be kept longer, it should be stored at no higher than 40 °F. At temperatures from 45° to 115 °F poison-producing microorganisms may grow rapidly. Foods can undergo a doubling of bacterial growth every 15 to 30 minutes, so it is important to prepare and serve perishable foods with as little time-lapse, as possible, after taking them from the refrigerator or freezer. Perishable food products, are those that are wholly or partially made of milk or milk products, or eggs, meat, poultry, fish, and shellfish.

Today's refrigerators are better engineered than ever, but to keep them working efficiently they need to be given some attention. Here are some suggestions:

1. Wash the inside of the refrigerator frequently.

2. Keep the areas around the motor and refrigerating unit clean. Lint and dirt on these parts cut off the supply of air causing the motor and refrigeration unit to overwork.

3. Check the gaskets around the doors. Be sure they are flexible and keep the cold air from escaping.

4. If your refrigerator is not self-defrosting, check the cooling area frequently, and defrost when needed. A buildup of ice on the cooling coils or even on the inside of the storage area prevents the refrigerator from working well.

5. Never cover the wire shelves with paper or foil, as this cuts down on air circulation within the refrigerator.

6. Avoid overcrowding your refrigerator if you are to achieve a maximum cooling effect.

While refrigeration will retard the growth of bacteria in food, another way to control bacterial contamination in foods is by cooking at high temperatures. High heat kills bacteria which might cause poisoning.

When food is taken from the refrigerator and cooked, it should reach a temperature of 140° in four hours or less. Because of the way various types of slow cookers function, cold or frozen foods may not always be heated to 140 °F within four hours.

Crockery cookers usually have a heating element only at the bottom. The heat must rise from the bottom through the mass of food to the top layer. Foods that are mostly liquid, such as soup, heat quickly all the way through. If the pot is filled to a depth of 2 or 3 inches with the same solid food, there should be no problem in reaching the proper temperature in four hours. But thicker foods, such as casseroles, take longer to heat thoroughly from bottom to top. If solid food is put into a slow cooker to a depth of 8 inches, it may not heat to 140° within four hours no matter how powerful the heating element at the bottom of the pot.

A deadly form of food poisoning, botulism, is caused by Clostridium botulinum. Home canned meats and low-acid preserved foods such as string beans, beets, and corn, which are prepared by the "cold pack" method, are the most common types of foods that can cause this illness. Temperatures used in the "cold pack" method cannot be relied on to destroy Clostridium botulinum spores (a dormant form of the bacteria). Even in an airtight, sealed jar, spores can grow and produce a toxin so potent that just tasting the food can be fatal. The ordinary home canner does not have reliable controls to assure that the internal temperature of every can reaches 240° to 260°F for the required time, as in commercial plants. Consequently, if you do any home canning, watch for evidence of swelling, decomposition, or abnormality in the food. If you find a jar or can in which the food does not seem right, destroy the entire can. Don't even feed it to animals or pets.

Another disease, trichinosis, is transmitted through raw or undercooked pork. Trichinella spirallis is a tiny worm frequently found in the muscle of pork. Unless destroyed, it can cause serious illness. All pork or pork products should be thoroughly cooked to an internal temperature of at least 170°F. Be certain the pork is cooked until there is no trace of pink in the meat or juices.

Cooked foods should be served as soon as possible. Avoid keeping for prolonged periods at room temperature. When warm-holding is necessary, the temperature should be kept at or above 140°F to prevent bacterial growth.

Contamination of food by Salmonella bacteria is a health hazard. When taken into the body, Salmonella microorganisms multiply in the gastrointestinal tract and produce irritation, with resulting nausea, vomiting, abdominal cramps and pain, diarrhea, and fever.

Salmonella organisms are often present in poultry, even when frozen. No matter what the final form the poultry may in (fried chicken, chicken salad, roast duck, etc.) every part of it should be heated to an internal temperature of at least 165°F to ensure that the Salmonella organisms are killed. Cooking is not the only precaution needed in the prevention of Salmonella poisoning. Poultry should always be washed carefully. Any utensils or work surfaces used in the preparation of uncooked poultry must be thoroughly cleaned before they are used for other purposes, to prevent Salmonella from contaminating other foods.

Eggs also have been the cause of Salmonella poisoning. Eggs with cracked shells should never be used unless they, or the products in which they are used, are thoroughly cooked.

When cream filled pastries and custards are not cooked or baked adequately, they pose a double hazard: food poisoning from both Staphylococcal and Salmonella infection. To protect against these disease organisms, cook the filling to at least 165°F immediately after it is prepared. Unless the cooked or baked custard or pastry is to be served immediately, refrigerate it at 45°F or below, and keep it at this temperature until served.

Many different kinds of bacteria will flourish in milk because it is such a good food. It is, therefore, important to be careful in its handling. Milk that we find in the supermarket is labeled "pasteurized". In the pasteurization process, milk is heated to 161 degrees F. for 15 minutes and then cooled very quickly to 45 degrees F. to preserve the flavor.

In the lab experience Testing Milk, you will examine milk from several sources and determine the quality of the milk by comparing its bacterial count to an accepted standard. In the test, the chemical methylene blue is added to the milk. The dye remains blue only when oxygen is present in the milk. Bacteria must use the oxygen present in the milk in order to live. By adding methylene blue to the milk and recording how long it takes for the dyed milk to return to its white color, we can tell approximately the number of bacteria present. If the discolorization time is over 5 1/2 hours, you have good milk.

In the Cottage Cheese experiment, we see an application of an enzyme. Enzymes are proteins which bring about a chemical reaction without themselves being affected by the change.

The enzyme rennin, in the form of a rennet tablet, causes the milk to curdle. The addition of buttermilk and citric acid help in the curdling action since both of the products increase the lactic acid content of milk. It is the lactic acid which hastens the curdling of milk. The resulting mixture will contain lumps of casein called curds and a liquid portion called whey.

In the Yogurt experiment, we will see the action of bacteria in converting milk to the thickened milk product called yogurt. The bacteria will grow very quickly in the milk when it is warmed by placing it in an incubator. The resulting change produces a product which has a flavor different from that of the original milk.

In the Milk to Glue experiment, we will see the action of acetic acid, vinegar, on skim milk. The results will be similar to the results in the cheese experiment. However, we will not sample the product of this experiment—just use it. Some industrial uses for casein include coating for papers, casein paints, plastic buttons and costume jewelry, and glues. We will make some casein glue.

LAB EXPERIENCE 2.15

TESTING MILK

Purpose: To determine the bacterial count in milk.

Materials:

Water bath or incubator maintained at 37 degrees C with a capacity to hold 6 test tubes
Thermometer
Timer
6 25-ml Sterilized test tubes with cotton plugs
Test tube rack
25-ml Graduated cylinder
20-ml Methylene blue solution (1:20 000) in a dropper bottle
1 Unopened container of fresh milk
1 Opened container of fresh milk, refrigerated 2 to 3 days
1 Opened container of fresh milk, at room temperature for 24 hours

Note to Teacher: Note the time frame in Step 6. This experiment may be used as an at-home experiment using a water bath or started first thing in the morning.

Procedure:

1. Label two test tubes "Fresh", 2 test tubes "Refrigerated", and 2 test tubes "Room temp". Then mark one of each pair MB (methylene blue). This will be the tested sample and the other test tube of each pair will be the control test tube.

2. Pour 10 ml of fresh milk into each container labeled "Fresh", and the appropriate milk into the other test tubes.

3. Add 2 drops of methylene blue solution to each test tube marked MB leaving the second of each pair (the control tube) without methylene blue.

4. Cap each tube with its sterilized cotton plug, and shake the tube carefully but thoroughly. Do not wet the cotton plug.

5. Place the six test tubes into the incubator or water bath and note the time of placement. Do not shake tubes again for the balance of the test.

6. Check test tubes every 1/2 hour for the first two hours. After that once an hour. The experiment may require 2 to 8 hours for completion.

7. The test is completed when the samples marked MB are as uniformly white as the control tube.

8. Evaluate your milk samples and complete the chart by comparing them with the reference table.

LAB EXPERIENCE 2.15 (Continued)

TESTING MILK

Sample	Time for Sample to Whiten	Quality of Milk
Fresh Milk		
Refrigerated Milk		
Room temp. Milk		

Reference Table for Bacterial Count

Time for Milk to Resume White Color	Quality of Milk	Approximate Number of Organisms per ml of Milk
Over 8 hours	Excellent	Variable, but very good
5 1/2 to 8 hrs	Good	Under 1/2 million
2 to 5 1/2 hrs	Fair	1/2 to 4 million
20 min to 2 hrs	Bad	4 to 20 million
Less than 20 min	Very bad	Over 20 million

Questions:

1. Which milk sample had the highest bacteria count?

2. Which sample had the lowest bacteria count?

3. What suggestions would you have in order to reduce the bacterial contamination?

4. At what bacterial count should milk be discarded?

Suggested Activity:

Discussion on good and bad bacteria in cheese, yogurt, and buttermilk.

LAB EXPERIENCE 2.16

COTTAGE CHEESE

Purpose: To make cottage cheese through the chemical action of rennin with liquid milk.

Materials:

Hot plate
Hot mitts
Thermometer
Ring stand and clamp
Large funnel
Knife
200-ml Beaker
4 2000-ml Beakers
50-ml Graduated cylinder
Cheesecloth
1 Rennet tablet
1 liter Skim milk
50 ml Fresh, cold cultured buttermilk
150 ml Distilled water
2 g Sodium chloride
5 ml Light cream
1 ml Citric acid

Note: You will be asked to taste the results in Step 15 so maintain cleanliness throughout.

Procedure:

1. Put 125 ml distilled water into a 200-ml beaker and dissolve one rennet tablet in it.

2. Put 1000 ml of fresh cold skim milk into a 2-liter beaker, put in thermometer, and place beaker on the hot plate. When the milk reaches 40 degrees C, remove it from hot plate.

3. Add 50 ml buttermilk to the rennet solution, stir and add this mixture to the heated skim milk of Step 2.

4. Add 1 ml citric acid to the heated skim milk and stir.

5. Cover the 2-liter beaker with a paper towel and let stand at room temperature for 2 hours.

6. The resulting mixture will contain lumps of casein which are known as curds. The liquid portion of milk is called whey. Stir gently again for 30 seconds.

LAB EXPERIENCE 2.16 (Continued)

COTTAGE CHEESE

7. Place the beaker with milk mixture on the hot plate and warm at low temperature setting to 44 degrees C.

8. Remove the beaker from the hot plate.

9. Set up the funnel with 2 or 3 layers of cheese cloth in it on a ring stand with the second 2-liter beaker beneath it.

10. Slowly pour the milk mixture through the funnel catching the liquid in the beaker. This may be a slow process for all the liquid must drain completely out of the mixture.

11. Divide the solids and put half into each of 2 clean 2000-ml beakers.

13. Put 1 g sodium chloride into one beaker and mix slightly. Taste a small sample of each.

14. Add 2.5 ml cream to each beaker and mix again.

15. Taste each mixture.

16. Divide the liquid in half, put 1 g of salt in one beaker of liquid, and stir. Taste the liquid with and without salt.

17. Complete the chart below by describing both solid and liquid portions of the mixture.

	Solid (curds)		Liquid (whey)	
	Salted	Unsalted	Salted	Unsalted
Taste sensation				
Texture				
Smell				
Appearance				

Questions:

1. What was the purpose of the rennet tablet?

LAB EXPERIENCE 2.16 (Continued)

COTTAGE CHEESE

2. What was the purpose of the buttermilk?

3. Is there any nutritional value to the whey?

4. How did salt effect the taste?

5. What is the purpose of adding cream?

Suggested Activity:

Library research on industrial uses of curds and whey.

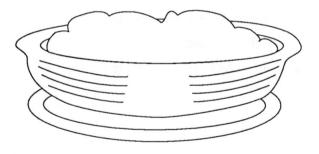

CLASS MADE COTTAGE CHEESE

LAB EXPERIENCE 2.17

YOGURT

Purpose: To prepare yogurt by converting liquid milk to a thickened milk product by bacterial action

Materials:

Incubator maintained at 36 degrees C
Hot plate
Hot mitts
Balance
Glass stirring rods
2 Thermometers
25-ml Beaker
2 1000-ml Beakers
25-ml Graduated cylinder
100-ml Graduated cylinder
Paper towels
200 g Powdered milk (skim or whole)*
1 liter Distilled water
1 pint (500 ml) Plain unflavored commercially prepared yogurt*
200 g Pureed frozen raspberries, blueberries, or strawberries*
40 ml Light cream*
10 g Powdered sugar or artificial sweetener*

Notes: 1. *Record the cost of these materials.

2. Note the time frame in Step 5 below.

3. You will be asked to taste some of the product, so maintain cleanliness at all times.

Procedure:

1. Put 500 ml of distilled water and 100 g of powdered milk into both 1000-ml beakers. Stir to dissolve.

2. Place the beakers on the hot plate and heat the mixture until it just boils. Turn the heat down and maintain the boiling for 1 minute.

3. Remove the beakers from the hot plate and allow to air cool to 36 degrees C.

4. Add 25 ml of commercially prepared yogurt to the mixtures in each of the beakers. Stir thoroughly and cover the beakers with a sheet of paper toweling.

LAB EXPERIENCE 2.17 (Continued)

YOGURT

5. Place the beakers in the incubator. Check the mixtures every hour until they thicken. Remove the beakers from the incubator.

6. Into one of the beakers stir in 200 g of pureed frozen berries, 10 g of powdered sugar or artificial sweetener, and 40 ml of light cream.

7. Distribute 2 ml of each of the lab prepared products to each student and 2 ml of the commercial yogurt. Note the texture, consistency, and taste sensation of each product in the chart below.

8. Calculate the cost of the laboratory prepared yogurt, both unflavored and flavored.

	Lab Plain	Lab Flavored	Commercial
Texture			
Consistency			
Taste sensation			
Cost/100 ml			

Questions:

1. Read the label of the commercial yogurt. What are the active ingredients?

2. Why was some commercial yogurt added to the laboratory prepared yogurt?

3. How does the taste sensation of each of the products compare?

4. Is it economically feasible to prepare yogurt at home?

Suggested Activity:

Library research to determine nutritional value and the calorie count of frozen yogurt, tofutti, ice milk, and ice cream. One source of reference would be the American Dairy Council. Give other sources.

LAB EXPERIENCE 2.18

MILK to GLUE

Purpose: To make glue from skim milk.

Materials:

Hot plate	200-ml Graduated cylinder
Hot mitts	Large funnel
Glass stirring rod	Cheesecloth
Ring stand with clamp	Wooden splints
Balance	Construction paper
Scissors	Distilled water
Safety glasses	2 g Sodium bicarbonate (baking soda)
2 500-ml Beakers	150 ml Skim milk
25-ml Graduated cylinder	30 ml 5% Acetic acid (white vinegar)

Procedure:

1. In one 500 ml beaker, put 150 ml skim milk and 30 ml 5% acetic acid.

2. Stir the mixture and place beaker on the hot plate. Heat at low temperature, stirring constantly.

3. As soon as the mixture begins to congeal and small lumps appear, remove the beaker from the hot plate. These lumps are called curds and the liquid is called whey.

4. Continue stirring the mixture until no more curds appear.

5. Allow the mixture to cool and the curds to settle to the bottom of the beaker.

6. Set up the ring stand with funnel. Put 3 layers of cheesecloth in the funnel. Place the second 500-ml beaker beneath the funnel.

7. Pour the mixture from Step 5 through the cheesecloth. Put the curds back into the first beaker.

8. Add 35 ml of distilled water and 1.5 g of sodium bicarbonate to the curds. Stir to a smooth consistency.

9. Should any small bubbles appear, add a few more grains of sodium bicarbonate until no more bubbles appear.

10. The residue in the beaker is glue.

LAB EXPERIENCE 2.18 (Continued)

MILK to GLUE

11. If desired, construct a triangular or square desk sign from construction paper. See diagram. Using a wooden splint, glue the sides of the construction together. Cut letters from another sheet of construction paper and glue them to the sign.

Questions:

1. Does the glue work well?

2. What is the purpose of adding acetic acid to the skim milk?

3. What is the natural process which is comparable to the addition of the acetic acid?

Suggested Activity:

Library research on the uses of casein and whey. Write to The Borden Company, manufacturers of casein glue, and inquire as to uses of casein.

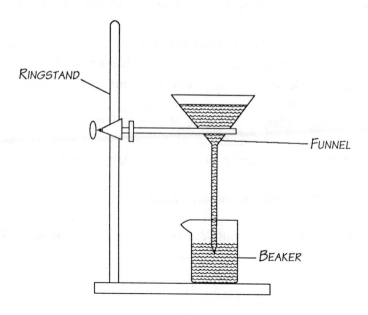

UNIT 2

BIOLOGY QUESTIONS

1. The body requires food for the following purposes: a) build and maintain tissue, obtain energy, and regulate body processes, b) satisfy hunger, c) so stored fat may be released, d) all of the above, e) none of the above.

2. The food we eat must be _____, _____, and _____before it can be utilized by the body.

3. The four food groups are: a) meat, dairy products, poultry, and bread and cereals, b) bread and cereals, meat, dairy products, and fruit and vegetables, c) milk, cheese, fruits, and bread and cereals, d) all of the above, e) none of the above.

4. The nutrients include_____, _____, and _____ and are found in the food we eat.

5. The building blocks of protein are called_____.

6. A complete protein of animal origin has _____ amino acids.

7. Amino acids are required by the body for _____ and _____ body tissues.

8. Name four foods which are good sources of protein: a) _____, b) _____, c) _____, d) _____.

9. Dried peas and beans are a good source of the nutrient _____.

10. What do proteins provide for in the diet? a) proper elimination of foods, b) enrichment in the diet, c) muscles and nerve tissue, d) extra calories.

11. Proteins are needed for the formation of: a) insulin, b) thyroxine, c) antibodies, d) all of the above.

12. Enzymes are necessary for: a) energy, b) digestion, c) blood sugar, d) none of the above.

13. What is the most important function of fiber in our diet?_____

14. Unrefined foods contain more _____ than refined foods.

15. Carbohydrates are made of the chemical elements _____, _____, and _____.

16. Name three foods which are important source of carbohydrate. _____, _____, _____.

17. A carbohydrate that occurs naturally in fruits, vegetables, and honey is called _____.

18. Sucrose, or common table sugar, is unusual because it is a _____ carbohydrate.

19. Before the body can use all carbohydrates, they must be broken down by _____ into _____.

20. Name three simple sugars. _____, _____, _____.

21. Enzymes break down carbohydrates into: a) glycogen, b) triglycerides, c) glucose, d) amino acids.

22. The body changes the starch in foods to _____ through _____.

23. Fiber in our diet comes only from _____ sources.

24. What is the minimum daily requirement for dietary fiber?

25. Fiber is the indigestible residue of the following foods: a) potatoes, bananas, b) apples, figs, strawberries, c) eggs and bacon, d) none of the above.

26. Fructose is less/more sweet than sucrose but has fewer/same/more calories per gram.

27. The major function of carbohydrates in the diet is to: a) produce amino acids, b) aid in digestion, c) produce energy, d) all of the above.

28. Fats in our diet provide _____ acid which is _____ for proper growth and healthy skin.

29. What amount of linoleic acid is required in our daily diet?

30. Name two oils rich in linoleic acids. _____, _____.

31. A fatty acid containing more than one double bond in the chain is called _____.

32. To test for sweetness we: a) drop in chemicals, b) compare calories, c) taste the food, d) all the above.

33. If saccharin or aspartame is used instead of sugar, it is because of: a) price, b) sweetness, c) calories, d) none of the above.

34. The four vitamins which are soluble in fat are: a) A, D, E, and K, b) A, B, E and D, c) D, E, K, and niacin, d) all of the above, e) none of the above.

35. Fats provide: a) the same, b) less, c) twice the energy value of carbohydrates or proteins.

36. Some fat in the tissue helps: a) cushion body organs, b) expel water, c) prevent heat loss, d) both a and c.

37. Name three foods with very high fat content. _____, _____, _____.

38. What is atherosclerosis? _____

39. What is cholesterol? _____

40. The normal well-balanced diet contains: a) 10-15% protein, 20-30% fats, and 55-70% carbohydrates b) 10-15% protein, 30-50% fats and 35-50% carbohydrates c) 30-40% protein, 10-20% fats and 40-60% carbohydrates d) none of the above.

Nutrients are listed in column I. Place the letter from column II into the space provided if you believe it is a true statement. *CAUTION:* Each class of nutrient may have more than one correct answer.

I	II
41. carbohydrate _____	A. can be burned to supply energy
42. fat _____	B. yields 9 calories per gram
43. protein _____	C. yields 4 calories per gram
	D. important tissue builder
	E. provides linoleic acid
	F. in complex form provides roughage
	G. contains nitrogen
	H. utilized as glucose

44. In the experiment, diet foods were found in many instances to be: a) less expensive than non-diet foods, b) more expensive than non-diet foods, c) the same price as non-diet foods, d) all of the above.

45. To achieve a weight loss, fat tissue must: a) release stored water, b) release stored fat, c) release stored waste, d) both a and c.

46. People who eat no meat are called _____.

47. The Biuret solution turns _____ if the test is positive for protein.

48. Testing for simple sugars requires: a) freshly prepared Biuret solution, b) results in a blue-black color if positive, c) requires the addition of heat and Benedict's solution, d) produces a shade of pink-violet.

49. Testing for sugar in foods will give you the following positive result: a) green, b) red, c) blue, d) orange.

50. The final color on a positive starch test is: a) gray, b) yellow, c) blue-black, d) red.

51. If the positive test on food results in a gray-white ash you are testing for _____.

52. The test solution for starch is Lugol's _____.

53. A simple test for fat is performed by rubbing the substance to be tested on brown paper. If fat is present the stain on the paper will be: a) opaque, b) greasy, c) transparent, d) translucent.

54. What do empty calories mean? a) absence of nutrients, b) absence of sugars, c) absence of space, d) all of the above, e) none of the above.

55. Margarine: a) has lower caloric value than butter, b) loses vitamin content when colored, c) is high in polyunsaturated acids, d) provides more than twice the energy value of protein.

56. Most vegetable oils (soy, sunflower, corn) are: a) saturated, b) polyunsaturated, c) unsaturated.

57. What are vitamins: a) food replacements, b) food supplements, c) essence of life, d) source of extra vitality.

58. Vitamins are needed for _____ and for _____.

59. In what way are vitamins similar?_____

60. Vitamins are _____ compounds.

61. How do synthetic and natural vitamins differ from each other?

62. Vitamin A: a) is converted from carotene, b) can cause adverse reactions if taken in excess, c) protects against eye diseases, d) all of the above.

63. Vitamin A is a _____ soluble vitamin.

Match the vitamin with the proper deficiency.

Vitamin	Deficiency Symptom
64. vitamin A	_____ anemia
65. vitamin C	_____ skin rash
66. vitamin B$_1$	_____ scurvy
67. vitamin K	_____ beriberi
68. niacin	_____ night blindness

69. The "sunshine vitamin" refers to _____.

70. What condition is caused by a lack of vitamin D?

71. The only vitamin that is not stored in the body is _____.

72. Ascorbic acid is another name given vitamin _____.

List the fat soluble vitamins and the foods in which they are most likely to be found.

73. _____   _____

74. _____   _____

75. _____   _____

76. _____   _____

Matching: Place the letter from column II into the appropriate space.

I		II
77. liver	_____	A. can be used as a substitute for salt
78. citrus fruits	_____	B. add bulk to diet
79. cellulose	_____	C. help regenerate red blood cells
80. mineral salts	_____	D. an important source of vitamin C
81. spices	_____	E. regulate osmosis

82. What vitamin controls production of collagen? _____.

83. What is collagen?_____.

84. What is the adult daily requirement for vitamin C? a) 10 mg, b) 5000 IU, c) 400 IU, d) 60 mg, e) none of the above.

85. Most measurable quantities of vitamin C are based on _____ properties.

86. When a substance loses hydrogen atoms or electrons it is _____.

87. To test for vitamin C, you would use: a) Biuret solution, b) Benedict solution, c) Lugol's iodine, d) none of the above.

88. Testing for vitamin C reveals: a) the cooking time has no effect on the amount present, b) the less food solution needed to change the color of the dye the greater the amount of vitamin C present, c) soaking the food has no effect on the amount present d) all of the above, e) none of the above.

89. In our experiment, vitamin C was detected in soaking water because the vitamin is _____ in water.

90. Excessive cooking _____ the loss of vitamin C.

91. The vitamin C content in foods is best preserved when the item is cooked by _____.

92. Since vitamin C cannot be stored in the body, what is the RDA for an adult?

93. Name two functions of the mineral elements in the body.

94. Some minerals are designated as "macrominerals." They are called this because: a) large amounts of them are in most foods, b) they are needed by people in large amounts, c) they can be taken in unlimited quantities, d) none of the above.

95. Calcium: a) has an RDA of 1 mg, b) is present in milk and milk products but not green leafy vegetables, c) is found with phosphorus in the bones and teeth, d) all the above, e) none of the above.

96. Calcium may be found in _____ and _____.

97. Which of the following is a mineral element? a) niacin, b) riboflavin, c) phosphorus, d) all of the above, e) none of the above.

98. Which of the following is a trace mineral? a) sulfur, b) iron, c) potassium, d) magnesium, e) none of the above.

99. _____ is an important trace element found mostly in the blood.

100. Liver is used in a diet for anemia because: a) it is easy to prepare, b) it is easy to digest and can be tolerated, c) it contains iron which is needed for red blood cells, d) the vitamin C content prevents excessive loss of blood.

101. _____ minerals are needed in small amounts in the diet.

102. Which one of the following is a trace element? a) lead, b) mercury, c) iron, d) all of the above, e) none of the above.

103. _____ helps to maintain normal water balance inside and outside the cells.

104. Everyone needs at least _____ of sodium per day.

105. A rich source of iodine is: a) seeds and nuts, b) whole and enriched grains, c) sea foods, d) liver, e) none of the above.

Matching: Place the letter from column II in the appropriate space.

	I			II
106.	*Mineral*			*Necessary for*
107.	calcium	_____	A.	normal behavior of nerves and muscles
108.	phosphorus	_____	B.	strong bones and teeth
109.	sodium	_____	C.	water balance of cells
110.	chlorine	_____	D.	food digestion
111.	potassium	_____	E.	regulate the volume and balance of body fluids
112.	magnesium	_____	F.	energy conversion
113.	sulfur	_____	G.	protein nutrition
114.	iron	_____	H.	red blood cells
115.	zinc	_____	I.	respiration
116.	selenium	_____	J.	growth
117.	manganese	_____	K.	muscle and bone structure
	iodine	_____	L.	thyroid gland

118. The minerals _____ and _____ when combined form table salt.

119. List five main disadvantages of fast foods. _____, _____, _____, _____, _____.

120. High blood pressure is called _____.

121. A doctor will measure your blood pressure by using an instrument called: a) a stethoscope, b) specific dynamic action gauge, c) sphygmomanometer, d) a blood spectroscope.

122. Essential hypertension: a) is very rare, b) is normal because the blood vessels cannot function without some degree of tension, c) can be permanently cured by medical treatment, d) exists for no apparent reason.

123. The pressure inside the arteries when the heart is contracting is: a) diastolic, b) systolic, c) diastolic and systolic, d) none of the above.

124. Blood pressure goes _____ during relaxing times and _____ with meals or excitement.

125. It is known that blood pressure goes _____ during sleep.

126. The measurement of the work the heart must do to pump blood through your body is called: a) blood pressure, b) systolic rate, c) diastolic rate, d) all of the above, e) none of the above.

127. High salt intake may result in the following: a) high blood pressure, b) kidney disease, c) cirrhosis of the liver, d) all of the above.

128. Generally speaking, people who are overweight tend to have a/an _____ blood pressure than people of normal weight.

129. Overweight: a) is usually a result of overeating and lack of exercise, b) is best treated by greatly increasing the protein in the diet, c) is normal for people over thirty-five years old, d) all of the above, e) none of the above.

130. A nutrition label tells the _____ of the serving and the _____ of servings in the container.

131. List three pieces of information required on all food labels. _____, _____, _____.

132. The only foods not required by the FDA to list all ingredients are so-called _____.

133. A/an _____ product is not as nutritious as the product it resembles.

134. If the nutrition label states that one serving provides four grams of protein, one gram of carbohydrate, and four grams of fat, then the food contains: a) 45 calories, b) 25 calories, c) 40 calories, d) none of the above.

135. The four types of open food dating are: _____, _____, _____, and _____.

136. The date a food product was manufactured, processed or packaged is _____.

137. The _____ date is the last date that food should be used.

138. The _____ date on canned foods tells how old the food is when it is bought.

139. Open dating: a) is required by the FDA to protect consumers, b) can tell the consumer the last day the food may be eaten or used, c) is meaningless to the customer but needed by the producer, d) all of the above, e) none of the above.

140. The freshness date: a) is the last date the product can be safely used without risk, b) can tell the consumer when to discard cans or packages from pantry shelves, c) is used on bakery products to inform the customer about when the product will be at its flavor peak, d) all of the above, e) none of the above.

Matching: Place the letter from Column II in the appropriate space.

I		II
141. pack date	_____	A. "best used by"
142. pull date	_____	B. last date food should be eaten
143. expiration date	_____	C. date food was manufactured
144. freshness date	_____	D. last date product should be sold

145. RDA means: a) Rural Diary Association, b) Recommended Daily Allowance, c) Redistributed Dietary Allotment, d) none of the above.

146. Nutrition labeling: a) was developed by the FDA and the food industry as a public service, b) is required on any food for which a nutrition claim is made, c) includes additives at the option of the producer, d) must be specific about what flavorings and colors are used, e) all of the above.

147. What are we able to find on a nutrition label? a) acid content, b) glucose content, c) nutrients, vitamin, mineral content, d) all of the above, e) none of the above.

148. Vitamins and minerals on a nutrition label: a) are followed by a number which is the amount of milligrams present, b) are followed by a number which is the percentage RDA, c) are a breakdown of the calorie content per serving, d) all of the above, e) none of the above.

149. Certain information is required on all food labels: a) name of the product, b) net contents or net weight, c) name and address of business or manufacturer, d) all of the above, e) none of the above.

150. The UPC: a) designates that the food complies with Jewish dietary laws, b) can tell store managers how fast the food is being sold, c) can easily be read by informed consumers, d) all of the above, e) none of the above.

151. Grades on labels tell the consumer: a) how nutritious the food is compared to all products of this type in the market, b) are required on milk and milk products because children and nursing mothers deserve only foods with the greatest nutrient value, c) that the food has met the requirements of the Department of Agriculture with respect to taste, appearance, and texture, d) all of the above, e) none of the above.

152. When comparing junk foods and fast foods: a) both types should be avoided since they provide nothing, b) they can do little harm because they are a source of fast energy and provide pleasure, c) try to balance off the fast foods you have eaten by eating fruits and vegetables in the other meals of the day, d) all of the above.

153. When the FDA "grades" milk and milk products, this grade is based on the FDA recommended _____ for the production and processing of these products.

154. The modern refrigerator is an important appliance which can be used to retard food contamination. Therefore: a) keep shelves clean by covering with foil, b) door gaskets should be flexible and intact, c) areas around the motor and refrigeration unit should be cleaned only by a trained repairman, d) all of the above, e) none of the above.

155. Bacterial contamination of food: a) requires that the bacteria have warmth, moisture, and a source of food, b) only occurs on warm summer days, c) is impossible because of modern food preparation techniques, d) all of the above, e) none of the above.

156. Bacterial contamination of foods can be reduced through _____ or _____.

157. Poison-producing microorganisms may grow rapidly in foods at temperatures from: a) 30 to 85 degrees F, b) 120 to 195 degrees F, c) 45 to 115 degrees F, d) all of the above, e) none of the above.

158. _____ is transmitted through raw or undercooked pork.

159. Botulism: a) is rarely fatal but very uncomfortable, b) is often associated with low-acid foods prepared by the cold-pack method, c) both of the above, d) none of the above.

160. Suspecting that a canned food is contaminated, you should: a) open it and smell, if it seems alright take a small taste, b) throw it away and lose money, c) if you are not sure, give some to the dog, d) none of the above.

161. 100 grams approximates: a) 5 tsp, b) 6½ tsp, c) 7½ tsp, d) none of the above.

162. How many calories are in a teaspoon of sugar? a) 8, b) 16, c) 32, d) 64.

163. How many calories are in a teaspoon of saccharine? a) 0, b) 5, c) 15, d) 20.

164. How many calories are in a teaspoon of aspartame? a) 0, b) 10, c) 20, d) 30.

Refer to the Calorie/Exercise chart to answer the following questions:

165. A medium size apple contains enough calories to walk for: a) 2 minutes, b) 11 minutes, c) 17 minutes, d) 23 minutes.

166. Two slices of bread and butter contain the calories to swim for: a) 2 minutes, b) 18 minutes, c) 30 minutes, d) 46 minutes.

167. A cup of ice cream contains enough calories to walk for: a) 49 minutes, b) one hour, c) all day, d) 24 hours.

168. Two doughnuts contain the calories to jog: a) 5 minutes, b) 13 minutes, c) 26 minutes, d) 52 minutes.

169. Which of these foods are excellent sources of fiber? a) oranges, b) salmon, c) kidney beans, d) bran cereals, e) white rice, f) peas, g) yogurt, h) round steak.

170. Which of the following fish contain the most heart-healthy oils? a) canned tuna, b) salmon, c) mackerel, d) sole, e) sardines, f) rainbow trout.

171. Two cups of tea contain more caffeine than one cup of coffee. a) True, b) False.

172. Which of the following are saturated fats? a) soybean oil, b) palm oil, c) butter, d) corn oil, e) fully hydrogenated soybean oil, f) sunflower oil, g) olive oil, h) coconut oil.

173. In Lab Experience 2.15, we sterilize the test tubes: a) in case we cut ourselves, b) not to contaminate the milk, c) because it is neater, d) all the above.

174. In Lab Experience 2.15, we open two of the milk containers: a) to drop in chemicals, b) to allow air to contaminate the milk, c) so that no one will drink the milk.

175. In the following statement, which is the incorrect answer.
The amount of bacteria in milk is affected by: a) time, b) storage temperature, c) exposure to air, d) brand of milk.

176. Cottage cheese must be: a) made in a cottage, b) bought in a store, c) made from milk and rennin, d) all the above.

177. Whey is: a) the way to go, b) spider food, c) the heavy part of anything, d) the liquid part of cottage cheese.

178. Curds are: a) a kind of hair, b) the solid part of cottage cheese, c) tribesmen of Asia, d) none of the above.

179. Cottage cheese can be made: a) with or without salt, b) only with salt, c) only without salt, d) none of the above.

180. Yogurt is made from: a) cheese, b) goats, c) milk and bacteria, d) none of the above.

181. Yogurt can be made at home: a) if you have the secret ingredients, b) if you take the time to do it, c) but it costs more than buying it, d) none of the above.

182. Glue: a) may be made of milk, baking soda, and vinegar, b) may be made into milk, c) can only be made out of milk, d) none of the above.

UNIT 3

PHYSICS

Physics is defined as the science that deals with matter, energy, motion and force. In this unit, instead of delving deeply into these phenomena, we will study their effects on our everyday life. Thus the topics to be covered include home appliances, television, microwaves, electric and gas meters, and the world energy crisis. As consumers we should understand some of the basic physical principles such as heat transfer, electricity and radiation.

MATTER AND ENERGY

The study of matter and energy, is a subject which affects us daily. For example, today's lunch will be metabolized, or converted, into cells, tissues, muscles, and organs. Thus, the matter in food changes into other matter and into the energy that allows us to move and think. This is also true for the process which takes place when green plants change water, carbondioxide, and the energy of the sun into fruit and wood. The fruit is eaten for food. The wood is used to build, heat, and light our homes.

Matter and energy cannot be created or destroyed, but can be converted from one form to another. It is this long sequence of events which makes our world.

POTENTIAL AND KINETIC ENERGY

Energy can be either potential (stored) or kinetic (moving and doing). We may further divide energy into several kinds: chemical, heat, electrical, and solar.

Mass is the amount of matter that goes to make up an object. Weight is the force or pull of gravity on an object. So when we hop on the scale in the morning to check our weight, we are really determining the pull of gravity upon our bodies. Weight is therefore proportional to mass. Weight is equal to mass times gravity (weight = mass × gravity).

If two equal and opposite forces act on a body, the two forces will neutralize each other and the body will remain motionless, or in equilibrium. If a force causes a body to move, then we say work has been done on the body. The unit of work is called the joule, or the foot-pound. For example, if we raise a one pound object a distance of one foot, we have used one foot-pound or one joule of energy. How long it takes to do work, or the rate of doing work, is called power. The unit of power is defined as a joule per second (joule/second) which is equal to the watt. In the English system the unit of power is horsepower, which is equal to 746 watts. For example, to raise a one pound object a distance of one foot in one second of time would require one horsepower (or 746 watts). To raise ten pounds a distance of one foot in ten seconds, still requires one horsepower. In summary, the unit of work is the joule, or the foot-pound; the unit of power is the joule/second (which is equal to the watt), or horsepower.

Assume that a boulder is carried from the bottom to the top of a cliff. If it is permitted to drop back down, the boulder will perform work as it falls to the bottom. This is kinetic energy. But if the boulder is resting at the top of the cliff it is performing no work: it merely possesses the potential to do work because of its position. This is potential energy. As the rock falls, potential energy is converted into kinetic energy; or, stored energy is converted into moving energy. Thus, energy can be changed from one kind to another. When the boulder strikes bottom, it sends objects flying (mechanical energy), it produces noise (sound energy), it causes the object that it hit to become warmer (heat energy), and it may strike sparks from another stone (light energy).

As we have said before, energy cannot be created or destroyed, but only changed from one form to another. If we were to add up all the energies in the case of the rock striking bottom after falling from the cliff, these energies would equal the amount of potential energy possessed by the boulder when it was at the top of the cliff. Where did this potential energy come from? The potential energy came from the muscular energy of the person who carried it to the top of the cliff. This muscular energy came from the chemical energy of the food he ate. The energy of the food came from the sun which is the source of all energy on this earth with two exceptions, nuclear and geothermal energy.

HEAT ENERGY

Suppose that a flame is applied to the bottom of a kettle containing water. The heat ultimately changes the water (liquid) into steam (gas). The motion of the molecules of the gas is greater than the molecules of the liquid, and the lid rattles. The flame was able to produce work. The flame possessed energy — this is called heat energy.

An object contains heat energy in an amount that depends on its mass, its temperature, and the specific material of which it is made. Heat is measured in calories or British Thermal Units (BTU). A calorie is the amount of heat needed to raise the temperature of 1 gram of water 1 degree Celsius. One calorie is equal to the energy required to lift a ten pound weight about 4 inches or 4.5 kg lifted about 10 cm.

The heat energy in the English measuring system is the British Thermal Unit (BTU). The BTU is the amount of heat needed to raise the temperature of 1 pound of water 1 degree Fahrenheit. One BTU is equal to the energy required to raise 778 pounds a distance of one foot. An example of the use made of the BTU is the air conditioner. The cooling capacity of a room air conditioner is defined as the amount of heat the unit is capable of removing from the air. The higher the BTU per hour rating of the unit, the greater is its cooling capacity.

The difference between heat and temperature is that heat describes the amount of energy needed to warm an area or object, while temperature is a numerical reading of how warm that area or object is.

Heat is produced by the constant movement of molecules. When heat is added to the object, the movement of the object's molecules is increased. The speed with which those molecules move determines the temperature of the body. The greater the speed of movement of the molecules, the higher the temperature.

Heat normally flows from a warmer to a cooler body. One object is giving off heat while the other object is gaining heat.

Many kinds of energy produce heat energy. For example, an electric current flowing through a wire (resistance) such as an electric light bulb or a heating coil will cause the wire to become hot.

LAB EXPERIENCE 3.1

HEAT TRANSFER AND TEMPERATURE

Purpose: This lab experience consists of four parts: three demonstrations and one experiment. The three demonstrations show the principles of heat transfer and temperature elevation. They are important for an understanding of the experiment which the students perform.

Part A - Demonstration 1

Place a block of metal heated to 65°C on a block of metal which had been kept in the refrigerator overnight. Note temperature of each metal. The hot block cools down, the cold block warms up. Eventually, both will reach the same temperature.

Heat flows from the warmer to the cooler body, and the flow stops when both are at the same temperature.

Part B - Demonstration 2

Prepare a source of heat, such as a hot plate, one beaker with 250 ml of water in it, one beaker with 500 ml of water in it. Note the temperature of the water in each beaker. Place them both on the hot plate. Measure the temperature rise of the water in each beaker. Allow the temperature to rise 20 degrees. The temperature rise in the beaker holding 500 ml will be half as fast as the temperature rise of the water in the other beaker. The beaker holding 500 ml will also cool more slowly.

The amount of heat in an object is related to both the temperature and the quantity of matter. A small pot filled with water will heat up sooner, and be at its boiling point sooner than will a larger pot filled with water, and heated to its boiling point. At the same temperature, a large sample of material contains more heat than a small sample of the same material.

Part C - Demonstration 3

A beaker with 250 g of water is placed on a hot plate; a second beaker with 250 g of ethyl alcohol is placed on the same hot plate. Be careful that no fumes or spills come in contact with the heated hot plate. Do not use a bunsen burner!! Note temperature of each liquid. Allow the temperature to rise 20 degrees. Both liquids are heated identically. The temperature of the ethyl alcohol will rise almost twice as fast as the temperature of the water even though both are of the same mass.

The amount of heat in an object is related not only to the temperature and the quantity of matter, but also to the type of matter.

LAB EXPERIENCE 3.1 (Continued)

HEAT TRANSFER AND TEMPERATURE

Part D - Experiment

Purpose: This experiment will demonstrate the effect of the nature of material on heat transfer. To determine if the nature of a substance influences its ability to transfer heat to water, select two objects of the same mass, volume, color, shape, etc. In addition, the objects must not be soluble in water. However, it is difficult to satisfy all these requirements, so compromise and select objects of equal mass.

Materials:

1	Double pan balance	2	250-ml beakers
2	Heat resistant plastic bags	1	400-ml beaker
10 to 15	Glass marbles	1	Hot plate
	(color is not important)	2	Thermometers
6	Lead balls	2	Styrofoam cups
		1	Safety goggles

Procedure:

1. The volume and color should not make any difference, but use equal masses of glass marbles and lead balls. To determine that they are equal in mass, balance them, as closely as possible on an equal arm balance. Don't break any marbles to achieve equality.

2. Put the marbles in one heat resistant plastic bag and the lead balls in another, and suspend the two bags in the same 400 ml beaker of boiling water. Leave them there long enough to make sure that each marble and each ball is at the same temperature as the boiling water (15 minutes at 100°C should be ample).

3. Meanwhile, put cool water into two styrofoam cups. The water should be at the same temperature, and the amount of water in the cups should be just enough to cover the marbles. Set the styrofoam cups into the 250 ml beakers for steadying support.

4. Place a thermometer in each cup and record the temperature.

5. When the marbles and balls have been heated for 15 minutes, remove the thermometers and quickly transfer the marbles to one cup and the lead balls to the other cup by pouring them out of their plastic bags. Replace thermometers.

LAB EXPERIENCE 3.1 (Continued)

HEAT TRANSFER AND TEMPERATURE

6. Read the thermometers immediately and at one minute intervals for ten minutes. Record the temperatures on the chart.

7. Be sure to record the maximum temperature before it starts to cool again to room temperature.

Materials	Water Temp. (Step 3)	Water Temp. (Step 5)	Max. Water Temp. (Step 6)	Final Water Temp. (Step 7)
Glass Marbles				
Lead Balls				

Question: Is there a difference in the maximum temperature attained by the water in the each cup?

Observations:

1. Equal quantities of different substances will generally absorb different quantities of heat for a given temperature rise, and give off different quantities of heat on cooling.

2. The specific heat of a substance determines the amount of heat required to change the temperature of 1 gram of the substance by 1 celsius degree.

   The specific heat value of lead is 0.031 cal/g °C.

   The specific heat value of glass is 0.20 cal/g °C.

3. Because glass marbles have a higher specific heat value, they were able to transfer more heat than the lead balls.

4. In effect, you used water as an instrument for measuring an amount of heat. This is the same exact method that is used to define heat. The calorie is the amount of heat necessary to raise the temperature of one gram of water one celsius degree.

5. When 1 calorie of heat is added to a substance, then 1 calorie of heat will be released when the substance is cooled.

CONCEPTS AND TERMINOLOGY

Heat is thermal energy which is being taken up by a body, given off by a body or being transferred from one body to another. Heat depends on the mass, the temperature, and the specific heat of a body.

Temperature is a numerical reading of how warm a body is.

Boiling point/vaporization point is the temperature at sea level, or one atmosphere of pressure, at which a liquid changes to a vapor or gas. This is a reversible condition, which occurs at 100 °C, or 212 °F, for water. Different materials have different boiling and vaporization points.

Melting point/freezing point is the temperature at which a solid changes to a liquid. This is a reversible condition which occurs at 0 °C, or 32 °F, for water at sea level. Different materials have different melting and freezing points.

Note that we use two different temperature scales: the Farenheit and Celsius scales. For both, the physical condition of the freezing of water or the boiling of water is the same. However, each scale gives these conditions a different value or number. On the Farenheit scale, water freezes at 32° and boils at 212°. On the Celsius scale, water freezes at 0° and boils at 100°. There are several convenient ways to convert from one scale to the other. Knowing the temperature in one scale and some conversion factors, it is simple to determine the temperature in the other scale.

  ° To convert from Celsius to Farenheit:
$$T_f = (1.8 \times T_c) + 32°,$$

  ° To convert from Farenheit to Celsius:
$$T_c = \frac{5}{9}(T_f - 32°),$$

  ° However, an equation that allows conversion either way is:
$$5F = 9C + 160$$
  where

T_f = Temperature in Farenheit
T_c = Temperature in Celsius
F = Farenheit temperature
C = Celsius temperature

The *boiling point* of a liquid is altered when another substance is dissolved in it. When salt is added to water it will require the water to boil at a temperature higher than 100 °C, or 212 °F. The resulting mixture is called a solution. Salt being dissolved is called a *solute,* and the water which is doing the dissolving is called the *solvent.*

The *freezing point* of a liquid is lowered when another substance is dissolved in it. The greater the amount of the substance dissolved in a fixed amount of liquid, the lower the freezing point of the solution. We apply this principle when we use rock salt to melt the ice on roads and sidewalks. The rock salt interferes with crystal formation as the water on the road cools.

At a higher altitude the air pressure decreases and the boiling point drops. The boiling point of water drops about one degree Celsius for every 1,000 feet of altitude. Pressure cookers boil water at pressures of up to two atmospheres and temperatures at about 120 °C. Keep in mind that at sea level we are normally subject to one atmosphere (15 lb/in²), and water boils at its normal 100 °C. Pressure cookers are useful for the rapid cooking of foods, thereby saving time, energy, and the nutritive value of the foods. In pressure cookers, the food is cooked by steaming.

Vacuum pans boil water at low pressure and at slightly above room temperature. They are used in the production of such things as sugar crystals, concentrated fruit juices and evaporated and powdered milk where a higher temperature would destroy the nutritive value of the food.

HEAT TRANSFER METHODS

Heat transfer occurs by several methods: conduction, convection and radiation.

CONDUCTION

Conduction is the transfer of heat from one molecule to another, in the same or different bodies, with no visible motion of the heated bodies. The molecules, however, are in violent motion, passing energy from one molecule to another. An example would be the heating of the metal handle of a pot as it is heated on the stove. In general, metals are good conductors of heat with aluminum and copper among the best. Stainless steel is not as good a conductor as the other two and therefore heats unevenly. Wood and glass are only fair conductors. Still air, held in tiny pockets of a porous substance, is a poor conductor. This is why fiberglass and urethane foam, enclosing as they do many tiny dead air spaces, make poor conductors and therefore good insulators for ranges and refrigerators.

CONVECTION

Convection is heat transfer by the motion of the medium as a whole. The medium is usually air or a liquid such as water which moves from one area to another carrying the heat with it. This is frequently described as a convection current. Heat is carried to the food in a gas oven by convection currents; in a refrigerator, heat moves from food by convection to the freezing unit.

When water in a saucepan is heated from room temperature to boiling, convection currents move through the liquid. As the liquid is heated, currents are formed by the expansion of the liquid, and its density is decreased. The heated lighter liquid rises while the cooler heavier liquid flows downward to take its place. Realize of course, that the liquid closest to the bottom of the pot is also being heated by conduction.

Convection currents bring the heated air from a hot-air furnace, through ducts, to the various rooms in the house, while at the same time the cooler air returns to the furnace through other ducts.

RADIATION

Radiation is electromagnetic wave motion, such as the passage of light through space. Radiant heat travels with the same speed as visible light, 186,000 miles per second, but is of longer wavelength. Like light, radiant heat travels in straight lines and can be reflected and absorbed as well as transmitted. Shiny, light-colored surfaces tend to reflect light; rough, dark surfaces to absorb it. Our sun is the most important source of radiant heat. It supplies slightly more than 6 BTU per square foot per minute to the earth during the hours when the sun's rays are perpendicular to the earth's surface.

Electric broilers and rotisseries are sources of radiant heat. Gas ovens as well as electric ovens, once the interior dark surfaces become heated, also give off radiations. These radiations are responsible for much of the browning of food while convection and conduction cook the inside.

RADIATION AROUND US

Since radiation is energy moving through space as invisible waves at the speed of light, the frequency of these waves — that is, the number of waves per second — helps to determine radiation characteristics and how radiation can affect people.

Frequency is also a basis for classifying different types of radiation such as x-rays, visible light, infrared rays, or microwaves. The frequency scale from least energetic to most energetic is called the electromagnetic spectrum. Man has found many ways to harness and safely use most of the different types or forms of radiation. In the order of longest to shortest wave length they are:

Radio/Television	Least energetic; lowest in frequency, longest in wave length
Microwaves	Radar
Infrared	Deep heat lamps
Visible Light	Sunlamps, lasers

Ultraviolet	Black light lamps, tanning lamps
X-rays	Medical science
Gamma rays	Most energetic; highest in frequency, shortest in wave length

Thus, the earth and its inhabitants are constantly being bombarded with all forms of radiation. But of all the forms bombarding us, we are most unconcerned about the most common one-sunshine. Ultraviolet radiation is the portion of the sun's electromagnetic spectrum which is harmful to our skin.

SUNSHINE

The earth's atmosphere acts as a shield and filters the burning ultraviolet rays. Dirt, smog, and other pollutants also act as filters. However, most people know that careless basking in the sun can result in a painful burn. The time of day, the location, the environment, and medications or other preparations affecting body chemistry should all be kept in mind when a person plans to be out in the sun. To judge how much suntime to take unprotected, consider the following situation.

Assume it is a calm, clear day, not too hot, and far from the pollution of the city. It's the first venture into the sun this year. A real tan is not expected on the first day, but a good start is desired. What do you do?

A good rule of thumb for "average" skin, without suntan preparation, is to begin the first day with about 40 minutes of sun, the second with 45, the third and fourth with about 50. After each time period, get out of the sun completely. Go indoors.

After this, most people should be able to stay out for a good part of the day because the melanin, or pigment of the average skin will have been built up to afford adequate protection. Building melanin must be done gradually or a burn will result. Be particularly careful of shoulders, knees, tops of feet, lips and ears. If there is little hair on the head, beware of sunstroke.

The best advice is not to push your luck. Remember that even small amounts of sun speed the aging process of the skin, and can increase the risk of skin cancer. However, there is a wide variety of creams and lotions on the market that can reduce the hazardous effect of the sun's ultraviolet rays. Even careful sunbathing, year after year, will bring out signs of aging because the effects are both insidious and cumulative. The people most susceptible to skin cancer are those with light-colored skin and eyes. The proper, regular use of sunscreens may help reduce the incidence of cancer in susceptible groups.

Sunscreens work by absorbing, reflecting, or scattering ultraviolet light, thus reducing the amount that reaches the skin. Sunscreens fall into two major categories: sunblocking products and suntanning products. In either case the claims made on the label are the best clue as to which is most suitable. The higher the "sun protection factor" (SPF) value, the more protection the product will give. The number indicates the amount of protection the product gives as compared to using none at all.

The SPF value ratings go from 2 to 15 or more. The highest numbers will almost completely prevent sunburn and suntan, while the lowest numbers give minimal protection. Each purchaser must evaluate how much protection is required.

One point to remember is that no product can make you tan faster than you would with no protection. The aim of such products is solely to help you stay outside a little longer without burning. Some preparations, such as baby oil, only keep you greased and more comfortable. A good skin preparation can help you, but it can't take the place of good judgement.

Although nature shields us from some of the sun's ultraviolet radiation by the ozone layer or other components in the atmosphere, we can still be exposed to these dangerous rays because they are also produced by certain artificial light sources.

Sunlamps are in wide use in the United States, but many people fail to recognize their potential danger. Many children, teenagers, and adults use sunlamps year round. Most devotees employ sunlamps to improve their appearance. However, sunlamp bathers should be aware that the ultraviolet radiation that tans and beautifies skin can also cause painful burns and possible lasting eye damage. People do not realize that under some lamps, one minute of ultraviolet radiation even at the specified distance between bather and lamp can be equivalent to one hour under the sun.

Case studies of sunlamp injuries show that although sunlamps and ultraviolet ray bulbs often come with instructions for proper use, many purchasers do not read the warning brochures or lose them. Therefore, the majority of users may not ever see a set of instructions or otherwise become aware of potential dangers in sunlamp use.

Here are suggestions for consumers from the Bureau of Product Safety for the safe use of ultraviolet bulbs and sunlamps:

1. Upon purchase, read and observe all instructions carefully. If instructions are not permanently attached to the lamp, tape them to the lamp's base or stand so that they will not be lost and will be available to successive users.

2. Be precise in measuring exposure time and distance from the lamp. Use a tape measure. Use a timer with an alarm bell so that if one's attention wanders, one will be alerted immediately to overexposure. Better still, purchase a sunlamp with a timing device to automatically turn off the lamp at the proper time.

3. Wear close-fitting eye protection.

4. Never stare directly at the lighted bulb.

5. Guard against mirrors that can reflect ultraviolet rays not only to the person using a sunlamp but also to persons nearby.

6. Never become so comfortable under a lamp that there is danger of becoming drowsy or falling asleep.

7. Remember, reading or similar activities under a sunlamp can be harmful to eyes.

8. Children should be carefully supervised under any form of ultraviolet light by responsible adults.

In summation, all radiation is potentially harmful and sunburn is painful. Pay attention and be careful.

TELEVISION RADIATION

There should be no health hazard in watching TV at a distance at which the image quality is satisfactory to the viewer.

Many of the components in television sets operate at thousands of volts, and are capable of generating x-rays. These components can produce x-rays capable of escaping from the receiver cabinet or picture tube. X-rays are produced when electrons, accelerated by high voltage, strike an obstacle while traveling in a vacuum, as in a TV tube. It is this kind of radiation that can make TV sets a potential hazard.

It was for this purpose that Congress enacted the Radiation Control for Health and Safety Act of 1968 which requires that TV receivers must not emit radiation above the 0.5 milliroentgen per hour level under the most adverse operating conditions. The roentgen may be considered as a measure of the radioactive dose received by a body. For example, a single dental x-ray gives about one roentgen, a full mouth x-ray series gives about 15 roentgen. The dose from natural radioactivity for a human being is five roentgen during the first 30 years of life. The milliroentgen is 1/1000 of one roentgen. It should be emphasized, however, that most TV sets have been found not to give off any measurable level of radiation.

When a TV set needs servicing, have it done by a qualified serviceman to assure that x-ray emissions are kept at a minimum. The primary cause of increased x-ray emission has been found to be an adjustment of operating voltages to levels higher than recommended by manufacturers. Qualified servicemen have been trained in the proper adjustment of the voltage to reduce the possibility of x-ray production.

MICROWAVE RADIATION

Microwaves are a type of electromagnetic radiation. Their use has soared in the past decade. Microwaves are used in police radar speed monitors, for telephone and television relay stations, and in diathermy machines for treating muscle soreness.

The microwaves in an oven are generated inside the cabinet by the electron tube called a magnetron. Because the metal interior of the oven reflects rather than absorbs microwaves, they bounce back and forth and are absorbed by food. Microwaves cause the water molecules in the food to vibrate, thus producing heat. This is what cooks the food. Foods high in water content cook more quickly than other foods.

Because microwaves penetrate the food and produce heat quickly, glass, paper, or plastic containers can be used to hold the food being cooked. The microwaves pass through these materials with minimal heating effect. Although the containers do not absorb nor are they heated by the microwaves, they can become hot from the food cooking in them. Be certain to use containers approved for microwave cooking and be careful when handling them. Metal pans or aluminum foil should not be used in a microwave oven. The microwaves will be reflected back to the magnetron, causing the food to cook unevenly and possibly damaging the magnetron tube.

In a conventional oven, the air in the oven compartment is heated and the heat is then transferred to the food, thereby cooking the food. In a microwave oven, all the heat is produced in the food so that the interior of the oven doesn't get hot. Consequently, microwave cooking is more energy-efficient than a conventional oven because the food heats quickly and the energy is used only to heat the food, not the compartment or the kitchen.

Microwave energy only heats the food. When thick foods such as a roast are cooked, the outer layers are heated and cooked primarily by microwaves while the inside is cooked mainly through the slower conduction of heat from the hot outer layers. Microwaves do not make the food radioactive or contaminated. Evidence also indicates that foods cooked in a microwave oven retain at least as many vitamins and minerals as those cooked in conventional ovens, perhaps retaining even more since the cooking is of much shorter duration.

Accidental exposure to high levels of microwaves could result in several types of injuries such as temporary sterility, burns, and cataracts. However, injuries can be caused only by exposure to very high levels of microwave radiation, levels much higher than users of microwave ovens can ever expect to receive.

To protect consumers from exposure to unnecessary hazardous levels of microwave radiation, the FDA has set safety standards for the performance of microwave ovens. These standards cover all microwave ovens manufactured after October 6, 1971. It sets a limit on the amount of microwave radiation that is permitted to leak from the oven wall, the seals around the door, and the window compartment. The limit is 5 milliwatts of microwave radiation per square centimeter, measured at 5 centimeters (2 inches) from the oven surface, and it is far below the level known to have adverse effects on people. As the distance from the oven increases, the level of microwave radiation decreases dramatically.

The FDA standard requires all ovens to be equipped with two independent interlock systems which prevent the oven from operating when the door is not securely fastened. In addition, a monitoring system stops the oven from operating if the interlock systems fail. These systems assure that emission of microwaves cease the moment the oven door is opened or the latch is released. Most important of all is that there is no residual radiation remaining once the oven door is opened.

There is little cause for concern unless the door hinges, latch, or seals are damaged. If the oven is suspected of leaking microwaves, contact your state or local health department. They usually have a program for inspecting ovens at no cost.

X-RAY RADIATION

Reports tell us that in 1895, Wilhelm Roentgen, a German physicist, discovered "a new kind of ray" which he called x-rays. They penetrated cardboard, wood, and cloth with ease. . . . Strangest of all, while flesh was very transparent, bones were fairly opaque". And so the discoverer, interposing his hands between the source of the rays and the screen, saw the bones of his hand projected in silhouette upon the screen. Since that discovery, x-rays have been one of our most valuable medical aids in saving lives.

Although a single x-ray examination is not likely to cause damage, all exposure involves some small risk. However, no one should be afraid to have a needed x-ray examination because the potential benefits of the x-ray far outweigh the possible damage from radiation exposure.

There are several ways to reduce unnecessary exposure to x-rays. The FDA establishes and enforces standards regulating x-ray equipment performance, conducts research into ways of reducing exposure, educates x-ray users in the proper use of equipment, and works with state and local radiation control programs and other federal agencies in promoting radiation safety. Most states have regulations requiring radiation safety surveys of x-ray facilities and machines.

There are some things that can be done to further protect the family. The American Dental Association has said that x-ray examinations should not be a standard part of every dental examination, but rather should be used only when necessary for proper diagnosis. We shouldn't insist on or reject x-rays but let the dentist be the judge.

The recommendation that everyone have an annual TB x-ray check is no longer applicable. A chest x-ray should be done only when recommended by a physician.

If there is any chance a woman might be pregnant, a physician usually will recommend that x-rays of the pelvic and abdominal regions be postponed, unless postponement would be detrimental to the woman's health. This precaution is especially important during the first three months of pregnancy because that is the time of extreme sensitivity to radiation of the rapidly developing cells.

It is wise to normally protect the reproductive organs with lead-lined rubber shields during x-ray examination unless these protective devices interfere with diagnostic procedures. Be sure your dentist covers you with a lead-lined shield before x-raying your teeth. Also close your eyes during the x-ray taking. Although the eyelids are not thick, they will offer one more thin layer of protection should there be any stray rays emanating from the machine.

To summarize, the use of x-rays holds great benefits for every individual, but also hold the potential for harm if not used properly.

RADON

Totally unrelated to nuclear power is the recently recognized home hazard due to radon gas. Radon is a naturally occurring by-product of uranium decay. It is an odorless, colorless gas that is found in small amounts in all soil and rock, particularly in shale and granite.

Radon is usually too diluted outdoors to be dangerous. When it seeps into buildings through basement floors and walls and through water pipes, it then can accumulate in concentrations high enough to be dangerous to the health of occupants of the buildings. The main hazard is increased lung cancer from radon "daughter" products which are the result of the normal decay of radon.

Radon in room air can be measured by a variety of methods. The most common uses a canister of activated carbon which absorbs radon from the air. The canister is sealed after a set period and the amount of radon absorbed can be measured in a professional laboratory.

Radon in water is measured in a similar way. Radon in well water is another serious radon hazard and should be checked by qualified personnel.

At the time of this writing, the Environmental Protection Agency has set 4.0 picocuries or greater per liter of air as the level requiring that steps be taken to reduce the amount of radon gas in a building. The effectiveness of any measures to accomplish this reduction depend upon the characteristics of the structure and the route of radon entry. Possible remedial action could include better sealing of foundations to decrease radon seepage into a building, or increased ventilation in areas with elevated radon levels to decrease the radon concentration. Professional consultation is a good idea before any action is taken.

RISK vs BENEFIT

There are two principal categories of radiation: ionizing and nonionizing. Ionizing radiation, such as x-rays, have the ability to strip electrons from atoms and create electrically charged ions capable of disrupting life processes. Nonionizing radiation lacks the ability to create ions, but can disrupt body processes through other mechanisms. Microwaves, light, and sound are classified as nonionizing radiation.

Most of what is known today about the effects of radiation on humans is the result of exposures to large amounts of radiation — some harmful such as the burn from a sunlamp, and some helpful such as the destruction of cancerous cells during radiation therapy. But not much is known about the effects of small amounts of radiation to which we are all subjected, such as the natural radiation from brick walls and electrical appliances that we all have in our homes. This is called "background radiation," and is measured in "millirems." This natural radiation can expose an individual to an average of about 140 millirems annually. People living at higher elevations receive even more. Radiation from man-made sources such as medical and dental x-rays and machinery, add a yearly average of 60 millirems. The rem is a measure of the effect on humans of exposure to radiation. The unit dosage includes the basic exposure plus the potential for biological damage from the radiation.

National and international scientific organizations have set a limit of 500 millirems per year of radiation which any member of the public may receive from a nuclear plant. In practice, nuclear plants release far less than that amount. It has been estimated that people living in the neighborhood of a power plant receive the same quantity of radiation that they would be exposed to from cosmic radiation during a single airplane flight across the United States.

The effects of radiation are categorized as either somatic or hereditary. Somatic effects directly affect the health of the person exposed to radiation. Hereditary effects occur in the genes of reproductive cells of the exposed individual, and may bring about changes in future generations.

The FDA has set safety standards for radiation-emitting products. These standards should be observed so that the benefits of the products will outweigh the risks.

HOME WEATHERIZATION

Weatherizing our homes to provide uniform comfort during the four seasons of the year has become a complex operation. Most of the problems, however, occur in cold weather. Our homes and business environments are heated by many different types of heating systems. However, only steam heat adds moisture to the home environment. All of the others provide very dry heat. In these cases, moisture can be added by a humidifier. Heating the air lowers the relative humidity of that air unless moisture is added. We are most comfortable at about 65 to 72 °F (18° to 22 °C), and at about 40 to 50% humidity. Humidity is the amount of moisture in the air, and proper humidity levels protect furniture as well as human skin and tissue.

When we speak of weatherizing a home, we mean making it more resistant to outside elements, and so insulation is very important. A better insulated house uses fuel more efficiently in order to maintain the desired interior climate.

Weatherization consists, first, of making the necessary repairs to cracks and holes that have no function except to permit unwanted drafts and increase your fuel bill. The second step is to wrap the house in a blanket of insulation, wherever it is cost-effective, to prevent heat transfers through walls, ceilings, and floors.

Eliminating these sources of air leakage is very cost-effective. Substantial reduction in heating and cooling loads can also be realized through a careful placement of grass, paving, shrubs, trees, and fences. Trees that lose their leaves in the fall let the sun shine in during the cold months and provide shade during the summer. Evergreens,

on the other hand, provide a constant windbreak on the north and west sides of a home.

INSULATION

The question of where to insulate can be answered by looking carefully at the living quarters. The ceiling with cold spaces above it, exterior walls and walls between living space and unheated garages or storage rooms, floors above cold spaces such as garages and open porches, and attic living space such as dormer walls and ceilings should be given first consideration.

The insulating materials available for use in existing homes are: mineral wool, cellulose fiber, vermiculite and perlite, plastic foams (polyurethane or polystyrene) and reflective foil. Mineral wool, either fiberglass or rock wool, is the most widely used type. It is available in blankets, batts, and loose insulation such as pouring wool or blowing wool. The amount of protection an insulating material can provide is indicated on a standard code known as the R-number. The R-numbers stand for resistance to winter heat loss or summer heat gain. These numbers are more accurate than inches as a means of designating insulation performance. One brand of insulation might be slightly thicker or thinner than another, but if they are marked with the same R-number they will resist heat transfer equally well.

To determine how much insulation is needed, calculate the overall area to be covered by multiplying the length by the width. Then adjust this number to allow for the area taken up by joists or studs. Mineral wool blankets and batts are available to fit 16-, 20-, and 24-inch joist and stud spacing. If pouring wool is to be used in an attic floor, then the bag label will tell how many square feet a bag of that particular insulation will cover. Divide that number into the number of square feet to be covered, and determine how many bags to buy. When installing insulation, take the following precautions:

1. Treat electrical wiring with care. Don't try to pull it or bend it out of the way.
2. Wear work gloves and loose fitting clothes, including a long-sleeved shirt because insulation fibers can cause temporary skin irritation.
3. Be wary of nails that stick through the roof sheathing.
4. Don't smoke in the attic.

CAULKING AND WEATHER STRIPPING

Although caulking and weather stripping are the simplest and usually the least expensive of home weatherization techniques, they are often overlooked. Both can be done in a short time and will pay for themselves in fuel savings during the first heating season. Studies indicate that a considerable amount of fuel can be saved* just by sealing the gaps in your home. Other studies show that the heat loss through cracks, loose windows, and doors can account for up to 55 percent of the heating load on a windy day.

It is also important to check all places where different building materials meet or where pipes or wires enter the house, and caulk these areas. All windows and doors, primary as well as storm, should be caulked around the frames. Only the top and sides of storm windows should be caulked, not the bottom. The putty around window panes should also be in good condition. The time to caulk is during the warmer months because caulk does not usually cure properly below 40°F (4°C). There are several types of caulking from which to choose: butyl rubber, acrylic latex and oil-base. Since caulking is an inexpensive material, it is wise to purchase more durable caulk although it may cost a little more. Oil-base sealants tend to harden more quickly than others, and therefore don't work well in areas where flexible materials are needed.

Also, oil-base sealants are more vulnerable to crumbling. A latex or acrylic latex caulk is easy to work with and can be painted almost immediately after application. However, it will not work well on fresh wood or new siding because it can dry out and crack within a few months. The best and most cost-effective sealant is a butyl type which stays flexible and durable for years. It shrinks only a little, adheres to almost everything, and is exceptionally resistant to shock, heat and cold. Although it costs a bit more than others, its life span is three to four times longer. Many caulks are available in toothpaste-type tubes which are good for small jobs. The cartridge caulk applied with a caulking gun usually gives best results for large jobs.

Windows and doors can be big energy-wasters. Windows are the third largest cause of heat loss in the home — after ceilings and walls. Doors and windows should fit tightly so they allow no drafts. Broken panes of glass should be replaced. While building or rehabilitating windows is the most thorough and longest-lasting method of weatherization, not everyone can afford it or has the tools and skill to do it. Weather stripping is a good alternative. There are many types: clay-like rope weather stripping is pressed into place; felt strips are glued or tacked into place; sponge or foam rubber with adhesive backing is glued over joints and cracks; neoprene covered sponge with wire mesh backing is generally the most durable and practical to install. Weather stripping and caulking are not a one-time effort. They need to be replaced every few years, depending on the quality of the material, the climate, and the construction of the house.

Most doors are installed with a space between the bottom of the door and the floor. This space can be as much as one-fourth inch or more, which in terms of heat loss can equal a nine square inch hole in the

---

*Fuel consumption can be reduced 10 to 30%.

wall of your home. If the space is a small crack, you can buy and install a door sweep. The door sweep should be low enough to ride along the floor and seal the crack when the door closes. If the space is one-half inch or more, you will need a saddle or threshold gasket. These are attached to the floor. The easiest to install is a bumper-type aluminum saddle, while the most effective is the two-piece adjustable interlocking type.

STORM WINDOWS

Storm windows can cut window heat loss from one third to one half, especially if your primary windows fit tightly. Storm windows cut heat loss by creating dead air space between storm and primary windows. This air space is the actual energy saver and should be at least half an inch wide. There are three types of storm windows: plastic, single pane, and combination screen and storm. All should be installed with weather stripping or caulking along the cracks between the storm unit and the window frame. Plastic sheeting is the least expensive and simplest project for the do-it-yourselfer. The plastic is available in different thicknesses and although eight or ten millimeters is easier to work with, four to six millimeters is sufficient. The sheeting is attached either to the primary window or to a wood frame. When attached to the primary window, masking tape or wood slats are used. Single pane storm windows are the most common. The storm window frames of most older homes are made of wood which provides the best protection although they are the heaviest to remove and install. Three panes of glass (two storms and one primary) will triple the R-value of a window. We can have three panes by using one plastic sheet on the inside of the house and a single pane storm window on the outside. The third type of storm window is the aluminum combination type which remains permanently in place. It has two storm windows and one screen which adjusts for usage. The units are also available in steel and plastic. Because combination units are most expensive, it is wise to very carefully check the quality of hardware, weather stripping and construction because a poorly constructed window offers little protection from the elements. When purchasing storm windows, look for the ANSI (American National Standards Institute) number that rates the efficiency of the window. The numbers range from one to four, with number one being most effective. A moderately priced window should have a 2 or 2.5 rating to be effective. Thermopane windows, a type of primary window with two glass panes, also is very effective. Storm doors serve the same purpose as storm windows. In addition to increasing the R-value of the primary door, they are particularly effective on windy days.

INDOOR CREATURE-COMFORT TIPS

Furnishings and surroundings have the potential of providing warmth in living quarters. Drapes and curtains should be left open on sunny days on all windows except northerly ones, so warm sunlight can enter. At sunset, the drapes should be closed to act as insulators, thus keeping the heat indoors.

The basic principle in preventing heat-loss through glass surfaces is to cover the glass tightly. One way this can be achieved is with modified roller-type shades. A study done by a research group at North Carolina State University found that light colored, opaque, vinyl-covered cloth shades were 22% more effective at cutting the annual energy waste than conventional draperies. The way to make simple shades more energy effective is to mount them inside the window frame, and hang them an inch or less out from the bottom sash, with only a one-quarter inch clearance on each side. Shades that are installed more than an inch from the window, or that don't close off air gaps, are less effective. Experiments have shown that tacking thin strips of wood to the sides of the window frame with a piece of stiff material such as denim left the window effectively sealed and the heat-reducing air flow cut off. This arrangement increased the heat savings of regular shades to 40%, and with a plastic-sheet shade the savings increased to 55%. This is about equal to the performance of storm windows.

For those who are reluctant to seal their windows for the duration of winter with plastic sheeting, there is window framing. Window frames use vinyl sheeting with light-weight wood frames. The clear vinyl plastic, 6 millimeters thick, is stapled onto a wood frame slightly smaller than the inside window area, with an inch and half of vinyl overlapping the frame. This vinyl frame is pressed into the window opening and is kept in place with latches. The vinyl then balloons out with the cold air that would otherwise seep inside. This insulates the window area by creating dead air space. The frame is easily made and easily removed, allowing for fresh air when wanted. The frames seem to work exceptionally well in older houses and loft apartments that have large windows.

There are some other things that can be done to make a home more comfortable and energy efficient.

1. When purchasing or recovering furniture, consider soft fabrics which feel warmer than leather, plastic or wood.
2. When painting use light colors on the walls and ceilings because light colors reflect heat and light back into the room.
3. Cold and drafty outside walls can be remedied by hanging large, thick tapestries or quilts on them.
4. Carpets are warm to the touch and offer more insulating value than tile, wood, slate or resilient floor coverings. The thicker and denser the carpet, the greater the insulating value. Wool and acrylic are the best insulators; nylon is least effective.
5. Avoid using radiator covers because they significantly restrict the flow of heat. If they must be used, be certain that at least 75% of the cover's surface has grill openings to allow for efficient heat flow. Keep the covers clean both inside and outside because dust acts as an insulator and wastes heat.
6. Furniture should be placed away from radiators, heat registers and air-return vents to allow for the easy circulation of heated air.
7. If the thermostat is located near a window, keep the window tightly shut and well insulated because air infiltration will lower the thermostat reading and keep the furnace working harder.
8. In winter each degree you lower the temperature of your house saves money. It is advisable to set the thermostat at 62°F (16°C) while at home, and turn it down to 55°F (13°C) overnight or when no one is home. If there are elderly persons in the home, or someone with circulatory problems, or someone taking medications such as tranquilizers, consult a physician before lowering the temperature.
9. Adding moisture to the air makes people feel warmer. Raising the inside humidity offers greater comfort and health for most people. A humidifier effect can be achieved by placing a pot of water on or near a radiator (not on an electric heater) or you can buy a portable room humidifier. Plants also act as minihumidifiers by adding small amounts of water vapor to the air.

10. The fireplace damper should be closed when not in use. Remember that a fireplace will permit heated air to flow up the chimney thereby bringing cool or cold air into the house to replace the warmed air. In addition, the fireplace will heat only the area directly in front of it while the rest of the room remains cold and drafty. This accounts for the highbacked chairs drawn up to the fireplace that are seen in early American homes. Fireplaces are more romantic than heat effective. A wood stove may be more effective than a fireplace, but there are many kinds and selection should be made carefully.

11. The kitchen is one of the greatest energy-using rooms in the home. Careful meal planning and energy-efficient appliances can result in money and energy savings. The refrigerator should be located in a cool spot with good air circulation around it. It should be away from heat sources or direct sunlight, the kitchen stove, and heating vents. It is advisable to open and close the refrigerator door as quickly and as infrequently as possible. Avoid putting hot foods in the refrigerator because they make it work harder. Allowing frozen foods to thaw in the refrigerator adds an extra cooling medium thereby requiring the refrigerator to work less hard. It is important to keep the refrigerator's condenser coils clean and be sure that the seals or gaskets on the refrigerator, freezer, and oven doors fit tightly.

12. Preheating the oven for only ten minutes is all that is necessary in most instances. Many dishes can be baked without preheating the oven at all. Everytime the oven door is opened, heat is lost. As long as the door stays closed, the oven is more efficient than the top burners. It is also a good idea to match the size of pots and pans to the size of the electrical burners or the size of the gas flames.

13. Exhaust fans should be used sparingly in the winter because they force your furnace to use energy to reheat the rooms. In addition, exhaust fans lower the humidity level that was elevated during cooking and bathing.

14. Water heating is the second most expensive item in the energy budget. Setting the temperature at a reasonably low number and using cold or warm, not hot, water whenever possible will result in energy savings. Wrapping the water heater with an insulation "blanket" will both cut heat loss and save money.

15. A faucet leaking one drop of water per second can waste over 3,000 gallons of water per year and if it was hot water, then a lot of fuel was also wasted. A water-flow restrictor on the showerhead will reduce water use by one-half without reducing the force of the water. Did you know the average shower requires only half as much hot water as an average tub bath, and even less if you install a showerhead flow restrictor?

16. The keys to saving energy in the laundry room are to use cold or warm water when washing clothes, and to rinse with cold whenever possible. It is best to operate washers and dryers with full loads to make the most efficient use of warm water or warm

air. It is advisable to clean the lint screen on the dryer after every use in order to keep the dryer running efficiently.

LIGHTING AND LIGHT BULBS

Three words are now printed on the paper sleeves in which your light bulbs are packaged are:

1. Watts: Wattage is the old standard that people had used for buying light bulbs because they were taught the brighter the bulb, the higher the wattage. But that isn't necessarily so, for the wattage only measures the amount of electricity being used by the bulb, not the amount of light you get out of it. Bulbs using the same amount of wattage don't always produce the same amount of light.
2. Lumens: Lumens are units for measuring the actual light output, the brightness, produced by the bulb. Saying "twice as many lumens" is the same as saying "twice as much light." The number of lumens printed on the paper sleeve tells you the average real light output of the bulb.
3. Bulb Life: The filament inside a bulb will last just so long; then it burns out. A listing on the bulb jacket now tells you how long the bulb is expected to last, on the average, before it burns out.

The long life bulbs or extended service bulbs are designed specifically to last longer than "standard" bulbs. For bulbs of the same wattage, longer life means less light, and a bulb has just so much "light life" and no more. This is because the filament eventually burns out after a certain amount of use. "Long life" filaments are heavier than those for standard bulbs, so they last longer. But, by their nature they don't give off as much light. The exception to this rule are the bulbs on the market which are filled with krypton gas. This gas increases bulb life by 50% over standard bulbs of the same wattage, with no loss in light output. Krypton bulbs are generally more expensive than "standards."

Incandescent bulbs come in one of two finishes: frosted and white. Frosted bulbs are etched inside the glass to reduce the concentrated glare of the filament, but they still have a visible bright spot. White bulbs eliminate the bright spot and they are recommended because they will "soften" shadows and reduce glare. It is recommended that frosted bulbs be used in translucent fixtures to eliminate glare.

Fluorescent tubes are now playing a major role in residential lighting. For applications where overall general illumination is needed such as in kitchens, recreation rooms, bathrooms, laundry rooms, and work shops fluorescent lighting is a good choice.

Some power companies charge the highest rates during their peak load period. This period is usually from 8:00 a.m. to 8:00 p.m., Monday through Friday. This is the time of greatest industrial and home usage. Many of the power companies will arrange to meter your electric energy usage if you could arrange to use your energy-intensive appliances at off-peak load periods. Energy-intensive appliances would be dishwashers, clothes dryers and washers. The power companies would charge a greatly reduced rate for off-peak time usage which would be 8:00 p.m. to 8:00 a.m. and weekends.

Some tips on economic use of light bulbs are:

1. Fluorescent lights are three to five times more efficient than incandescent bulbs, and cost much less to operate.
2. Dimmer switches reduce energy use when brightness is not important.

3. Remember to dust bulbs and shades regularly to obtain more light.
4. Most important of all, turn off all lights, stereo systems, and TV sets when leaving a room.

ELECTRICITY

Perhaps you've walked across a carpet in wintertime, or touched a door knob or metal railing, and experienced a nerve-tingling shock. Or after shampooing your hair, you've noticed sparks crackling as you brush your dry hair. Both of these experiences are related, and similar effects were observed long, long ago. As a matter of fact, the early Greeks are usually credited with discovering this phenomenon. It is called static electricity. Early experimenters found that substances such as rubber and amber acquired the ability to exert forces on other objects whenever the rubber or amber were rubbed vigorously with pieces of wool or fur. These substances were said to be "electrified." It was thought that a special fluid had flowed from one body to another. Today we say that the object is charged, and use the term electric charge.

Benjamin Franklin investigated electrical phenomena, and suggested that electrical effects were due to a surplus or deficiency of some fluid. He assigned the terms "positive" to represent a surplus and "negative" to represent a deficit of this fluid. Franklin believed that when a hard rubber rod was rubbed with fur, electrical fluid flowed from the rod to the fur. Thus the charge on the rod was negative. The basic discoveries made by Franklin and others have been extended until we understand a great deal about electricity and have made many applications of it. Whenever we turn on an electric light, use the telephone, or watch television, we are utilizing the end results of a very long chain of scientific discoveries and investigations.

Electric charge is no longer viewed as being a fluid. Experiments have shown that electricity is composed of particles that move in wave-like fashion. Experiments have also shown that there is a negative charge on the orbiting electron of the atom, while there is a corresponding positive charge on the proton of the atom. The proton is located in the nucleus of the atom, and the quantity of positive charge is equal in magnitude to the quantity of negative charge present. The amount of charge on one electron is extremely small and so we use a larger unit, the coulomb, to describe electric charge. One coulomb is equal to the charge on 6.24×10^{18} (or over six billion billion) electrons!

It has been found that some materials can hold an electric charge stationary and keep it from moving. Such materials are called insulators. Other materials allow electric charges to move through them freely and these materials are called conductors. Glass, rubber, and wood are examples of insulators, while copper, gold, aluminum, and salt water are examples of conductors. Not all materials fit neatly into these two categories. Some materials, known as semiconductors, are intermediate between conductors and insulators. Modern technology uses these materials extensively. The transistor and integrated chip that are used in the calculator and transistor radio are two examples of semiconductors.

Efficient transmission of energy over long distances is very practical and efficient. Thermal energy, from fossil fuels or nuclear reactors, is converted into electrical energy which is carried by conducting wires (transmission lines) to our homes and factories. The movement of electrical charge is responsible for the transmission of electrical energy. A stream of moving electrical charges is called current. The unit of current is the ampere, more commonly referred to as "amps."

Because electric current carries energy,

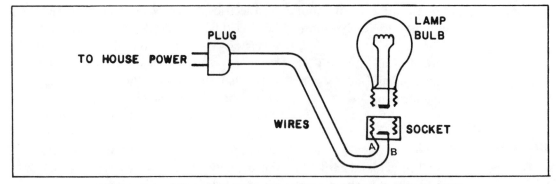

Figure 3.1 *Diagram of Electric Current Through a Light Bulb*

this energy can be extracted and changed into heat and work. As an example, look at Figure 3.1. Electric current flows into terminal A, moves through the filament of the bulb (a poor conductor with a high melting point), and flows out at terminal B. It moved between points A and B. In addition to the light produced, some of the energy possessed by the electric charge was transferred into heat.

To maintain the flow of electric current in a complete system (a circuit), an energy source such as a battery or electric generator is required. The power source provides the force to drive the electric current and is called an electromotive force or EMF. This EMF is measured in volts such as a 12-volt automobile battery. In this case the battery changes chemical energy into electrical energy, and vice versa. The concepts of voltage and amperage were known and used long before the electron was discovered. Although the negative pole of the battery is the side possessing an excess of electrons, it is still named negative. The current or electrons flow from negative to positive from a point of excess of electrons to a point deficient in electrons from the negative pole of the power source through the external path (the light bulb, etc.) back to the positive pole of the power source. In general, all electrical circuits consist of two basic types: series circuits and parallel circuits.

SERIES CIRCUITS

In a series circuit the electrons can follow only one path, from the high-potential to the low-potential point. Figure 3-2 shows such a circuit. In this figure, the high-potential (negative) point is indicated by the symbol − and the low-potential (positive) point by the symbol +. The direction of electron flow is indicated by the symbol e →.

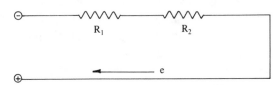

Figure 3.2 *The Series Circuit, Showing Two Resistors Connected in Series*

Although all substances offer some resistance to the current, we sometimes wish to introduce a concentrated, or lumped, resistance into a circuit. This is indicated by the symbol —⋀⋀⋀—. A light bulb is an example of a resistance, and so is any heating element doing work.

In Figure 3.2 you will notice two resistors (marked R_1 and R_2) connected together. (For this discussion we will ignore the resistance offered by the connecting wires.) Since there is only one path, all the electrons must flow through the entire series circuit. Thus, the current is the same in all parts of the circuit.

This is explained mathematically as:

$$I_t = I_1 = I_2 = \ldots$$

where I = current, measured in amps.

The amount of voltage or EMF required to push the current through each resistor is called the voltage drop across that resistor. The total voltage of the circuit is the sum of the individual voltage drops. The total electric pressure, or voltage, required to force the electrons from the negative to the positive end of the circuit is expressed mathematically as:

$$V_t = V_1 + V_2 + \ldots$$

where voltage is measured in volts.

In the circuit of Figure 3.2 assume that the total voltage is 90 volts and that the resistance of R_2 is twice that of R_1. The voltage drop across R_1 will then be 30 volts, and the voltage drop across R_2 will be 60 volts.

When individual resistances are connected in series, the total resistance is equal to the sum of the resistances of the individual resistors. This is expressed as:

$$R_t = R_1 + R_2 + \ldots$$

where resistance is measured in ohms.

If one resistance is burned out, then no current can flow because the current path is incomplete. This condition is called an open circuit.

Figure 3.3 illustrates a circuit with two different measuring devices, an ammeter and a voltmeter. The ammeter is a device that measures the flow of current, and the voltmeter measures the voltage across the circuit or battery. The circuit could represent two light bulbs in series with the power source.

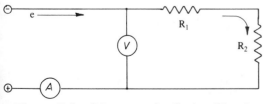

Figure 3.3 *Diagram of a Series Circuit*

PARALLEL CIRCUITS

In a parallel circuit, the electrons can follow two or more paths simultaneously from the high to the low-potential point. Figure 3.4 shows such a circuit.

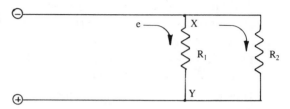

Figure 3.4 *The Parallel Circuit, Showing Two Resistors Connected In Parallel*

The current flowing from the high-potential (negative) point divides at X. Part flows through resistor, R_1. The balance flows through resistor R_2. Both parts of the electron stream join at Y, and the combined stream then flows on to the low-potential (positive) point.

Since current will flow more readily through a low-resistance than through a high-resistance path, if R_2 has twice the resistance of R_1, twice as much current will flow through R_1 as through R_2. (We disregard here the resistance of the connecting wires.) Thus, if the total current is equal to 9 amperes, then 6 amperes will flow through R_1 and 3 amperes through R_2. The total current is simply the sum of the separate resistor currents, and the amperage increases as additional resistors are connected in parallel. This is expressed mathematically as:

$$I_t = I_1 + I_2 + \ldots$$

Because each resistor has the same difference of potential across it, the voltage drop across each resistor is the same. This means that the voltage is constant throughout the circuit.

$$V_t = V_1 = V_2 = \ldots$$

When two or more lamps are connected in parallel, the total equivalent resistance is less than that of any single lamp, so that the resistance is a reciprocal of the total resistance, and is equal to the sum of the reciprocals of the individual resistances.

$$\frac{1}{R_t} = \frac{1}{R_1} + \frac{1}{R_2} + \ldots$$

Resistance is a measure of a substance's ability to resist the flow of electric current. It is measured in units called ohms. If in Figure 3.4, we assume R_1 to be equal to 15 ohms and R_2 equal to 30 ohms, the total resistance of the circuit can be computed as follows:

$$\frac{1}{R_t} = \frac{1}{15} + \frac{1}{30} = \frac{2+1}{30} = \frac{3}{30}$$

$$R_{total} = \frac{30}{3} = 10 \text{ ohms}$$

An example of series wiring comes to mind when you think of strings of Christmas tree lights. If you have had such a string, you know that if one bulb burns out all the other bulbs go out too, and it is often quite a task to locate the faulty one. More recently, most Christmas tree lights are wired in parallel, so that the bulb not operating can easily be located. All outlets on general purpose and appliance circuits are wired in parallel. If a bulb burns out or a toaster fails to operate, no other outlets on the circuit are affected. Only when a fuse opens or a circuit breaker pops (opens) is the entire circuit dead. The fuse is in series with the rest of the circuit.

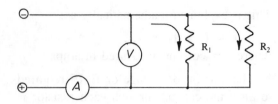

Figure 3.5 *Diagram of a Parallel Circuit*

As you can see there is a relationship between voltage (V), resistance (R), and current (I). The relationship between them is given by Ohm's law:

$$V = IR$$

If the voltage is known to be 120 volts and the current is 10 amps then R = 12 ohms. Power in watts (W), is found by:

$$W = IV.$$

Thus, a circuit of 5 amps at 120 volts uses 600 watts (0.6 kw). In an hour this would consume 0.6 kilowatt hours (kwh).

Most of the home appliances are known as small appliances and only require 115-volt power. However, some of the appliances that draw large amounts of current require 230-volt power. From Ohm's Law it can be seen that for a given appliance when R is constant, if the voltage goes up then the current needed goes down. Therefore, home circuits use both 115-volt and 230-volt circuits.

3-PRONG PLUG

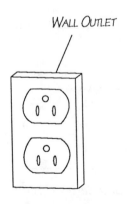

WALL OUTLET

LAB EXPERIENCE 3.2

ELECTRICAL CIRCUITS

Purpose: To study electrical circuits.

In order to produce a steady electrical current, we must provide an unbroken conducting path which begins and ends at an energy source such as a generator, battery, or power pack.   This complete conducting path is called an electrical circuit.   Power sources move existing charges around the electrical circuit, much the same way that a pump moves water in a pipe.   As we can control the flow of the water by means of a valve, so we can control the flow of electrical current by means of a switch, which is simply a convenient device for making a break in a circuit.

NOTE: A 12-volt battery can shock you.   The household voltage of approximately 115 volts is dangerous.

Materials:

2 1.5-volt batteries	Wire leads with alligator clips
2 1.5-volt bulbs	1 switch
2 bulb sockets	

Procedure:

Part A: Simple Series Circuit

1. Connect a wire from one pole of a battery to one terminal of a switch. Be certain the switch is in an open position.

2. Connect a wire from the other terminal of the switch to one terminal of a socket into which you have placed a light bulb.

3. Now connect a wire from the other terminal of the socket to the other pole of the battery.   In each of the connections, be certain that the metal part of the wire is connected rather than the outer covering.

4. Close the switch.   The bulb should light since you have completed the circuit.

5. Draw a diagram of the circuit.

LAB EXPERIENCE 3.2 (Continued)

ELECTRICAL CIRCUITS

Questions:

1. If the clip of the connecting wire is attached to only the outer covering and you close the switch, does the bulb light?

2. What is the purpose of the outer covering on the wire?

Part B: Batteries in Series

1. Remove the wire connected to the positive pole of the first battery, and connect it to the positive pole of the second battery.

2. Connect another wire from the positive pole of the first battery to the negative pole of the second battery. The batteries are now connected in series.

3. Close the switch. How does the brightness of the bulb compare with its brightness in Part A?

4. Draw a diagram of this circuit.

Question:

What explanation can you give for the comparison in brightness in Step 3 above?

Part C: Bulbs in Series

1. Repeat Part B but add a second bulb in series with the first bulb.

2. Close the switch. Is the brightness of each bulb closer to that of Part A or Part B? What conclusion(s) can you come to from this comparison?

3. Unscrew one of the bulbs. What happens to the other? Why?

LAB EXPERIENCE 3.2 (Continued)

ELECTRICAL CIRCUITS

Part D: Batteries in Parallel

1.   Go back to the circuit in Part A.

2.   Connect a wire from the positive pole of the first battery to the positive pole of the second battery.

3.   Connect another wire from the negative pole of the first battery to the negative pole of the second battery.   The batteries are now connected in parallel.

4.   Close the switch.   How does the brightness of the bulb compare with that of Part A?

5.   Draw a diagram of the circuit.

Question:

What conclusion(s) can you come to from the comparison made in Step 4 above?

Part E: Bulbs in Parallel

1.   Repeat Part D but add a second bulb in parallel with the first.

2.   Close the switch.   Is the brightness of each bulb closer to that of Part A or Part B?   What conclusion(s) can you come to from this comparison?

3.   Unscrew one of the bulbs.   What happens to the other?   Why?

GROUNDING

For safety, one point in an electrical circuit is connected to a "ground" wire which is connected to a rod driven into the earth. This permits stray charges to be safely removed. Electric current is carried to and from an appliance through a plug and a cord, which contains two insulated wires. One prong and wire carries current to the appliance. The other prong and wire carries current from the appliance back through the house circuit and is connected to the "ground."

The flow of current to and from the appliance should be the same or be "in balance." This is another way of saying that all of the current leaving the power source must return to the source. However, if the insulation on a wire inside the appliance is broken, the current tries to leak out to any good conductor, such as the metal casing of the appliance. That makes the appliance "live." This leaking current is waiting to move to a ground. If you touch a live appliance at the same time you touch a ground, the electricity will flow through you to get to that ground, giving you a shock. Standing on a wet or damp floor is the same as touching ground. You will not get a shock if you touch the "live" appliance but not touch anything else at the same time. This is the reason that birds can sit on high voltage wires and not be affected. They have not completed a circuit, and thus no electricity flows through their bodies.

Look closely at a wall outlet. Notice that one of the two slots for the plug is longer than the other. It is common practice to connect the grounded side of the line to the longer slot and the live side of the line to the shorter slot. In most installations, the screw in the center of the wall plate is also connected to ground. Although the slots are of different lengths, the plugs on most lamps and some appliances are of the same length and may be inserted into the outlet either way. Some appliances have plugs that match the uneven slots. In this case, the plug must be inserted into the wall outlet in the correct matching slot. Never use an extension cord on these appliances.

In industrial applications or in applications where safety is a critical feature, it is best to attach the case of the appliance to the ground. This is done by using a three prong plug and a special outlet. A wire from the case of the appliance is connected to this plug so that the case is grounded whenever the appliance is connected to the circuit.

FOR SAFETY SAKE

Electricity can kill. Always approach the repair of an electrical appliance with extreme caution. Give the job your undivided attention and think constantly of the potential danger.

- Do not touch any bare wire which is connected to an electrical outlet.
- Never work on anything "live."
- Always check to make sure that there is no voltage between the case of the appliance and ground.

If there is trouble in the appliance, disconnect it from the source of electricity by pulling out the plug. Make it a habit to pull the plug and have it lying in sight whenever working on the appliance. If the plug is kept in sight then no one can accidently plug it back into the receptacle.

SAFETY DEVICES

Fuses or circuit breakers are safety devices to prevent an excess amount of current. Such an excess always generates too much heat and could cause a fire. A fuse contains a thin bridge (a resistor) of low melting alloy that melts when excess current flows through it. Circuit breakers are made of strips of two different metals fastened together, each with a different coefficient of expansion. When too much current flows through a breaker, one metal expands more than the other so that the strip bends and opens or breaks, the circuit. When the trouble is righted, flip a switch on the circuit breaker and reconnect the circuit. Fuses should be replaced with new fuses of the same size — not larger — nor by putting in a penny and then the burned-out fuse. When a fuse "pops" or a circuit breaker "trips" that means the circuit is being overloaded. Determine what is causing the overload, and fix it. Only then replace the fuse or reset the circuit breaker. Home building codes require an appliance using more than 1,650 watts to have a separate circuit.

AC AND DC CIRCUITS

A circuit in which the charges flow in one direction half the time and then flow in the opposite direction for the second half of the time is called an alternating current (ac) circuit. Alternating current is generated in over 90% of the central power plants in the United States and is, accordingly, widely used. Alternating current is more readily transmitted over long distances at reasonable cost. Our homes and most businesses operate with alternating current.

A circuit in which current flows in only one direction is called a direct current (DC) circuit. It is used for electroplating metals and for charging batteries. In instances when DC is needed, but not available, an AC source can be used and the current is changed, or rectified, to DC. In other instances, special DC generators are used to generate the DC current directly.

ELECTRICAL POWER USAGE

About 25 percent of the energy used in the United States is in the form of electrical energy. How much electrical energy do you and your family use? You can find out by reading your electric bill. It tells the number if kilowatt hours of electrical energy used in the home each month. A kilowatt hour, like a calorie, is a measure of energy.

(1 kilowatt hour = 860 calories).

In purchasing electrical appliances, we are not usually interested in the total energy consumed but in the rate of energy consumption. The rate of energy consumption is power, and power is equal to work divided by time, or how long it takes for work to be done.

$$\text{Power (watts)} = \frac{\text{work (joule)}}{\text{time (sec)}}$$

or

$$\text{Power (watts)} = \text{volts} \times \text{amps}$$

Now we can't do much with one watt-hour, but how much energy is a kilowatt hour? An hour is a measure of time. so 1 kilowatt hour of energy is the amount of energy needed to operate a 1,000-watt electric toaster for 1 hour. Or, 1 kilowatt hour is the amount of energy needed to light ten 100-watt bulbs for one hour.

HOW TO COMPUTE YOUR ENERGY CONSUMPTION

Primarily, we use electric and gas in our homes for heating, cooking and washing. Electrical ranges, electric water heaters, and most electric clothes dryers require the largest amount of power for operation. Certain other appliances such as automatic clothes washers, dishwashers, furnace fans, and freezers do not have high power ratings even though they are motor driven. These appliances require a large surge of current when the motor first starts to operate. After this first surge, the current required is fairly small. In general, motor-driven appliances use much less electricity than appliances that use electricity for heat production. Regular meter readings enable you to determine the progress of your conservation measures. This section will show how to compute the cost for the amounts used at home.

HOW TO READ AN ELECTRIC METER

Electric meters record kilowatt-hours

(kwh), the standard unit used in computing electric costs. One kilowatt-hour of electricity equals 1,000 watt hours of usage. The following four-step guide to reading an electric meter was adapted from "How to Understand Your Utility Bill," a pamphlet published by the Department of Energy and available free from the Office of Public Affairs, U.S. Department of Energy, Washington, DC 20585.

1. Read dials from left to right. (Note that numbers run clockwise on some dials and counterclockwise on others.)
2. The figures above each dial show how many kilowatt-hours are recorded each time the pointer makes a complete revolution.
3. If the pointer is between numbers, read the smaller one. For example, in Figure 3.6 the pointer on the first dial is between 0 and 9 — read 9. The pointer on the second dial is between 5 and 4 — read 4. The pointer on the third dial is almost directly on 5, so the reading on the third dial is 4. The fourth dial is read 9. Thus, the total reading is 9,449.
4. This reading is based on a cumulative total since the meter was last set at zero. The reading 9,449 kwh of electricity shows the total used since the zero setting.

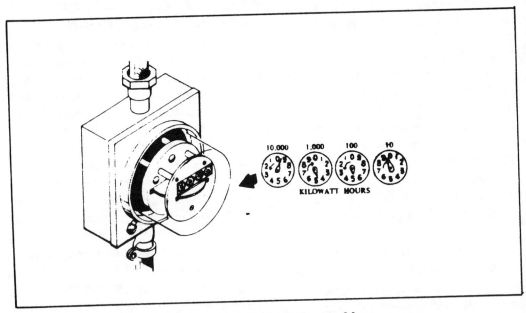

Figure 3.6   *A Typical Electric Meter*

LAB EXPERIENCE 3.3

ELECTRIC METER READING

Purpose: To monitor electric usage in your home for a 24 hour period and for a 7-day period.

Procedure:

1. Locate meter. It is usually located on the outside of the house so that it can be read by the power company without disturbing the occupants.

2. Take one meter reading. Note time of day. Also record the appliances used in the ensuing 24-hour period, and the length of the time they were in use.

3. Take second meter reading 24 hours later.

4. Subtract first reading from second.

5. Repeat reading 7 days after the first reading was taken.

6. Complete chart.

	1st meter Reading (kwh)	2nd meter Reading (kwh)	Electric Usage (kwh)
For 24 hours			
For 7 days			

Questions:

1. What appliance(s) were used during the 24-hour period? For how long?

2. Can any of these appliances be used during evening hours?

3. What appliances run 24 hours per day?

4. Can you give a reason for the large electric usage on a particular day?

HOW TO COMPUTE YOUR ELECTRIC BILL

To figure your kilowatt-hour cost per month, look at your bill to determine the total dollar figure in the column headed "amount for service" and divide that amount by the kilowatt-hours used which is found in the column headed "your use was."

Example: Assume the total amount was $90 and you used 1000 kilowatts, then

90.00	÷	1,000	=	$0.090
(total $ amt.)		(kwh used)		(per kwh)

(By using the total dollar amount, you automatically include the energy adjustment charge. Remember, your kilowatt-hour charge may change each month.)

This figure ($0.090 per kilowatt-hour) multiplied by the rating in kilowatts of each appliance or motor, tells the cost to operate that appliance or motor each hour it is used during the month.

Most appliances are rated in one of three ways: amps, horsepower or watts. These ratings are found on the nameplate somewhere on the appliance or motor. Since you are charged for kilowatt-hours of use, the first two (amps or horsepower) must be converted into watts.

amps × volts = watts

(The voltage rating is also found on the nameplate and is normally 115 V or 230 V with slight variations.)

The following examples will help with the computation.

1. A refrigerator rated at 5 amps × 110 volts = 550 watts or 0.55 kilowatt × $0.09 per kilowatt-hour = $00.0495. For every hour this refrigerator operates, the cost will be $0.0495. (Remember, refrigerators are thermostatically controlled and do not operate every hour during the month.)

2. An air conditioner rated at 2 kilowatts × $0.09 per kilowatt-hour = $0.18. The cost per hour of operation of this unit is $0.18. (Central units will have circulating fans which must be added to the cost of operation.)

3. A 100-watt light bulb = 0.1 kilowatt × $0.09 = $0.009. One hour of operation will cost $0.009. This bulb could operate for 10 hours for $0.09. (100 watts × 10 hours = 1,000 watts or 1 kilowatt.)

4. What would it cost to operate a 1/2 horsepower motor on a pool filter for one hour if the power company charges $0.09 per kwh? (One horsepower = 746 watts.)

FUEL COST ADJUSTMENT CHARGES

The fuel cost adjustment or energy adjustment charge is a fee, also called a "passthrough." These charges are added to an electric bill to compensate the power company for the increased cost of the coal, gas, oil, or nuclear fuel which it uses to generate electricity.

Table 3.1 was prepared by the Edison Electric Institute. It may be used in conjunction with the following Lab Experience 3.4, although it would be preferable for each student to look at appliances and then determine the wattage of the appliances. The "average hours used" represents hours at full power; an oven, for example, cycles on and off rather than running continuously.

TABLE 3.1

APPLIANCE POWER CONSUMPTION

Appliance	Average Wattage	Average Hours Used Per Year	Approximate kwh Per Year
Air Cleaner	50	4,320	216
Air-conditioner (room)*	860	1,000	860
Blanket	177	831	147
Blender	300	3	1
Broiler	1,140	75	85
Carving Knife	92	87	8
Clock	2	8,760	17
Clothes Dryer	4,856	204	993
Coffee Maker	1,200	177	140
Deep Fryer	1,448	57	83
Dehumidifier	257	1,467	377
Dishwasher	1,201	302	363
Egg Cooker	516	27	14
Fan (attic)	370	786	291
Fan (circulating)	88	489	43
Fan (roll-away)	171	807	138
Fan (window)	200	850	170
Floor Polisher	305	49	15
Freezer (16 ft^3)	340	3,504	1,190
Freezer (frostfree 16.5 ft^3)	455	4,002	1,820
Frying pan	1,196	84	100
Furnace fan	500	1,300	650
Germicidal lamp	20	7,050	141
Hair Dryer	600	42	25
Heat Lamp (infrared)	250	52	13
Heater (portable)	1,322	133	176
Heating Pad	65	154	10
Hot Plate	1,200	75	90
Humidifier	177	921	163
Iron (hand)	1,100	55	60
Mixer	127	16	2
Microwave Oven	1,450	131	190
Radio	71	1,211	86

*Figures for room air-conditioner will vary widely, depending on area and size of unit.

TABLE 3.1 (Continued)

APPLIANCE POWER CONSUMPTION

Appliance	Average Wattage	Average Hours Used Per Year	Approximate kwh Per Year
Radio/record Player	109	1,000	109
Range with Oven	12,200	57	700
Range with Self-cleaning Oven	12,200	60	730
Refrig/Freezer (12.5 cu. ft.)	450	3,488	1,500
Refrig./freezer (frostfree 17.5 cu. ft.)	757	2,974	2,250
Roaster	1,333	45	60
Sandwich Grill	1,161	28	33
Sewing Machine	75	147	11
Shaver	15	33	0.5
Sunlamp	279	57	16
Television (black and white, tube)	100	2,200	220
Television (black and white, solid-state)	45	2,222	100
Television (color, tube)	240	2,200	528
Television (color, solid-state)	145	2,207	320
Toaster	1,146	34	39
Toothbrush	1.1	909	1
Trash compactor	400	125	50
Vacuum cleaner	630	73	46
Waffle iron	1,200	17	20
Washing machine (automatic)	512	201	103
Washing machine (non-automatic)	286	266	76
Waste Dispenser	445	16	7
Water Heater	2,475	1,705	4,219
Water Heater (quick-recovery)	4,474	1,075	4,811

LAB EXPERIENCE 3.4

YOUR HOME APPLIANCE POWER USAGE

Purpose: To determine the cost of several home appliances. Select six appliances in your home from the following list and complete chart.

Conditioner
  (window)
  (central)
Electric blanket
Circular hand saw
Electric clock
Clothes dryer
Clothes washer
Coffee pot
Dehumidifier
Dishwasher
Drill
Fan
Frying pan
Hair dryer
Humidifier

Iron
Light bulbs-5
  Incandescent
  bulbs of
  varying wattage
Light bulbs-2
  fluorescent
  bulbs of
  varying wattage
Microwave oven
Range
Radio
Refrigerator/Freezer:
  manual defrost,
  Auto defrost

Sewing machine
Stereo
Television
  (solid state)
  Black & white,
  color
Television
  (tube type)
  black & white,
  color
Toaster
Vacuum cleaner

	APPLIANCE					
	1	2	3	4	5	6
Average Wattage						
Hours Used Daily x Wattage = Watt-hours						
$\dfrac{\text{Watt-hours}}{1000} = \text{kwh}$						
Rate Charged By Power Company						
Kwh x Rate = Cost per Day						
Cost/Day x 30 Days = Cost/Month						

Appliances are:

1. _____   4. _____
2. _____   5. _____
3. _____   6. _____

HOW TO READ THE GAS METER

Reading the gas meter regularly is another way of checking the amount of energy you use.

A gas meter tallies the number of cubic feet of natural gas that you have used. Read it as you would an electric meter. (Refer to Page 3-37.)

From left to right, the dials register 3,177. This is not the final reading, however. It must be multiplied by 100 because each time the pointer on the right-hand dial moves from one number to another, the use of 100 cubic feet of natural gas has been recorded. Thus, the total reading is 317,700. Since the meter was last set at 0, it has recorded the use of 317,700 cubic feet of natural gas.

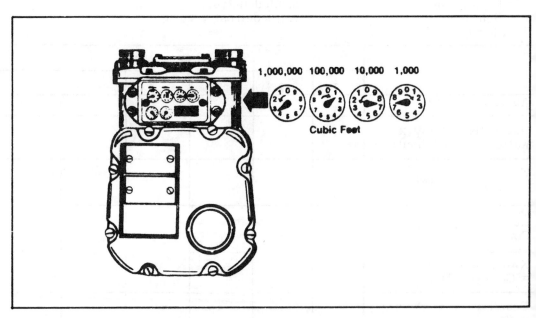

Figure 3.7   *A Typical Gas Meter*

LAB EXPERIENCE 3.5

READING YOUR GAS METER

Purpose: To estimate how much gas your family uses.

Procedure:

The gas meter is located either outside the house or in the basement.

1. Read the gas meter immediately after your family goes to bed, and again before they get up. During this time only your heating system should be operating. Take another reading 24 hours later.

2. Read the gas meter before and immediately after cooking and baking.

3. Subtract the evening reading from the morning reading.

4. Subtract the reading before cooking and after cooking.

5. Divide the difference between the readings by the number of hours between readings. The resulting answer would tell you the number of cubic feet of natural gas used per hour.

6. Complete chart.

Time Interval	1st Meter Reading (ft^3)	2nd Meter Reading (ft^3)	Gas Usage (ft^3)
One Night			
One Meal			
24 Hours			

Questions:

1. Would your gas consumption vary from season to season?

2. How could you cut your gas consumption?

REGULATION OF NATURAL GAS

Natural gas (which is primarily methane) and propane has many applications for commercial and residential uses. Because of the political and economic factors in its production and distribution, natural gas is subject to many governmental controls. State regulatory commissions usually control the retail price of electric power and natural gas, and establish the conditions of service under which utilities operate. Most commissions set prices on the basis of a cost-plus formula. This reflects the cost of providing service at a level deemed sufficient plus a fair return on investments made in plants and equipment. If you have a question about your utility company's adjustment charge, contact your company or the regulatory commission in your state or provincial capital.

Some of the terms used in describing the quantity of gas, the amount of heat or energy supplied, and other cost factors are described here:

- Cubic Foot (cu. ft) — A quantity of natural gas is measured by its volume, hence in cubic feet.
- Therm — The ability of natural gas to produce heat is measured in therms. Power companies sell gas in cents per therm. A therm is equal to 100,000 BTU. The amount of heat or the number of BTU in a cubic foot of natural gas varies, but 100 cubic feet of natural gas usually contains a little more than 1 therm. Some gas companies bill their customers by the number of cubic feet used, and some bill by the number of therms used.
- Purchased Gas Adjustment Charge (PGA) — A fuel-cost adjustment charge appearing on a natural gas bill. It compensates the gas company for the increased cost of the natural gas it buys to sell to its customers.
- Rate Schedule — This schedule describes how the utility company determines the cost of each therm or cubic foot of gas you use. Rate schedules are not usually shown on the bills. If you want to know your rate schedule, call the utility company. Typically, the first group of cubic feet or therms used in a billing period costs more than the second group; the second group costs more than the third, and so on. Some companies, however, are experimenting with different approaches.

Major home appliances contribute to the high cost of energy. Starting in 1980, energy standards for these appliances were established and energy-use labels are now attached to appliances. They can be used in comparison shopping in the same manner as you would compare the gasoline efficiency of automobiles. Table 3.2 is from the pamphlet "How to Understand Your Utility Bill," published by the DOE. From the table you can estimate whether an appliance with a high price tag but low operating cost would be more economical in the long run than a low-priced model with high operating cost.

TABLE 3.2

AVERAGE ANNUAL ENERGY CONSUMPTION AND COST ESTIMATES FOR MAJOR APPLIANCES

Appliance	Unit Efficiency			
	High		Low	
Electricity (at 5 cents/kwh)	kwh	Cost($)	kwh	Cost($)
Air conditioner				
Room: 10,000 BTU/hr, 750 hr	645	32	1,400	70
Central: 30,000 BTU/h, 1,000 hr	3,000	149	5,769	287
Clothes dryer, 416 cycles	880	44	960	48
Clothes washer, electric water heater, 416 cycles	1,250	62	1,440	71
Dehumidifier, 20 pints/day, 1,300 hr	485	31	618	24
Dishwasher, electric water heater, 416 cycles	1,240	69	1,780	87
Freezer, 16 cu. ft.				
Chest-type, manual defrost	807	40	955	48
Upright, manual defrost	919	46	--	--
automatic defrost	--	--	1,643	82
Furnace, 50,000 BTU/hr, 2,080 hr	23,360	1,152	23,360	1,152
Heater				
Space, 1,000 watt, 1,600 hr	1,600	--	1,600	--
Water, 64.3 gals/day	6,020	300	7,400	368
Heat pump, 50,000 BTU/hr, 2,080 hr (efficiency varies with climate and dwelling design)	9,395	467	14,655	728
Lighting	900	45	1,100	55
Oven, microwave, 600 watts	80	4	140	7
Range, conventional, 30-in. oven	675	34	825	41
Refrigerator-freezer, 17 cu. ft., automatic defrost	1,008	50	1,908	95
Television:				
black & white, 19 in., 2,200 hr	107	5	150	7
color, 19 in., 2,200 hr	170	8	366	18

TABLE 3.2 (Continued)

AVERAGE ANNUAL ENERGY CONSUMPTION AND COST ESTIMATES FOR MAJOR APPLIANCES

| Appliance | Unit Efficiency | | | |
| | High | | Low | |
Gas (at 37 cents/therm)	Therms	Cost($)	Therms	Cost($)
Clothes dryer, 416 cycles	45	16	65	24
Furnace, 50,000 BTU/hr, 2,080 hr	1,003	390	1,360	488
Heater, water, 64.3 gals/day	345	126	460	168
Range, conventional, 30-in. oven	60	23	130	53

ENERGY WASTE

A little drip means a big energy waste. Although each drop of water is small, when you add all the drops together you may find that more than a hundred gallons of water have gone down the drain. One drip per second from a leaky showerhead or faucet drips about 175 gallons per month down the drain. If hot water is dripping, then more than water is being wasted. Costly energy used to heat the water is also being tossed down the drain.

The following lab experience The Cost of a Drip will give the student an opportunity to figure the cost of a leaky faucet.

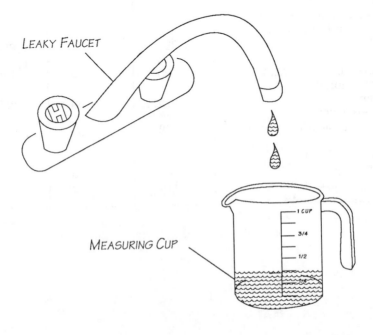

LEAKY FAUCET

MEASURING CUP

LAB EXPERIENCE 3.6

THE COST OF DRIP

Purpose: To determine the cost of a leaky faucet.

Materials:

Timer
8 fluid ounce measuring cup
Paper
Pencil
Calculator (optional)

Procedure:

1. Turn on the cold water faucet so that a steady drip is produced.

2. Place the measuring cup under the faucet to catch the drip, and set the timer for 10 minutes.

3. After 10 minutes turn off the water and carefully remove the measuring cup with the water.

4. Calculate the amount of water lost by a leaky faucet using the following steps:

   a. Since 10 minutes is 1/6 of an hour, multiply the number of ounces by 6 to estimate the amount of water lost in 1 hour.

   b. Since there are 24 hours in a day, multiply the value from Step 4a by 24 hours to obtain the total number ounces of water lost in one day.

   c. Since there are 365 days in a year, multiply the number of ounces from Step 4b by 365 days to obtain the total number of ounces of water lost in one year.

5. At this point convert ounces into gallons by dividing the number of ounces/year (Step 4c) by 128 ounces/gallon (gal).

6. For example, if we assume that in the measuring cup you have collected 3 ounces of water in 10 minutes, which equals 1/6 of an hour, then the calculations proceed as follows:

   a. 3 ounces/10 minutes x 6 = 18 ounces/hour x 24 hours/day = 432 ounces/day.

   b. 432 ounces/day x 365 days/year = 157 680 ounces/year.

   c. 157 680 ounces/year divided by 128 ounces/gal = 1231.875 gal/yr. Then round-off this number to 1 232 gal/yr.

LAB EXPERIENCE 3.6 (Continued)

THE COST OF DRIP

7. Using this estimate we find that a leaky faucet can cause the loss of more than 1 200 gallons of water. This is costly especially since most of us buy our water from a water company.

   If this drip was the hot water faucet, then we would have to add the cost of heating the water which is dripping down the drain.

8. To find the number of BTUs used to heat the water, make an assumption that the cold water is at 40 degrees F when it goes into the water heater which is set to heat water to 140 degrees F for home use. This 100 degree difference requires energy.

   The number of gallons used per year times the weight of 1 gallon of water times the number of degrees difference between cold and hot water will give the amount of energy needed to heat the water. The heat capacity of water is 1 BTU equals 1 degree F per pound.

   For example, 1 232 gal/yr x 10 pound/gal x 100 degrees F = 1 232 000 BTUs.

9. Once you know the number of BTUs required to heat the lost water, and you know the method of heating water in the home—oil, natural gas, or electricity—then it is possible to calculate the amount of fuel it took to heat the water, and finally to calculate in dollars and cents what it cost to heat the water that dripped down the drain.

10. The teacher will provide you with a series of conversion values that will enable you to calculate the number of gallons of oil, or cubic feet of natural or propane gas, or the kilowatt-hours of electricity used to heat the water.

Suggested Activity:

At the rate which you pay the power company, calculate on a daily basis what it costs your family to heat water.

FUELS

Energy is a much discussed and much misunderstood subject. This text cannot solve the question of whether we should heat our homes by burning oil, gas, wood, or use electricity or converted sunshine. We also cannot solve the question whether to build nuclear plants or not.

However, we can provide you with some information about the major forms of fuels presently in use. The teacher and student should calmly and rationally discuss the information keeping in mind the following questions:

1. How comfortably would you like to live?
2. What are you willing to pay for this level of comfort?
3. What are you willing to give up to attain this comfort?
4. What would be the effect on the environment for you to achieve this degree of comfort?
5. How would your level of comfort impact on the billions of other people living on this planet Earth?
6. For how long can you continue to live comfortably along with the billions of other people all drawing upon the same finite resources?
7. How do we balance safety, health and environmental concerns against the ever-growing need for energy?

There is no free lunch, and you can't get something for nothing. We are all passengers together on this one fragile planet and it is all we have.

WOOD

Wood is the oldest form of fuel. Wood is composed primarily of cellulose which is the basic component of trees. It is a chemical combination of carbon, hydrogen and oxygen known as an organic compound or hydrocarbon. Cellulose contains moisture, inorganic salts, and resinous substances such as sap and pitch. The lower the mois-ture content of the wood, the more heat produced when it is burned. A pound of dry wood will yield 7,500 to 9,000 BTU of heat.

Dry, seasoned wood will produce about twice as many usable BTU as unseasoned (wet) wood. It takes at least a year to dry wood properly after it has been cut. The denser species of wood (hardwoods), such as hickory, oak, ash, maple, and beech produce more BTU than the softwoods such as white pine, cedar, and poplar.

Wood that is burned with air supply closed off produces charcoal. This method is called destructive distillation. Charcoal is almost pure carbon and gives off more heat than wood.

FOSSIL FUELS

The fossil fuels, predominantly coal, petroleum, and natural gas are indeed fossils. Like all other forms of energy, they originated in solar activity. They are the remains of plant and animal life that thrived in a time of extraordinary photosynthetic activity eons ago and were buried or inundated before they had a chance to decompose. The hydrocarbon molecules remain in varying grades of richness.

COAL

Coal is found in several forms, from lignite to bituminous to anthracite. In each successive stage, more carbon has been concentrated and consequently more high-quality energy is available per pound. The different kinds of coal are:

- *Anthracite* — This type is the hardest coal, contains the most carbon, is the cleanest burning, and is best for home use. It yields about 12,000 to 14,000 BTU/lb.
- *Bituminous* — This type is less hard than anthracite, possesses less carbon, is a soft coal suitable for industry, and yields about 12,000 to 13,500 BTU/lb.
- *Lignite* — This type of coal or

"brown coal" as it is called, is even younger than bituminous coal, possesses less carbon, is a smoky fuel, and yields about 7,000 to 10,500 BTU/lb.

- *Peat* — This type of coal or "green coal" has the least amount of carbon, is very smoky and is rarely used in the United States except in rural areas where it is readily accessible. It yields about 7,000 to 9,000 BTU/lb.

As recently as early in this century, coal was the leading source of energy in the U.S. Trains ran on it, homes were heated by it, industry operated machinery with it. With the discovery of vast fields of oil, coupled with the growth in importance of the gasoline-burning internal combustion engine, coal fell into disfavor. Coal was difficult to mine, expensive to transport, dirty to use. Quite simply, we stopped using it. Now, some look to coal as the partial salvation to the oil and gas shortages.

But before we can utilize coal extensively, a number of associated problems must be solved. Environmental laws in many areas require precipitators and scrubbers to remove pollutants from coal. New combustion technology and equipment must be developed to make coal a more efficient fuel. New coal deposits must be discovered.

Coal, as fuel in power generating plants, offers great potential as an electrical energy producer. In addition to its direct combustion use, we need to refine the technology to liquify and gasify coal whereby it would serve as a substitute for oil and gas.

LIQUID FUELS

Liquid fuels are obtained from crude petroleum, and are separated by fractional distillation. Fractional distillation is the heating of the petroleum, and as each part or fraction of the whole is vaporized, it is tapped off until all that remains is a material thick and viscous such as tar. Fuel oil, such as home heating fuel, is one of the fractions and produces about 18,000 BTU/lb.

The crux of the petroleum problem is the imbalance between production and consumption. While demand is increasing, U.S. production of oil is decreasing. In the 1980's the U.S. imported about one third of the oil we consumed. The amount we import in the 1990's is rising steadily.

In 1980, the United States imported 5,177,000 barrels a day of foreign oil. This is nearly half the quantity imported in 1977, but the cost was very high. Energy conservation and smaller cars have reduced the amount imported but while the demand is rising at a slightly lower rate, it is still increasing. As the standard of living throughout the world rises, the demand for fuels is certain to rise accordingly. Domestic oil production has not changed significantly in many years, and estimated reserves of U.S. oil are much lower each year in spite of new oil discoveries. Another worrisome aspect is the source of foreign oil. Some 88% of the oil we must import comes from the same OPEC countries that cut off our supplies in 1973. Because of our reliance on foreign oil, the U.S. is still vulnerable to an embargo, should one be declared again. Those who looked to the Alaskan pipeline for the solution to our oil shortage problems have been disappointed. The North Slope oil flowing through the pipeline provided only about 1.2 million barrels per day initially. By now, production has reached about two million barrels per day. However, the field's maximum production has begun to decline.

Petroleum can be found in various media. The richest deposits of petroleum usually are saturated sandstones, where the liquid crude oil flows freely to the wells. Other forms of petroleum such as kerogen, which is found in U.S. oil shale reserves in three western states, cannot be exploited by drilling oil wells because the kerogen is a solid and does not flow. We may look to other potential drilling areas, particularly the outer continental shelf. But a number of obstacles have blocked extensive continental shelf drilling. As a result of uncertain environmental and economic climates, the petroleum companies are reluctant to commit funds for exploration.

We must face these unpleasant facts: our U.S. reserves are decreasing at the rate of 3.5% annually while consumption is increasing by 4.8% per year. We have no choice but to develop alternative fuel sources for our energy needs.

GASEOUS FUEL

Several different types of gases are used for countless industrial and agricultural processes, heating, and the production of electricity.

- *Artificial Gas* is made by the destructive distillation of bituminous coal. It is then purified and sold as coal gas. Artificial gas is a mixture of hydrogen, methane and carbon monoxide and has a disagreeable, nauseous odor. It yields about 11,000 to 20,000 BTU/lb.
- *Water Gas,* also an artificial gas, is made up primarily of hydrogen and carbon monoxide. Since it is odorless, coal gas is added to water gas to make detection easier and to increase heat output.
- *Natural Gas* is composed primarily of methane, and burns with a very hot blue flame. It yields about 20,000 to 28,000 BTU/lb.
- *Propane* and *Butane* are bottled forms of natural gas, and can be used where natural gas is not available.

The price of natural gas is dependent upon the time when it was produced. It has ranged from a pre-1973 price of 52¢ per thousand cubic foot to $2.40 per thousand cubic foot in early 1977. With prices pegged so low, it comes as no surprise that our natural gas reserves have declined rapidly. Low prices simultaneously encouraged waste and discouraged exploration for new reserves.

In 1976, the U.S. reserves of natural gas, including known Alaskan fields, was determined to be 218 trillion cubic feet. We are consuming more natural gas each year then we can replace with new discoveries and at an annual consumption rate of about 20 trillion cubic feet, our reserves could be depleted in a decade or two.

Ironically, the two fuels (oil and gas) which are in shortest supply are also in greatest demand, accounting for over three-fourths of the present energy use in the U.S. Each year this demand for oil and gas increases. To further the irony, the energy resource of which there is the greatest supply — coal — is in relatively limited demand due to the environmental problems associated with obtaining and using it.

TABLE 3.3

SUMMARY OF FOSSIL FUELS

FUELS	BTU/LB
Dry Wood	7,500 - 9,000
Anthracite	12,000 - 14,000
Bituminous	12,000 - 13,500
Lignite	7,000 - 10,500
Peat	7,000 - 9,000
Natural Gas	20,000 - 28,000
Artificial Gas	11,000 - 20,000

SYNTHETIC FUELS

The methods for obtaining synthetic fuels are for the most part well understood. From the turn of the century into the 1920's when oil became plentiful, a coal gasification process was used to produce a low-grade fuel called "town gas." This was used to light cities and warm ovens. In World War II, Germany fueled its Messerschmitts and Panzer divisions with coal-derived gasoline. Since 1960, South Africa has been producing oil from coal (albeit on a small scale) in their Sasol I plant and by the end of the 1980's hopes to generate some 60% of its petroleum this way.

The term "synthetic" is actually something of a misnomer. The oil is there. It's just difficult to take it out of the shale and tar sands or to convert it from coal, another carbon-based organic material. Each of the four principal technologies for obtaining synthetic fuels has its own peculiar characteristics and associated problems.

In *coal gasification,* some 400 billion tons of coal are considered to be economically recoverable. Because coal is plentiful, the aim is to process it so that it is a better source of heat energy. Thus, both the gasification and liquefaction processes endeavor to produce hydrogen-enriched coal. Ordinary coal has 16 atoms of carbon for every single atom of hydrogen, and heavy fuel oil has six carbon atoms to one hydrogen atom. Natural gas, on the other hand, has four hydrogen atoms for every carbon atom. Under temperature and pressure, the chemical structure of coal breaks down to admit more hydrogen atoms to its molecular structure. The trick then is to enrich pulverized coal with hydrogen atoms. In coal gasification, steam and oxygen in the presence of high temperatures and under pressure, react with coal to form a gaseous mixture of hydrogen and carbon monoxide. This can be used as a low-grade boiler fuel. However, if the mixture is also passed over a nickel-based catalyst then methane, the chief constituent of natural gas, is the result.

Coal liquefaction relies on the same chemical principles as gasification, namely the addition of hydrogen to coal. However, it differs in that it produces a liquid fuel which has a lower carbon-to-hydrogen ratio that can be burned as a substitute for oil or gasoline.

There are two approaches to liquefaction: indirect and direct. Indirect liquefaction is a two-step process by which coal is first converted to a gas. This is then chemically changed into a variety of synthetic liquids, including fuels and chemicals. There is only one commercial-scale indirect liquefaction plant in the world, South Africa's Sasol I, which was mentioned earlier.

Direct liquefaction is presently the preferred technique. In this process, the coal is dissolved under high temperature and pressure with a coal-derived solvent, say a light oil — and in some cases a catalyst — that chemically transfers the hydrogen to the coal to form either a heavy oil or a refinable liquid fuel.

Two direct liquefaction pilot plants are in operation. One, in Fort Lewis, Washington, is run by a Gulf Oil subsidiary for the Department of Energy and processes 50 tons of coal a day, to produce 150 barrels of fuel oil while the other, in Wilsonville, Alabama, is owned and operated by a subsidiary of the Southern Company and processes six tons daily for an output of 18 barrels of oil. These are not large quantities and do not begin to meet our needs. However, the technique is there and efforts along these lines need to be pursued and encouraged.

SHALE OIL

Although there 1.8 trillion barrels of shale oil in an area bounded by Colorado, Wyoming and Utah, only about 600 billion are considered recoverable. When cooked at 900°F, the pulverized shale yields up an organic material called kerogen that recombines chemically into oil. But shale, too, has its problems. For one thing, a commercial-sized plant producing 100,000 barrels of oil a day, would require a daily disposal of 150,000 tons of shale. The shale cannot simply be returned to the earth since crushing it causes the volume to increase by 20% of its former size. Shale processing also requires great amounts of water, a fact that worries conservationists.

A way around these problems is to process the shale underground, without ever bringing it to the surface. The "in situ" process, as it's called, entails drilling down to the shale seam, perhaps no more than 200 to 300 feet below ground level or in many cases into a mountain, and fracturing it with an explosive charge. Then a slow-burning fire would heat the shale, releasing the oil. This would then flow to the bottom of the explosion chamber cavity and be pumped out. Shale produces a fuel that can be burned in a boiler, and with proper conditioning can be upgraded to a product that could be refined for consumer use.

TAR SANDS

Recovery of oil from tar sands requires a technology in which Canada has the most experience. Much of the work in extraction and refining of bitumen, a form of petroleum deposit, is being performed by Canadian subsidiaries of American oil companies. In this process, the gooey sands are mined by a large drag line and moved by conveyor belt into the extraction plant, where they are mixed with hot water and steam to form a slurry. It is put into extraction vessels where the material breaks down into sand and bitumen. This is then cleaned, cracked and upgraded with hydrogen and a catalyst. The first plant was opened 10 years ago in Alberta by a Sun Company subsidiary, and is producing 50,000 barrels of oil a day.

THE ALCOHOLS

Methanol (methyl alcohol) is made from wood. Methanol is highly toxic and corrosive. It has a high affinity for water and contains only half the energy content of an equal volume of gasoline. Straight methanol cannot be used in an automobile. The methanol can cause "hesitation" in a car's engine in winter and "vapor lock" in summer. Concentrations of more than 10 to 15% of methanol in gasoline would require an extensive redesign of automobile engines in order to compensate for methanol's lower heat content.

Ethanol (ethyl alcohol) is made from grains. Gasohol, an ethanol blend, is better for cars than methanol. The 1979 crop of wheat and corn was 8 billion bushels. This would make enough alcohol to replace 5% of the country's oil consumption. Certainly, farmers should be encouraged to utilize gasohol to run their farm equipment. The distillation of grains to produce ethanol from which gasohol is derived is a natural for that industry. The use of food to run machinery is questioned.

Of course, it takes energy to produce energy. This energy is used while producing the steel and other materials that go into constructing a plant, and the electricity and oil needed to run the equipment in the plant. This is the so called "net energy" concept and by this measure synthetic fuels are considerably less efficient than domestic oil. The energy yield for synthetic fuels produced from coal, for example, is about 17 to 1 BTU while for shale oil the ratio drops from 6.5 BTU to 1 BTU. Domestic oil returns about 50 BTU of energy for every 1 BTU that is used in producing it. This is one reason we are still involved with oil rather than an alternative energy source.

NUCLEAR POWER

Nuclear power is produced by two methods: fission and fusion.

NUCLEAR FISSION

A nuclear power plant relies on fissioning uranium 235 to produce the necessary heat energy to make steam which is then used to generate electricity. Uranium 235 is an element made up of atoms, each of which has a nucleus containing neutrons and protons. When the U-235 nucleus is struck by a neutron originating from an outside source, it splits apart, releasing two or three identical neutrons. If these neutrons strike another fissionable atom, its nucleus also splits, releasing more neutrons. This chain reaction produces the necessary heat to produce steam which drives a turbine. Since nothing is burned to produce this heat, no smoke or combustion products are released to the environment.

A nuclear power plant that relies upon the fission of U-235 operates in the following way. The core of a nuclear reactor consists of several hundred fuel bundles. These bundles are made up of 12-foot metal tubes each containing a stack of hard ceramic-like pellets made of uranium oxide. The arrangement and dilution of this fuel is exactly opposite that needed to produce a nuclear explosion. A nuclear reactor cannot explode because its fuel contains only 3% of fissionable U-235. Therefore, a nuclear power plant cannot blow up like a bomb.

Since the fuel pellets tend to retain most radioactive by-products of the fission process, they form the first in a series of barriers to prevent the uncontrolled release of radioactive materials from the plant. The second barrier is the sealed metal tubes which enclose the pellets. These tubes, which make up the fuel bundles, are inside a third barrier, a 6 to 8 inch thick steel reactor vessel weighing several hundred tons. Surrounding this, in a multiple-barrier containment concept, is a steel shell and a concrete structure which is at least three feet thick. This last barrier provides further protection against such forces as earthquakes and tornados.

The water in which the fuel core is immersed serves two purposes. First, it is heated by the fission process to form steam to drive the turbine. Second, it makes the fission process possible by acting as a "braking agent" to slow down the neutrons. The slow-moving neutrons make the nucleus of the U-235 atom fission, or split, more readily. In the event that all of the water were lost, fission would cease. A complete loss of water from the reactor vessel, however, would allow a buildup of residual heat in the reactor that could damage or melt the core. To prevent this, there are standby core cooling systems which would automatically reflood the reactor vessel, and simultaneously spray the core from the top with thousands of gallons of water per minute. A duplicate back-up system provides a further measure of safety. These systems have their own power supplies. They are not dependent on electricity from an outside source for their operation.

NUCLEAR WASTE

Every year or so, a nuclear plant must be shut down and one-third to one-fourth of the depleted fuel bundles in its core must be replaced with new fuel. Although only 2% of fuel has been used, oxides and other contaminants, which are the result of the fissioning process, cause the action to become inefficient. This requires a replacement of a portion of the fuel bundle each year. Up to 97% of this depleted fuel is recoverable, and can be recycled again as reload fuel.

At this time, the spent fuel rods are stored on site. Some of these stored radioactive rods have been stored this way for years. In France, the spent fuel rods are reprocessed and sold at great profit for nuclear fuel all over the world. The U.S. does not allow any reprocessing at this time.

A refinement of nuclear fission — the breeder reactor — could achieve optimum efficiency, because it has the ability to provide more nuclear fuel than it consumes. It is estimated that we have some 3.5 million tons of uranium in the U.S. that can be recovered. Should breeder reactors become commercially available, the uranium supplies in the U.S. would be extended and provide us with additional fuel.

The other side of the story regarding the long term safety of nuclear energy is the fear of an accidental release of radioactive materials regardless of safety precautions. The problem of disposing of nuclear waste remains to be settled. Also, the problems involving security and safety in transporting nuclear fuels have to be resolved.

We cannot settle the question of whether nuclear power is worth the risk. It is suggested that the student obtain literature from both the advocates of nuclear power and those opposed to it. Attending a debate on the subject should prove interesting.

It is the aim of this text to enable people to discuss the topic in as factual a manner as possible.

NUCLEAR FUSION

Fusion is the process by which the sun and other stars generate their energy. The sun is composed of very hot gases. It is so hot that atoms in it have been ionized. This means that the negatively charged electrons have become separated from the positively charged nucleus of the atom. The "naked" atom is called an ion. Matter consisting of ions is known as plasma and has some very special properties. One of these properties is that the ions frequently collide with each other. The hotter the plasma, the harder they collide.

The major problem facing researchers is how to hold and heat this plasma in a suitable container so that the ions, which are moving more than a million miles per hour, will not strike the walls of the container and lose their energy. One method of confinement is to keep the plasma inside a magnetic field called a "magnetic bottle." This method is safe because if the magnetic field fails for any reason, the fusion process stops and no material is released.

Fusion is one form of energy being looked at for electrical power production. The process would be environmentally attractive. The basic fuel for fusion is plentiful. Some fusion plants would operate using deuterium, which is an isotope of hydrogen. Deuterium is found in seawater. Other fusion plants would use tritium, another isotope or variety of hydrogen, which can be produced in a reaction with lithium. Lithium is a chemical element found in granite rocks and in seawater. This too is in plentiful supply.

Early fusion power plants would generate electricity by means of a thermal energy conversion cycle, which would obtain heat energy from the fusion of deuterium and tritium. Eighty percent of the energy released by this reaction would be carried by neutrons. This requires that the reaction chamber be surrounded by a region in which the neutrons can slow down and release their energy, as heat to a working fluid. The fluid would in turn be used to generate steam to drive an electric turbine-generator.

If fusion power comes to fruition, it would replace most other forms of electric power in the United States by the middle of the 21st century. This would free the nation forever from the need to use the precious and dwindling supplies of fossil fuels in power plants.

Almost all power plants, whether they be fossil or nuclear fueled, draw water from a nearby lake, river or ocean to cool the turbine condenser. This external water is isolated from, and never mixes with, the water used to generate steam. Cooling towers, ponds, or other methods are used to minimize the effect of temperature on the aquatic environment.

SOLAR ENERGY

It has long been man's dream to harness the energy of the sun. Every day, the sun floods the earth with a hundred thousand times more energy than produced by all the electric generating plants in the world. When we speak of solar energy, we are referring to two distinct modes of energy production — the solar thermal power plant and the individual solar system.

One limitation to the practicality of solar energy for power plants is the large land areas required for reflectors to collect the sun's rays. Another limiting factor is that the sun shines only part of the day on any one spot, and on many days the sun is obscured by cloud cover. A third difficulty is the immense cost involved to construct a solar thermal plant. The cost is about a thousand times higher than the cost of conventional generating systems. Many experts see solar energy providing no more than 8% of our total energy needs by the year 2000.

The individual solar energy system, using the sun's direct radiant energy to heat water for household uses and to warm living and working areas of one building, will probably be the most significant application of solar energy during the remainder of this century. This system is technically practical right now, although it is expensive. It does require stand-by energy systems for those days when the sun doesn't shine. The individual solar energy system seems most practical for new construction where site, window orientation, insulation and landscaping can be controlled at the outset.

Most solar systems can be characterized as either active or passive in their operation. Active solar systems are characterized by collectors, thermal storage units and transfer media, in an assembly which requires additional mechanical energy to convert and transfer the solar energy into thermal energy. This additional energy, generated on or off the site, is required for pumps or other heat transfer devices for the system's operation. Generally, the collection, storage, and distribution of thermal energy is achieved by moving a transfer medium throughout the system with the assistance of pumping power. The transfer medium is frequently a liquid such as water.

A passive solar system, on the other hand, is generally classified as one where solar energy alone is used for the transfer of thermal energy. Pumps and other mechanical heat transfer devices are not required for the operation of the system. The collection, storage, and distribution of heat are achieved by natural phenomena which use convection, radiation and conduction of heat energy. The basics of solar energy utilization is shown in Figure 3.8.*

The basic function of a solar domestic hot water system is the collection and conversion of solar radiation into usable energy as illustrated in Figure 3.9.

Solar radiation is absorbed by a collector, placed in storage, with or without a transfer medium, and distributed to the point of use. The performance of each operation is maintained by automatic or manual controls. An auxiliary energy system is usually available both to supplement the output provided by the solar system, and to provide for the total energy demand should the solar system become inoperable.

The simple flat-plate collector has the widest application. It consists of an absorber plate, usually made of metal and coated black to increase absorption of the sun's energy. The plate is insulated on its underside and covered with one or more transparent cover plates to trap heat within the collector and reduce convective losses from the absorber plate. The captured heat is removed from the absorber plate by means of a heat transfer fluid, generally air or water. The fluid is heated as it passes through or near the absorber plate and then transported to points of use, or to storage, depending on the energy demand.

---

*"Solar Hot Water & Your Home" Publication, National Solar Heating and Cooling Information Center, P.O. Box 1607, Rockville, MD. 20850.

Operational Description. The solar hot water system usually is designed to preheat water from the incoming water supply prior to passage through a conventional water heater. The domestic hot water preheat system can be combined with a solar heating system or designed as a separate system. Both situations are illustrated below.

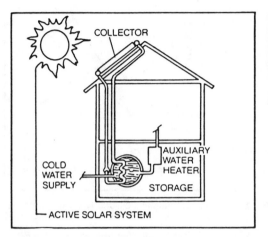

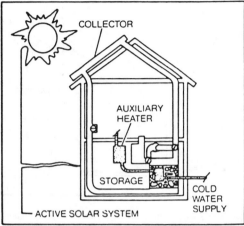

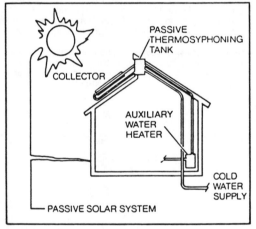

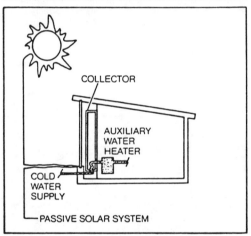

Domestic Hot Water Preheating—Separate System. Domestic hot water preheating may be the only solar system included in many designs. An active solar system is shown in the upper figure and a passive thermo-syphoning arrangement in the lower.

Domestic Hot Water Preheating—Combined System. Domestic hot water is preheated as it passes through heat storage enroute to the conventional water heater. An active solar system using air for heat transport is shown in the upper figure and a passive solar system in the lower.

Figure 3.8 *Basics of Solar Energy Utilization in Solar Hot Water Systems*

162

Collector Orientation and Tilt. Solar collectors must be oriented and tilted within prescribed limits to receive the optimum level of solar radiation for system operation and performance.

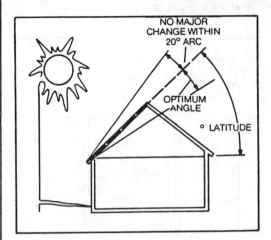

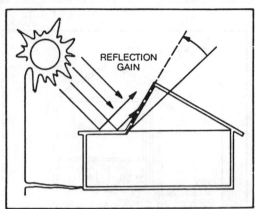

Collector Tilt for Domestic Hot Water. The optimum collector tilt for domestic water heating alone is usually equal to the site latitude. Variations of 10 degrees on either side of the optimum are acceptable.

Modification of Optimum Collector Tilt. A greater gain in solar radiation collection sometimes may be achieved by tilting the collector away from the optimum in order to capture radiation reflected from adjacent ground or building surfaces. The corresponding reduction of radiation directly striking the collector, due to non-optimum tilt, should be recognized when considering this option.

Snowfall Consideration. The snowfall characteristics of an area may influence the appropriateness of these optimum collector tilts. Snow buildup on the collector, or drifting in front of the collector, should be avoided.

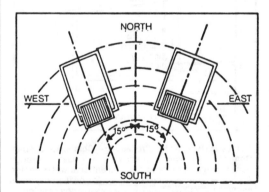

Collector Orientation. A collector orientation of 15 degrees to either side of true South is acceptable. However, local climate and collector type may influence the choice between East or West deviations.

Figure 3.9   *Solar Hot Water Systems, Operational Description*

PRESENT FUEL CONSUMPTION AND FORECAST

It was estimated in 1970 that the world coal supply would last 2300 years, but at the present rate of use this estimate has been foreshortened to only 111 years. Natural gas should last 37 years but at the present rate of use, 22 years are projected. Oil should last 31 years but at the present rate of use, only 20 years are projected. The United States with about 6% of the world's population is using almost 50% of the world's supply of oil, coal, and natural gas. As the standard of living rises throughout the world, so will energy demands rise. What is the alternative? Alternative energies.

Moving water is a source of energy. The most abundant form of moving water is to be found in ocean tides. Since they are limitless, the tides hold hope as a usable energy source. But no practical method has been developed.

Another naturally occurring phenomenon, geothermal energy, is created by the build-up of intense heat beneath the earth's surface. Although geothermal might seem to offer an attractive source of energy, it will probably be developed and used in areas close to sources. Heat losses occurring over long distances make transmission impractical.

As to wind power, windmills large enough to supply the energy needs of any sizable area would have to be gigantic, expensive, and have a dependable source of wind to power them. This too has limitations for wide usage.

Nuclear fission and fusion, coal, and synthetic fuels have been discussed elsewhere in this unit.

To maintain our present living standards while using energy wisely requires conservation, the improvement of the usefulness and efficiency of present fuels, and the development of new energy sources as rapidly as possible.

As a first step, we have embarked on a program of conservation. One group of experts contends that conservation could take care of about 17% of our total energy demands by the year 2000.

The second step is the development of new technologies to improve the usefulness and efficiency of presently available fuels. Fossil fuels are non-renewable resources. Each of us in our personal and working lives consumes, directly or indirectly, about 1300 gallons of oil, 11,000 cubic feet of natural gas and 2½ tons of coal each year. At this astounding rate of consumption, the world's supply of oil and gas will be totally exhausted by the 21st century. It isn't as if we have time to think about what we should do — the 21st century is almost here! It is urgent that positive action be taken now. We must decide how we want to live out our lives and the kind of world we want our children to inherit. We must choose now.

UNIT 3

PHYSICS QUESTIONS

1. The science that deals with matter, energy, motion, and forces is called _____.
2. _____ is the amount of matter that goes to make up an object.
3. _____ and _____ cannot be created or destroyed.
4. _____ and _____ can be converted from one form to another.
5. With regard to the study of matter: a) it is too complicated to have any bearing on our everyday lives,   b) if wood is burned for heat, it is thereby destroyed,   c) the matter in food changes into other matter and energy,   d) none of the above.
6. If a boulder is resting at the top of a hill it merely possesses: a) kinetic energy, b) potential energy,   c) heat energy,   d) all of the above.
7. As the boulder falls, it is demonstrating: a) potential energy,   b) kinetic energy,   c) mechanical energy,   d) all of the above.
8. Kinetic energy: a) is the same as potential energy,   b) is the same as moving energy,   c) is another term for stored energy,   d) all of the above.
9. Kinetic energy may be converted to: a) mechanical energy,   b) heat energy, c) light energy,   d) both a and b,   e) all of the above.
10. Energy is described as: _____ (stored), _____ (moving and doing).
11. Four kinds of energy are: _____,   _____, _____,   _____.
12. Heat: a) and temperature are the same thing,   b) is a form of energy based on molecular motion,   c) depends on humidity,   d) all of the above,   e) none of the above.
13. A measurement of heat is: a) calories or BTU's   b) grams,   c) degrees,   d) milligrams.
14. Temperature is described as _____.
15. When heat is added to an object, the movement of the molecules is   a) decreased,   b) increased,   c) stays the same.
16. The temperature, at sea level, at which a liquid changes to vapor is called: a) melting point,   b) boiling point,   c) freezing point,   d) none of the above.
17. The temperature at which a solid changes to a liquid is called: a) boiling point, b) freezing point,   c) melting point,   d) all of the above.
18. 75°C corresponds to: a) 41.7°F,   b) 167°F,   c) 135°F,   d) 137°F.
19. 10°C is the same as: a) 38°F,   b) 50°F,   c) 54°F,   d) none of the above.
20. 104°F is the same as: a) 40°C,   b) 26°C,   c) 12°C,   d) none of the above.
21. Heat flows from a _____ to a _____ body.
22. In the heat transfer experiment, which material was a better heat conductor? _____.
23. The specific heat of a substance: a) is equal to its density,   b) is always measured in

calories, c) is the amount of heat needed to raise the temperature of water one degree celsius, d) determines the amount of heat needed to change the temperature of one gram of the substance by one celsius degree, e) none of the above.

24. Salt being dissolved is called a _____, and the water which is doing the dissolving is called the _____. The resulting material is described as a _____.

25. The three major forms of heat transfer are _____, _____, and _____. An example of each form is _____, _____, and _____.

26. Conduction is: a) transfer of heat from one molecule to another, b) transfer of heat by the motion of the medium as a whole, c) electromagnetic wave motion, d) none of the above.

27. Which is the largest source of radiant heat? a) the sun, b) x-rays, c) microwaves, d) all of the above.

28. Different types of radiation are: a) x-rays, b) visible light, c) infrared rays, d) microwave, e) all of the above.

29. What is the definition of SPF? _____.

30. Sunscreens work by absorbing, reflecting, or scattering: a) radiation, b) ultraviolet light, c) infrared light, d) ocean spray at the beach, e) x-rays.

31. _____ light rays are used for tanning.

32. The microwaves in a microwave oven are generated by the electron tube called a/an _____.

33. In a microwave oven, all the heat is produced in the _____.

34. X-rays: a) are so called because they are 10 times more powerful than ordinary sunlight, b) have resulted in governmental requirements with regard to safety precautions, c) are medically important tools which therefore can be freely used without protective devices, d) all of the above, e) none of the above.

35. "Background radiation" is measured in: a) roentgen, b) millirems, c) milliroentgen, d) a and c.

36. An example of ionizing radiation is _____. An example of nonionizing radiation is _____.

37. The limit of millirems per year of radiation which you may safely receive is: a) 1,000 millirems, b) 300 millirems, c) 500 millirems, d) none of the above.

Matching: Place the letter from column II into the appropriate space for column I.

I		II	
38. conduction	_____	A.	electric broilers a source
39. convection	_____	B.	explains why fiberglass is a good insulator
40. radiation	_____	C.	basis of the hot-air furnace
41. radio/television	_____	D.	most energetic
42. microwaves	_____	E.	medical science use
43. infrared	_____	F.	black light lamps

44. visible light _____ G. radar
45. ultraviolet _____ H. sunlamps
46. x-rays _____ I. deep heat lamps
47. gamma rays _____ J. least energetic
48. coulomb _____ K. measure of effect on humans of exposure to radiation
49. roentgen _____ L. measure of radioactive dose received by body
50. rem _____ M. pigment of skin
51. "C" _____ N. kilocalorie
52. melanin _____ O. energy unit
53. "c" _____ P. describes electric charge
54. heating coil _____ Q. foot-pound
55. solvent _____ R. resistance to heat transfer
56. joule _____ S. ohms
57. R-number _____ T. water

58. Electromagnetic wave motion, such as the passage of light through space, is called: a) convection, b) conduction, c) radiation, d) none of the above.

59. _____ is the measure of moisture in the air.

60. The amount of protection an insulating material can provide is indicated on a standard code known as the _____.

61. Insulating material: a) can be best judged by the thickness of the material, b) should be chosen with regard to its R-number code, c) should be purchased in the amount determined by multiplying the length times the width of the area to be covered, d) all of the above.

62. _____ is/are the third largest cause of heat loss in the home.

63. At a higher altitude, air pressure decreases and the boiling point of a liquid _____.

64. For a more comfortable and energy efficient home: a) use light colors on walls and ceilings to reflect heat and light back into the room, b) place furniture as close to the radiator or heat register as possible so as to obtain maximum benefit, c) be sure to use only metal radiator covers since most metals are good conductors of heat, d) all of the above.

Match the items in column I with the most appropriate statement in column II.

I   II

65. wooden frame storm windows _____ A. second most expensive energy user

66. insulation _____ B. effective around doors and windows

67. caulking _____ C. protect arms and hands while installing

68. water heater   _____   D.   may provide substantial reduc-
tions in heating/cooling loads

         E.   good protection but heavy

69. ANSI numbers are used to rate the _____ of windows.

70. What are the three words printed on the package of light bulbs?
_____, _____, _____.

71. The amount of electricity being used by a bulb is measured in _____.

72. The amount of light given out by a bulb is measured in _____.

73. When purchasing light bulbs: a) the wattage is the most important to check because the higher the watts the brighter the light, b) longlife filaments in light bulbs may be more expensive, but they last longer and give off more light than standard bulbs, c) lumens will tell you the actual light output of the bulb, d) all of the above, e) none of the above.

74. The unit of current is called: a) amperes, b) watts, c) volts, d) none of the above.

75. Glass, rubber, and wood are examples of: a) insulators, b) conductors, c) semiconductors.

76. Copper, gold, and aluminum are examples of: a) insulators, b) conductors, c) semiconductors.

77. Electron flow in a complete circuit is from _____ to _____.

78. The current, or electrons, flow from _____ to _____ or from a point of _____ of electrons to a point _____ in electrons.

79. In a _____ circuit, the electrons can follow only one path.

80. In a _____ circuit, the electrons can follow two or more paths simultaneously.

81. A _____ wire is necessary to safely remove stray charges.

82. A circuit in which the charges flow in one direction half the time and then in the opposite direction the other half is called: a) alternating current, b) direct current, c) neither.

83. A circuit in which the current flows in only one direction is called: a) alternating current, b) direct current, c) neither.

84. _____ are safety devices to prevent an excess amount of current.

85. If two bulbs are part of a series circuits: a) both will go out if one blows or is loosened, b) only the affected or malfunctioning one will be out, c) none of the above.

86. If two lighted bulbs are part of a parallel circuit and one blows out, the other one will: a) go out, b) remain lit, c) none of the above.

87. In a parallel circuit: a) the electrons can follow two or more paths at the same time, b) parallel circuits are too complex to be utilized in private homes, c) parallel circuits are different in that they function from a low to a high potential.

88. If one resistance is burned out and no current can flow, the circuit is a/an: a) closed circuit, b) open circuit, c) series circuit, d) none of the above.

89. In a simple series circuit with an EMF of 12 volts and a resistance of 6 ohms, the current would be: a) 2 amps, b) 2 volts, c) 0.5 amps, d) 0.5 watts, e) 0.

90. Calculate the total resistance of a series circuit where R_1 = 6 ohms and R_2 = 12 ohms.

91. Calculate the total resistance of a parallel circuit where R_1 = 6 ohms and R_2 = 12 ohms: a) 18 ohms, b) 2 ohms, c) 4 ohms, d) 6 ohms, e) 0.5 ohms.

92. A circuit of 2 amps at 120 volts would consume how many kilowatts in one hour. a) 24, b) 0.24, c) 60, d) 40, e) 0.6.

Matching: Place the letter in column II in the most appropriate space.

I		II
93. energy source	_____	A. unit of current
94. ampere	_____	B. keeps electric charge from mo~ ing
95. insulator	_____	C. flow of electric current in a con plete system
96. conductor	_____	D. best material for this use is co per
97. circuit	_____	E. can be an electric generator
98. lumens	_____	F. current flow
99. static electricity	_____	G. volts × amps
100. amperage	_____	H. surface charge
101. ohms	_____	I. kwh
102. watts	_____	J. brightness
103. electric meters	_____	K. 100,000 BTU
104. gas meter	_____	L. cubic feet
105. therms	_____	M. resistance
106. volt	_____	N. moving energy
107. calorie	_____	O. negative particle of atom
108. electron	_____	P. stored energy
109. kinetic energy	_____	Q. unit of heat measurement
110. potential energy	_____	R. electrical pressure

111. Power companies sell _____ in cents per therm.

112. When too much current goes through the circuit: a) the power company will charge at a higher rate, b) the fuse is said to "pop" or a circuit breaker "trips," c) the overloading can be corrected by wise use of extension cords, d) none of the above.

113. Some power companies have plans which can save you money: a) but you must use energy-intensive appliances at off-peak times only, b) peak times are evenings and weekends when everyone is at home using all sorts of electric appliances, c) in order to take advantage of such a plan you must agree to purchase special washers and dryers, d) none of the above.

114. You can keep track of the kilowatt-hours of electricity consumed in a particular time

period by: a) calling an electrician, b) by subtracting the dial reading at the beginning of the period from the reading at the end, c) both a and b, d) none of the above.

115. PGA or Purchased Gas Adjustment Charge is: a) the price you have agreed to pay the power company for service, b) determined by the varying rates the company charges for usage, c) what compensates the company for higher costs of gas, d) none of the above.

116. _____ is the oldest form of fuel.

117. Coal: a) was never a common source of energy since it was dirty, b) does not give as much heat as well-seasoned dry wood, c) is being looked to as a salvation from gas and oil shortages, d) none of the above.

118. Fuel oil: a) is an exhaustable supply, b) can be obtained from crude petroleum, c) is a product unique to the U.S., d) none of the above.

119. The following statement regarding natural gas is true: a) the demand is greater than the supply, b) low prices which encourage use are a spur to further exploration of new sources by suppliers, c) our reserves will never be depleted, d) none of the above.

120. Natural gas is primarily: a) methane, b) methanol, c) neither.

121. Methanol (methyl alcohol) is primarily made from: a) wood, b) grains, c) neither.

122. Ethanol (ethyl alcohol) is primarily made from: a) wood, b) grains, c) neither.

123. What is geothermal energy? _____.

124. What two things can we do to maintain our present living standards with reference to energy? _____, and _____.

125. Name four types of gases used for industrial heating and the production of electricity.
_____, _____, _____,
_____.

Match column I with the appropriate term from column II.

I		II
126. wood	_____	A. contains carbon, hydrogen and oxygen
127. coal	_____	B. lignite
128. petroleum	_____	C. propane
129. gas	_____	D. kerogen

130. Nuclear power plants draw water from nearby sources in order to cool the turbine condenser: a) this water is not dangerous, b) this water is extremely toxic, c) the water is cooled by the process and must be heated before it can be released, d) none of the above.

131. Nuclear wastes: a) are completely harmless due to modern technology and no cause for public concern, b) the disposal of nuclear wastes is a serious problem, c) used or spent fuel rods have no value and should be discarded, d) none of the above.

132. Radiation from a nuclear plant: a) is bad for local residents so they should increase their vitamin intake to play it safe, b) residents receive no radiation since the plants

are airtight,   c) residents get about as much radiation as they would from single airplane trip across country,   d) none of the above.

133. Which one is not associated with nuclear fusion?   a) plasma,   b) uranium, c) "magnetic bottle,"   d) deuterium,   e) lithium.

134. _____ are intermediate materials between conductors and insulators.

135. A quantity of natural gas is measured in: a) kwh,   b) watts,   c) cubic feet,   d) all of the above.

136. Give two examples of fossil fuels: _____ , _____

137. Coal is found in several forms: a) peat,   b)bituminous,   c) lignite,   d) all of the above.

138. Give two examples of synthetic fuels _____ , _____

139. The two methods of producing nuclear power are: a) gasification and liquefaction,   b) vaporization and condensation,   c) fission and fusion,   d) none of the above.

140. A nuclear reactor cannot explode because its fuel contains only 3% of fissionable __.

141. With regard to nuclear power: a) nuclear power plants produce energy by fissioning U_{235},   b) nuclear power plants produce energy by fusing U_{225},   c) melting of the "core" is an essential part of the process of creating energy,   d) none of the above.

142. Most solar energy systems can be characterized as either _____ or _____ in their operation.

143. Solar energy systems for home use: a) depend on a transfer medium such as water,   b) are relatively easy and inexpensive to install,   c) are not affected by snow since the heat already collected melts it,   d) all of the above,   e) none of the above.

144. Construction of solar energy plants: a) is minimal in cost because the sun's energy is free,   b) is extremely expensive for the amount of energy obtained,   c) would provide about 65% of our energy needs,   d) none of the above.

145. Since energy demands are always increasing and the world's supply of fuel is being depleted: a) the only answer is conservation,   b) there are no other possibilities so we will just go as far as we can and stop,   c) research into such power sources as wind and moving water should be expanded,   d) all available energy sources should be researched and expanded while conservation is practiced.

UNIT 4

CHEMISTRY

Logically, to discuss chemistry it is necessary to learn about elements, mixtures, compounds, atomic masses, and many more basic principles. Here, we plunge directly into a study of food additives, soaps and detergents, shampoos, cosmetics, antacids, drugs, aspirin, fibers, fabrics, and household safety. Not everyone will understand the nature of each chemical process, or even be able to pronounce the names, but the lab experiences should be clear to all. This hands-on approach is also elementary chemistry. We hope that the reader may wish to learn more from other sources.

Hydrogen and oxygen, two very common gases, when mixed together properly yield water which is a completely new substance. A substance that is necessary for our daily lives. Because there are so many substances or chemicals, both natural and man made, that impact upon our lives, the government has established rules and regulations to safeguard us. This watchdog action is provided under the jurisdiction of the U.S. Food and Drug Administration (FDA).

In each instance, the FDA has some rule or law that impacts upon us and what we buy. It is hoped that evaluation skills will be developed so that there is an understanding of the role of food additives, the complexities of water and its interaction with soaps, detergents, and shampoos, the manufacture of cosmetics, the effect of antacids, and of drugs, both brand name and generic. If we look at food, medicine, cosmetics, fabrics, and detergent labels, it is astonishing how much of what we accept as commonplace is based in chemistry.

The question is raised as to what these chemicals do for and to us. Which of the food additives enhance the product favorably? What do phosphate-based detergents do to us and our environment? What happens to you if you take two different drugs simultaneously? How do you tell the difference between cotton and wool? How may different kinds of fabrics be dyed? What are the conditions necessary for combustion? What are the ways of putting out fires?

FOOD ADDITIVES

Food additives are defined as substances added directly to food or to packaging materials. Food additives are also substances that might otherwise affect food without becoming a part of it, such as various forms of radiation that are used in food processing.

The use of additives is not new. When people first learned that fire would cook meat and salt would preserve it without cooking, then the use of additives began. As our knowledge of food improvement and preservation has increased, so has our use of additives. Food additives are used to enhance flavor. Some examples are spices and natural and synthetic flavors. Additives are also used to stabilize and thicken foods. Starch, pectin, gelatin, gum arabic, and agar are among those used for these purposes. The production of many types of baked goods, soft drinks, and candy require the addition of additives to neutralize or alter the acidity or alkalinity of the food.

Other additives may retain moisture, or add nutrients such as vitamins and minerals, or mature and bleach flour, or increase volume and smoothness, or act as propellants for food in pressurized cans. Modern science has developed preservatives such as sodium and calcium propionate to retard the growth of bread molds. Butylated hydroxytoluene (BHT) and butylated hydroxyanisole (BHA) are used as preservatives and antioxidants for fats and oils contained in foods frequently found on the grocery shelves. Additives are also used for hardening, drying, coloring, leavening, antifoaming, noncaloric sweetening, disease prevention, creaming, firming, antisticking, shipping, and sterilizing. As you can see, additives are used for many reasons.

The U.S. Federal Food, Drug, and Cosmetic Act was modified in 1958 by the Food Additives Amendment. Under the amendment, two major categories of additives are exempt from the testing and approval process. The first is a group of some 700 substances "generally recognized as safe" (GRAS) by qualified experts. The idea behind what has come to be known as the GRAS List was to free the FDA and manufacturers from being required to prove the safety of substances already considered harmless because of past extensive use with no known harmful effect. The second group is simply referred to as food additives. Any substance newly proposed for addition to food must undergo strict testing designed to establish the safety for the intended use.

The information must be presented to FDA in the form of a petition as to the identity of the new additive, its chemical composition, how it is manufactured, and analytical methods to be used to detect and measure its presence in the food supply at the levels of expected use. The data must establish that the proposed analytical method adequately determines that the additive is in compliance with the regulations.

It must be established that the additive will accomplish the intended effect in the food. Also, the level sought for approval is not higher than that reasonably necessary to accomplish the intended effect. Finally, data must establish that the additive is safe for its intended use. This requires experimental evidence ordinarily derived from feeding

studies and other tests, using the proposed additive at various levels, in the diets of two or more approved species of animals.

A basic rule is a 100-fold margin of safety for anything added to food. This means that the manufacturer may use only 1/100th the maximum amount of an additive that has been found not to produce any harmful effects in test animals. A special provision of the 1958 and 1960 food additives amendments, the so-called Delaney Clause, states that a substance shown to cause cancer in man or animal may not be added to food in any amount.

There is no real difference under the law between those substances we call "foods" and those we call "food additives." Meat and potatoes, for example, clearly would be considered as additives instead of "food" when served in a stew, except that they are more appropriately considered as GRAS (generally recognized as safe). Preservatives such as sodium and calcium propionate are produced naturally in Swiss cheese. Citric acid, a widely used additive to foods, is present in all citrus fruit. Many so-called "natural foods" contain toxic substances. Safrole is found in sassafras roots, oxalic acid in spinach and rhubarb, and certain goiter inducing substances are found in certain vegetables. In addition, modification of agricultural products through breeding and selection may significantly increase the concentration of a toxicant naturally present in them.

Some of the food additives and complex carbohydrates have specific benefits. Pectin for example, is found naturally in apples oranges and grapefruit. It is also made commercially from citrus peels, and is used for thickening processed foods such as jellies jams and marmalades. Chemically, pectin is a polysaccharide, meaning it has 10 or more types of sugars linked together. It's also a nondigestible fiber, and studies show that it tends to lower the blood cholesterol level Scientists at the U.S. Department of Agr culture's (U.S.D.A.) Carbohydrate Nutrition Laboratory cite several studies in which cholesterol levels were reduced in the blood of males after they ate from 6 to 36 grams of pectin daily for two to four weeks. Cholesterol was not lowered when these same men ate equivalent amounts of cellulose or wheat fiber. The key to the difference may be that pectin absorbs more bile salts in the gastrointestinal tract then cellulose does. While studies are being done, pectin appears to be an important supplement to the diet. One good way to add it to the family menu is to use it in homemade salad dressing.

Guar gum is another polysaccharide fiber additive used as a food binder, thickener or texturizer. It is made from bean-like plants grown in the United States, India and Pakistan. Guar gum is used in many breakfast foods, processed vegetables, sweet sauces, cheese-imitation dairy products, milk products, fruit ices, snack foods, processed fruits, gelatin puddings, and fats and oils. According to studies noted by the U.S.D.A. scientists, guar gum may be even more effective than pectin in reducing cholesterol levels in the blood.

Two other polysaccharide fibers with anticholesterol effects are gum ghatti and carrageenan, an extract of red algae. Gum ghatti is obtained from trees found in India and Sri Lanka. It is used primarily as a stabilizer in frozen dairy products and nonalcoholic beverages. Carrageenan is used chiefly as a suspending agent in foods, as a clarifying agent in beverages, and as a control on crystal growth in frozen confections.

These food additives not only provide fiber in the diet but in addition, they have the added benefit of being helpful in reducing the cholesterol that tends to clog the body's arteries. They also possess the potential for reducing high blood pressure and the health problems that accompany it as discussed in the biology unit.

The addition of nitrite compounds to meats, fish, and poultry goes back to medieval times — long before refrigeration was known. It was noted by travelers, on land and sea, that meats treated with nitrite compounds remained edible for long periods of time. At first they were added to the food because their interaction with bacteria gave the food a nice pink or red color. Later, it was found that nitrites act as a preservative slowing down the growth of bacteria that can cause food poisoning in human beings.

Although both nitrate and nitrite compounds are common food additives, our thoughts of them are changing. Scientists have confirmed that nitrates are changed, either in the mouth or digestive tract, into nitrites which can then combine with amines (the by-products of protein digestion) to form nitrosamines. There is some evidence that nitrosamines have caused cancer in laboratory animals. Keep in mind that animals used in experiments are fed massive doses of the additives.

Saccharin is another additive that is kept in our food supply. Studies over the past 3 or 4 years indict saccharin as causing bladder cancer. But once again, the amount fed to the lab rats was enough to cause damage to many organs and be exceedingly harmful to the entire animal. One of the questions raised by these studies is whether we can deprive diabetics and dieters from foods that are presently available to them because the foods contain saccharin.

Benzoic acid is one of the oldest chemical preservatives used in foods, having been described as a preservative in the 1800s. Both it and the related chemical compounds sodium benzoate and potassium benzoate are on the FDA's list of generally recognized as safe (GRAS) preservatives and are permitted for use in foods up to a maximum of 0.1%. Benzoic acid is widely used in food products, especially beverages, fruit products, bakery products and condiments.

The sorbates are relatively new in the area of food preservatives. The first U.S. patent on sorbic acid was granted in 1945.

Sorbates are active against yeast and molds and are generally recognized as safe by the FDA without any restriction in use. The major food categories that use sorbates are: dairy products, bakery products, vegetable salads, dried fruits, fruit juices and fruit salads, carbonated and noncarbonated beverages, condiments, confectionery products, and smoked fish.

There are many reasons for the use of food additives. Foods, which had to be shipped long distances from source to consumer, had to be protected from spoiling. The spoilage could be caused by the food itself undergoing changes or from molds and bacteria in the air. Other additives cause baked goods to have a finer texture or even to rise uniformly, or to keep foods like shredded coconut from becoming wet and sticky, or to increase the vitamin and mineral content of foods. The use of salt, sugar, vinegar, heat, freezing, smoke and spices to prevent or delay food spoilage has been in existence for a long time. However, in the most cases, manufacturers do not list the exact amount of additive included in their product.

How can we balance the benefits against the risks?

There is no way in which absolute safety can be guaranteed. Premarketing clearance under the Food Additives Amendment does assure that risk of adverse effects occurring is at a low level. Since many GRAS substances were not subjected to modern laboratory testing, the FDA in 1972 began an extensive review of the safety of each item on the GRAS list. Upon completion of this review, the FDA will have an up-to-date analytical and toxicological file for the safe uses of all substances listed for use in food either as a GRAS substance or as a food additive.

At present the addition of sulfites as a preservative for packaged foods must be declared on the label. All packaged foods that contain more than 10 parts per million of sulfites—regardless of why they are added—must also be declared. The use of sulfites as a preservative on raw fruit and vegetables was banned in July 1986. The ban was applied to salad bars where the sulfite was used to preserve the crispness and color of raw fruits and vegetables sold loose or packaged in cellophane. While the 1986 ban applies specifically to raw fruits and vegetables, there are many other foods which contain the sulfites and the FDA is now required to determine their safety as well.

LAB EXPERIENCE 4.1

FOOD ADDITIVES

Purpose: To determine the food additives in your favorite foods.

Procedure: Read the labels of canned and packaged foods and determine if any food additives are in your favorite foods.

Canned Foods	Food Additive(s)	Quantity of Additive(s)
Packaged Foods	Food Additive(s)	Quantity of Additive(s)

Questions:

1. What criteria would you use to permit additives to food products?

2. In order to eliminate additives from your food, would you be willing to limit your diet to food grown only in your area?

LAB EXPERIENCE 4.1 (Continued)

FOOD ADDITIVES

Evaluate five snack foods by comparing the major nutrients and additives present in the foods.

Snack Food	Major Nutrients/ Serving	Additives/ Serving
1.		
2.		
3.		
4.		
5.		

Questions:

1. Do the additives enhance the flavor?

2. Do the additives enhance the nutritive value of the food?

3. For what purpose are the additives included?

WATER, SOAPS, DETERGENTS

Water, which covers three fourths of the earth, is one of the basics of life. We drink it, we bathe in it, we use it for transportation, we use it to grow and prepare our food, and for processing. While some communities get their water from their own wells and lakes, most communities rely on public and private water companies for their source. Large scale purification methods have been developed to protect people's health. These methods use a variety of techniques to accomplish their purpose. In the lab experience Water Purification, you will duplicate, on a small scale, some techniques for purifying water.

In one method, a mixture of chemicals to form a precipitate called "floc" causes particles of dirt or other solid matter to coagulate and settle to the bottom of a basin or tank. A filter removes additional matter. In some processes the combination of filters and chemicals speed up the clarification and purification process.

In large-scale water purification, the water is filtered through coarse and fine rock, gravel, and sand so that large and small particles are trapped by the natural material. Bacteria grow in organic matter and the presence of organic matter in water may make it unfit for drinking. This is what is being tested in Part C of the Water Purification experiment. Copper sulfate is added to water in an early stage of water purification. The Environmental Protection Agency's drinking water standards requires that it be added in concentration well below levels that are detrimental to human beings but is sufficient to kill organisms that live in water.

Water is described as being soft or hard. All tap water has a broad variety of inclusions in it: minerals, both disease and non-disease causing bacteria, dust particles and pollutants. The difference between hard and soft water is the number and kinds of minerals that are to be found in the water. Hard water has a larger proportion of calcium, magnesium, and iron compounds in it than is to be found in soft water. These chemical compounds disassociate so that they form ions. These calcium, magnesium, and iron ions inhibit the lathering action of soap. Soap, an alkali salt of fatty acids, works well in removing dirt and grease from surfaces. But in hard water which contains a relatively high amount of minerals in solution, these chemicals react with the soap to form deposits of a gummy material called soap scum or soap curd. The familiar ring in the bathtub is composed of these deposits to which dirt and other undissolved matter in the water may adhere. It is this soap scum which also settles back on fabric, fibers, and skin, and tends to "grey" clothing. It also prevents us from rinsing the shampoo or soap off ourselves. In the lab experience Hard Water, you will study the properties of hard water and some techniques for softening it. Some hard water can be softened just by boiling, other kinds of hard water can only be softened by the addition of chemicals.

Soap, in one form or another, has been around for a very long time. Colonial women and pioneer women all made their own soap by heating scrap fat till it melted, and then adding lye (sodium hydroxide which came from wood ashes) to the melt. This was allowed to cool, harden, and then cut into bars of soap for household use. The addition of herbs, scents, and colorings came much later, but the original basic product was serviceable if not exactly kind to the hands and skin. Soap will lather well in water that has a reasonable amount of dissolved minerals in it, but it causes many problems in hard water. Because much of the water we use has an excess amount of minerals in it, soap manufacturers turned to the chemist for assistance. Hard water washing was made possible by the formulation of synthetic detergents which could be used for cleaning purposes.

The chemical formulation of a detergent

involves many compounds that can be grouped into three general categories: the surfactant, the builder, and miscellaneous.

- The surfactant of a detergent acts as a wetting agent. Its job is to make the water interact with the fabric so that dirt will be lifted out of the fiber.
- The second category, the builder, ties up the hard water ions so these chemicals cannot interfere with the action of the surfactant. The builder of a detergent also reacts with the wash water making it more alkaline. This alkalinity is necessary for the effective removal of dirt. The most common builders are phosphate compounds.
- The third grouping, the miscellaneous ingredients, includes brighteners, perfumes, and anti-deposition agents. Brighteners are dyes which absorb invisible ultraviolet light and emit white or blue light making the wash look whiter. Anti-deposition agents keep dirt in suspension, once it has been removed from a fabric, so that it may be readily rinsed away.

The water pollution problems resulting from the use of detergents involve either the surfactant or the builder. Problems involving the surfactant were observed first and they have largely been solved. Surfactants now in use are biodegradable, or readily broken down into the simpler compounds of carbon dioxide and water, by bacteria present in the environment.

Those involving the builder are still of great concern. The detergents with builders containing phosphates initially caused enormous problems. The phosphate compounds in waste water caused a vast and rapid growth of vegetation in the brooks and rivers into which the waste water flowed. This rapid growth of plants used up the oxygen faster than it was produced, and caused the aging and finally the killing of all life in that body of water. This process is called eutrophication. Detergent manufacturers found it necessary to modify their products and limit the amount of phosphates, or remove them entirely from the detergents. The manufacturers lowered or removed the phosphate compounds from their products, and their packages proclaim this fact today.

The laundry industry is now asking consumers to take a more critical look at nonphosphate alternative detergents. They claim that these products don't clean as well as phosphate products, and cause mechanical as well as physical problems. Sodium carbonate, or old-fashioned washing soda, used in place of the phosphates can precipate the calcium ions. This can cause an abrasive film of lime to clog the steel parts of the washing machine and eventually damage the machine. Use of nonphosphate detergents also results in wash water with a pH of 10.5 to 11.* This is a very alkaline water solution which can cause skin and eye irritation. Finally, the industry feels that hotter water is necessary to thoroughly clean clothes thereby increasing energy costs.

Despite the difficulties with detergents, we cannot return to a broad use of soap. Soap is totally unsuitable for use in automatic dishwashers and our present day washing machines are specifically designed for use with detergents. Research is in progress for the reformulation of detergents and for the modification of our water treatment systems so that we would not be faced with the problem of eutrophication.

If only hard water is available in the home for washing, drinking and cooking, it is possible to convert it to soft water by the use of an ion exchange system in the basement of the house. The ion exchange system

---

*for a discussion of pH see Acids and Alkalines

ses a sodium-rich resin which exchanges he sodium for the calcium and magnesium ions in the water. Periodically, it is necessary to recharge or replace the sodium in the resin, and sodium chloride (salt) is used for this purpose.

This conditioned or softened water now proceeds into the water lines of the rest of the house. Soaps and detergents lather well, leaving almost no ring or scum. The presence of sodium is not apparent at all. However, there is some controversy as to whether the additional sodium significantly affects humans.

In the following lab experiences, there are a series of experiments in which you will compare the effectiveness of bleaches on various kinds of stains.

- The first set of experiments calls for an evaluation of the so called "all-fabric" bleaches.
- The second set is a comparison of all-fabric bleaches with chlorine bleaches.
- The third and fourth sets call for an evaluation of the effectiveness of all-fabric bleaches as compared to chlorine bleaches on stained polyester-blend fabrics. The same questions follow each experiment. Will the answers always be the same?

Bleaches contain sodium hypochlorite which acts as an oxidizing agent on stains. The reaction reduces or removes the stain from the fabric.

In the making of soap, lye or sodium hydroxide is added to an oil or fat. This process is called saponification. When salt is added to the oil and sodium hydroxide mixture, glycerin is a by-product in this soap making process.

Soap solutions help in removing dirt, grease, and oil from clothing by first wetting the fabric and then mixing between the particles of grease and dirt. The soap breaks the grease into tiny particles that become suspended in the water without dissolving. The water with the grease particles in it is called an emulsion. When you rinse the fabric, the rinsing water flushes away the grease and dirt emulsion.

Did you know that the first commercial floating soap was made by accident when the soap mixer was left on too long? Extra air was beaten into the mixture thereby producing a soap that floats.

In one lab experience, you will have an opportunity to make soap but remember that the product may be harsh to your skin. This can happen if one ingredient, sodium hydroxide, has not reacted completely with the fat, or if too much sodium hydroxide or too little fat was used. After you make the soap, save it for another lab experience.

The degree of harshness is determined by the alkalinity of the soap. Phenolphthalein is used to detect alkalinity or acidity. This is determined by knowing the pH of the substance. The pH scale ranges from 0 to 14 and is based on the number of hydrogen ions present in solution. The midpoint, 7, is the pH of water, which is neutral. A pH of less than 7 is acid while a pH greater than 7 is alkaline. The pH can be measured by strips of paper saturated with acid-base indicators. The higher the pH value, the more alkaline and the more irritating the product is to the skin. An additional explanation of pH can be found under the topic of antacids.

LAB EXPERIENCE 4.2

WATER, SOAPS, DETERGENTS

Purpose: To compare the cleaning ability of three all-fabric bleaches.

Materials:

1. Swatches (7 cm x 7 cm) of white cotton cloth, which have been stain with a fruit juice, fat or grease, and a beverage such as tea, coffee, cola. These stained clothes should be at least 2- to 3-weeks old. Ea group is to have 9 swatches.

2. Three brands of all-fabric bleaches including one store brand. Transf bleach to another box or jar so that its identity remains unknown. Gi each box a code number for identification.

3. A heavy duty detergent with no additives such as brighteners softeners.

4. Basin.   5. Rubber gloves.   6. Safety glasses.   7. Thermomete

Procedure:

This lab experience is conducted in two parts. In the first part, you w wash the soiled swatches without soaking them. In the second part, you w soak the swatches for a given amount of time and then wash them.

1. For each stained cloth, use a quantity of detergent plus one of t bleaches, and hot water. Wash without soaking.

2. If you use a basin or the sink, use the same amount of water, at t same water temperature, give it the same amount of time, and the sa number of dunkings, swishings and scrubbings for all three bleache (Use rubber gloves to protect your hands.)

3. Complete the chart. Rate bleach effectiveness as follows:

     0 = not effective (worst)   3 = good
     1 = poor   4 = most effective (best)
     2 = fair

Swatch	Stain	Bleaches		
		1	2	3
1.				
2.				
3.				

LAB EXPERIENCE 4.2 (Continued)

WATER, SOAPS, DETERGENTS

Swatch	Stain	Bleaches		
		1	2	3
4.				
5.				
6.				
7.				
8.				
9.				

4. Soak the stained swatches for at least 12 hours in a solution of the test bleaches, detergent and room temperature water.

5. Wash them in the same water, using the same number of dunkings, swishings and scrubbings for each of the bleaches.

6. Complete chart. Rate bleach effectiveness.

Swatch	Stain	Bleaches		
		1	2	3
1.				
2.				
3.				
4.				
5.				
6.				
7.				
8.				
9.				

LAB EXPERIENCE 4.2 (Continued)

WATER, SOAPS, DETERGENTS

7. Examine both sets of swatches, and evaluate how well the stain was removed from each one.

8. Unwrap boxes and record the names of each product.

    Bleach 1:
    Bleach 2:
    Bleach 3:

Questions:

1. Were you surprised by the results? Why or why not?

2. What advertising claims were made for bleaches selected?

3. Did your test results support the advertising claims?

4. Was the store brand product as effective as the brand name products?

5. What is the price difference between store brand and brand name product?

6. Would you change your brand?

LAB EXPERIENCE 4.3

BLEACHES FOR COTTON FABRICS

Purpose: To compare all-fabric bleaches with chlorine bleaches in the ability to remove stains from white cotton fabrics.

Materials

1. Swatches (7 cm x 7 cm) of white cotton cloth, which have been stained with a fruit juice, fat or grease, and a beverage (tea, coffee, cola). These stains should be allowed to age 2 to 3 weeks.   Each group is to use 18 swatches.

2. Three brands of all-fabric bleaches, include one store brand. Three brands of chlorine bleaches, include one store brand. Transfer bleach to another box or jar so that its identity remains unknown. Give it an identifying code number.

3. A heavy duty detergent with no additives.

Procedure:

This lab experience is conducted in two parts.   In the first part, you will wash the soiled swatches without soaking them.   In the second part, you will soak the swatches for a given amount of time and then wash them.

1. For each stained cloth, use a quantity of detergent plus one of the bleaches, and hot water.   Wash without soaking.

2. If you use a basin or sink, use the same amount of water, at the same water temperature, give it the same amount of time, and the same number of dunkings, swishings and scrubbings for all of the bleaches. (You use rubber gloves to protect your hands.)

3. Complete the chart.   Rate each bleach's effectiveness as follows:

        0 = not effective (worst)   3 = good
        1 = poor   4 = most effective (best)
        2 = fair

Swatch	Stain	Bleaches					
		1	2	3	4	5	6
1.							
2.							
3.							

LAB EXPERIENCE 4.3 (Continued)

BLEACHES FOR COTTON FABRICS

Swatch	Stain	Bleaches					
		1	2	3	4	5	6
4.							
5.							
6.							
7.							
8.							
9.							
10.							
11.							
12.							
13.							
14.							
15.							
16.							
17.							
18.							

4. Soak the stained swatches for at least 12 hours in a solution of tes bleaches, detergent and room temperature water.

5. Wash the swatches in their soaking water, using the same number o dunkings, swishings and scrubbings for each of the test bleaches.

6. Complete the chart. Rate bleach effectiveness.

Swatch	Stain	Bleaches					
		1	2	3	4	5	6
1.							
2.							

LAB EXPERIENCE 4.3 (Continued)

BLEACHES FOR COTTON FABRICS

Swatch	Stain	Bleaches					
		1	2	3	4	5	6
3.							
4.							
5.							
6.							
7.							
8.							
9.							
10.							
11.							
12.							
13.							
14.							
15.							
16.							
17.							
18.							

7. Examine both sets of swatches, and evaluate how well the stain was re-moved from each one.

8. Unwrap boxes and reveal the names of each product.

Bleach 1: _____   Bleach 4: _____

Bleach 2: _____   Bleach 5: _____

Bleach 3: _____   Bleach 6: _____

LAB EXPERIENCE 4.3 (Continued)

BLEACHES FOR COTTON FABRICS

Questions:

1. Were you surprised by the results? Why or why not?

2. What advertising claims were made for the bleaches selected?

3. Did your test results support the advertising claims?

4. Was the store brand product as effective as the brand name products?

5. What is the price difference between store brand and brand name products?

6. Would you change your brand?

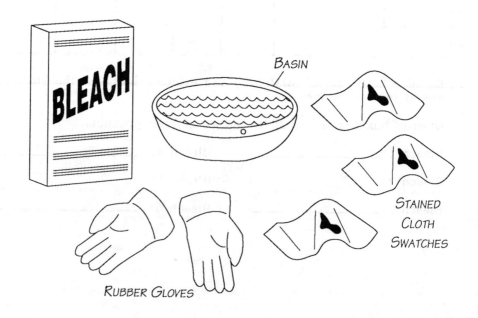

LAB EXPERIENCE 4.4

BLEACHES FOR WHITE POLYESTER FABRICS

Purpose: To compare the cleaning ability of all-fabric bleaches with chlorine bleaches when used on white polyester-blend fabrics.

Materials

1. Swatches (7 cm x 7 cm) of white polyester cloth which have been stained with a fruit juice, a fat or oil, and a beverage (coffee, tea, cola). These stains should be 2-3 weeks old. Each group is to use 18 swatches.

2. Three brands of all-fabric bleaches. Include one store brand.

3. Three brands of chlorine bleaches. Include one store brand. Transfer bleach to another box or jar so that its identity remains unknown. Give it an identifying code number.

4. Heavy duty detergent with no additives.

Procedure

This lab experience is conducted in two parts. In the first part, you will wash to soiled swatches without soaking. In the second part, you will soak the swatches for a given amount of time and then wash them.

1. For each stain cloth, use a quantity of detergent plus one of the bleaches, and hot water. Wash without soaking.

2. If you use a basin or sink, use the same amount of water, at the same water temperature, give it the same amount of time, and the same number of dunkings, swishings and scrubbings for all of the bleaches. (You will use rubber gloves to protect your hands.)

3. Complete the chart. Rate each bleach's effectiveness as follows:

       0 = not effective (worst)   3 = good
       1 = poor   4 = most effective (best)
       2 = fair

		Bleaches					
Swatch	Stain	1	2	3	4	5	6
1.							
2.							
3.							
4.							

LAB EXPERIENCE 4.4 (Continued)

BLEACHES FOR WHITE POLYESTER FABRICS

Swatch	Stain	Bleaches					
		1	2	3	4	5	6
5.							
6.							
7.							
8.							
9.							
10.							
11.							
12.							
13.							
14.							
15.							
16.							
17.							
18.							

4. Soak the stained swatches for at least 12 hours in a solution of test bleaches, detergent and room temperature water.

5. Wash the swatches in their soaking water, using the same number of dunkings, swishings and scrubbings for each of the test bleaches.

6. Complete the chart. Rate bleach effectiveness.

Swatch	Stain	Bleaches					
		1	2	3	4	5	6
1.							
2.							
3.							

LAB EXPERIENCE 4.4 (Continued)

BLEACHES FOR WHITE POLYESTER FABRICS

Swatch	Stain	Bleaches					
		1	2	3	4	5	6
4.							
5.							
6.							
7.							
8.							
9.							
10.							
11.							
12.							
13.							
14.							
15.							
16.							
17.							
18.							

7. Examine both sets of swatches, and evaluate how well the stain was re-
    moved from each one.

8. Unwrap boxes and reveal the names of each product.

    Bleach 1: _____   Bleach 4: _____

    Bleach 2: _____   Bleach 5: _____

    Bleach 3: _____   Bleach 6: _____

LAB EXPERIENCE 4.4 (Continued)

BLEACHES FOR WHITE POLYESTER FABRICS

Questions:

1. Were you surprised by the results? Why or why not?

2. What advertising claims were made for bleaches selected?

3. Did your test results support the advertising claims?

4. Was the store brand product as effective as the brand name products?

5. What is the price difference between store brand and brand name products?

6. Would you change your brand?

LAB EXPERIENCE 4.5

BLEACHES FOR COLORED POLYESTER FABRICS

Purpose: To compare the cleaning ability of all-fabric bleaches with chlorine bleaches when used on colored polyester-blend fabrics.

Materials

1. Swatches (7 cm x 7 cm) of colored polyester-blend cloths which have been stained with a fruit juice, a fat or oil, and a beverage (coffee, tea, cola). These stains should be 2-3 weeks old. Each group is to use 18 swatches.

2. Three brands of all-fabric bleaches-one a store brand.

3. Three chlorine bleaches - one a store brand. Transfer bleach to another box or jar so that its identity remains unknown. Give it an identifying code number.

4. Heavy duty detergent with no additives.

Procedure

This lab experience is conducted in two parts. In the first part, you will wash the soiled swatches without soaking. In the second part, you will soak the soiled swatches for a given amount of time and then wash them.

1. For each stain cloth, use a quantity of detergent plus one of the bleaches, and hot water. Wash without soaking.

2. If you use a basin or sink, use the same amount of water, at the same water temperature, give it the same amount of time, and the same number of dunkings, swishings and scrubbings for all of the bleaches. (You must use rubber gloves to protect your hands.)

3. Complete the chart. Rate each bleach's effectiveness as follows.

0 = not effective (worst) 3 = good
1 = poor   4 = most effective (best)
2 = fair

Swatch	Stain	Bleaches					
		1	2	3	4	5	6
1.							
2.							

LAB EXPERIENCE 4.5 (Continued)

BLEACHES FOR COLORED POLYESTER FABRICS

Swatch	Stain	Bleaches					
		1	2	3	4	5	6
3.							
4.							
5.							
6.							
7.							
8.							
9.							
10.							
11.							
12.							
13.							
14.							
15.							
16.							
17.							
18.							

4. Soak the stained swatches for at least 12 hours in a solution of test bleaches, detergent and room temperature water.

5. Wash the swatches in their soaking water, using the same number of dunkings, swishings and scrubbings for each of the test bleaches.

6. Complete the chart. Rate bleach effectiveness.

Swatch	Stain	Bleaches					
		1	2	3	4	5	6
1.							

LAB EXPERIENCE 4.5 (Continued)

BLEACHES FOR COLORED POLYESTER FABRICS

Swatch	Stain	Bleaches					
		1	2	3	4	5	6
2.							
3.							
4.							
5.							
6.							
7.							
8.							
9.							
10.							
11.							
12.							
13.							
14.							
15.							
16.							
17.							
18.							

7. Examine both sets of swatches, and evaluate how well the stain was removed from each one.

8. Unwrap boxes and reveal the names of each product.

Bleach 1: _____   Bleach 4: _____

Bleach 2: _____   Bleach 5: _____

Bleach 3: _____   Bleach 6: _____

LAB EXPERIENCE 4.5 (Continued)

BLEACHES FOR COLORED POLYESTER FABRICS

Questions:

1. Were you surprised by the results? Why or why not?

2. What advertising claims were made for bleaches selected?

3. Did your test results support the advertising claims?

4. Was the store brand product as effective as the brand name products?

5. What is the price difference between store brand and brand name products?

6. Would you change your brand?

LAB EXPERIENCE 4.6

BLEACHES, PRICE COMPARISON

Purpose: To do a price comparison of non-liquid all-fabric vs chlorine bleach products.

Procedure:

1. Determine the unit price (cost per pound) for each of the following products?

Brand of Bleach	Cost/ Pound	Cost/ Gram
Store Brand All-Fabric		
Brand Name All-Fabric		
Brand Name All-Fabric		
Store Brand Chlorine		
Brand Name Chlorine		
Brand Name Chlorine		

Questions:

1. If there are price differences, how would you account for them?

2. On the basis of the preceding lab experiences, is the price per pound a realistic basis for determining price per use?

LAB EXPERIENCE 4.7

MAKING SOAP

<u>Purpose</u>: To make soap by mixing a fat with an alkali.

Materials:

Hot plate
Hot mitts
Low metal pan with rack
Tongs
25-ml Test tube
Test tube rack
Spatula
Rubber gloves

Safety glasses
2 250-ml Beakers
25-ml Graduated cylinder
100-ml Graduated cylinder
Petri dish
Glass stirring rod
pH Indicator paper
Vegetable oil or fat such as shortening
6M Sodium hydroxide (NaOH) (lye)
Sodium chloride (NaCl) (salt)

<u>Procedure</u>:

1. Put 100 ml of tap water into a 250-ml beaker (Beaker 1) and bring to a boil.

2. Reduce heat, slowly add 25 g of NaCl, and stir mixture with a glass rod. Keep warm over low heat.

3. In a low pan with rack, put sufficient water to cover the rack. Bring to a boil. This will be the water bath for the experiment.

4. Put 15 ml of oil or fat into a second 250-ml beaker (Beaker 2).

5. Carefully add 15 ml of 6M NaOH to the oil in Beaker 2.

6. Note the volume of liquid in Beaker 2. Place this beaker containing oil and NaOH onto the rack in the water bath prepared in Step 3.

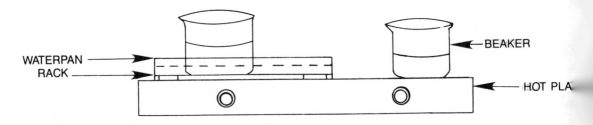

Figure 4.1 Lab Setup for Making Soap

LAB EXPERIENCE 4.7 (Continued)

MAKING SOAP

7. Carefully and constantly stir the contents of the beaker containing the oil and NaOH (Beaker 2). Maintain the original volume by adding distilled water to the beaker.

8. Continue to heat the water bath and the beaker containing the oil and NaOH (Beaker 2) for 30 minutes.

9. After 30 minutes, fill a test tube half full of warm water and place it in a test tube rack.

10. Then using a stirring rod, remove a small amount of the solution from Beaker 2 and dip rod into the test tube half full of warm water.

11. Shake the test tube and note reaction:

    a. If fat globules are present and no suds form, continue to heat the solution in Beaker 2 for another 15 minutes.

    b. If no fat globules are present and suds form, then add 25 ml of water to the beaker (Beaker 2) and stir.

12. Add 50 ml of the warm salt solution from Beaker 1 to Beaker 2. Stir the solution. Test the pH.

13. Remove Beaker 2 from the water bath and allow to cool.

14. Using the spatula, remove the solid material from the beaker and place into the petri dish. Pat it into a smooth mass.

15. When the solid material in the petri dish is cold, rinse it in cold water, and allow to dry and harden.

    CAUTION: This soap may be very harsh because excess sodium hydroxide may not have mixed completely with the other materials. Do not use this product on the skin.

16. Cover the petri dish and save for Lab Experience 4.8.

LAB EXPERIENCE 4.7 (Continued)

MAKING SOAP

<u>Questions:</u>

1. Describe the product in the petri dish.

2. What is the pH of the product? Is this acid or alkaline?

3. Where could such a soap be used?

4. Where did pioneer settlers obtain the oil and lye for soap making?

    a. oil

    b. NaOH (lye)

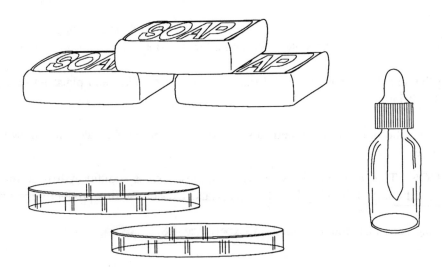

LAB EXPERIENCE 4.8

TESTING SOAP

Purpose: To test soaps for harshness or alkalinity.

Materials:

Metric ruler
Safety glasses
4 to 6 Petri dishes
25 ml Phenolphthalein in a dropper bottle
3 to 5 different kinds of bath or bar laundry soap
Soap made in Lab Experience 4.7

Procedure:

1. Cut a 1 cubic centimeter piece of lab-made soap and place in a petri dish.

2. Place one drop of phenolphthalein on the soap. If pink-red coloring results, the soap is alkaline.

3. Note result on the chart below.

4. Repeat Steps 1 through 3 for the other samples of soap.

Soap Brand	Phenolphthalein Result	Unit Price/oz
1. Lab soap		
2.		
3.		
4.		
5.		

Questions:

1. Why is strongly alkaline soap undesirable?

2. Is there any difference in texture and alkalinity between toilet and bar laundry soap.

LAB EXPERIENCE 4.9

FLOATING SOAP

Purpose: To make soap that floats.

Materials:

Hot plate	Evaporating dish
Hot mitts	Egg beater
Safety glasses	Knife
Balance	1 bar of commercial laundry soap
2 1000-ml Beakers	1 bar of commercial toilet soap
100-ml Graduated cylinder	

Procedure:

1. Cut about 1/3 of a bar of toilet soap into thin slices and weigh it on a balance.

2. Place remainder of bar in a 1000-ml beaker filled with 600 ml of tap water. If soap floats, obtain a different brand of soap and repeat Steps 1 and 2.

3. Measure a quantity of tap water which is 1/3 by volume the amount of soap from Step 1 and place both soap and water into a1000-ml beaker.

4. Place beaker and contents on a hot plate at low temperature and slowly melt the soap.

5. When the material is liquid, remove it from the hot plate and beat the soap with an egg beater at low speed. Be careful not to spatter the hot mixture.

6. When the soap becomes too stiff to beat, empty the soap into an evaporating dish and let it stand at room temperature until cold.

7. Remove the soap from the dish, and place it in a 1000-ml beaker filled with 600 ml of tap water. Note if soap floats.

8. Wash hands with soap and note feel of lather.

9. Repeat Steps 1 through 8 using a laundry soap.

Questions:

1. What is the difference between soaps that float in water and those that sink?

2. Are there any advantages to floating soap?

3. Are there any disadvantages to floating soap?

LAB EXPERIENCE 4.10

TESTING SCOURING POWDERS*

<u>Purpose</u>: To determine the composition and properties of scouring powders.

*Teacher demonstration: test under hood. Chlorine gas may be liberated.

<u>Materials:</u>

Hot plate
Hot mitts
Ring stand
Funnel
Tripod magnifying glass
Balance
6 100-ml Beakers
500-ml Beaker
100-ml Graduated cylinder
Glass stirring rod
Glass slides
3 Watch glasses

Thermometer
Spatula
Safety glasses
Rubber gloves
Aluminum or copper metal strips (2 cm x 10 cm)
Filter paper
Paper towels
3 Commercial scouring powders
Washing soda
Phenolphthalein in a dropper bottle
3M Hydrochloric acid (HCl) in a dropper bottle

<u>Procedure:</u>

<u>Part A: Test for Alkalinity</u>

1. Label the scouring powders 1, 2, 3, and washing soda (WS).

2. Place 5 g of the first dry scouring powder into one watch glass. Place under hood.

3. Add 1 drop of phenolphthalein to the powder and note reaction. Record any color change in the chart below.

4. Put 2 to 3 drops of 3M HCl on the powder. Do you see any bubbles or gas given off? Record on the chart below. CAUTION: Don't breath in the fumes. Chlorine gas may be liberated.

5. Repeat Steps 1 through 3 for each of the remaining scouring powders and washing soda.

LAB EXPERIENCE 4.10 (Continued)

TESTING SCOURING POWDERS*

6. Enter results on the chart below.

	Phenolphthalein Reaction	Dilute HCl Reaction
Brand 1		
Brand 2		
Brand 3		
Washing Soda		

Questions:

1. A pink-red reaction spot to phenolphthalein indicates the presence of _____ _____.

2. The giving off of gas when dilute HCl was put on the scouring powder indicates that some carbonate compounds were present. Did any of the brands have this reaction? _____ Which ones? _____, _____, _____.

Part B: Test for Carbonates

1. Put 200 ml of tap water into 500-ml beaker along with a thermometer and heat to 90 degrees C.

2. Put 5 g of scouring powder into a 100-ml beaker.

3. Using a hot mitt, add 50 ml of hot water to beaker in Step 2. Stir carefully and thoroughly. Allow to cool slightly.

4. Filter the mixture, saving both filtrate and solid residue on filter paper for use in Parts C and D.

5. Add 5 drops of 3M HCl to the filtrate. Note if any gas is given off? If so, then sodium carbonate is present. The common name for sodium carbonate is washing soda and it is a frequent component of scouring powders.

LAB EXPERIENCE 4.10 (Continued)

TESTING SCOURING POWDERS*

Part C: Examine the Residue

1. Using the spatula, place a few particles of residue from the filter paper onto a glass slide.

2. Place the slide and residue under the magnifying glass and examine the residue.

3. Note the size and shape of the particles. Draw some representative particles of the scouring powders below.

<u>Brand 1</u>   <u>Brand 2</u>   <u>Brand 3</u>   <u>Washing Soda</u>

Part D: Test for Abrasiveness

1. Place some particle residue on a strip of aluminum or copper. With a paper towel folded over several times to act as a buffer, vigorously rub for 1 minute 1/3 of the metal surface with the residue.

2. Reserve the remainder of the strip of metal to use with the remaining brands.

3. Examine the metal strip under the magnifying glass particularly the depth of the scratches on the surface of the metal.

Part E:

Repeat Parts A, B, C, D with each of the remaining scouring powders and washing sodas.

Part F: Analysis of Product

1. From Part C, list the scouring powders from the smallest or smoothest particles to the largest or sharpest particles.

Powder 1

Powder 2

Powder 3

Washing Soda

LAB EXPERIENCE 4.10 (Continued)

TESTING SCOURING POWDERS*

2. From Part D, list the scouring powders from the products producing the finest to the deepest scratches.

Powder 1

Powder 2

Powder 3

Washing Soda

Questions:

1. How could you tell if the scouring powders contained both an abrasive, such as calcium carbonate and washing soda which is sodium carbonate?

2. From the drawings of the residue, what conclusions would you come to after seeing the sharp edges and corners of the particles?

3. Are the scouring powders listed in the same order on both lists in Part F?

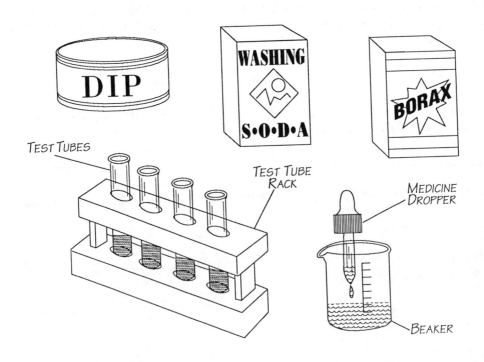

LAB EXPERIENCE 4.11

HARD WATER

Purpose: To study the properties of hard water and techniques of water softening.

Materials:

Hot plate   Glass marking pencils
Hot mitts   100-ml Beaker
Safety glasses   400-ml Beaker
Ring stand with clamp   500-ml Beaker
Medicine droppers   Distilled water
4 25-ml Test tubes   1 liter 1% Hard water
Test tube rack   1 liter 1% Soap solution
Funnel   1 liter 1% Dishwashing or laundry detergent
10-ml Graduated cylinder   Water softeners:
50-ml Graduated cylinder   1 box Trisodium phosphate (Dif)
Filter paper   1 box Sodium carbonate (Salsoda)
pH Paper   1 box Sodium tetraborate (Borax)

Procedure:

Part A: Effectiveness of Soap in Different Kinds of Water

1. Label 3 test tubes: one Tap Water, one Distilled Water, and one Hard Water.

2. Put 10 ml of each water in their respective test tubes.

3. Put 50 ml of a 1% soap solution into a 100-ml beaker.

4. Using a medicine dropper, add 5 drops of the soap solution to the test tube. Shake the test tube thoroughly. If suds do not form, or form but do not last 1 minute, repeat adding 5 drops and shaking until the suds last for 1 minute. Record the number of drops in the chart below.

5. Repeat Step 4 for the distilled water.

6. Repeat Step 4 for the hard water.

Solution	Number of Drops of Soap for Suds
Tap water	
Distilled water	
Hard water	

LAB EXPERIENCE 4.11 (Continued)

HARD WATER

Part B: Effectiveness of Liquid Detergent in Different Kinds of Water

1. Clean the test tubes and beaker in prepartion for the next part of the experiment.

2. Label 3 test tubes: one Tap Water, one Distilled Water, and one Hard Water.

3. Put 10 ml of each water into respective test tubes.

4. Put 50 ml of 1% liquid detergent solution into a 100-ml beaker.

5. Using a medicine dropper, add 5 drops of the liquid detergent solution to the test tube. Shake the test tube thoroughly. If suds do not form or form but do not last 1 minute, repeat adding 5 drops and shaking until the suds last for 1 minute. Record the number of drops in the chart below.

6. Repeat Step 4 for distilled water.

7. Repeat Step 4 for hard water.

Solution	Number of Drops of Soap for Suds
Tap water	
Distilled water	
Hard water	

Part C: Effectiveness of Soap and Detergent in Boiled and Filtered Hard Water

1. Prepare boiled and filtered water by putting 200 ml of 1% hard water into 500-ml beaker. Place beaker on hot plate and boil for 10 minutes. Some solid material will settle out of solution. Allow the solution to cool slightly.

2. Set up ring stand with clamp, funnel, filter paper, and a 400-ml beaker beneath funnel.

3. Pour boiled water through filter into the 400-ml beaker. Use this water for Parts C, D, and E.

4. Put 10 ml of clear boiled water into a test tube labeled "Clear Boiled Water". Test pH and record in chart below.

LAB EXPERIENCE 4.11 (Continued)

HARD WATER

5. Using a medicine dropper, add 5 drops of soap solution to the test tube. Shake the test tube thoroughly. If suds do not form or form but do not last 1 minute, repeat adding 5 drops and shaking until the suds last for 1 minute. Record the number of drops in the chart below.

6. Repeat Steps 4 and 5 using the liquid detergent.

	Number of Drops of Soap	pH	Number of Drops of Detergent	pH
Boiled and Filtered Hard Water				

Part D: Effectiveness of Liquid Soap in Boiled Hard Water with Commercial Water Softeners

1. Label 3 test tubes: one Dif, one Salsoda, and one Borax.

2. Put 10 ml of the clear boiled water into each of the 3 labeled test tubes.

3. To the test tube labeled "Dif", add a few grains of the water softener Dif (about 0.1 g). Shake until dissolved. Take the pH of the solution and record on chart in Part E.

4. Using a medicine dropper, add 5 drops of soap solution to the test tube. Shake the test tube thoroughly. If suds do not form or form but do not last 1 minute, repeat adding 5 drops and shaking until the suds last for 1 minute. Record the number of drops on chart in Part E.

5. To the tube labeled "Salsoda", add a few grains (about 0.1 g) of the water softener Salsoda and shake until dissolved. Take the pH of the solution and record on chart in Part E.

6. Repeat Step 4 adding the soap solution and note the results on the chart in Part E.

7. To the test tube labeled "Borax" add a few grains (about 0.1 g) of the water softener Borax and shake until dissolved. Take the pH of the solution and record on chart in Part E.

8. Repeat Step 4 adding the soap solution and note results on chart in Part E.

LAB EXPERIENCE 4.11 (Continued)

HARD WATER

Part E: Effectiveness of Liquid Detergent in Boiled and Filtered Hard Water with Commercial Water Softeners

1. Label 3 test tubes: one Dif, one Salsoda, and one Borax.

2. Put 10 ml of the clear boiled and filtered tap water into each of the labeled test tubes and place in a test tube rack.

3. Add a few grains (about 0.1 g) of Dif to the test tube so labeled. Shake until dissolved. Take pH of solution and record in chart below.

4. Using a medicine dropper, add 5 drops of the liquid detergent solution to the test tube. Shake the test tube thoroughly. If suds do not form or form but do not last 1 minute, repeat adding 5 drops and shaking until the suds last for 1 minute. Record the number of drops in the chart below.

5. Repeat Steps 3 and 4 using Salsoda in place of Dif.

6. Repeat Steps 3 and 4 using Borax in place of Dif.

Solution	Part D Number of Drops of Soap for Suds	pH	Part E Number of Drops of Detergent for Suds	pH
Clear boiled water with Dif				
Clear boiled water with Salsoda				
Clear boiled water with Borax				

Questions:

1. Which water sample needed the least soap solution to make suds?

2. Which water sample needed the most soap solution to make suds?

3. Which water sample needed the least liquid detergent solution to make suds?

LAB EXPERIENCE 4.11 (Continued)

HARD WATER

4. Which water sample needed the most liquid detergent solution to make suds?

5. How effective as a softening agent is boiling hard water ?

6. How effective was each of the commercial water softening products in the soap solution?

7. How effective was each of the commercial water softeners in the liquid detergent solution?

8. What effect do the commercial water softening products have on the pH of the solution?

9. What is the pH of soap as compared to liquid detergent?

10. Name some of the solids that settle out of hard water when it is boiled.

11. How do dish detergent rinse-aids work?

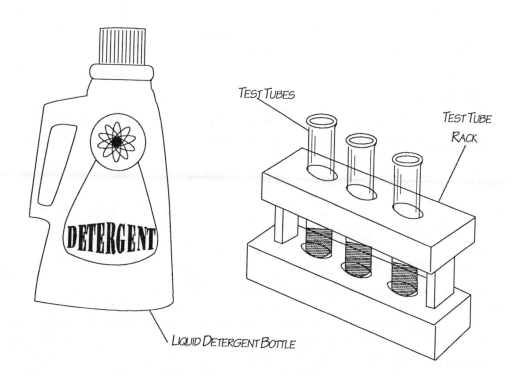

LAB EXPERIENCE 4.12

WATER PURIFICATION

Purpose: To learn some water purification methods.

Materials:

Hot plate	25-ml Graduated cylinder
Hot mitts	100-ml Graduated cylinder
Balance	6 25-ml Test tubes
Ring stand	Test tube rack
Funnel	Clay soil
2 Glass stirring rods	Tap water
Filter paper	3M solution of Aluminum sulfate
3 50-ml Beakers	3M solution of Sodium hydroxide
2 500-ml Beakers	3M solution of Potassium permanganate

Procedure:

Part A: Precipitation

1. Put 10 ml of 3M sodium hydroxide solution into a test tube.

2. Add 10 ml of 3M aluminum sulfate solution to the test tube, and describe the results

   _____.

   The precipitate is aluminum hydroxide. It is insoluble and is called "floc" when the two chemical compounds are used for water purification.

Part B: Settling

1. Label one 500-ml beaker AS for aluminum sulfate, and the second 500-ml beaker SH for sodium hydroxide. Label 2 test tubes similarly.

2. Put 10 g of clay soil into each of the 500-ml beakers.

3. Add 300 ml of tap water to each of the beakers and stir thoroughly. Let the beakers stand at room temperature for 5 minutes.

4. After 5 minutes, describe any change. _____

   In water purification, this process is called settling.

5. To the beaker labeled AS, add 20 ml of aluminum sulfate solution. To the beaker labeled SH, add 20 ml of sodium hydroxide solution. Stir each beaker and allow the beakers to stand at room temperature for 15 minutes.

LAB EXPERIENCE 4.12 (Continued)

WATER PURIFICATION

6. After 15 minutes note the change in each beaker. In which beaker have the particles settled faster? _____

7. Put filter paper in the funnel, stir the AS beaker again and immediately pour off 15 ml of water into the test tube marked AS.

8. Put a clean piece of filter paper into the funnel and repeat Step 7 for the beaker marked SH.

9. From which beaker is the filtrate clearer and freer of particles? _____
_____.

In large-scale water purification, the water is filtered through coarse and fine rock, gravel, and sand so that large and small particles are trapped by the natural material.

Part C: Test for Organic Material

1. Put 20 ml of water into a 50-ml beaker and place on hot plate.

2. Put 10 ml of tap water into a test tube, add 2 drops of dilute potassium permanganate and place test tube in beaker.

3. Heat the solution and note any color change. If the mixture loses its color, then organic material is present. How long did it take before the color began to change?
_____

Part D: Distilled Water Tests

Repeat Part C Steps 1 to 3 using distilled water instead of tap water for the experiment.

Questions:

1. How would you describe what happens in the change that occurs in Part B Step 4?

2. Have you seen this change before? What is it called?

3. What explanation would you have to describe what occurs in Part B Step 9?

Suggested Activities:

1. Library research on how your town or city purifies its water supply.

2. Invite a representative from the local water company to describe its operation.

SHAMPOOS

The hair strand is divided into two parts. The root or hair follicle, is buried in the scalp. This is the living portion of the hair strand. The portion that is visible to us is the hair shaft which is the dead portion of the strand of hair. Hair grows from the root outward, and so the part we see, cut, shampoo, and maybe even color is no longer alive. This is why you can trim and cut your hair without experiencing pain.

If you are considering coloring your hair, then be aware of the cautions and warnings which appear on hair dyes. They are not to be taken lightly, and whether you are going to do it yourself or have a professional hairdresser color your hair it is best to do the patch test first.

The patch test will indicate any allergic reaction you might have to the product. Once a person develops an allergy to a particular type of dye, the allergy remains for life. There are other types that might be used, but it might be best to consult with a dermatologist and bring a sample of the first dye product with you. The FDA has published a highly recommended pamphlet entitled "If You're Coloring Your Hair" by Jane Heenan.

A shampoo is a special preparation for cleansing the hair of dirt, oil, and dead skin scales. Today there are many advertised shampoos which are touted as an aid to success in work, social and sexual settings.

Back in 1938, the primary cleansing agent in shampoo was soap, so the shampoos of that era were not covered by the Food, Drug and Cosmetic Act. Today, the cleansing agent in most shampoos is a synthetic detergent rather than soap. Because shampoos containing synthetic detergents fall within the legal definition of a cosmetic, most of the products that dominate today's shampoo market are so classified.

All synthetic detergents have the capacity to break down the barrier between water and dirt, or other material on the surface which is to be cleaned. The surface can then be rinsed clean.

From our discussion about Water, Soap, and Detergent (see Page 140), we know the problem of hard water and soap which leads to soap scum formation. This soap scum can also form on the hair when shampooing with soap and hard water. This dulls the hair and makes it difficult to comb unless rinsed with some substance that will redissolve the scum.

When soap was still the thing for hairwashing, the scum that formed to dull the hair's luster was often reduced or eliminated by following up with a rinse of such acidic substances as vinegar and lemon juice. The scum, as we know, is caused by the insoluble calcium and magnesium salts. Acid substances such as vinegar or lemon juice lower the pH of these salts to they become soluble fatty acid salts and eventually become fatty acids. In this form they are easily rinsed-off and out of the hair. The belief still persists among some consumers that vinegar and lemon juice are needed, even when a synthetic detergent shampoo is used. Synthetic detergents do not react with the calcium in the water. Scum deposits do not form, even in the hardest water, though the detergent or cleaning action may itself vary depending on the kind of synthetic detergent used and the kind of foreign material to be removed.

Sometimes a lathering agent is added to a synthetic detergent just so that it would appear to the user that it is "working." The manufacturer assumes the consumer wants to see suds.

The biggest problem with a synthetic detergent is that the more thoroughly it removes dirt and other unwanted material, the more likely it is to irritate the scalp, strip off hair dyes and tints put on by the consumer at some effort and expense, remove the natural oil left on the hair from the hair gland secretions, or neutralize the intended effects of some conditioning ingredients in the shampoo.

Some shampoos contain conditioning agents. Among conditioners that have been used in shampoos to produce various cosmetic effects are eggs, or protein derivatives, glycerin or propylene glycol, and ethyl alcohol. These conditioners give hair the appearance or feel of softness; create or enhance luster and sheen; impart smoothness to the touch and make combing or brushing easier; give the hair "body," or somewhat more bulk; retain "set"; and control static electricity or frizziness resulting from excessive dryness.

It should be understood that protein materials used in shampoos, or for that matter any other conditioning ingredients, cannot feed the hair roots to make the hair "alive." The visible hair strand is dead tissue, and the roots cannot be reached by the application of any product. Other ingredients in the products may be about 20% alcohol and up to 75% water. Optional ingredients may include shellac, silicone, lanolin, and vegetable gums. These ingredients do no particular harm to the hair, not any more than polish harms the nails.

Have you wondered how those "texturizers" texturize and where all that "extra body" comes from? It comes from coating the hair with a plastic. Plastic resins are used in hair lacquers and wave sets. It is comparable to putting three coats of polish on your nails. Your nails get thicker — three coats of polish thicker, and that's how plastic coating makes your hair thicker.

The conditioners in shampoos are not normally adequate to conceal damage to hair that may result from the use of chemicals such as dyes, bleaches, waving or straightening mixtures, or from the intense heat used to curl or straighten the hair strands. Special conditioners usually are needed, after shampooing to mask such damage. Shampoos labeled for use on normal, dry, or oily hair are formulated by controlling the strength or amount of the synthetic detergent, included in the shampoo.

Oiliness and flaking of the scalp is normal. The human scalp, even at its healthiest, shows a mild degree of scaling. This exists because the skin all over the body continually sloughs off bits of its dead outer layer. On the scalp, sebacious glands add their oily secretions (sebum) to the dead skin scales. This combination forms dandruff. Most dandruff is nothing more than this normal condition, and a reasonably clean and healthy scalp can be maintained by shampooing once or twice a week. When dandruff is shed from the scalp in scales larger than normal, it becomes unsightly, either in the hair itself or when it falls and clings to the outer clothing. A medicated shampoo, labeled for dandruff control should be considered if flaking is very heavy. There is no evidence that changes in diet, or the addition of vitamins or minerals to the diet, can control the development of dandruff.

The law holds the manufacturer of a synthetic detergent shampoo or other cosmetic solely responsible for safety in its use. The manufacturer is expected to use ingredients about which there have been no questions of safety, and to perform adequate studies with test animals and humans for new ingredients or combinations to make sure the product is safe to use before it is put on the market.

LAB EXPERIENCE 4.13

SHAMPOOS

Purpose: Experiment and judge shampoos in order to determine which
products work best.

Procedure:

1. Select four advertised shampoos that claim some special characteris
   (such as protein or low pH), and four shampoos that do not adverti
   these special characteristics.   Put two advertised brands and two una
   vertised ones into an "A" batch, and the remaining four into a "
   batch.

2. Divide the class into groups of four students.   Assign half the groups
   buy the four "A" shampoos, and the remaining groups to buy the "
   shampoos.   Also ask students to bring in empty shampoo bottles.

3. In class, groups should pour the test shampoos into different containe
   and give each container a code number.   By exchanging "A" shampoos f
   "B" shampoos, each group will have unfamiliar coded shampoo samples f
   testing.

4. Test the pH of each shampoo using universal pH paper.

5. Each student should then use a test sample for two weeks, rate it, a
   pass it along.   Over eight weeks, four samples should be rotated amo
   the four students in each group.

6. Each student should rate each shampoo in several categories:

   a.   How effectively it cleans the hair?
   b.   How easily the shampoo rinses out of the hair?
   c.   How the hair feels and behaves after shampooing?
   d.   Any comments.

Rate the product on a 1 to 4 basis: 1-terrible, 2-poor, 3-fair, 4-excelle

Brand	Unit Price	Cleaning	Rinsing	Feels	Behaves	pH
1.						
2.						
3.						
4.						
5.						

LAB EXPERIENCE 4.13 (Continued)

SHAMPOOS

Brand	Unit Price	Cleaning	Rinsing	Feels	Behaves	pH
6.						
7.						
8.						

Questions:

1. Is there any difference between the shampoos tested?

2. What type of shampoo did you think you needed before this test? Which of the test shampoos was that type? Did you like that one better than the other test shampoos?

3. Do you think some of the judgments might have been different if you'd known the shampoos' brand names?

4. What advertising claims were made for some of the shampoos tested? Did your evaluations support or refute these claims?

5. Why is it important to be unaware of the names of test-samples while testing?

6. Do you compare prices before choosing a shampoo? Why or why not?

TOOTHPASTE

Dental disease includes the decay of teeth and the deterioration of the soft tissue surrounding the teeth. It is possible to prevent dental disease by reducing the food for bacteria that live in the mouth and strengthening the tooth surface.

Sugars in the food we eat combine with saliva to form plaque. The bacteria that ordinarily live in the mouth use the sugars for food. In the process acids are given off which attack the teeth causing tooth decay. It is evident then that the way to reduce tooth decay is by eating less sugars and reducing the amount of bacteria present in the mouth. Flossing and brushing, at least once a day, dislodges the plaque which tends to build up on teeth. Getting rid of the plaque will also prevent the swelling and bleeding of the gums.

In the lab experience, you will prepare some toothpaste and compare it with a commercial brand. You will be evaluating both toothpastes for alkalinity or acidity and abrasiveness. You want to use a toothpaste reasonably close to the pH of your mouth, and not harsh or abrasive to your teeth. A pH too different from your mouth will leave it feeling strange, and a harsh toothpaste will scratch your teeth exposing them to deterioration.

The components of toothpaste are:

1. Flavors and color for taste and attractiveness.
2. Sweeteners, such as saccharin, for flavor.
3. Humectants, such as glycerine, for moistening.
4. Detergents or soap for foaming action.
5. Binders, such as alginates or gums, for smoothness.
6. Abrasives, such as chalk, for scouring action.
7. Therapeutic ingredients such as fluorides.

Toothpaste advertising is monitored by both the Food and Drug Administration and the American Dental Association.

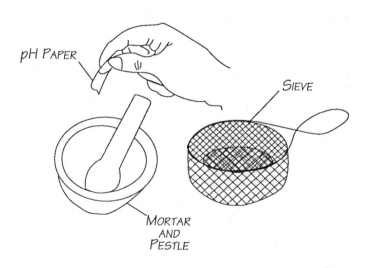

pH PAPER

SIEVE

MORTAR
AND
PESTLE

LAB EXPERIENCE 4.14

TOOTHPASTE

<u>Purpose:</u> To make toothpaste and compare it with a commercial brand.

<u>Materials:</u>

Mortar and pestle or Number 50 sieve
Balance
50-ml Beaker
500-ml Beaker
1000-ml Beaker
pH paper
New glass slides
Distilled water

125 g Precipitated calcium carbonate
   (extra-fine grade chalk)
95 g Precipitated calcium phosphate
   (extra-fine grade)
20 g Sodium saccharin
30 g Powdered white soap
10 to 15 drops Oil of peppermint or wintergreen
Glycerin
Favorite brand of toothpaste

<u>Procedure:</u>

1. In the 50-ml beaker, mix the oil of peppermint with a small quantity of saccharin, and then mix with the rest of the saccharin.

2. In the 500-ml beaker, combine the chalk and calcium phosphate with the soap.

3. Add the mixture from Step 1 to the mixture from Step 2.

4. Mix thoroughly in a mortar and pestle or force it through the number 50 sieve.

5. Add equal quantities of glycerin and distilled water to make a paste similar in consistency to the commercial toothpaste.

6. With a strip of pH paper, check the pH of the product just made. The pH is _____.

7. With another piece of pH paper, check the pH of the individual's saliva. The pH is _____.

8. Check the pH of your favorite brand of toothpaste. The pH is _____.

9. Place 2 cm of the laboratory prepared toothpaste on a glass slide. Cover with a second slide and rub the two slides together for 30 seconds. Do not use too much pressure.

10. Rinse toothpaste off the glass slides and check them for scratches. Record condition of slides in chart below.

LAB EXPERIENCE 4.14 (Continued)

TOOTHPASTE

11. Using new slides, repeat Steps 9 and 10 with the favorite brand of toothpaste. Record condition of slides in chart below.

	Lab-made Toothpaste	Commercial Product	Mouth
pH			
Scratches			

Questions:

1. Do you see any scratches:

   a. on the first set of slides?

   b. on the second set of slides?

2. What quality of toothpaste does this evaluate?

3. What was the reason to check the pH of your saliva?

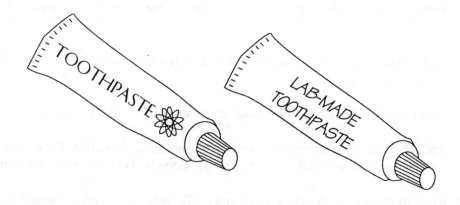

COSMETICS

Cosmetics have been around for thousands of years in just about every country and culture. Even the tombs of the Egyptian rulers contain jars and pots of what were evidently cosmetics. We have more recent records of European ladies and gentlemen of the 17th and 18th centuries lavishly using cosmetics.

The cosmetic industry is big business. Each year we spend billions of dollars on everything from creams and oils to shampoos and shave creams. About one-fifth of the sales go for toothpaste, shampoo, mouthwash, talcum powder, hand lotion, and soap while the remainder goes for the perfumes, lipstick, rouges, eye shadows, etc. Manufacturers would have you believe that only their currently advertised product will magically change the purchaser into a princess, or more recently a prince. The vanishing creams of yesterday that were widely used in the hope of wiping away wrinkles—the telltale signs of aging—have become the preventers, repairers, cell renewers, and anti-aging complexes of today. They are advertised to diminish wrinkles, prevent future signs of aging, and preserve the youthfulness of the skin. There are products for both men and women. Dermatologists describe these products as moisturizers. Actually, moisturizers simply coat the skin so that water cannot evaporate out, leaving the skin dry. The only way to moisturize the skin is to get water inside of it by drinking, soaking or bathing.

Wrinkles result from the wearing down of the protein fibers that lend elasticity to the skin. Other factors such as dehydration and a slowdown of the cells to renew themselves, heredity, overexposure to the sun, general health, and the environment also contribute to the process. In other words, wrinkles are inevitable.

Cosmetics cannot cure or remove wrinkles. Cosmetics are, however, able to smooth the skin's appearance. When you use a moisturizer, the skin's outer cells absorb the material and balloon up, pressing against each other. This smooths and softens fine wrinkles, such as crow's feet around the eyes. The deeper wrinkles, such as frown wrinkles or genetic creases, hardly respond to cosmetics. The injection of collagen into these deeper wrinkles just smooths the surface. The collagen molecule is too large to be absorbed into the skin. It coats the surface and fills in the creases. The injection may give the surface of the face a smoothed-out look and feeling.

Petroleum jelly does not prevent wrinkles. It will prevent moisture from evaporating from the skin, but it too cannot penetrate the skin. Most wrinkle products on the market contain humectants, such as glycerol, which act as water retainers. These will help the skin from looking and feeling dry. Wrinkle products contain the same basic ingredients: water, emulsifiers, and oily materials. After these basic components, each company adds its special ingredients such as fragrance and color. None of the products will prevent wrinkles. The only way to postpone wrinkles is to stay out of the sun and use a sunscreen according to directions.

Differences between cosmetics are mostly the result of packaging and advertising. In most cases, chemical analysis shows that all products in any one category are basically of the same composition. The price is the result of the package and the "hype." Many of the men's skin care cosmetics presently being advertised are basically the same as women's products. The fragrance, color and packaging are changed to appeal to men, and the price varies accordingly.

The question of how cosmetics are manufactured, promoted and regulated in the U.S. is addressed by the Food, Drug, and Cosmetic Act of 1938. This law was passed to prohibit the trading of adulterated and misbranded foods, drugs, cosmetics, and medical devices. The law was supplemented by the Fair Packaging and Labeling Act to include cosmetics. This addition ensures that the packages and labels on cosmetics give accurate information about the identity of the product, the net contents, and the name and address of the distributor. In the U.S., authority for enforcing the provisions of the Food, Drug, and Cosmetic Act is vested in the Food and Drug Administration (FDA).

The Food, Drug and Cosmetic Act defines a cosmetic as any product which may be "rubbed, poured, sprinkled, or sprayed on, introduced into, or otherwise applied to the human body for cleansing, beautifying, promoting attractiveness or altering the appearance without affecting the body's structure or functions."

The most significant difference between a product classified as a cosmetic and one classified as a drug is that drugs must be tested and proven safe and effective before they are marketed. A cosmetic does not require pre-market testing. Most cosmetic manufacturers do test their products for safety before putting them on the market, but the FDA does not have the authority to require this of them. The law does not require the manufacturer to make known to the FDA any adverse reactions of the products. However, the agency can take legal action to have a product removed from the market if it is a proven health hazard. It is only in recent years that manufacturers have voluntarily registered their product formulations with the FDA. The listing of ingredients is very important. The consumer has the right to know what is in any product. If an adverse reaction occurs, then the patient and doctor can determine what ingredients to avoid. The components must be listed in order of amount contained, with the major ingredient first. Constituents that constitute less than 1% of the product need not be listed by amount, and color ingredients can be listed in any order regardless of the amount used in the product. Components

must be listed by uniform names, which have been established especially for ingredient labeling. This rule is intended to prevent consumers from being confused or misled by the use of different names for the same constituent. Color additives in cosmetics must be FDA approved. For eye products, only inorganic pigments are allowed.

The law does not require manufacturers to list any special component or trade secret.

Antiperspirants are legally drugs, not cosmetics, because they alter a body function by reducing the flow of perspiration. The flow of perspiration is reduced by certain substances called astringents. Antiperspirant properties are found in the salts of a number of metals, but the most commonly used antiperspirants are the salts of aluminum. These include aluminum chloride, aluminum sulfate, and aluminum chlorhydrate. These aluminum salts also have antibacterial properties.

Unlike antiperspirants, deodorants are cosmetics designed merely to prevent body odor, not to stop perspiration. Since most body odor is the result of bacterial action on perspiration, most deodorants contain an effective antibacterial agent — a substance that can kill bacteria or prevent their growth. Deodorant powders consist mostly of talc and perfumes. Often they contain ingredients such as zinc oxide and zinc stearate to make them adhere better or feel more comfortable on the skin. Whatever antibacterial agent is used, it generally comprises a very small percentage of the deodorant. The other ingredients either provide a cosmetic benefit, such as fragrance, or make application easier, i.e., the propellant in an aerosol, or water in a roll-on product.

Many deodorants and antiperspirants contain alcohol, which has a potential for stinging or burning, and these products may carry a warning statement on the label that they should not be used immediately after shaving the underarms.

CHOOSING COSMETICS

Knowing some basic facts will help you choose cosmetics wisely.

- Creams and lotions can't keep skin from wrinkling. Dry skin doesn't cause wrinkling although it often goes along with it. Wrinkling is caused by damage to the supporting fibers of the skin. The fastest way to damage these fibers is to expose the skin to sun.
- The best sunscreen is para-aminobenzoic acid (PABA). This material absorbs the light from the ultraviolet range, and emits it at a lower wavelength. Thus, PABA acts as a good screen against the sun. Baby oil doesn't give the skin any protection from the sun's ultraviolet rays.
- Skin is dry because it lacks water. To correct dryness, get water inside the skin by soaking or bathing. Then apply a moisturizing cream or lotion to keep the water where you want it.
- Unusual ingredients, such as mink oil, turtle oil, or royal jelly, do not help a cream or lotion hold moisture on the skin. Nor do they prevent wrinkles. They just raise the price. Many dermatologists favor water and unscented soap for cleansing. Most make-up is easily removed with cleansing cream. Then use soap and water.
- No one has proven that natural ingredients are better for the skin just because they're natural.

HOMEMADE COSMETICS

Making your own cosmetics can be fun and economical. There are several books on the market such as the "The Complete Book of Natural Cosmetics," by Beatrice Traven, Simon & Schuster: New York City, "Cosmetics from the Kitchen," by Marcia Donnan, Holt, Rinehart & Winston: New York City, and "Down to Earth Beauty," by Catherine Palmer, St. Martin's Press: New York City. The ingredients are readily obtainable from a supermarket or pharmacy. The equipment for measuring and preparation are ordinary household items. The creams may vary in their ingredients, but they basically consist of an oil, a wax, and some liquid.

The oil may be coconut, almond, olive or sesame. The wax would probably be beeswax because it is easily obtainable and will make a firmer product. Lanolin or cocoa butter will thicken the product. Liquids such as rosewater, fruit juices, ethyl alcohol or isopropyl alcohol may be used.

In all instances, the oils, wax, lanolin, or cocoa butter are heated in a double boiler container. When they have melted, they are removed from the heat and vigorously stirred. The liquid is added, drop by drop, beating it in after each addition. The substance will solidify as it cools. It should be placed in a dark or opaque container with a close fitting lid. Label the container and it is ready for use. Because homemade cosmetics do not have any preservatives they should be kept refrigerated and used quickly.

The FDA does not require that a cosmetic fulfill all the hopes and dreams of users. It does require that a cosmetic be labeled without false or misleading representations, with information about the product, its maker and the quantity of its contents. It must be free of substances that may make it injurious. It must be produced in a sanitary plant and it must be packaged in a safe and nondeceptive container.

Good health is still the best foundation for good looks. The skin is nourished by proper diet and not by any vitamins, minerals or hormones contained in cosmetics. Proper nutrition, exercise, sufficient sleep, and a minimum of exposure to the sun will

222

all contribute to longlasting attractiveness.

You will have an opportunity to make several cosmetics: a skin freshener, cold cream, and hand lotion. Cold creams are used as a skin cleanser. They are oil and wax emulsions which contain large amounts of water. When applied to the skin, the emulsion breaks down allowing the water to separate. As the water evaporates, the skin feels cool. The dirt and grease on the skin dissolve into the wax emulsion. When the cream is removed, dissolved particles of make-up, grease and dirt are removed with it.

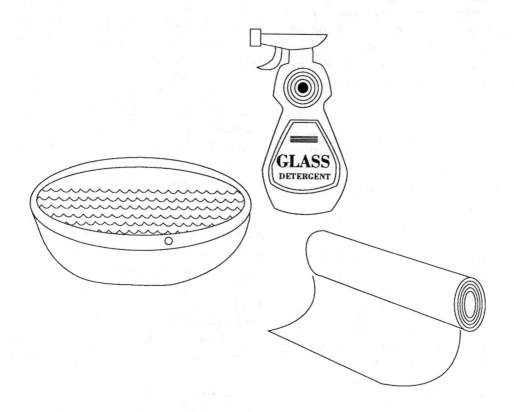

LAB EXPERIENCE 4.15

SKIN FRESHENERS

Purpose: To make a skin freshener - a homemade cosmetic.

Materials:

    60-ml fruit juice, unsweetened, and preferably fresh
    30-ml water
    60-ml alcohol
    A few drops of extract such as lemon or peppermint
    150-ml Ehrlenmeyer flask with rubber stopper or another container with a
    tight-fitting cap
    Basin
    Glassware detergent
    Paper towels
    50-ml graduated cylinder or beaker

Procedure:

1.   Combine the ingredients in a stoppered 150-ml Ehrlenmeyer flask.

2.   Shake vigorously.

3.   Label the product, and store in refrigerator.

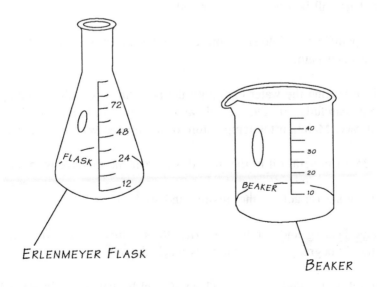

ERLENMEYER FLASK

BEAKER

LAB EXPERIENCE 4.16

COLD CREAM

Purpose: To prepare a cleansing cream and compare it with a commercial product.

Materials:

Hot plate	10-ml Graduated cylinder
Hot mitts	100-ml Graduated cylinder
Glass stirring rod	200-ml Graduated cylinder
Balance	Distilled water
Low metal pan with rack	20 g Paraffin wax
Small empty food jar	125 ml Mineral oil
with lid (baby food)	1.5 g Sodium borate (Borax)
Thermometer	1.5 g Stearic acid
Safety glasses	3 to 5 ml favorite fragrance*
100-ml Beaker	Commercial brand of cold cream
500-ml Beaker	

*Have some groups make unscented cream. Fragrances may be extracts of lemon or orange, cologne, perfume, or oil of lavender or peppermint.

Procedure:

1. Put sufficient water in metal pan to cover rack and place on hot plate. Begin heating the water. This will be used as a water bath.

2. Cut the paraffin wax into small pieces and place it in the 500-ml beaker. Put the beaker into the water bath.

3. Continue heating the water bath until the paraffin wax melts. Holding the beaker with hot mitt, carefully stir the melted wax with glass rod. Put the thermometer into the melted wax. Maintain the temperature of the melted wax at 70 degrees C.

4. Add 125 ml mineral oil to the melted wax. Stir the mixture with the stirring rod.

5. Add 1.5 g stearic acid to the mixture and stir.

6. Continue heating and carefully stirring the mixture of paraffin, oil, and stearic acid until the 70 degree C. temperature is reached again.

7. Put 70 ml of distilled water in a clean 100-ml beaker, place in water bath, and heat to 70 degrees C.

8. Add 1.5 g Borax to heated 70 ml of water. Stir until the Borax is mixed with the water.

LAB EXPERIENCE 4.16 (Continued)

COLD CREAM

9. Remove the beaker and mixture of Step 8 from the hot plate and while stirring constantly, slowly add all the oil-water-Borax solution to the wax-oil-stearic acid solution. Cool slightly.

10. At this point add the fragrance.

11. Stir the mixture and allow it to cool a little more. Before the mixture hardens, pour it into the small jar and cover. Keep it in a cool place.

12. Compare the texture and list of ingredients of the lab product and the commercial product on the chart below.

	Lab Product	Commercial Product
Texture		
Ingredients		

Questions:

1. How does the appearance of the lab cleansing cream compare with the commercial product?

2. Are there any preservatives in either of the cold creams?

3. What is an emulsion?

LAB EXPERIENCE 4.16 (Continued)

COLD CREAM

4. Which federal agency oversees the commercial production of cosmetics?

5. Put some lipstick on the back of each hand. Use the lab product to cleanse your right hand and the commercial product to cleanse your left hand. Compare cleansing action and note results.

Lab product _____

Commercial product _____

LAB EXPERIENCE 4.17

HAND LOTION

Purpose: To make a hand lotion and compare it to a commercial brand.

Materials:

Hot plate	500-ml Beaker
Hot mitts	Distilled water
Glass stirring rod	60 g Anhydrous lanolin
Balance	80 g Petroleum jelly
Thermometer	60 g Glycerol
Safety glasses	2 g Boric acid
Low metal pan with rack	0.5 to 1 ml favorite fragrance*
1-ml Graduated cylinder	Commercial brand of hand lotion

*Fragrances may be spices, oil of peppermint or lavender, extracts of orange or lemon, or any cologne or perfume. Have some groups make fragrance-free lotion.

Procedure:

1. Put sufficient tap water into pan with rack to cover the rack, place on hot plate, and bring the water to a boil. This is the water bath.

2. Place the lanolin, petroleum jelly, and glycerol in the 500-ml beaker. Stir the components.

3. Put the beaker onto the rack in the water bath. Place the thermometer into the mixture in the beaker. Heat the mixture in the beaker to 70 degrees C. Stir the mixture carefully.

4. When the mixture reaches 70 degrees C, remove the beaker from the water bath and add 2 g boric acid to it. Stir and let the mixture air cool slightly.

5. Add fragrance to the mixture and allow it to cool to room temperature.

6. Compare the product with the commercial brand and note below.

	Lab-Made Lotion	Commercial Lotion
Color		
Texture		
Covering Ability		

LAB EXPERIENCE 4.17 (Continued)

HAND LOTION

Questions:

1. How would you compare the scented with the unscented lotion?

2. What is the function of glycerol in the mixture?

3. How does the lab-made lotion compare with the commercial brand with respect to texture and covering ability?

4. How would you change the consistency to make it thicker or thinner?

5. Would you use it in place of the commercial brand?

ANTACIDS

Over-the-counter medications for the relief of stomach distress are taken by many people. Most of these products are antacids. To discuss these, we must define acids and alkalines (bases).

ACIDS AND ALKALINES

We've mentioned the term pH before and this would be a good time to describe what we have been talking about. The pH is an intensity factor describing the strength of acidity or alkalinity. The pH scale is based on the number of hydrogen ions that are in solution. The substance used to standardize the scale is water. The pH scale goes from 0 to 14; the midpoint, 7, is the pH of water, which is considered to be neutral. A pH of less than 7 has more hydrogen ions (H^+) than hydroxide ions (OH^-), and is considered to be acidic in nature. If the pH is above 7, then there are more hydroxide ions (OH^-) than hydrogen ions (H^+) present, and the substance is a base or alkaline.

The pH is measured by pH papers which are strips of paper impregnated with acid-base indicators. These indicators are chemical compounds which exhibit one color in an acid solution and a different color in a more alkaline solution. Litmus papers, which turn blue in a base and red in acid, are common examples. Universal indicator papers show a continuous change of color over a wide pH range, usually from very red for a pH of 1 to very blue for a pH of 14.

An acid can be produced by living organisms. For example, milk can be made sour by the action of bacteria. An acid will turn the dye called litmus from blue to red. An acid will neutralize an alkaline or base producing water and a salt. If you mix equal quantities of sodium hyroxide and hyrodchloric acid, you get water and sodium chloride (table salt). Some household acids are citric acid (lemon juice) and acetic acid (vinegar).

Some examples of bases are sodium hydroxide (NaOH) and potassium hydroxide (KOH). A base feels soapy when rubbed between the fingers.

In chemical terms, an acid is a substance which can donate a proton. The hydrogen ion (H^+) represents the proton an acid can release. A base is any substance which accepts protons.

ANTACID ACTION

Antacids are taken to neutralize excess stomach acid which is said to cause upset stomach and heartburn. All antacid medications are alkaline in nature and act upon the gastric juices. These juices consist of hydrochloric acid and the enzyme pepsin. Both are produced in the stomach as part of the digestive process.

Most antacids are made to dissolve slowly in the stomach so that carbon dioxide will be given off gradually as the antacid does its job.

Antacids contain aluminum hydroxide, calcium carbonate, sodium bicarbonate, and magnesium compounds. Although they all act on the excess acidity, some of them present problems. Aluminum hydroxide is a good antacid but tends to cause constipation. Sodium bicarbonate, or baking soda, is effective and quick acting but its antacid effect is quickly dissipated. Also, some people cannot consume large quantities of sodium. The magnesium compounds have a laxative effect. Calcium carbonate (chalk) is included because while it reduces excess acidity, it causes neither constipation nor diarrhea.

Consequently, a good antacid contains both aluminum and magnesium compounds along with the carbonates. These compounds are all insoluble in water and tend to coat and soothe the irritated lining of the stomach. They thereby increase comfort as well as generating carbon dioxide. The effervescence of the carbon dioxide allows the entrapped gas to be released. Although the gastric juices are normally acid and are neutralized by the antacid, they rapidly redevelop their acid content. The neutralization effect should relieve the discomforted individual.

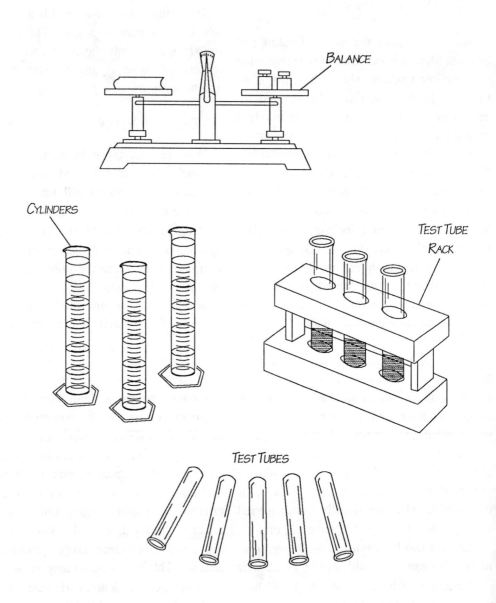

BALANCE

CYLINDERS

TEST TUBE RACK

TEST TUBES

LAB EXPERIENCE 4.18

ACIDS AND ALKALINES

Purpose: To determine how acid or alkaline these everyday substances are by performing the following lab experience.

Materials:

Test tubes   Vinegar (10% solution)
Test tube rack   Grapefruit juice
Stirring rods   Club soda (diluted half with water)
Universal pH paper   Ordinary shampoo (10% solution)
Graduated cylinders, 5 ml, 10 ml   Liquid laundry detergent (5% solution)
Distilled water   Household ammonia
5 150-ml Ehrlenmeyer flasks   Baking soda (10% solution)
2 50-ml beakers   Acetylsalicylic acid (Aspirin) tablet,
Rubber gloves   dissolved in 20 ml of distilled water
Safety glasses   Buffered acetylsalicylic acid tablet, dis-
Milk   solved in 20 ml of distilled water
Mortar and pestle   Test tube brushes
Glass marking pencils   Balance
Paper towels   Basin
Glassware detergent

Preparations:

1. To make a 10% vinegar solution, measure 10 ml of vinegar and place in an Ehrlenmeyer flask.   Add distilled water to the 100 ml marking of the flask.

2. To make 100 ml of a 10% shampoo solution, measure 10 ml of the shampoo and place in the Ehrlenmeyer flask.   Add distilled water to the 100 ml marking of the flask.

3. To make 100 ml of a 10% baking soda solution, weigh 10 g of sodium bicarbonate (baking soda).   Place in flask. Add a small amount of distilled water to dissolve the baking soda, and then add distilled water to the 100 ml marking.

4. To make 100 ml of a 5% laundry detergent solution, weigh 5 g of laundry detergent into a flask.   Add distilled water to the 100 ml mark.

Procedure:

1. Pour 2 ml of each of the substances into a separate properly labeled test tube.

2. Dip the stirring rod into a test tube containing one of the substances you are testing, and transfer a drop to a piece of pH paper.

LAB EXPERIENCE 4.18 (Continued)

ACIDS AND ALKALINES

3. Match the color of the moistened pH paper with the color chart on the pH paper dispenser. Record number.

4. Wash the stirring rod with water and dry thoroughly after each use. Continue the testing.

5. Complete the chart below.

Substances	pH
Vinegar	
Grapefruit juice	
Club soda	
Shampoo	
Laundry detergent	
Ammonia	
Baking soda	
Aspirin	
Buffered aspirin	
Milk	

Questions:

1. What does pH mean?

2. What is the pH of a neutral solution?

3. Would any of the solutions be considered to be neutral?

LAB EXPERIENCE 4.19

EFFECTS OF ANTACIDS

Purpose: To observe the neutralizing effect antacids have upon hydrochloric acid and to compare various brands of antacids.

Materials:

Test tubes
Test tube rack
3 to 4 brands antacids
3 10-ml graduated cylinder
2 200-ml dropper bottles
Balance
Phenolphthalein solution
Distilled water
Rubber gloves
Safety glasses
Glassware detergent
Paper towels

Universal pH paper
(100 ml) 1 M hydrochloric acid (HCl)
(100 ml) 1 M sodium hydroxide (NaOH)
(500 ml) 0.1 M hydrochloric acid (HCl)
(100 ml) 0.1 M sodium hydroxide (NaOH
Mortar and pestle
Stirring rods
Glass marking pencils
18 50-ml dropper bottles
Test tube brushes
Basin

Procedure:

Have students work in groups of 3. Weigh powdered antacids against a tablet
and establish a comparable dose. This lab is divided into two parts A and B.
Part A determines the pH level of a dose. Part B determines how well the
antacids neutralize hydrochloric acid as it relates to stomach juices.

Part A:

1. Place one antacid tablet or equivalent in each of three test tubes.

2. Add 10 ml of water to tube 1.
    Add 10 ml of 1 M hydrochloric acid to tube 2.
    Add 10 ml of 1 M sodium Hydroxide to tube 3.

3. What happens?

4. After the reactions have ceased, check the pH of each solution by
    dipping a stirring rod into each solution, placing a drop of solution on a
    piece of pH paper. Compare the result with the color chart on the pH
    container. Record in Step 5.

LAB EXPERIENCE 4.19 (Continued)

EFFECTS OF ANTACIDS

5. pH Tube 1: _____

   pH Tube 2: _____

   pH Tube 3: _____

Question:

   Which solution most closely resembles the conditions of the stomach?

Part B:

1. Read label of antacid package for recommended dosage.

2. Crush the recommended dosage of antacid tablet in a mortar and pestle and place into dropper bottle.

3. Add 100 ml of 0.1 M hydrochloric acid to the crushed tablet in the dropper bottle. Shake thoroughly till the tablet dissolves.

4. What happens?

5. Transfer 5 ml of the 0.1 M hydrochloric acid plus antacid mixture (from Step 3) into a test tube. Position over a piece of white paper.

6. Add 1 drop of phenolphthalein solution to the test tube. Is there any change in color of the solution? Yes ____ No ____. If the solution remains colorless, then it is acidic.

7. Now add 0.1 M sodium hydroxide, counting drops, to the test tube. Swirl contents of tube after each added drop.

8. When the first pink color appears and persists for 30 seconds after swirling, stop adding sodium hydroxide. You have reached the neutralization point where the excess hydrochloric acid (the acid not neutralized by the crushed antacid tablet) has been finally neutralized by the addition of a certain number of drops of sodium hydroxide or milliliters of NaOH. Record the number of drops added in Step 11.

9. This entire procedure may have to be repeated, at least once, so that you can catch the appearance of the first pink color.

LAB EXPERIENCE 4.19 (Continued)

EFFECTS OF ANTACIDS

10. Repeat the experiment with the other antacid products.

11. Complete chart. Note that 1 ml = 20 drops.

Brand	No. Drops of NaOH	No. ml of NaOH for Neutralization
1.		
2.		
3.		
4.		

Questions:

1. What is the relationship between the amount of NaOH added and the ability of the antacid to neutralize hydrochloric acid?

2. Is one product any more effective than another?

3. Do you agree with the advertising claims of each antacid product?

4. Phenolphtholein is liquid acid-base indicator. Can you see where the term pH comes from?

DRUGS — GENERIC vs BRAND NAME

In the U.S. all drugs, whether they are sold under their brand names or their generic names, must meet the same FDA standards for safety, strength, purity, and effectiveness. All drug manufacturers large or small, are subject to FDA inspection and must follow their Current Good Manufacturing Practice Regulations. This is why the FDA believes there is no significant difference in quality between generic and brand name drugs.

All drugs have a generic name, also called the "official" or "nonproprietary" name. A generic name is assigned to a drug when it appears that the drug has some medicinal value. Newly developed drugs are also given brand or trade names. Unlike generic names which usually are contractions of a complex chemical name, brand names generally are short, easy to remember, and often devised to suggest the therapeutic usefulness of the drug.

It is the brand name that is used to advertise a drug to the medical profession. The generic name must appear in advertising and in letters at least half as large as that of the brand name. Aspirin, for example, is the generic name in the U.S. for the leading nonprescription pain killer. Bayer and St. Joseph's are the brand names for different manufacturers' aspirin. Whether you buy a bottle of store brand aspirin or a name brand, there will be no difference in the pain killing quality of the medications. Any drug that claims to be aspirin must meet the official FDA standards for that drug. This same principle applies to prescription drugs.

It is a popular misconception that name brand drugs are produced only by large, well-known firms, while generic drugs are made by small, unknown companies. A small drug company can put a brand name on its products just as a large company can market a drug under its generic name. Further, many large drug firms distribute, under their own brand names, products that have been manufactured, packaged, and labeled by firms that make generic drugs. As a matter of fact, some manufacturers may make a drug and sell it under both a brand name as well as its generic name. Or, a drug firm may make the final dosage of its products from drugs purchased in bulk from other companies. All of this is well within the rules and regulations of the FDA. Since the name of the actual manufacturer of a drug does not have to appear on the product label, neither consumers nor pharmacists may be aware that a drug carrying the brand name of one company actually was made by another firm.

Before a new drug can be put on the market, the manufacturer must submit an application to FDA. It must include the results of tests carried out by the manufacturer in several phases: in the laboratory, on animals, and finally on human volunteers. The results must prove that the drug is safe and effective for its intended use. If the application is approved, the manufacturer may market the drug.

Because generics generally are cheaper than their brand name equivalents, purchasing is one way to help hold down the rising cost of medical care. Physicians should be asked to prescribe drugs by their generic names, and pharmacists should be permitted to fill prescriptions with the lowest cost version of the prescribed drug. In some cases the physician and pharmacist will want to use a brand they have experience with and trust, but in others they may be able to save you money by using a different brand.

PRESCRIPTION DRUGS

A prescription drug is any medicine that requires an Rx or prescription from a doctor. Prescription drugs may be sold only by licensed pharmacists. Drugs bought without a prescription are called patent medicines or over-the-counter (OTC) medicines.

Prescription drugs are generally more

potent than medicines available without a prescription. Should the doctor consider a medicine necessary and safe for continued use, the label will state it can be refilled.

When a doctor prescribes a medicine, ask him what the drug is supposed to do for you, what possible undesirable effects to watch for and how to handle them if they happen. Get his specific instructions for taking the drug. Besides asking questions, tell your doctor about any special drug problem you have, such as allergies or side effects from drugs taken in the past. Also tell him of any other medicines you may be using now. Any reaction to a drug should be reported to the doctor immediately. You should also ask him for the manufacturer's specification sheet for the drugs he is prescribing.

If you are taking medicines:

a. Don't drink alcoholic beverages without first asking the doctor whether the combination could be dangerous.

b. Don't stop taking a prescription drug just because you are feeling better and think you no longer need it. Follow the doctor's instructions.

c. Don't keep prescription drugs that are no longer needed. Clear out your medicine cabinet regularly and get rid of all medicines that are no longer needed.

d. Do read labels carefully for storing instructions. Some drugs should be kept cool and dry, others refrigerated. Always store medicines out of the reach of children.

A prescription is prescribed for you and only you. Don't share it with anyone else even if the symptoms seem to be the same. The medical problem might be entirely different, and the medication could be dangerous. Never take a medicine that "looks like" yours, always read the label to be certain you are taking the correct one.

Don't mix different pills in the same container.

DRUG/DRUG INTERACTION

Be cautious about taking several medicines at the same time. As factual information emerges about potentially dangerous drug interactions, the FDA requires that such information be indicated on the label that accompanies a nonprescription (OTC) medicine. They also require that labeling information be available to pharmacists and physicians for prescription drugs. The FDA publishes a monthly collection of data about such interactions.

Drugs interact in a number of ways. One drug may make another drug act faster or slower, or more powerfully or less powerfully than it normally would. One drug may change the effect another drug has on the body.

Frequently one drug acts on another by affecting the way it is absorbed, distributed, or broken down (metabolized) by the body. For example, assume that there is a circulatory problem which is the result of a blood clot in an artery or vein. The physician may prescribe an anticoagulant medicine — a medicine that "thins" the blood and thus helps dissolve the clot. If, at the same time, an antacid is being taken, even a nonprescription antacid, the anticoagulant could be absorbed at a slower rate than required in order to do its job properly. This could be a very dangerous situation.

The combination of anticoagulants and alcohol can be very serious. Although chronic alcohol abuse speeds up the rate at which the liver metabolizes the anticoagulant, and thereby reducing its effect, drinking a great deal of alcohol in a short period can slow down the rate of metabolism. This latter effect can magnify the impact of the anticoagulant to the point where the blood becomes so thin that it may be difficult to halt bleeding caused by an injury. Remember that alcohol is a drug.

One drug can also either inhibit or hasten the excretion of another drug from the body, and thus either exaggerate or reduce the effect of the drug. Prescription medicines are formulated on the basis of a normal level of acid in the urine (the pH of the urine). But certain nonprescription drugs such as antacids which contain ammonium chloride, sodium bicarbonate, or citrates, change the pH of the body. This can interfere with the beneficial impact of the prescription medicine.

Other drugs when combined produce unusual reactions. In these cases, the end result is greater than the sum of the parts. This type of action, in which the effects of two or more drugs are not simply added to each other but are multiplied, is called potentiation. Potentiation can greatly accelerate the helpful effect of a drug, as when the antibiotic trimethoprim is used to enhance the activity of the antibiotic sulfamethoxazole in combating certain infections. The combination is used to treat respiratory tract infections. However, potentiation also can be one of the most dangerous forms of drug interaction. For example, phenytoin (which is Dilantin) is used as an antiepileptic drug and when taken with small amounts of barbiturates may result in a faster clearance of phenytoin from the body. This could lead to lower blood levels of phenytoin, and result in seizures. A number of deaths of otherwise healthy persons have been reported which resulted from potentiation. The situation commonly occurs by mixing alcohol with sleeping aids, pain relievers, or tranquilizers.

Even commonly used nonprescription medicines can have potentiating effects. Acetylsalicylic acid greatly increases the blood thinning effect of oral anticoagulants. Therefore, a person who is taking such medication may risk hemorrhage if aspirin were used to alleviate a headache.

Another kind of drug reaction affects the body chemistry in a way that skews or confuses the results of diagnostic tests. For example, a laboratory test to determine a patient's calcium metabolism can be affected by excess use of laxatives. Also, large doses of vitamin C can produce false negative urinary glucose tests which can mask a diabetes condition. Because the words "drugs" and "medicine" mean the same thing, tell the physician what medications, prescription or over-the-counter, are being taken. No medicine is too insignificant to mention when the doctor is prescribing a medication.

Don't start taking a second drug unless the doctor knows about it. Tell the pharmacist, when he fills a prescription, what other drugs are being taken. A personal drug record could then be set up so that a possibly dangerous drug interaction can be avoided.

Read the label and remember that drugs have three names: (1) the chemical name, which is usually not given on the label; (2) the generic name, which is the official name for the drug; (3) the proprietary name or the trade-marked brand name for that drug. It is critical to remember that the warnings printed on labels give only the generic name, which in all probability will be different from the brand name. A single generic drug can be packaged under different brand names. Knowing the generic name for the prescription drug, and reading the label on nonprescription drugs, can keep the consumer from experiencing a drug interaction.

FOOD/DRUG INTERACTION

Foods can and often will increase or decrease the therapeutic effectiveness of many prescription and nonprescription drugs. It is only within recent times that this dangerous combination has come to the public's attention. A few drugs and their food reactions are mentioned here:

1. *Acetaminophen* — This is the same as Tylenol and Datril, and should not be eaten with crackers, dates, jelly and

other foods high in carbohydrates. These foods can slow the initial rate at which the drug is absorbed, and markedly increase the time it takes for the drug to act as a pain reliever or fever suppressant.

2. *Demeclocycline* — This is tetracycline. It should not be taken with milk, dairy products, or any food products high in calcium compounds. These foods inhibit the absorption of the drug. Antacids also significantly inhibit the absorption of tetracycline and should not be taken with the drug.

3. *Erythromycin* — This drug should not be eaten with acidic fruit juices, wines, syrups, or soft drinks. Acidic beverages promote the rapid breakdown of the drug in the stomach, and often decrease the antibacterial action of the drug.

4. *Iron Compounds (Ferrous Sulphate or Ferrous Chloride)* — These iron compounds are found in iron-fortified vitamins and should not be eaten with milk, eggs, cereals and dairy products. These foods significantly inhibit the absorption of iron through the formation of insoluble iron salts.

5. *Levodopa* — This is a component of Dopar and Larodopa. It should not be eaten with bacon, bran products, beef kidney and liver, lentils, pork, sweet potatoes, tuna or walnuts because these foods contain large quantities of Vitamin B_6 (pyridoxine). Foods high in pyridoxine impair the drug's ability to control Parkinson's disease for which it is prescribed.

6. *Phenytoin* — This drug is Dilantin and should not be taken with food flavor enhancers containing monosodium glutamate (MSG). The drug can enhance the rate of absorption of MSG which can increase the incidence of generalized weakness, a numbness at the back of the neck, and heart palpitations.

7. *Thyroid* — Any thyroid medication should not be eaten along with kale, cabbage, carrots, cauliflower, spinach, peas, peaches, brussel sprouts or turnips. These foods tend to inhibit thyroid hormone activity and interfere with the drug's activity.

ANTIHISTAMINES

There is an active campaign against drinking and driving — a very dangerous combination. An equally dangerous and lethal practice is the combination of driving after taking drugs. Many of the medicines we take to ease pain, reduce tension, or to combat a disease can interfere with an individual's ability to react quickly. They can cause drowsiness, dizziness, lightheadedness, or blurred vision.

Antihistamines are regularly taken for allergies, but they are also an integral component of cough remedies. Antihistamines, along with scopolamine, are components in daytime sedatives which are sold to combat "simple nervous tension." These ingredients in OTC products will calm you down and make you downright sleepy. Therefore, you shouldn't be operating machinery or driving if you are taking a sedative. Drugs such as Darvon and Demerol, Valium and Librium, and amphetamines which are pain killers, tranquilizers, and a group of weight reducing aids, respectively, can cause dizziness, drowsiness, visual disturbances, tremors, and uncoordinated muscle movements. These drugs and others of a similar nature can impair an individual's efficiency for as long as 14 hours. Taking the drug the night before can still affect the individual driving to work the next day!

The FDA's bulletin on "Self Medication" nicely sums up the rules to follow for your own safety:

1. Don't be casual about taking drugs.
2. Don't take drugs you don't need.
3. Don't overbuy and keep drugs for long periods of time.

4. Don't combine drugs carelessly.
5. Don't continue taking OTC drugs if symptoms persist.
6. Don't take prescription drugs not prescribed specifically for you.
7. Do read and follow directions for use.
8. Do be cautious when using a drug for the first time.
9. Do dispose of old prescription drugs and outdated OTC medications.
10. Do seek professional advice before combining drugs.
11. Do seek professional advice when symptoms persist or return.
12. Do get medical check-ups regularly.

PAIN RELIEVERS

Pain relievers or analgesics are heavily advertised. The commercial messages about brand-names' superiority, about self-medication, and the overall use of drugs are messages that we all must contend with. The questions arise as to how advertising has influenced our understanding of the over-the-counter medications. How informed are the self-medication decisions we make? How complete is the information in current pain-reliever ads and commercials? How can imcomplete information in ads make a brand-name pain reliever seem special? Incomplete information can hide the fact that a brand-name is really an acetylsalicylic acid or acetaminophen product.

ACETYLSALICYLIC ACID

This substance, acetylsalicylic acid (aspirin), has been around since the turn of the century helping people cope with their aches and pains. What is it? How does it work? Why does it work? Is it good or bad? These are some of the questions that will be discussed in the following paragraphs.

HISTORY OF ACETYLSALICYLIC ACID (ASPIRIN)

At first, the salts of salicylic acid were administered in a water solution, but this had a very disagreeable taste. The search for a more palatable form led to the discovery of acetylsalicylic acid, or aspirin, which was first sold by the German company Bayer in 1899. This company still owns the name Aspirin as a trademark worldwide. In the U.S., aspirin is the generic name for acetylsalicylic acid products. Aspirin is the most widely used drug in the world. However, aspirin's easy availability frequently leads people to underestimate both its effectiveness and, if used improperly, its potential for being very toxic and dangerous. It is more effective than most people realize.

It is well known that acetylsalicylic acid lowers fever temperatures rapidly, although it does not affect normal temperatures. During fever, acetylsalicylic acid dissipates the body's excess heat by increasing sweating and blood flow in the skin, thus lowering body temperature.

Acetylsalicylic acid, as a pain killer, does not lead to physical addiction as with other analgesics (or pain killers). Acetylsalicylic acid is effective, and less toxic than more powerful pain killers.

Acetylsalicylic acid works best on pain of mild to moderate severity, such as muscular aches and pains, backaches, toothache, and headache. Acetylsalicylic acid works at the site of the pain by two actions. First, it reduces the swelling that occurs at a site of injury or infection. Second, it directly blocks the pain-causing chemicals that the body releases at the site of an injury, which in turn act upon the pain nerves.

Any use of acetylsalicylic acid for aches and pains should be for a short period unless otherwise directed by a doctor.

Acetylsalicylic acid works well for arthritic pain. It also does something even more useful: it can reduce the inflammation in joint tissues and in surrounding structures. Damage to joints is the most difficult aspect of rheumatoid arthritis to manage. Any drug that reduces inflammation is important, for it can lessen or delay crippling. Acetylsalicylic acid's effectiveness in reducing inflammation also helps in the treatment of rheumatic fever. There are several new anti-inflammatory drugs for treating arthritis, but acetylsalicylic acid is much cheaper, and for most patients, at least as effective. Most physicians still consider acetylsalicylic acid the drug of first choice for rheumatoid arthritis.

Acetylsalicylic acid is readily absorbed from the stomach in whatever form it is taken. Its onset time varies from 10 to 45 minutes, depending upon what else is in the stomach and the form of the aspirin. Acetylsalicylic acid combined with sodium carbonate or some other buffering substance or a carbonated acetylsalicylic acid — one that fizzes — tends to be absorbed fastest. But dissolving acetylsalicylic acid in hot water doesn't speed up the rate of absorption by the body at all. Acetylsalicylic acid should always be taken with a full glass of water. The effect of a normal dosage will last for about four hours.

Many over-the-counter cold preparations contain acetylsalicylic acid, although it has no effect on viruses or bacteria. Thus, it won't cure a cold or the flu, or even shorten its duration. Acetylsalicylic acid will make the cold sufferer more comfortable by reducing the fever and relieving the headache and muscle aches. Gargles containing acetylsalicylic acid have no benefit at all for a sore throat.

There is some evidence that acetylsalicylic acid and large doses of vitamin C taken together may be more damaging to the stomach than acetylsalicylic acid alone. People with colds who want to take both should make sure the stomach is empty of acetylsalicylic acid before taking vitamin C, or use enteric-coated acetylsalicylic acid which doesn't dissolve in the stomach, but dissolves further down the digestive tract. It is important to understand that the excretion of large amounts of vitamin C in the urine can interfere with the excretion of acetylsalicylic acid from the body. This, in turn, would raise the levels of acetylsalicylic acid in the bloodstream.

HOW IT WORKS IN THE BODY

Aspirin appears to produce many of its effects by interfering with the body's production of prostaglandins, a specialized group of hormone-like compounds.

Prostaglandins occur in all body tissues and in many body fluids such as the blood, urine, and semen. The body's cells seem to create small amounts of prostaglandins in order to perform specific tasks, and then the prostaglandin breaks down and disappears. The prostaglandins perform a variety of functions. They stimulate the contraction of the smooth muscles of the uterus and the gastrointestinal tract; they promote conception; they regulate the transmission of nerve impulses; they inhibit the flow of gastric juices; they regulate blood pressure and affect clotting; they play a role in inflammation. Because prostaglandins can produce fever, can sensitize pain receptors, and can intensify inflammation, aspirin's antiprostaglandin action helps to explain some of its longstanding therapeutic benefits.

It is known that certain prostaglandins promote blood clotting. By interfering with the production of prostaglandins, aspirin may help reduce unwanted clots that contribute to heart attacks and strokes. Research is being done in this area to see if aspirin can be used in the prevention of heart attacks.

Along with the discoveries of new uses for aspirin, there is increasing evidence that it can cause side effects which may be serious. Many of these effects are gastrointestinal in nature. Aspirin may cause some bleeding of the stomach lining. In most cases this is painless and it is not related to symptoms of stomach distress. But when aspirin is taken over a long period, there is sometimes enough loss of blood to cause iron-deficient anemia.

A number of studies have confirmed the association in humans between regular aspirin consumption and chronic gastric ulcer. Aspirin, if not the cause of duodenal ulcers, certainly exacerbates them. Needless to say, anyone who already has an ulcer should should not take acetylsalicylic acid. Other studies have shown that buffering does not prevent injury to the stomach lining. Enteric coatings for aspirin (which would delay the absorption of acetylsalicylic acid until it reaches the intestine) do reduce damage to the stomach, and are less likely to cause ulcers and erosions in the stomach than would plain or buffered aspirin.

Acetylsalicylic acid definitely prolongs bleeding. It has been found that a pin prick wound will usually bleed for about two minutes, but a single dose of two regular 5 grain aspirin tablets doubles that bleeding time for the next four to seven days. In the normal individual this causes no problem. However, aspirin should be avoided by patients who are anticipating surgery, or have a vitamin K deficiency, or hemophilia. People taking drugs which thin the blood should avoid aspirin as should those with liver disease. Chewable aspirin should not be taken for at least seven days after a tonsillectomy or oral surgery unless directed by a doctor.

People with gout should also avoid taking OTC medications which contain aspirin because it can decrease the elimination of uric acid by the kidneys, thereby interfering with the action of certain gout medications. Aspirin enhances the effects of drugs used to lower the blood sugar, so diabetics should not take aspirin without consulting their physicians.

Studies have shown that pregnant women are another group who should avoid aspirin. There is some evidence that birth defects and infant mortality is linked to expectant mothers who took aspirin during their pregnancies. It is now disapproved for the entire period of pregnancy.

No one really knows how many people are allergic to acetylsalicylic acid. This allergy can appear at any time, and an absence of such an allergy is no guarantee that it can't happen in the future. A first reaction is rarely fatal, but people allergic to acetylsalicylic acid have to make a major effort to avoid the more than 200 products on the market that contain it. Acetylsalicylic acid when used properly, can be a valuable medication for the treatment of many conditions. However, every time you take it, remember it affects many biological functions in ways that are only moderately understood. It should not be taken unnecessarily or indiscriminately.

ANALGESICS

There are only three analgesics available in OTC preparations: aspirin, acetaminophen, and phenacetin. There are some differences between aspirin and acetaminophen as well as some risks. Aspirin may help to reduce inflammation and swelling; acetaminophen does not. Aspirin may cause some stomach bleeding; acetaminophen does not. Both however, are equally effective in reducing fever and relieving pain.

Phenacetin is suspected of being involved in kidney damage. Medications containing phenacetin have been banned in Canada, and in the United States they must carry a warning.

There are no ingredients in any of the OTC pain relievers that are any stronger or more effective than aspirin or acetaminophen.

What is the major difference between store-brand and name brand pain relievers? Price! Name brands may be several hundred times more expensive than store brands.

When a drug is described as being "effective and safe," what does it mean?

And what doesn't it mean? It does mean that the drug is capable of treating certain symptoms, but it doesn't mean that the drug will work all the time. It does mean that the drug, if used as directed on the label, is not likely to be harmful, but it doesn't mean that there are no side effects or risks involved in taking the drug.

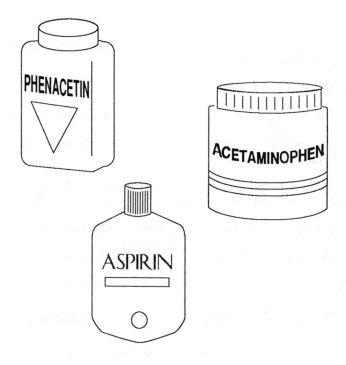

LAB EXPERIENCE 4.20

ACETYLSALICYLIC ACID (ASPIRIN)

Purpose: To look at various brands of acetylsalicylic acid and determine the pH and percentage of the compound in each brand.

Materials:

6 different acetylsalicylic acid brands, include store-brand and buffered aspirin
Universal pH paper
Stirring rod
Basin

Balance: to read 3 or 3 places
Mortar and pestle
1 50-ml beaker
Distilled water
Paper towels
Glassware detergent

Procedure:

NOTE: The tablets contain substances such as sugars or starches which are added to keep it from crumbling.

1.   Note the odor of each tablet.

2.   Note the number of grains per aspirin tablet from the label.

3.   Weigh each aspirin tablet to two or three places, and record weight (in grams) on chart.

4.   Calculate the number of grams of aspirin per tablet.   The conversion factor for converting the number of grains to grams is: 15 grains = 1g.

$$\frac{15 \text{ Grains}}{1 \text{ gram}} = \frac{\text{Number of Grains of Aspirin/Tablet}}{X \text{ grams}}$$

5.   Record the number of grams on the chart in Step 12.

6.   Calculate the percentage of aspirin in each product.

$$\frac{\text{Mass of aspirin (grams)}}{\text{Mass of single tablet}} \times 100\% = \% \text{ aspirin in tablet}$$

7.   Record percent of aspirin for each brand.

LAB EXPERIENCE 4.20 (Continued)

ACETYLSALICYLIC ACID (ASPIRIN)

8. Crush the aspirin tablet in the mortar and pestle, place in beaker, and add 20 ml of distilled water to it. Aspirin tablets are not soluble in water. They form a suspension when mixed with water.

9. Dip a stirring rod in the suspension and place a drop of the solution on a piece of pH paper.

10. Match the color of the pH paper with the color chart on the universal pH paper container. Record on chart.

11. Wash and dry beaker and stirring rod, and repeat experiment with each brand of aspirin.

12. Complete chart below.

Brand	Grains of Each Tablet (from label)	Mass of Tablet (grams)	Calculated Mass of Aspirin (grams)	% Aspirin in tablet	pH	Odor
1.						
2.						
3.						
4.						
5.						
6.						

LAB EXPERIENCE 4.20 (Continued)

ACETYLSALICYLIC ACID (ASPIRIN)

Questions:

1. Is there any difference in the amount of aspirin per tablet among the brands?

2a. Which is lowest?

 b. Which is highest?

3. Is there any difference in the percentage of aspirin per tablet among the brands?

4a. Which is lowest?

 b. Which is highest?

5. Did any of the aspirin tablets smell like vinegar? Acetylsalicylic acid tablets kept too long mix with the moisture in the air, and form acetic acid (vinegar). They should not be used.

6. Is there any difference in pH between regular and buffered aspirin?

7. Is there any difference in aspirin content between store brand and name brand aspirin?

8. Would it be economically worthwhile to buy extra large bottles of aspirin?

9. Calculate price per 100 tablets, and also the unit price per tablet.

	Brand	Price/100 Tablets	Price/Tablet
1.			
2.			
3.			
4.			
5.			
6.			

10. Would you change your brand?

LAB EXPERIENCE 4.21

HOME MEDICINE CABINET INVENTORY

Purpose: To keep in mind that the words drug, medicine or medication all mean the same thing. By reading labels, the consumer may avoid unnecessary or inappropriate medications.

Procedure:

Perform a medicine cabinet inventory and include age of the item.

Rx Drugs	Name Brand	Over-the-Counter Medicines			Date
		Store Brand	Generic Name	Brand Name	

Questions

1. Were you surprised at the number of medications found and date of purchase?

LAB EXPERIENCE 4.21 (Continued)

HOME MEDICINE CABINET INVENTORY

2. How many medications were identified by brand name rather than by generic name?

3. What label information was a surprise?

4. Were you familiar with the main ingredients in most of the medications?

5. What information, if any, might stop you from using a particular medication?

6. How many of the medications presently in your medicine cabinet are name-brands, and how many are store-brands?

7. Are you aware of the warnings and cautions for most of the medications you have used?

8. How informed do you think most consumers are about the OTC medications they use?

LAB EXPERIENCE 4.22

PAIN RELIEVER PRICE COMPARISON

Purpose: To perform a price comparison of OTC pain relievers. Because prices for the acetylsalicylic acid or acetaminophen pain relievers may vary widely, students should visit a local pharmacy and a local discount drug store in order that they may compare prices of name-brand and store-brand acetysalicylic acid and acetaminophen.

Procedure:

1. Select 4 to 6 different pain relievers, including a store-brand of aspirin and acetaminophen. Choose the same size or quantity for all the brands selected, if possible.

2. Compute the price per tablet (unit price), and also the price per two-tablet dose (if that would be the dose normally taken.)

3. Complete the following chart.

Brand	Acetylsalicylic Acid Compounds	Acetaminophen Compounds	Price Per Tablet	Price Per 2 Tablets
1.				
2.				
3.				
4.				
5.				
6.				

LAB EXPERIENCE 4.22 (Continued)

PAIN RELIEVER PRICE COMPARISON

Questions

1. What is the price difference between the most and the least expensive brands containing aspirin?

2. What is the price difference between the most and the least expensive brands containing acetaminophen?

3. If you have been using one of the above pain relievers, would the price difference make you think about changing to a store-brand rather than the name-brand?

4. What pain reliever claims provided only partial information? What information was missing?

5. What warnings do analgesic ads give?

6. From a consumer's point of view, do you think ads should warn consumers about an OTC medication's risks and side effects?

TEXTILES

While fashions may not be of interest to all of us, we all buy and wear clothing. To be assured of good value, it is important to know something about fibers, fabrics, and textiles.

In 1958, a law called the Textile Fiber Products Identification Act was passed in the United States. The law requires that an information tag be attached to all merchandise sold in the United States. This tag is to stay in place until the consumer removes it. The information tag includes the percentage by weight of each fiber used in the item, the name and address or registered identification number of the manufacturer, and the country of origin if the fabric has been imported. The Textile Fiber Products Identification Act was intended to give the consumer information about qualities to be found in the merchandise. In 1972, the Federal Trade Commission required another label giving care instruction be attached to merchandise. This was additional information for the consumer.

Before continuing with classifications and standards, let's define some terms that we need to use when talking about fabrics and textiles:

1. Fiber: The basic unit used to make textile yarns and fabrics.
2. Yarn: May be called thread. When used in weaving, the correct term is yarn.
3. Single yarn: A strand of threads or fibers grouped or twisted together.
4. Ply: A yarn composed of more than one single yarn twisted together.
5. Thread: A type of tightly twisted multi-ply yarn used for sewing and weaving.
6. Cloth: Refers to material or fabric formed by fibers that may be woven, knitted, braided, bonded or laminated.
7. Textiles: All materials that have been formed into yarns or fabricated into cloth.
8. Textures: The surface effect of a fabric, that is, the softness, dullness, luster, roughness or smoothness, of the surface.
9. Warp: The lengthwise yarns of a fabric.
10. Weft, woof, or filling: The crosswise yarns in woven cloth.
11. Sheeting: A cloth used mostly for bed sheets.

A fabric that has the same number of warp and filling threads per inch is said to be "square". The number of yarns per inch is a measure of quality. Usually, the higher the count the better the fabric. For example, the type numbers for sheeting is determined by adding the number warp and filling threads per inch. In the case of muslin sheeting, $72 + 68 = 140$ threads per square inch, or $80 + 80 = 160$ threads per square inch. A 160 thread count sheet would be smoother and softer than the 140 threads per square inch sheet.

A yarn count applies to wool, cotton and spun man-made yarns. A yarn count can be made on these fabrics using a device called a yarn counter. The student will have an opportunity to do this in the lab experience Determine the Thread Count of Different Fabrics. Keep in mind that the finer the yarn, the higher the count.

When performing the lab experience Determine the Strength of a Single Fiber and Thread, remember that a thread is made up of several tightly twisted fibers while a single fiber is just that—a single fiber. Can you guess which one would be stronger? Most fibers get weaker when wet. The exceptions are cotton and linen which get stronger when wet. Care must be taken when handling fibers which weaken when wet.

Fibers may be classified in several ways:
1. With a generic name as designated by the Textile Fiber Products Identification Act. This would apply to all manufactured man-made fibers such as acetate and polyester.
2. With the origin of the fiber, as to whether it is natural such as cotton and silk, or a man-made fiber such as acrylic and nylon.
3. With common names of fibers such as linen and wool, and trade names such as Orlon* and Lycra*.

The guidelines for textiles include:
1. The testing of fabrics for color fastness to sunlight, laundering, and perspiration.
2. The control of shrinkage. Years ago this process was called "Sanforizing."
3. Crease resistance.

Several associations including the National Retail Merchants, American Standards, and the Neighborhood Cleaners have developed washing and dry cleaning instructions for the consumer.

When examining fibers under the microscope, notice that cotton fibers are flat, twisted, and look like hollow tubes which have collapsed. Linen fibers are uneven in appearance with projections extending along the shaft. Wool fibers are scaly, and silk resembles bamboo. Acetate fibers are smooth, and viscose rayon fibers are smooth with stripes on them.

The illustrations that follow show the differences and similarities between some natural and man-made fibers.

*Registered trademark: E.I. DuPont Co., Inc, Wilmington, DE

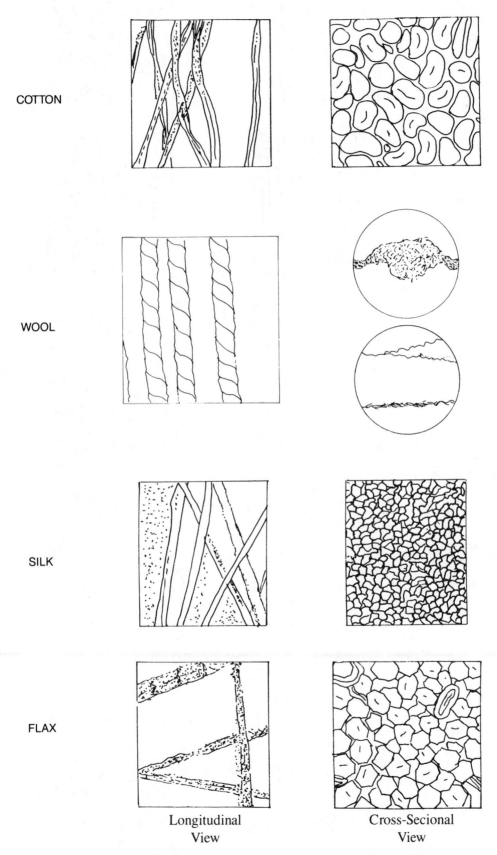

COTTON

WOOL

SILK

FLAX

Longitudinal
View

Cross-Secional
View

Figure 4.2 Illustrations of Natural Fibers

254

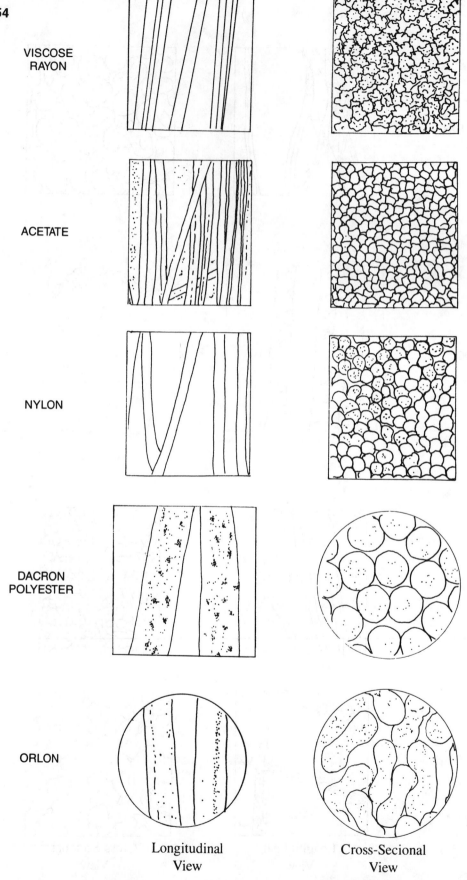

VISCOSE
RAYON

ACETATE

NYLON

DACRON
POLYESTER

ORLON

Longitudinal
View

Cross-Secional
View

Figure 4.3 Illustrations of Man-made Fibers

NATURAL FIBERS

Most fibers contain the chemical elements hydrogen, oxygen, and carbon. The animal fibers, silk and wool, contain these elements plus nitrogen while wool also contains sulfur. These animal fibers can be described as proteins while cotton and linen are cellulose plant fibers. Natural fibers—animal, vegetable, and mineral occur in nature while man-made fibers are made from basic raw materials.

The vegetable fibers, cotton and linen, are plant fibers. Cotton is a cellulose fiber that comes from the boll of the cotton plant. Its desirable properties include softness and the ability to absorb and evaporate body moisture. Cotton's strength depends on the yarn and weave of the fiber and it lends itself to a variety of finishes which can be made to resemble all the other fibers.

SILK

Silk is produced from wild and cultivated silk worms. Silk is the longest natural fiber and there are 3 grades of silk. "Pure silk" has no imperfections, it is very light in weight, and is the most expensive silk. "Spun silk" is short fibers spun together. It is of lower quality and should be less expensive than the highest grade "pure silk". "Silk noil" is the lowest quality of silk. It is the waste product of the next grade "spun silk" and must be labeled as "silk noil". It is imported from Japan, Italy, and China.

Silk burns slowly with a yellowish flame. It melts and fuses together and is self extinguishing. The odor is similar to burning feathers. Because silk is an animal fiber, the alkaline fumes change red litmus to blue. The residue appears as brittle, black beads which are easily crushed.

WOOL

Wool is the sheared hair of sheep. The Wool Products Labeling Act 1939, was passed to "protect producers, manufacturers, distributors, and consumers from substitutes and mixtures of unknown fibers in spun, knitted, woven, or otherwise manufactured wool products." The law requires that products containing wool, with the exception of upholstery and floor covering, have a label attached that specifies the kind of wool used in the product. The grades of wool are:

1. New: This is wool that is being used for the first time. Virgin wool is a phrase used by manufacturers for new wool.
2. Reprocessed: This refers to fibers reclaimed from fabrics which were never used. They are shredded back into fibers and then used to make other yarns and fabrics.
3. Reused: This refers to fibers that have been reclaimed from used fabrics. It is frequently used for interlinings and inexpensive articles where warmth is necessary.

Animal fibers such as merino from merino sheep, alpaca from domesticated llama, camel hair, cashmere from Indian or Chinese goat, and mohair from the Angora goat may be called wool. All wool products must be labeled with fiber content in percentage amounts.

Wool fibers burn slowly and curl away from the flame. The flame dies out when the wool is removed from the source of fire and the fibers smell like burning feathers. The residue looks like shiny, black, hollow beads which are easily crushed. The alkaline fumes turn red litmus blue. The fumes turn moist lead acetate paper brown-black indicating that wool contains sulfur.

COTTON

Cotton has many advantages. It can be made wrinkle-resistant, fire-resistant, mildew-resistant, water-repellent, wash and wear, and perspiration-resistant, mercerized for added strength and luster, and preshrunk. The disadvantage of cotton is that it is not elastic and creases readily. Also it will shrink unless preshrunk.

Cotton blends which mix percentages of cotton with synthetic fibers such as polyester, make for fabrics which have most of the desirable properties of cotton while reducing the disadvantages. Cotton is described as having more uses than any other textile fiber.

Cotton bursts into flames when brought near to a flame. It burns with a yellow glow, a smoky flame, and appears scorched. The odor is similar to burning paper, and the residue is a light gray ash. Since cotton is a plant product, the acid fumes turn blue litmus red.

LINEN

Linen is manufactured from the fibers of the flax plant. Its desirable properties include its coolness for its weight, its ability to readily absorb moisture, its strength, and ease of laundering. The disadvantages are that linen crushes and wrinkles easily. It can be made fire-resistant, water-repellent, wrinkle-resistant, perspiration-resistant, and given a wash and wear finish. Because there is a good deal of "synthetic linen" on the market, only a fabric made entirely of linen may be labeled "100% Linen". Any blends of linen and other fibers must be stated on the information tag.

Linen, also a plant fiber, burns in a manner similar to cotton. It bursts into flames, has a yellow glow, and smolders after being extinguished. The odor is similar to burning paper, and it leaves a small amount of fine gray ash. The acid fumes turn blue litmus red.

MINERAL FIBERS

The mineral fibers include asbestos and metal threads. Because asbestos is suspected of causing cancer when inhaled or ingested, it can no longer be used in fabrics despite its excellent fire-resistant quality.

Threads of gold and silver are drawn (pulled) from rods until they are very fine. They are frequently mixed with other fibers for flexibility and lower cost.

SYNTHETIC FIBERS

The man-made fibers such as rayon, nylon, polyester, and Orlon were first made as substitutes for natural fibers. They come under the regulation of the Federal Trade Commission and the Textile Fiber Products Identification Act which provide that the percent of man-made and natural fibers must be listed on the merchandise information tag.

Rayon is derived from cellulose. Nylon, polyester and Orlon are derived from petroleum. These synthetics are widely used in clothing, rugs and many types of home decorations. One advantage of these fibers is that fabrics made from them are moth resistant.

VISCOSE RAYON

Viscose rayon is made from cellulose. It has the strength of silk when dry but is weaker when wet. Rayon has the ability to absorb moisture which makes it comfortable to wear. It is receptive to dyes and blends well with many fibers. Rayon needs to be treated with resins for washability and requires a finish for wash and wear.

Rayon bursts into flames when ignited and burns rapidly with sputtering. It has an odor similar to burning paper, and leaves a small amount of a light, fluffy residue. The acid fumes will turn blue litmus to red.

ACETATE

Acetate is made from cellulose. Acetate has only fair wrinkle resistance and holds a crease poorly. It has limited wet strength. Because it does not absorb moisture readily, it dries quickly. It tends to accumulate static electricity. Fabrics made of acetate do not pill.

Acetate fibers melt and burn rapidly giving off small sparks. The odor is reminiscent of vinegar, and the residue consists of irregularly-shaped beads that do not crush easily. Its fumes change blue litmus to red.

NYLON

Nylon is made from coal, water and air. Nylon is very strong and resists abrasion and wrinkling well. It's low moisture absorbancy make nylon fabric easy to wash and dry. This property often makes it uncomfortable to wear. Nylon resists crushing, holds it shape, and is light in weight. It takes dyes well.

Nylon melts and drips while burning. The smoke is white but not sooty. The burning odor is similar to celery, and it leaves a residue bead which is sticky while hardening. Nylon's alkaline fumes change red litmus to blue.

DACRON* POLYESTER

Polyester is made from petroleum, coal, air and water. Some good qualities of polyester include its outstanding wrinkle-resistance and resiliency, wash and wear ability, the ability to blend with other fibers, strength and resistance to abrasion. A disadvantage is that oil and grease stains tend to cling to the fibers.

Polyester burns slowly and melts producing a dark and sooty smoke. It usually is self-extinguishing. When burning, it produces a "chemical" odor and leaves a hard black or dark brown bead.

ORLON

Orlon is a trademark name for acrylic fibers and is a synthetic substitute for wool. Orlon is light in weight although it provides excellent warmth. It is colorfast, resistant to moths and sunlight, and possesses good wash and wear qualities.

Orlon ignites readily, burns rapidly, smokes, sputters, and burning pieces may fall away. It has an acidic odor when burning, and leaves a black, gummy, brittle, irregular bead.

---

* Registered trademark: E.P. DuPont Co., Inc, Wilmington, DE

LAB EXPERIENCE 4.23

DETERMINE THE THREAD COUNT OF DIFFERENT FABRICS

Purpose: To recognize different textile materials according to thread count.

Materials:

Magnifying lens, 1 per student
Yarn counter, 1 per pair of students
5 cm square swatches of labeled cotton fabrics including:
    Gingham
    Broadcloth
    Percale 180 thread count
    Percale 200 thread count
    Muslin 120 thread count
    Muslin 160 thread count

Procedure:

1. Using the yarn counter, count the number of threads per square inch of warp and woof (weft) of each sample and record in chart below.

2. Using the magnifying lens, examine and draw each of the fibers present in the warp and woof. Sketch each fiber in chart below.

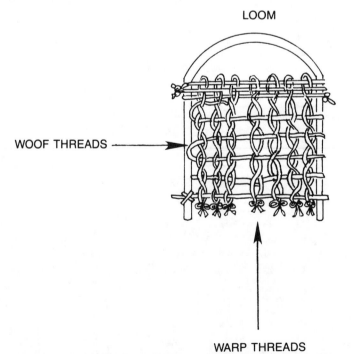

Figure 4.4 Identifying Warp and Woof (Weft) Threads

LAB EXPERIENCE 4.23 (Continued)

DETERMINE THE THREAD COUNT OF DIFFERENT FABRICS

3. Complete the chart.

Fabric	Thread Count per Inch		Sketch of Each Fiber
1.	Warp		
	Woof		
2.	Warp		
	Woof		
3.	Warp		
	Woof		
4.	Warp		
	Woof		

Questions:

1. Describe the apparent characteristic of each fabric.

2. Do you consider them to be tightly or loosely woven?

3. Do the two types of percale appear to be woven equally tight? Why?

4. Do the two types of muslin appear to be woven equally tight? Why?

5. For what purposes would a closely woven fabric be desirable?

6. Is there any advantage to loosely woven cloth? Name some examples.

LAB EXPERIENCE 4.24

DETERMINE THE STRENGTH OF SINGLE FIBERS AND THREADS

Purpose: To determine the strength of single fibers as opposed to single threads.

Materials:

Double pan balance	Labels
Gram masses (weights)	Labeled samples of washed types
from 1 gram to 1 kilogram	of cotton (10 cm x 5 cm) including:
Ring stand	Gingham
Overflow bucket with handle	Percale 180 thread count
Scissors	Percale 200 thread count
Sponge pads 12 cm x 12 cm x 1 cm	Broadcloth
Sewing threads	Muslin 120 thread count
of same diameter of 6 different kinds	Muslin 160 thread count
Masking tape	
Metric ruler	

Procedure:

Part A: Testing Individual Fibers

1. Separate a single thread from a labeled swatch and untwist it to get an individual fiber. Repeat for each swatch but do not mix them up.

2. Pull each fiber to see which ones break most readily. Record on chart below.

3. Soak swatches in room temperature water overnight.

4. Repeat Steps 1 and 2.

5. Record results on chart below.

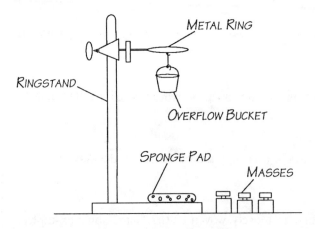

LAB EXPERIENCE 4.24 (Continued)

DETERMINE THE STRENGTH OF SINGLE FIBERS AND THREADS

Fibers	Relative Strength of Single Fibers	
	Dry	Wet
Gingham		
Percale 180		
Percale 200		
Broadcloth		
Muslin 120		
Muslin 160		

Part B: Testing Individual Threads

1. Cover the metal ring of the stand and the handle of the overflow bucket with masking tape. This is to keep the sewing thread from being rubbed when it experiences excessive weight exerted upon it.

2. Attach the metal ring close to the top of the stand.

3. Weigh the overflow bucket.

4. List and number six kinds of thread. Use the number as reference in the chart below.

   1. _____

   2. _____

   3. _____

   4. _____

   5. _____

   6. _____

5. With scissors, cut a 50 cm length of one of the sewing threads.

6. Tape one end of thread to the metal ring of the ring stand and wind the thread 4-5 times around the tape covering the metal ring.

LAB EXPERIENCE 4.24 (Continued)

DETERMINE THE STRENGTH OF SINGLE FIBERS AND THREADS

7. Pull the free end of the thread through the ring of the ring stand and gently raise the bucket until the bottom is approximately 10 cm above the ring stand base. Wind the thread around the ring and tape the thread so that it cannot slip.

8. Measure the distance from the bottom of the bucket to the table and record on chart below. It should be approximately 10 cm.

9. Place a sponge pad under the overflow bucket to cushion the falling bucket.

10. Gently add the masses to the bucket, one at a time, until the thread breaks. After each mass is added:

    a. Record mass added on lines 2 through 7 on chart below.

    b. Record distance from bucket to table on lines 9 through 14 on chart below.

11. Determine the total mass that caused the thread to break. Include the mass of the bucket and record on the chart below.

12. Repeat the experiment with other threads.

13. With scissors, cut 50 cm lengths of thread samples and label them. Do not pull thread to break it.

14. Soak threads overnight in room temperature water.

15. Repeat Steps 5 through 12 using wet threads.

LAB EXPERIENCE 4.24 (Continued)

DETERMINE THE STRENGTH OF SINGLE FIBERS AND THREADS

	Threads											
	Distance (cm) Dry						Distance (cm) Wet					
	1	2	3	4	5	6	1	2	3	4	5	6
1 Mass of Bucket (g)												
Added Masses (g)												
2												
3												
4												
5												
6												
7												
Distance of Bucket to Table												
8 —Empty												
—After Each Mass												
9												
10												
11												
12												
13												
14												
Total Mass to Cause Break												
Total Distance Stretched												

LAB EXPERIENCE 4.24 (Continued)

DETERMINE THE STRENGTH OF SINGLE FIBERS AND THREADS

Questions:

1. Did any dry threads stretch before breaking? Which ones and how much?

2. Did soaking in water have any effect on the thread samples?

3. About how much more did the wet threads stretch than the dry ones?

LABORATORY EXPERIENCE 4.25

IDENTIFY ANIMAL, VEGETABLE, and MANMADE FIBERS — VISUAL TEST

Purpose: To examine under the microscope various fabrics made of animal, vegetable, and manmade fibers, and learn to identify them.

Materials:

2-power microscopes, 1 per pair of students
Labels
Swatches of the following fabrics
    (if possible they should be white):

Cotton	Acetate*
Linen	Viscose Rayon*
Wool	Dacron polyester*
Silk	Nylon*
	Orlon*

Procedure:

1. Label each fabric swatch.

2. Pull a 7 cm thread out of each swatch of fabric. Keep it with the swatch.

3. Untwist the thread to obtain several single fibers.

4. Examine each fiber with the naked eye, especially the ends of the broken fibers. Note if the end is smooth cut or jagged.

5. Place a few fibers of one material on a microscope slide. Moisten the fibers slightly so that they lie flat.

6. Examine each fiber under the high power of the microscope. Be sure you have single fibers of each material and not a thread made up of several fibers twisted together.

LABORATORY EXPERIENCE 4.25 (Continued)

IDENTIFY ANIMAL, VEGETABLE, and MANMADE FIBERS — VISUAL TEST

7. Complete the chart below:

Kind of Material	Description of Fiber as Seen Under Microscope	Drawing of Fiber	Condition of Fiber End
Cotton			
Linen			
Wool			
Silk			
Acetate*			
Viscose rayon*			
Dacron polyester*			
Nylon*			
Orlon*			

* Trade names: E. I. DuPont de Nemours & Co., Inc., Wilmington, DE.

Questions:

1. When you take a garment to the dry cleaners, why is it advisable to tell the cleaner what kind of material is in the garment?

2. What facts should you look for on the labels of garments you buy?

3. What is the relationship between the fiber and the feel of the cloth?

4. How would you describe the difference between the vegetable fibers (cotton and linen)?

5. How would you describe the difference between the animal fibers (wool and silk)?

LABORATORY EXPERIENCE 4.25 (Continued)

IDENTIFY ANIMAL, VEGETABLE, and MANMADE FIBERS — VISUAL TEST

. What are some similarities between manmade fibers?

. Why does linen become very soft after many washings?

Suggested Activities:

Library research

. What is the process that converts the linen plant to linen cloth?

. How is the cotton plant converted to cotton fabric?

. What is the difference between long staple cotton and short staple cotton, and how is each used?

LAB EXPERIENCE 4.26*

IDENTIFY ANIMAL, VEGETABLE, and MANMADE FIBERS — SMELL TEST

* TEACHER DEMONSTRATION

Purpose: To identify animal, vegetable, and manmade fibers by direct burning and by testing vapors released in decomposition.

Materials:

Bunsen burner
Forceps or tweezers
Matches
10-ml Test tubes
Test tube holders
Test tube racks
Safety glasses
Plexiglass shield
Scissors

10 3-inch Petri dishes
Filter paper
Solution of lead acetate
Red and blue litmus paper
Marked swatches of
   the following washed fabrics:

Cotton	Acetate**
Linen	Viscose rayon**
Wool	Dacron polyester**
Silk	Nylon**
	Orlon**

SAFETY CAUTIONS:

1. Place plexiglass shield between you and the experiment.

2. Wear safety glasses.

3. Hold test tube away from face.

4. Avoid breathing the fumes.

5. Remove all unnecessary flammable material from work area.

6. Wear lab coat to protect clothing.

Procedure:

Part A: Burning in Direct Flame

1. Cut fabrics in pieces measuring 2.5 cm square and label them. Cut sufficient fabric for Parts A and B.

2. Using forceps or tweezers, hold a piece of fabric in contact with the flame of the Bunsen burner until it ignites.

3. Once it is burning well, place the burning fabric in a petri dish and let it burn out.

LAB EXPERIENCE 4.26* (Continued)

IDENTIFY ANIMAL, VEGETABLE, and MANMADE FIBERS — SMELL TEST

4. In the chart below note:

a. the way the fabric burns

b. how fast or slow the fabric burns

c. the amount and kind of residue that remains after burning

d. any obvious odor

e. keep the dish and contents until the end of the experiment to compare with other samples.

5. Repeat Steps 2 through 4 for each fabric.

Part B: Destructive Decomposition

1. Using fabric cut in Part A, place a piece of material in a dry test tube.

2. Cut filter paper into strips 1 cm by 4 cm .

3. Turn the mouth of the test tube slightly downward and heat the test tube over a Bunsen burner flame until fumes are generated.

4. With forceps or tweezers, dip a piece of filter paper into a solution of lead acetate.

5. Hold this saturated paper in the opening of each test tube as fumes are being given off. Note any color change that occurs to the paper.

6. In turn, hold a piece of moist red litmus paper and a piece of moist blue litmus paper in the fumes. Once again, note any color change on the litmus papers and record on chart below.

7. Note the appearance of the sample.

8. Repeat Steps 1 through 7 for each piece of fabric.

LAB EXPERIENCE 4.26* (Continued)

IDENTIFY ANIMAL, VEGETABLE, and MANMADE FIBERS — SMELL TEST

	Cotton	Linen	Wool	Silk	Acetate**	Viscose Rayon**	Dacron Poly-ester**	Nylon**	Orlon**
Rate of Burning									
Odor Produced									
Kind of Flame									
Lead Acetate									
Litmus: Red									
Blue									
End Product Produced									

** Trademark of E.I. DuPont Co., Inc., Wilmington, DE.

Questions:

1. What instrument may be used to identify various textiles?

2. What does the odor produced by burning fibers indicate?

3. Name three elements that most fibers contain.

4. Animal fibers contain a group of compounds known as _____.

5. What substance collects in the cool portion of the test tubes?

6. What effect do the fumes have on the lead acetate paper?

LAB EXPERIENCE 4.26* (Continued)

IDENTIFY ANIMAL, VEGETABLE, and MANMADE FIBERS — SMELL TEST

7. What effect do the fumes have on red litmus paper?

8. What effect do the fumes have on blue litmus paper?

9. What chemical elements are to found only in animal fibers?

10. How do the residues in Part A differ from those in Part B?

11. In Part B, did the fabrics really burn?

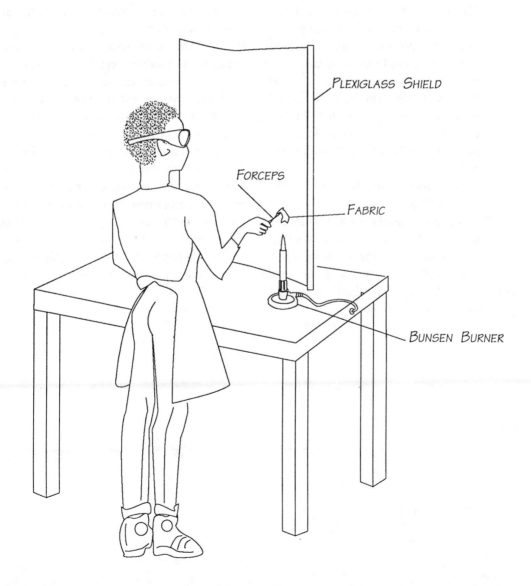

DYES

Natural dyes have been used for thousands of years. People used berries, leaves, minerals, insects and shellfish to color and beautify their surroundings and clothing.

In the last hundred years, chemists have created many beautiful colors. Some of these synthetic dyes resist sunlight, bleaches and detergents better than do the natural dyes.

In the Textile Dyeing experiment, the student will have an opportunity to color different fabrics with dyes and note the results. Some definitions might be helpful before we proceed:

1. Mordant: A chemical substance which unites with a dye making it colorfast or more able to adhere to cloth.

2. Direct dye: Produces colorfastness on cloth without the use of a mordant. Wool and silk may be dyed directly with malachite green and fuchsin. Cotton and other cellulose derived fibers may be dyed directly with Congo red.

3. Colorfastness: The ability of a dye to resist fading.

The type of dye used on a textile depends upon the color desired and the kind of textile. What is the advantage in using a mordant before the dye? Dyes may be made colorfast by the use of mordants. A mordant give permanence to color.

INKS

With the invention of writing, it became apparent that the written word needed to be preserved. A substance had to be created and a permanent dye called ink came about.

Synthetic dyes derived from coal tar are used in the manufacture of ink. Coal tar is a black gummy substance which is a by-product in the manufacture of coke. All of the commercial dyes and inks on the market today are made from either coal tar or are chemical combinations such as you will use in the lab experiences to follow.

The student will have another opportunity to remove stains. This time the stains will be ink stains. Bleaches are compounds that contain either oxygen or chlorine, or both. These compounds react with colored materials to produce colorless products.

Paper chromatography is a technique for analyzing the colored components of ink. It is a method of separating and identifying the composition of the mixture.

The chemical compounds or pigments that make up the ink are dissolved in the water, and are carried up the filter paper. Since these pigments are chemically different from each other, they are separated out and deposited at different levels as the water climbs the paper. It is then possible to determine the number of components in ink.

LAB EXPERIENCE 4.27

TEXTILE DYEING

Purpose: To dye different kinds of fabrics using a variety of dyes.

Materials:

Hot plate	White cotton cloth
Hot mitts	White woolen cloth
Safety glasses	Distilled water
24 25-ml Test tubes	Mild laundry detergent
Test tube holders	Congo red solution
Test tube racks	Malachite green solution
6 1000-ml Beakers	Fuchsin solution
4 250-ml Beakers	3 or 4 packages of
500-ml Beaker	commercial dyes (Tintex, etc.)
100-ml Beaker	Tartar emetic solution
3 10-ml Graduated cylinders	(potassium antimony tartrate)
50-ml Graduated cylinder	Tannic acid solution
Glass rods	100 ml Aluminum sulfate solution
Scissors	100 ml Ammonium hydroxide solution

Note: See Teachers Manual for preparation of solutions.

Procedure:

Part A: Preparation of Cloth

1. Cut 8 pieces of cotton cloth and 8 pieces of woolen cloth 2.5 cm square.

2. To remove the sizing, grease, and dirt, place 7 pieces of cotton in a 1000-ml beaker containing 200 ml of tap water to which has been added 2 g of mild laundry detergent.

3. Boil for 5 minutes, remove the cloth pieces and rinse them thoroughly in cool tap water.

4. Repeat Steps 2 and 3 using 7 pieces of wool.

5. Leave 1 piece of cotton and 1 piece of wool unwashed for comparison purposes.

Part B: Direct Dye Method

1. Put 10 ml of Congo red solution into each of 2 clean labeled test tubes.

2. Place a piece of washed cotton cloth into one of the test tubes and a piece of washed wool cloth into the other test tube.

3. Put 10 ml of malachite green solution into each of two clean labeled test tubes.

LAB EXPERIENCE 4.27 (Continued)

TEXTILE DYEING

4. Place a piece of washed cotton cloth into one of the test tubes and a piece of washed wool cloth into the other test tube.

5. Put 10 ml of fuchsin solution into each of two clean labeled test tubes.

6. Place a piece of washed cotton cloth into one of the test tubes and and a piece of washed wool cloth into the second test tube.

7. Place the six test tubes into a 1000-ml beaker half filled with tap water and put on hot plate.

8. Boil for 8 minutes. Make certain that the cloths remain completely covered by the solutions.

9. Remove test tubes from the boiling water bath, and remove the cotton and wool cloths from the test tubes using a different glass rod for each color.

10. Drain off the dye solutions.

11. Rinse the cloths thoroughly with cool tap water until there is no visible color in the rinse water.

12. Examine the cloths and compare the cotton and wool cloths from each dye color. In each color group, which cloths appear to have absorbed the most dye? Overall, which type of cloth appears to have absorbed the most dye? Record on chart below.

13. Air dry the samples and save.

Part C: Test for Colorfastness

1. Place each color sample of cotton cloth from Part B Step 13 into a 500-ml beaker containing 100 ml of cold water and stir vigorously with a glass rod.

2. If the water remains colorless, then the cloth is colorfast.

3. Doublecheck for colorfastness by pouring some of the water into a clean test tube, hold the test tube vertically over a piece of white paper, and look directly into the water.

4. Air dry the cotton cloths and paste them on the chart below.

5. Repeat Steps 1 through 4 using the wool cloths.

LAB EXPERIENCE 4.27 (Continued)

TEXTILE DYEING

Part D: Use Mordant Antimonyl Tannate in the Dyeing Process

1. Place 2 pieces of clean white cotton cloth and 2 pieces of clean white woolen cloth in a 250-ml beaker containing 50 ml of tannic acid solution.

2. Boil gently for 3 to 4 minutes.

3. Remove the pieces of cloth from the solution and squeeze out the excess water. DO NOT RINSE THEM.

4. Put 50 ml of tartar emetic solution in a 100-ml beaker and place on the hot plate to warm. Place the same 4 pieces of cloth from Step 1 and place into this beaker.

   Note: The combination of tartar emetic and tannic acid produces the mordant antimonyl tannate.

5. Stir thoroughly. Be sure the samples of cloth are submerged, and allow to stand for 1 minute.

6. Remove and rinse the cloths in tap water.

7. Allow the cloths to air dry. They are now mordanted with antimonyl tannate.

8. Fill, about half full, two clean test tubes with a cold solution of the dye malachite green.

9. Place a sample of cotton cloth into one of the test tubes and a sample of wool cloth into the other test tube.

10. Fill, about half full, two clean test tubes with a cold solution of fuchsin dye.

11. Place one sample piece of cotton cloth and a sample of wool cloth into each of the test tubes.

12. Place the 4 test tubes in a 1000-ml beaker half full of tap water on the hot plate and heat the contents to boiling. Allow to stand 5 to 6 minutes in the boiling water.

13. Remove the cloths, rinse them thoroughly in running water and allow to air dry.

14. Test for colorfastness as in Part C.

15. When the samples are dry, paste them in the chart below.

LAB EXPERIENCE 4.27 (Continued)

TEXTILE DYEING

Part E: Use the Mordant Aluminum Hydroxide in the Dyeing Process

1. Place 2 clean cotton and 2 clean wool samples in a 1000-ml beaker and cover with a solution of aluminum sulfate. Boil the contents for 4 to 5 minutes.

2. Remove the pieces of cloth with a glass rod and squeeze out the excess liquid.

3. Place the pieces of cloth into a second 1000-ml beaker and cover them with a solution of dilute ammonium hydroxide. Heat gently for 5 minutes. Remove the cloths with glass rod, and rinse thoroughly in cold water. Let dry. They are now mordanted with aluminum hydroxide.

   Note: The combination of ammonium hydroxide and aluminum sulfate produces the mordant aluminum hydroxide.

4. Fill two clean test tubes half full with malachite green dye and place a sample of cotton into one test tube and a sample of wool into the other test tube.

5. Fill two more clean test tubes half full with fuchsin dye and place a sample of cotton in one test tube and a sample of wool into the other test tube.

6. Allow the four samples of cloth to remain in the cool dye solutions for half an hour. Do not heat.

7. Use a clean glass rod or clean it before removing the cloth samples from the dye solutions. Rinse each cloth thoroughly in cold water.

8. Test for color fastness as in Part C, and allow to air dry.

LAB EXPERIENCE 4.27 (Continued)

TEXTILE DYEING

9. Paste the samples in the chart below.

Part B: Step 12

Fabric	Malachite Green	Congo Red	Fuchsin
Cotton			
Wool			

LAB EXPERIENCE 4.27 (Continued)

TEXTILE DYEING

Part C: Step 4

Fabric	Malachite Green	Congo Red	Fuchsin
Cotton			
Is it colorfast?			
Wool			
Is it colorfast?			

LAB EXPERIENCE 4.27 (Continued)

TEXTILE DYEING

	Part D		Part E	
	Mordanted with Antimonyl Tannate		Mordanted with Aluminum Hydroxide	
	Malachite Green	Fuchsin	Malachite Green	Fuchsin
Cotton				
Is it colorfast?				
Wool				
Is it colorfast?				

Part F: Commercial Dyes

1. Look at the directions on the packages of commercial dyes. Note the kinds of fabrics they may be used on.

2. Do these dyes contain mordants?

3. If you use dyes at home, why is it necessary to know the kind of material being dyed?

Questions:

1. What is the difference in colorfastness between nonmordanted fabrics and mordanted fabrics?

2. What are acid and alkaline dyes?

LAB EXPERIENCE 4.27 (Continued)
TEXTILE DYEING

3. Why must fabrics be thoroughly cleaned before dyeing?

4. Define the terms :

   a. mordant

   b. direct dye

   c. indirect dye

   d. vegetable dye

   e. coal tar dye

5. Which of the cloths, cotton or wool, absorb the most dye?

6. What is meant by a commercial all-purpose dye?

Suggested Activities:

Activity A: Make Vegetable Dyes

This requires boiling the vegetables in small quanties of water and then reducing the liquid to strengthen the color. The resulting solutions are suitable for dyeing fabrics and can be used to color food.

Red Dye:

1. Wash 2 to 3 unpeeled beets, and cut into 1/2 inch cubes.

2. Place the pieces in a beaker with sufficient water to cover the beets.

3. Place beaker and contents on a hot plate and boil the beet cubes for 1/2 hour, making certain that the water level continues to cover the pieces.

4. After 1/2 hour, remove beets from beaker. Allow the liquid to cool and settle so that solid particles present may settle out of solution.

5. Carefully pour the liquid into a suitable sized beaker and heat without boiling until the contents of the beaker is reduced by half.

LAB EXPERIENCE 4.27 (Continued)

TEXTILE DYEING

6. The solution is now ready to be used to dye cloth. The red coloring is due to a combination of iron and magnesium compounds.

Green Dye:

1. Place 1/2 pound of washed spinach in a beaker with sufficient water to cover the vegetable.

2. Boil for 4 to 5 minutes.

3. Pour the spinach liquid and solids through a filter into another beaker. Save the liquid.

4. Scrape spinach and other solid material into a clean beaker and cover with 2 to 3 cm of ethyl alcohol.

5. Place the beaker with the spinach from Step 4 into a larger beaker containing 5 to 6 cm of water.

6. Put the beakers on a hot plate and heat water until it just begins to bubble. Keep the heat low so that the alcohol in the small beaker does not boil. CAUTION: ALCOHOL VAPOR IS HIGHLY FLAMMABLE!!!!

7. Stir and mash the spinach with a glass rod.

8. After 15 minutes, filter the mashed spinach liquid and vegetable into a clean beaker. Save the liquid.

9. If the vegetable still has green coloring, scrape the solids from the filter paper back into the warm alcohol, and repeat Steps 6, 7, and 8.

10. When as much green coloring as possible has been removed from the spinach, combine the "saved" liquids from Steps 3 and 8, and allow to stand for 24 hours so that the alcohol evaporates.

11. The solution is now ready to be used to dye cloth. The green coloring is the chlorophyll extracted from the spinach.

Activity B: Tie Dyeing

1. Prepare a one meter square piece of cotton, as in Part A, to remove all sizing, grease, and dirt.

2. Using the direct dye method, as described in Part B, prepare 2 or 3 dyes.

LAB EXPERIENCE 4.27 (Continued)
TEXTILE DYEING

3. Cut 4 or 5 pieces of cotton string 15 cm long for tieing cloth.

4. Pick up the cotton square at its center and allow it to hang freely.

5. About 10 cm from the center of the dropped cloth, tie the cloth with cotton string. Continue to tie the cloth every 10 cm thereby making a number of separate sections as shown below.

6. Pour a dye solution into a 1000-ml beaker. If available, use several different dyes each in its own beaker.

7. Dip each section of the cloth, one at a time, into a different colored dye.

8. Rinse throughly, remove the strings, and allow to dry.

9. A pattern of colored concentric circles will result as shown below.

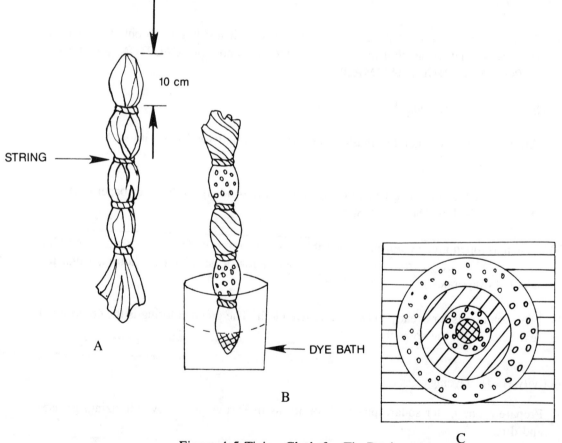

Figure 4.5 Tieing Cloth for Tie Dyeing

LAB EXPERIENCE 4.28

MAKING INK

Purpose: To learn how to prepare blue-black ink.

Materials:

Balance	White paper
2 25-ml Test tubes	Distilled water
Corks to fit test tubes	Ferrous sulfate
Test tube rack	Tannic acid
Glass rods	Blue dye
Pencil	Household chlorine bleach

Procedure:

Part A: Basic Ink

1. Label a test tube FS. Add 10 ml of distilled water and dissolve 2 grams of ferrous sulfate in it. Place in test tube rack.

2. Dip a glass rod in the solution and use it to print your name on a piece of white paper. Using a pencil, identify the paper.

3. Label a second test tube TA. Add 10 ml of distilled water and dissolve 2 grams of tannic acid in it. Place in test tube rack.

4. Dip a clean glass rod in the solution and use it to print your name on a second piece of white paper. Using a pencil, identify the paper.

5. Set the signature papers aside for 3 to 4 days.

6. Cork the test tubes and save both solutions for Part B.

Questions:

1. What is the color of the ferrous sulfate solution?

2. What is the color of the tannic acid solution?

3. Is there any insoluble sediment in either of the solutions?

4. Which one?

LAB EXPERIENCE 4.28 (Continued)

MAKING INK

5. Can you read your name just after the liquid has dried on the white paper?

6. After 2 to 3 days, can you read your name on the white paper? Which one is sharper or clearer?

7. Paste the labeled samples on the chart below.

Part B: Blue Ink

1. Add 4 to 5 drops of blue dye to the tannic acid solution.

2. Print your name on a clean piece of white paper with this solution. Save the solution for Lab Experience 4.29.

3. Let this printing stand for 2 to 3 days.

4. Using a pencil, label and place the printed sample on the chart below.

Questions:

1. Is the first sample easy to read?

2. How easy is it to read the second sample after it has been standing 2 to 3 days?

Ferrous Sulfate Solution	Tannic Acid Solution	Tannic Acid and Blue Dye Solution

LAB EXPERIENCE 4.29

REMOVING INK STAINS

Purpose: To learn how to remove ink stains from fabric.

Materials:

Test tubes	Blue dye
Test tube rack	Blue-black ink
Glass rods	Oxalic acid*
2 pieces of white cloth 8 cm square	Household chlorine bleach
Tannic acid solution with blue dye	(5 % sodium hypochlorite solution)
(from Lab Experience 4.28)	Laundry detergent
India ink	

*Oxalic acid may be purchased at the pharmacy or a chemical supply house.

CAUTION: Liquid bleach and oxalic acid are poisonous. Wash hands and all equipment thoroughly.

Procedure:

1. On a piece of cloth, place three ink spots: the first of India ink, the second of the blue dye ink from Lab Experience 4.28, Part B, and the third of blue-black ink. Below each spot label them A, B, C.

2. Wash this cloth immediately with detergent and water.

3. Let cloth dry, label it, and paste it on the chart below.

4. On a second piece of cloth, place three spots of ink as in Step 1 and let these spots dry until the next lab class.

5. Put household chlorine bleach on these dried ink spots. Household chlorine bleach is used to remove stains by oxidation.

6. If the spots remain, rinse the cloth from Step 5, and place oxalic acid on the spot locations. Oxalic acid is a reducing agent used for stain removal.

7. Wash the cloth in detergent and water and let it air dry. Identify sample.

8. Paste the cloth sample below. Indicate types of ink used for A, B, and C.

LAB EXPERIENCE 4.29 (Continued)

REMOVING INK STAINS

Cloth with ink not dried   Cloth with dried ink

Ink A _____   Ink A _____

Ink B _____   Ink B _____

Ink C _____   Ink C _____

Questions:

1. Were the ink spots readily removed when washed immediately?

2. What effect does bleach have on the ink spots?

3. What effect does oxalic acid have on the ink spots?

4. Were any of the spots resistant to either bleach or oxalic acid?

5. What was the effect of washing the cloth after allowing the ink to dry?

6. Which of the inks would be considered a permanent ink?

Suggested Activity:

Repeat the experiment using different brands of ball point or felt tipped pens.

LAB EXPERIENCE 4.30

ANALYZING INK IN BALL POINT PENS

Purpose: To ascertain the number of chemical components in a ball point pen using chromatography.

Materials:

3 Ring stands	Scissors
3 Test tube clamps	Forceps
3 25-ml Test tubes	Filter paper
3 Corks to fit test tubes	Cotton swabs
10-ml Graduated cylinder	3 Thumbtacks
Test tube rack	Distilled water
Metric ruler	

Procedure:

1. Label ball point pens A, B, and C.

2. Label three test tubes A, B, or C.

3. Do not touch the paper with hands. Hold the filter paper with forceps and cut three strips each 21 cm long and 2 cm wide. Cut one end of each into a "V" shape as shown in Figure 4.5.

4. Using Brand A pen, draw a band 0.5 cm wide across one piece of filter paper about 1.5 cm above the "V" end as shown in Figure 4.5. Allow the ink to dry and repeat this procedure over the same line two more times. Make the line darker not wider or thicker. Let the ink dry between applications.

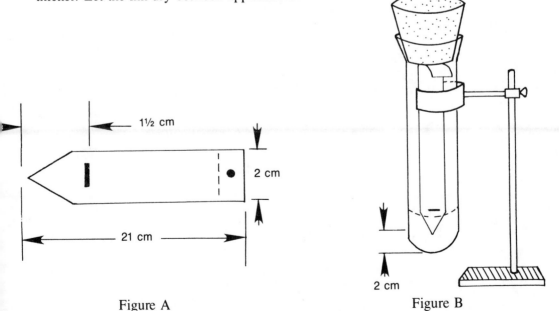

Figure A   Figure B

Figure 4.6 Chromatography Lab Setup

LAB EXPERIENCE 4.30 (Continued)

ANALYZING INK IN BALL POINT PENS

5. Holding the filter paper with forceps, tack the square end to the bottom of the cork and bend the paper so that it will fit into the test tube without touching the sides of the test tube, and the pointed tip is 2 cm above the bottom of the tube as shown in Figure 4.5. Remove cork and paper from test tube.

6. Carefully pour 10 ml of distilled water into the test tube. Do not let any water splash against the inner sides of the test tube. If any water does so, dry the water away using a swab.

7. Clamp the test tube in an upright position to the ring stand.

8. Put cork with filter strip into the test tube so that the pointed end of the paper is just beneath the surface of the water, and the inked line is about 1 cm above the surface of the water.

9. Note the progress of the water up the filter paper. When it is about 3 cm from the top, remove the strip from the test tube, and allow the paper to air dry.

10. Tape Brand A paper chromotography sample below.

11. Repeat Steps 2 through 10 for pen B.

12. Repeat Steps 2 through 10 for pen C.

    Brand A   Brand B   Brand C

LAB EXPERIENCE 4.30 (Continued)
ANALYZING INK IN BALL POINT PENS

Questions:

1. How many color separations are there for Brand A, Brand B, and Brand C?

   Brand A:

   Brand B:

   Brand C:

2. What caused the color separation?

3. Is there a practical application for paper chromatography?

Suggested Activity:

Research Question 3.

COMBUSTION

Combustion is the process of burning. For burning to take place, three conditions must be present:

1. There must be a fuel or some material to burn.
2. The fuel must be heated to a temperature high enough so that it will begin to burn. This is called the kindling temperature. Every fuel has a specific kindling temperature.
3. Oxygen must be present to support the burning. When oxygen combines with a fuel, the process is called oxidation. Without oxygen, the material is not able to burn.

When all three conditions are present, combustion is possible.

There are several ways of extinguishing fires. They are all based on the concept of removing the fuel, lowering the temperature, or cutting off the supply of oxygen. Any one of these conditions will stop a fire from burning or even prevent it from occurring in the first place.

Methods of putting out fires may be as simple as pouring sand or throwing a heavy cloth over the fire to the use of a fire extinguisher. There are several kinds of extinguishers and each is used to put out different kinds of fire. Fires are described as Class A, B, or C and the types of fire extinguishers are pressurized water, pressurized soda-acid, foam, carbon dioxide, dry chemical, and the newest one, the halon extinguisher.

CLASSIFICATION OF FIRES

Class A fires involve burning wood, paper, and cloth. These materials usually form hot coals which sustain the fire. Water works best to cool and thereby lower the temperature of the material.

Class B fires involve flammable liquids such as gasoline, oil, paint, and cooking fat. You would not use water extinguishers on Class B fires for water would cause the burning material to float and spread the fire. Burning liquids need to have their oxygen supply cut off.

Class C fires involve electrical and electronic equipment, and it would be suitable to use either the carbon dioxide, dry chemical, or halon extinguishers on such fires.

TYPES OF FIRE EXTINGUISHERS

The types of fire extinguishers are:

1. Pressurized water: This type works best on Class A fires. It contains water and compressed air. When the handle is squeezed, a valve opens and a stream of water is forced out.
2. Pressurized soda-acid: This type is also good for a Class A fire. It contains sodium bicarbonate dissolved in water and a small container of sulfuric acid. When the extinguisher is turned upside down, the chemicals mix and generate carbon dioxide. As the carbon dioxide expands, it forces water out through the hose to put out the fire.
3. Foam: The foam extinguisher works best on Class A and Class B fires. It contains sodium bicarbonate and aluminum sulfate dissolved in water. When the extinguisher is turned upside down, the chemicals mix and form a foam. The foam comes out of the extinguisher, covers the burning material, and keeps the air from reaching it. This smothers the fire.
4. Carbon dioxide: This type is best used on Class B and Class C fires. It uses carbon dioxide already stored inside the extinguisher. When you press the handles, a valve opens and sprays the carbon dioxide through a large horn onto the fire, thereby smothering it.
5. Dry chemical: This extinguisher is suitable for Class B and Class C fires. When a valve on the extinguisher is opened, powdered sodium bicarbonate is forced out through a hose. The powder smothers the fire.

6. The newest fire fighting device is the halon system which uses the chemical compound bromotrifluoromethane. This compound is odorless, colorless, electrically nonconductive, noncorrosive, and leaves no residue. The halon compound is stored as a liquid in a special fire fighting system. When it is needed, the liquid changes to a vapor as it is released. It can be used on all three classes of fires and would be particularly effective around sensitive electronic equipment where corrosion caused by water or dry chemicals would pose problems.

Halon, like freon, has been implicated as an environmental hazard to our ozone layer. This concern needs to be taken into consideration in the selection of equipment.

PRECAUTIONS

Fires are dangerous for three reasons: heat is produced, smoke is produced, and oxygen is used up. It is important to remain calm and get help quickly. Should clothing catch on fire, it is essential to know what to do, and even more importantly, what not to do.

DO: Drop to the floor, cover with a heavy blanket or coat, remove clothing, remain calm, get help, use cold water to lessen pain and prevent further body damage.

DON'T: Run, panic, touch burn areas, tear clothing from burned areas, use grease, break blisters.

The best approach is fire prevention:

1. Never overload electric outlets.
2. Never leave a connected iron.
3. Never let rubbish pile up.
4. Never use flammable cleaners.
5. Never leave an open fire.
6. Never let children get at matches.
7. Never smoke in bed.
8. Never wear loose fitting sleeves when cooking.
9. Use extra caution when broiling.

PULL
THE RING OR LOCK PIN

POINT
THE EXTINGUISHER AT THE BASE OF THE FIRE

PRESS
THE DISCHARGE LEVER

LAB EXPERIENCE 4.31

COMBUSTION

Parts A, B, and C are teacher demonstrations; Part D may be a student lab or teacher demonstration.

Purpose: To study the conditions required for burning and the methods of extinguishing fires.

Materials:

Bunsen burner	800-ml Beaker
Hot mitts	Candle 5 cm long
2 Aluminum pans	500 g Sand
Forceps	Piece of clay 2.5 cubic cm
Safety glasses	100 g Sodium bicarbonate
Matches	25 ml Acetic acid
Wooden splints	Spray bottle filled with tap water
Glass plate	Heavy cloth or old towel 20 cm square
2 400-ml Beakers	

Procedure:

Part A:

1. Place the clay in a 400-ml beaker and insert the candle into it. The clay acts as a support for holding the candle upright.

2. Light the candle and blow out the flame.

3. Light the candle again and when it is burning well, cover the beaker with the glass plate.

4. Repeat Step 3 but put a wooden splint between the beaker and glass cover.

Questions:

1. Did the flame go out immediately?

   Step 3 _____

   Step 4 _____

LAB EXPERIENCE 4.31 (Continued)

COMBUSTION

2. Describe what happened to the flame.

Step 3 _____

Step 4 _____

Part B:

1. Put a wooden splint into the 800-ml beaker and set one end on fire.

2. Put one drop of water on the flame. If the flame does not go out, put several drops on flame. Why did water make the flame go out? _____

3. Attach the Burnsen burner to the gas jet and light the burner.

4. Turn the gas jet off. Explain what happens. _____
_____

Part C:

1. Place a wooden splint in the foil pan and set the splint on fire.

2. Gently pour sand over the flames until the fire is extinguished. What made the flame go out?

3. Place another wooden splint in the second foil pan and set it on fire.

4. Put on the hot mitts and quickly press the towel or cloth over the fire to snuff out the flames. What made the flames go out?

Part D:

1. Use the candle-beaker setup from Part A.

2. Light the candle.

3. Put 100 g of sodium bicarbonate in another 400-ml beaker. Gently shake to form an even layer.

4. Slowly pour 25 ml of acetic acid over the sodium bicarbonate. The bubbles that form are carbon dioxide gas. This gas is heavier than air and will fill the beaker forcing out the air.

LAB EXPERIENCE 4.31 (Continued)

COMBUSTION

5. Hold the second beaker containing the carbon dioxide gas over the candle flame and slowly pour the carbon dioxide gas over the candle flame. Note the results.

Questions:

1. What are the three requirements for burning to take place?
   a. _____ b. _____ c. _____

2. The temperature at which a substance begins to burn is called its _____.

3. What condition is removed when you blow out a fire?

4. What condition was removed when you placed a glass plate over the beaker?

5. Why can water be used to put out a wood burning fire?

6. What condition was removed when the gas jet was turned off?

7. What condition is removed when sand is used to extinguish a fire?

8. What condition is removed when a towel or cloth is used to put out a fire?

9. What effect does the carbon dioxide gas have on a fire?

10. What would be the most apppropriate method to use to extinguish the following fires:
    a. a small stack of wood
    b. a pan of oil on the stove
    c. clothing
    d. a stack of newspapers stored in the garage
    e. automobile engine or electrical wires.

11. Define the term combustion.

HOUSEHOLD SAFETY

The home has areas of potential accidents. We have listed some of the key precautions to be observed in the main areas of your home.

In the kitchen:

1. Don't mix:
   a. chlorine bleach and ammonia
   b. ammonia and iodine
2. Products like furniture polishes, drain cleaners and some oven cleaners should have safety packaging to keep little children from accidentally opening the packages.
3. Keep all cleaning and chemical products in their original containers. Labels on these containers often give first aid information in the event someone swallows or comes in contact with the product.
4. Harmful products should be stored away from food. If harmful products are placed next to food, someone may accidentally get a food and a poison mixed up and swallow the poison.
5. All potentially harmful products should be put up high and out of the reach of children. Locking all cabinets that hold dangerous products is the best poison prevention.

In the bathroom:

1. Don't smoke while using pressurized sprays such as hair or deodorant sprays.
2. Aspirins and other potentially harmful products should have child-resistant covers.
3. As medicines get older, the chemicals inside them can change. Look for the expiration dates. Flush all old drugs down the toilet. Rinse the container well, then discard it.
4. Only give drugs to the person for whom the doctor has prescribed. It is illegal to give prescription medicine to someone other than the patient for whom it was prescribed.
5. Keep all medicines in their original containers with the original labels. Prescription medicines may or may not list ingredients. The prescription number on the label will, however, allow rapid identification by the pharmacist of the ingredients should they not be listed. Without the original label and container, you can't be sure of what you're taking.

In the garage or storage area:

1. Violent reactions may occur to people who swallow such everyday substances as charcoal lighter, paint thinner and remover, antifreeze and turpentine. Therefore, keep them in well-marked and closed containers that are out of children's reach.
2. Gasoline, kerosene, and chlorine should not be stored close together.
3. Never store gasoline, kerosene or other flammable substances in glass containers. Gasoline, kerosene and other volatile substances should be stored in approved storage containers and clearly marked.
4. All poisons should have child-resistant caps and be stored in the original labeled containers.
5. No poisons should be stored in drinking glasses or soda pop bottles.
6. Harmful products should be locked up and out of reach.

To prepare for an emergency, look up the phone number of the local Poison Control Center and post it near the telephone. If you live in an area not covered by a Center, then keep the phone numbers of the local rescue squad, fire and police departments, and your doctor close to the telephone.

If an accident happens, save the container and some of its contents. This will help the rescue people determine the appropriate treatment.

Keep calm, be careful, get help quickly.

UNIT 4

CHEMISTRY QUESTIONS

Matching: Place the letter from column II into the appropriate space.

1. mass of the proton	_____	A. atom
2. zero charge	_____	B. proton
3. positive charge	_____	C. neutron
4. smallest unit of matter	_____	D. ion
5. atom without electron	_____	E. electron
6. orbits the nucleus	_____	F. 1800 times greater than mass of electron
7. equal to number of protons	_____	G. equal to the mass of the neutron
8. mass of the proton	_____	H. number of electrons

9. The FDA is a term commonly used to describe the: a) Federal Dairy Association, b) Food and Drug Administration, c) Fair Drug Accreditation, d) none of the above.

10. The Federal Food, Drug, and Cosmetic Act of 1958: a) requires that all additives must be accepted and approved, b) states that a group of "generally recognized as safe" substances are exempt from testing and approval, c) does not require any additives to be tested and is concerned only with weights and packaging, d) all of the above, e) none of the above.

11. Food additives are defined as _____.

12. Food additives are added to: a) enhance flavor, b) give more bulk to food, c) both d) neither.

13. Food additives are used for: a) coloring, b) firming, c) sterilizing d) all of the above.

14. The accepted rule for additives: a) is that producers may not add more than 1/10th of the maximum dose of an additive that is free from harmful effects, b) not more than 1/100th of the maximum amount may be added, c) manufacturers may add the substance in any amount, d) none of the above.

15. Food additives are essential in packaged goods and canned foods: a) to stabilize and thicken foods, b) to neutralize or alter the acidity or alkalinity of the food, c) to retain moisture, d) to raise the pH factor, e) none of the above.

16. What is the definition of GRAS? _____.

17. What is the meaning of polysaccharide? _____.

18. Guar gum is a polysaccharide fiber additive which is used as a: a) food binder, b) thickener, c) texturizer, d) all of the above, e) none of the above.

19. Which of the following is *not* true of pectin? a) used for thickening processed foods, b) found in apples, oranges and grapefruits, c) nondigestable fiber, d) raises blood cholestrol level.

20. Which of the following is a polysaccharide fiber? a) guar gum, b) gum ghatti, c) carrageenan, d) both a and b, e) all of the above.

21. Saccharin: a) has been proven to be harmful to humans when taken in small quantities, b) is not harmful to humans and animals in any amount, c) allows people suffering from diabetes to have a more varied diet, d) none of the above.

Matching: Place the letter from column II in the appropriate space.

I			II
22. nitrite	_____	A.	an extract of red algae
23. citric acid	_____	B.	improves the color of certain foods
24. pectin	_____	C.	linoleic acid
25. guar gum	_____	D.	found naturally in food
26. carrageenan	_____	E.	lowers blood cholesterol levels
27. GRAS	_____	F.	found in citrus fruits
28. polysaturates	_____	G.	antioxidants for fats and oils
29. sodium and calcium	_____	H.	generally recognized as safe
30. BHT or BHA	_____	I.	found in spinach and rhubarb
31. oxalic acid	_____	J.	produced in Swiss cheese
32. Delaney clause	_____	K.	states any substance shown to cause cancer in animals may not be added to food.

33. How much of the earth's surface is covered by water? _____.

34. The two gases which chemically combined form water are _____, and _____.

35. What is the difference between hard and soft water? _____.

36. An alkali salt of fatty acids is called _____.

37. Hard water contains a large proportion of the following minerals: a) calcium, magnesium, iron, b) calcium, phosphorus, zinc, c) magnesium, iodine, copper, d) none of the above.

38. How would you convert hard water into soft water? _____.

39. Sodium chloride is used in an ion exchange system which exchanges ions of _____ for the minerals found in water.

40. A chemical which combines with particles in water and settles to the bottom is called: a) filter media, b) floc, c) Fullers cleaner, d) all the above.

41. Hard water is measured by: a) striking it with a paddle, b) seeing how soap reacts to it, c) swallowing it, d) all the above.

42. Hard water makes detergents clean: a) better, b) worse, c) the same, as softened water.

43. Water with particles of grease mixed in it is called: a) an emulsion, b) dishwater, c) mulch, d) none of the above.

44. Soap does not contain: a) fat, b) lye or sodium hydroxide, c) sand.

45. Floating soap will wash: a) as good, b) better, c) worse, than nonfloating soap.

46. Soap harshness is caused by: a) lack of secret ingredients, b) the way it is mixed, c) the alkalinity of the soap, d) all the above.

47. Scouring powder is: a) less abrasive, b) as abrasive, c) more abrasive, than soap.

48. A pH scale measures: a) acidity/alkalinity, b) the weight of pH, c) the cost of pH, d) none of the above.

49. What are the three groups that go into the chemical formulation of a detergent? _____ , _____ , _____ .

50. The _____ acts as a wetting agent in detergents.

51. The most common builders in a detergent are _____ .

52. The builder of a detergent: a) acts as a wetting agent, b) softens the water, c) ties up hard water ions, d) none of the above, e) all of the above.

53. Name one problem which is caused by the phosphates in detergents. _____ .

54. The water pollution problems resulting from the use of detergents involve either the _____ or _____ .

55. The pH scale is based on: a) number of hydrogen ions in a solution, b) number of carbon ions in a solution, c) number of chloride ions in a solution, d) none of the above.

56. In regard to the term pH: a) if the pH is over 7, excess hydrogen ions cause the substance to be a base, b) if litmus paper turns blue, the substance is a base, c) the pH scale is based on normal atmospheric pressure, d) none of the above.

57. The substance that has a pH of 7 is: a) chlorine, b) water, c) salt, d) all of the above.

58. Sodium hypochlorite is found in _____ .

59. Bleach acts as a/an _____ on stains.

60. Calcium, magnesium and iron compounds found in hard water disassociate and form ions. These ions cause the following condition: a) raises the pH factor, b) converts hard water to soft water, c) creates a process called "eutrophication," d) stops the lathering action of soap, e) none of the above.

61. Washing soda used in place of phosphates: a) is harmless to washing machines, b) is a great deal safer than sodium carbonate, c) requires hotter water to clean clothes, d) none of the above.

62. The hair strand is divided into the _____ and the _____ .

63. The living portion of the hair is called the _____ .

64. A/an _____ test indicates any allergic reaction you may have to certain hair coloring products.

65. Shampoo available in the market today: a) is really only liquified soap and scent, b) eliminates the need for acid rinses, c) cleans better because it is very sudsy, d) all of the above.

66. Conditioners and conditioning shampoos: a) nourish the hair by feeding its roots, b) are specially filtered to penetrate into the scalp, c) are used for cosmetic effect, d) none of the above.

67. The "texturizers" and "extra body" in shampoos work because they coat the hair with a _____ material.

68. Dandruff: a) can be controlled by proper diet and adequate vitamin intake, b) is really a symptom that should be observed with care, c) is a normal occurrence, d) none of the above.

Match: Place the letter from column II in the appropriate space.

	I			II
69.	surfactant	_____	A.	an alkali salt of fatty acids
70.	alkalinity	_____	B.	basic to life
71.	soap	_____	C.	acts as a wetting agent
72.	hair shaft	_____	D.	ties up hard water ions
73.	dandruff	_____	E.	necessary for effective removal of dirt
74.	builder	_____	F.	buried in scalp
75.	water	_____	G.	dead portion of hair strand
76.	moisturizer	_____	H.	oiliness and flaking of scalp
77.	cosmetics	_____	I.	controls water evaporation
78.	hair follicle	_____	J.	requires no premarket testing

79. The difference between a product classified as a cosmetic and one classified as a drug is that: a) drugs must be tested and proven safe and effective before they are marketed, b) the law requires manufacturers to list any special component or trade secret, c) color additives in cosmetics do not have to be FDA approved, d) none of the above.

80. The difference between a cosmetic and a drug is: a) drugs are taken internally, b) you do not need a prescription for eye shadow, c) a drug can change some body function, d) none of the above.

81. Regarding cosmetics, it can be said: a) the higher the price the better the product, b) some products can reverse the aging process, c) higher prices are really the result of better marketing plans, d) all of the above.

82. With regard to cosmetics, the FDA: a) can remove a product from the market if it is a health hazard, b) requires the producer to report any and all consumer complaints about the product, c) insists upon extensive and monitored pre-market testing, d) all of the above.

83. Moisturizers simply do what? _____.

84. The only way to moisturize the skin is to: a) drink more water, b) soaking in water, c) bathing, d) all of the above, e) none of the above.

85. A cosmetic is defined as any product which may be _____ on the body.

86. Differences between cosmetics are mostly the result of _____.

87. Skin is dry because it lacks _____.

88. _____ additives in cosmetics must be FDA approved.

89. How cosmetics are manufactured, promoted, and regulated in the U.S. is addressed by the _____.

90. Vanishing creams: a) were used by Houdini, b) are a skin moisturizer, c) makes people weigh less, d) all of the above.

91. Cosmetics can: a) remove wrinkles from a face, b) make the face look better, c) make the skin healthier, d) all of the above.

92. Which of the following would not be found in a hand lotion: a) lanolin, b) petroleum jelly, c) glycerol, d) scouring powder.

93. Antiperspirants are legally considered _____.

94. Deodorants are legally considered _____.

95. Antiperspirants: a) prevent body odor, b) reduce flow of perspiration, c) prevent growth of bacteria, d) all of the above, e) none of the above.

96. Deodorants: a) prevent body odor, b) reduce flow of perspiration c) prevent bacterial growth, d) both a and b, e) both a and c.

97. If the pH of a product is less than 7, it is considered to be a/an _____.

98. If the pH of a product is more than 7, it is considered to be a/an _____.

99. The pH factor describes the strength of _____ or _____ and is based on _____ in a solution.

100. Litmus papers are one example of how to measure _____.

101. What is the primary action of antacids? _____.

102. Antacids are composed of: a) aluminum hydroxide, b) calcium carbonate, c) sodium bicarbonate, d) all of the above.

103. Aluminum hydroxide is a good antacid but tends to cause _____.

104. Magnesium compounds tend to have a/an _____ effect.

105. Name three things that the FDA requires on a cosmetic. _____, _____, _____.

106. The best sunscreen contains _____.

107. PABA stands for _____.

108. Homemade cosmetics basically consist of _____, _____, _____.

109. The difference between generic and brand name drugs is: a) brand name drugs are produced by big companies, b) generic drugs can only be obtained with a prescription, c) there is no difference.

110. The test for a new drug must be submitted to the FDA with the results of the test conducted as follows: _____, _____, and _____.

111. Drugs bought without a prescription are called _____.

112. What three names do drugs have? _____, _____, _____.

113. The difference between prescription and over-the-counter drugs is: a) the average consumer does not know what to ask for, b) patent medicines do not require a

prescription, c) it is wasteful to throw away prescribed medicines since they may be used again if the same symptoms reoccur, d) all of the above.

114. When you are taking more than one medication at the same time: a) you will have no problems if each drug is for a different symptom, b) don't worry about it needlessly since the doctor would not advise you to take anything dangerous, c) tell the doctor everything you are taking including home and patent remedies, d) none of the above.

115. Good advice for anyone taking drugs is: a) read and follow directions, b) purchase in large quantities for greater economy, c) if the doctor prescribes a drug, have confidence in his decision and do not pester him with needless questions, d) all of the above.

116. Drug and food interactions: a) are not serious since food is a natural substance and it can not cause any bad reactions, b) never occur, c) have been reported so consumers should be aware of special precautions when taking drugs, d) none of the above.

117. When taking antihistamines: a) they are excellent for relieving allergy symptoms and do not have any side effects, b) some of these medicines which require a prescription can cause reactions but over-the-counter types do not cause problems because they are made by FDA standards, c) the best thing is to read the label and package insert, ask your doctor, and avoid driving or operating machinery, d) none of the above.

118. Generics are _____ than brand name equivalents and can be used in place of _____ drugs.

119. Acetaminophen (Tylenol) should not be taken with: a) foods high in carbohydrates, b) acidic beverages, c) foods high in calcium, d) none of the above.

120. Demeclocycline (Tetracycline) should not be taken with: a) foods high in calcium, b) foods high in vitamin B_6, c) foods high in carbohydrates, d) none of the above.

121. Name 3 effects cause by antihistamines. _____,
_____, _____.

122. Aspirin interferes with the body's production of: a) ulcers, b) prostaglandins, c) acids, d) all of the above.

123. Name two side effects of aspirin. _____, _____.

124. Name three analgesics. _____, _____,
_____.

125. Phenacetin is suspected of being involved in: a) kidney damage, b) stomach ulcers, c) heart disease, d) none of the above.

126. What is the risk of taking aspirin and vitamin C together? _____.

127. How could aspirin reduce heart attacks? _____.

128. OTC stands for _____.

129. Name two groups of people who should avoid aspirin. _____,
_____.

130. Action in which the effects of two or more drugs are multiplied is called: a) generic, b) potentiation, c) anticoagulant, d) all of the above.

131. Acetylsalicylic acid is another name for: a) aspirin, b) antihistamines, c) acetaminaphen, d) dilantin.

132. Aspirin: a) is the most widely used drug in the world, b) is not addictive and can be used freely for long periods, c) has no side effects and can be used by anyone without danger, d) all of the above, e) none of the above.

133. If you have a cold and take aspirin or a remedy containing aspirin: a) aspirin will cure a cold for most people, b) gargling with an aspirin solution will relieve the sore throat discomfort often associated with a cold, c) aspirin will relieve the headache and fever of a cold, d) none of the above.

134. Regarding the use of aspirin for other illnesses: a) people suffering from gout should avoid it, b) it is safe to take aspirin if you have a stomach ulcer, c) diabetics and people with liver problems can take aspirin without fear, d) all of the above, e) none of the above.

135. Aspirin works by interfering with the body's production of prostaglandins. This substance: a) is produced in the brain and spinal cord, b) prevents strokes, c) is found in all body tissues, d) all of the above, e) none of the above.

136. Allergic reactions to aspirin: a) have not been reported at any time since the drug was introduced in 1899, b) will appear the first time you take the drug, c) can appear at any time, d) all of the above, e) none of the above.

137. The difference between aspirin and acetaminophen is: a) acetaminophen helps reduce inflamation and swelling while aspirin does not, b) aspirin helps relieve inflammation and swelling while acetaminophen does not, c) acetaminophen causes stomach bleeding, d) none of the above.

138. When purchasing over-the-counter drugs such as aspirin: a) buy brands such as as Bayer and St. Joseph because they contain important stabilizers, b) remember there is no difference between brands except price, c) name brands are produced under higher standards, d) none of the above.

139. FDA regulations require that: a) all drug producers make and package drugs bearing their name on their own premises, b) large companies (since they market in a wider area) must follow more stringent good manufacturing practices, c) before a new drug can be put on the market, it must be proven that the drug is safe and effective for its intended use, d) none of the above.

140. If you have stopped taking a drug, the unused protion should be: a) stored in the refrigerator, b) mixed with other unused drugs, c) given to a friend who might be able to use it, d) thrown away, e) all of the above.

Matching: Place the letter from column II in the appropriate space

I		II
141. anticoagulant medicine	_____	A. aspirin
142. antacid	_____	B. alkaline in nature and acts on gastric juices
143. potentiation	_____	C. two drugs are not added to each other but are multiplied in effect
144. acetylsalicyclic acid	_____	D. when the body breaks down a substance

145. metabolized   _____   E.   contain ammonium chloride, sodium bicarbonate or citrates

                                                      F.   thins the blood

146. Warp refers to: a) the way a thread bends,   b) the threads that are held in place by a loom frame,   c) the threads that are threaded in and out of the others in a loom, d) none of the above.

147. Woof (or weft) refers to: a) the way a thread bends,   b) the threads that are held in place by a loom frame,   c) the threads that are threaded in and out of the others in a loom,   d) none of the above.

148. Most threads: a) are made up of several fibers,   b) are a single fiber,   c) none of the above,   d) all the above.

149. At home, the following should never be mixed: a) ammonia and chlorine bleach, b) ammonia and iodine,   c) none of the above,   d) all the above.

150. At home, keep household chemicals and cleaners in: a) new containers,   b) identical glass jars,   c) the original containers,   d) none of the above.

151. Which of the following statements are incorrect: a) keep dangerous items high and away from children,   b) do not put poisons in soda pop bottles,   c) keep all old unused medicines in a jar,   d) all the above.

UNIT 5

CONSUMERISM

EVOLUTION OF CONSUMERISM

Contemporary consumerism evolved in the mid-1960's. It was triggered by the concerns expressed in Rachel Carson's book "Silent Spring," followed by Ralph Nader's auto safety investigation. These concerns were most clearly expressed by President Kennedy's efforts to establish the four rights of consumers: the right to safety, the right to be informed, the right to choose, and the right to be heard.

From the mid-sixties to the late seventies, the field that consumerism encompassed steadily expanded. The trend was apparent in increased spending for federal regulatory activities, as the government addressed long-standing consumer problems. The movement was concerned with the protection of the rights of the consumer against infringement by business and even governmental agencies. Eventually, environmental concerns and consumerism became entwined on many common issues.

Looking at the regulatory or legislative scorecard, the strength of the consumer movement seems to have subsided. This judgement may be premature for consumer protection is solidly entrenched in the legal system. It includes provision for private parties to sue for redress of violations of governmental regulations. However, in spite of all of the advances, many of the initial dissatisfactions have not been remedied.

RIGHT TO SAFETY

The right to safety implies protection against the marketing of goods that are hazardous to health or life. Thus, laws relating to foods, textiles, drugs, cosmetics, and tires demand that the products not endanger health or safety and that if a potential exists for dangerous misuse, a clear warning be provided such as those on poisonous cleaning fluids.

The right to safety has been broadened to include mandatory protection of people from themselves. Consequently, people are not permitted to select an automobile which does not have seat belts and other mandatory safety features.

RIGHT TO INFORMATION

The right to be informed implies that the consumer should not be deceived. For example, the Federal Trade Commission (FTC) has taken the position that an advertising claim should be unique to the advertised product. Even slogans like "best buy" and "most significant breakthrough" are now being challenged.

The right to be informed goes well beyond a protection against deception. It requires that the consumer be given sufficient information to make wise purchase decisions. Legislation has been enacted to provide useful comparative information, such as truth in lending, unit pricing, product ingredients, and nutritional information. However, advertisements and point-of-sale information still provide much of the product data upon which the consumer relies. This is not always unbiased information.

RIGHT TO CHOOSE

Concern over the right to choose goes back to the end of the last century, when the Sherman Anti-trust Act was enacted to break the monopoly power of the giant firms of that era. Antitrust legislation and enforcement encouraged competition. A major effort is now directed at increasing the number of competitors and ensuring that competitors do not make agreements among themselves that would be detrimental to the long term interests of consumers. Price fixing continues to be the most significant threat to a consumer's right to choose.

RIGHT TO BE HEARD

The right to be heard involves an assurance that the consumers' interest would be considered in the formulation of government policy and in regulatory proceedings. Back in 1964, Lyndon Johnson created the Office of Special Assistant to the President for Consumer Affairs to give the consumer a voice within government. Business lobbies argued that it would only increase the harassment of businessmen and disrupt the work of other government units, but it continues to operate.

This does not mean that nobody is listening to us. Many business firms have created consumer affairs departments to coordinate consumer programs, and to permit a new type of representation of consumer interests. Most of these departments handle customer complaints. However, the political realities of large organizations tend to inhibit any efforts by these departments to sponsor consumer interests in the policymaking process of the firm.

RIGHT OF RECOURSE

There is now a fifth right, the right to recourse and redress which means a fair settlement of just claims. A variety of innovations, including free legal services for the poor, consumer class action suits, and arbitration procedures have enhanced this right. The Magnuson-Moss Warranty Act of 1975 is an example. This Act reformed warranty practices.

Since the buyer has the right to expect a level of quality based on advertising and warranty, any deviation from this level is the basis for complaint. The Act defines the legal obligations of the warrantor, and the recourse procedures available to the buyer.

RIGHT TO QUALITY ENVIRONMENT

It is suggested that there be a sixth right. The right to a physical environment that will enhance the quality of life. Environmental problems differ from other consumer concerns because many of today's problems were not created by a present action. Rather, the conditions were caused by an action taken many years before or many miles away. In the long run however, what each of us does to his immediate environment does affect the world at large. As the song says, sewage dumped in the water in Troy, New York will end up in the cups of the people in Perth Amboy, New Jersey.

ACTION GROUPS

A number of private organizations now provide impetus and support to the consumer movement. There are national organizations such as Consumer Federation of America. There are local groups such as the "Action Line" which is an effort by local media to assist in resolving consumer complaints. There are also special interest groups such as GASP (Group Against Smoking and Pollution) and ACT (Act for Children's Television). Then there are organizations, not especially identified with the consumer movement, that have and will continue to play a major role in the 1980's. For example, AARP (American Association of Retired Persons) took an active part in making generic drugs available to the public.

The Better Business Bureau (BBB) in their book "A Guide to Wise Buying" states that although we have all kinds of organizations lobbying for government action, consumers owe it to themselves to shop carefully and choose dealers that are reliable.

WARRANTIES

We should consider the quality of the

service department that is responsible for in-warranty repair of purchases as carefully as we look for quality, and as carefully as we evaluate price. If a local dealer or service affiliate has been reluctant to, or proved incapable of, providing effective service in the past, then this factor should play a part in where we make our purchases. Check the service record maintained at your local BBB. Comparing warranties (guaranties) should be an important part of the shopping process. Comparing the reliability of the company behind the warranty is equally important. The terms warranty and guaranty are often used interchangeably, and legally mean the same thing.

The time to become familiar with the terms of the warranty is before you buy the item. Warranties should be in writing. A businessman who is unwilling to put his promises in writing is not the person to do business with. Also do not be misled by the terms "limited" or "full" on a warranty, because some "limited" warranties will afford more protection than some "full" warranties. For example, a "full" warranty assures service everywhere in the U.S., a "limited" warranty covers a specific geographic area. Some smaller manufacturers may not have the capability to offer a "full" warranty, but their warranty may be better if you stay in the area where you bought the product.

Check written warranties to see whether these key points are covered:

- What is covered? The entire product or only certain parts? Is the warranty full or limited?
- Whom do you call for in-warranty repairs? The manufacturer? The dealer? A service agency?
- Must repairs be made by either a "factory representative" or "authorized dealer" to keep the warranty in effect? Is an authorized repair center located near you?
- Who pays shipping charges for mer-chandise returned for repair?
- Who pays for parts? For labor?
- How long does the warranty last on the entire product, on parts, and assemblies?
- If pro-rata reimbursement is provided, what is the basis for it? Is it for the time you have owned the product, or the amount of usage, or for the original cost?
- If the warranty provides for a refund of a defective product, do you get the refund in cash or in credit toward a replacement?
- Will a substitute product be provided for your use while yours is being repaired?

Remember:

- Before you use a product, read the owner's manual or instruction sheet. Follow the operating instructions, and be sure that any specific routine maintenance or service is done as suggested or required by the warranty.
- Keep your warranty and the sales receipt for future reference. Make a note of the date of purchase and the date of installation. Register your appliance or other purchase with the card provided. Keep a record of the dates of all in-warranty repair work.
- Your best guaranty of a good warranty is the care you take in making your purchase.

COMPLAINTS

Consumer service organizations, such as the BBB, use complaint correspondence as an effective indicator of problem areas. This correspondence provides the BBB network with solid evidence of the manufacturers' or retailers' performance. This, in turn, shows the need for industry-wide adoption of advertising and selling standards.

HOW TO COMPLAIN

You can register your complaint about a product in many ways. It may be in person, as when you return an item to the place of purchase. It may be by phone, which is a poor method because it leaves no trail of proof of complaint or response. A clear concise letter is by far the best method, and if you doubt the sincerity of the dealer then send it by registered mail.

Your letter should contain the following information:

1. What you bought. Supply information that will enable the company to identify the product according to size, color, model number, serial number, etc.
2. Where you bought it. Include the complete address of the retailer.
3. When. The date of purchase is important.
4. How you paid for it. Specify cash, check, credit card or money order. Include copies (never send originals) of receipts, canceled checks, sales contract, etc.
5. Describe the problem. Be objective. Allow the facts to speak for themselves.
6. What do you want? State whether you expect a refund, a partial refund, repair or replacement of the product, or delivery of merchandise.
7. Keep a copy of your letter. You should have a response within three weeks. Even if the problem is not solved in that period of time, you should at least have an acknowledgement from the firm indicating that the matter is being investigated.
8. If you fail to receive any action or satisfaction, contact your local BBB or even the local district attorney. Do not just let the matter drop.

COMPLAINTS ABOUT COSMETICS

Complaints about cosmetics are handled in a slightly different manner from other merchandise. The BBB recommends the following action:

1. Register your complaint exactly in the same manner as for any other product. Save the remains in case you are asked to return it to the manufacturer or dealer.
2. If you are complaining about advertising, send a copy of the letter to your local Better Business Bureau.
3. If you are reporting an allergic reaction or problem caused by a cosmetic, send a copy of the letter to FDA.

FEDERAL AGENCIES

Federal agencies do not usually handle individual consumer complaints. However, most agencies have established offices of consumer affairs which are responsible for communicating consumer concerns, the consideration of consumer issues, and for direct response to consumers. The federal government has established the following agencies:

- Office of Consumer Affairs, Old Executive Office Building, Washington, DC 20506. This office coordinates federal activities in the area of consumer protection. The Office carries on an extensive public information program, conducts investigations, holds conferences and conducts surveys on consumer issues.
- Consumer Product Safety Commission (CPSC), 1750 K Street, NW, Washington, DC 20036. This commission has the power to:

  Set safety standards for all common household and recreational products

Seize and ban hazardous products from the market place

Ban from the market any product that presents an unreasonable risk of injury

Order manufacturers, distributors, or retailers to notify purchasers about hazardous products and to repair, replace or refund the cost of such products.

- Federal Trade Commission (FTC), Washington, DC 20580. This commission has the responsibility of administrating the Fair Packaging and Labeling Act, the Truth-in-Lending and Fair Credit Reporting Acts, and warranty regulations.
- Food and Drug Administration (FDA), 5600 Fishers Lane, Rockville, MD 20852. This agency is responsible for overseeing the marketing of food, drugs, cosmetics, and medical devices.
- U.S. Postal Inspection Service, Washington, DC 20260. This service is the oldest law enforcement agency in the U.S. The office processes complaints of fraudulent use of the mails, and conducts field investigations.

STATE, MUNICIPAL AND PRIVATE AGENCIES

Consumer protection is often a function of the Office of the Attorney General at the state level. Some states have established statewide toll-free telephone lines to receive complaints and requests for information from consumers.

Many local television stations and newspapers have assigned special reporters (Trouble Shooters) to assist with and report on a wide range of consumer problems.

The range of services of local consumer protection agencies varies with the powers and responsibilities included in the enabling legislation, and with the funds budgeted for staff and services.

The Better Business Bureau (BBB) system checks advertising claims, receives complaints concerning advertising and works with industries to develop standards in advertising and selling.

The BBB responds to inquiries and complaints. They urge consumers to check the reputations of local firms before making a purchase or entering into a contract. Although they do not recommend specific firms, they do respond to inquiries with information including the number of years the firm has been in business, whether customers have had problems, the nature of the problems, and how the firm resolved them. They provide facts from extensive file records and you must draw your own conclusions.

Better Business Bureaus also attempt to resolve consumer complaints through mediation — the intervention of an interested, concerned third party. Your complaint must be presented in writing, preferably with copies of relevant correspondence (including your original complaint letter). The Bureau will then seek a fair adjustment of the complaint by the business.

OPEN QUESTIONS

A decade ago government regulation was the accepted solution to a variety of ills. In response to public demand, the Consumer Product Safety Commission (CPSC) was established in 1972, and the Magnuson-Moss Consumer Product Warranties Act came into effect in July 1975.

However, a backlog of consumer issues remains unresolved by the federal government particularly in the areas of consumer safety and health. Certainly the performances and omissions of the service industry, frivolous advertising, and unresponsive business organizations sustain the consumer movement. The housing shortage, the crippling impact of inflation on people with fixed incomes, and the difficulty of funding all necessary public services accelerate consumer concerns.

Along with the foregoing we need to look at the problems of the manufacturers. In other words, let's look at both sides. Often, when we examine problems from the other's point of view, the solutions are neither clear cut nor black and white. All aspects of problems should be considered.

Today, political and public support for new regulations is no longer easily obtained and existing regulations are being challenged.

Although the role of regulation will continue to be examined, it will not necessarily be reduced. In some situations, further regulations are appropriate and justifiable. Some instances still to be resolved are:

1. Products and services with hidden costs that are difficult to detect. For example, unnecessarily high energy costs due to poorly installed insulation.
2. Hazards unknown to the manufacturer and to the public at the time the product was made and sold. For example, the damage done to the unborn by the drug thalidomide. What are the responsibilities of a seller when later evidence shows that the items sold are now dangerous?
3. The question arises as to how much damage to the environment may be allowed in the production of a given product. Unhappily, the answer cannot be zero because all people and all processes pollute. We must decide on the limits we can live with. For example, would we give up autos, steel manufacturing, or even farming because of environmental damage.

During the 1980's the role of governmental agencies and legislation is expected to decline. However, there will probably be a corresponding growth in the importance of consumer and private organizations, business firms, and individual consumers.

The consumer's rights, the price and quality of the product, and the reliability of the seller, should be evaluated. The best protection for a buyer is knowledge.

UNIT 5

CONSUMERISM QUESTIONS

1. The Sherman Anti-Trust Act was enacted to: a) protect consumers against deception, b) protect against goods hazardous to health, c) break monopolies, d) all of the above, e) none of the above.

2. Important rights of consumers were established by: a) Lyndon Johnson, b) J. F. Kennedy, c) D.D. Eisenhower, d) none of the above.

3. The right to safety does not apply to: a) toxic cleaning chemicals, b) automobile safety features, c) minimal vitamin requirements.

4. The right to information implies that: a) the government is responsible for conducting brand comparison studies, b) producers are responsible for comparative studies, c) the consumer be given enough information to act wisely, d) none of the above.

5. Price fixing: a) is advantageous to the consumer since it allows the government to set a fair range of prices, b) gives stability to the economy, c) has an impact on free choice, d) all of the above, e) none of the above.

6. The right to choose is related to: a) encouraging competition, b) listings of product sources by manufacturers made available to the public, c) the individual and has never been impinged upon, d) none of the above.

7. The fifth and newest right of the consumers' rights is: a) right to recourse and redress, b) right to safety, c) right to choose, d) right to be heard, e) none of the above.

8. The new or suggested sixth right is: a) right to recourse and redress, b) right to choose, c) right to quality environment, d) right to safety, e) none of the above.

9. The right to be heard means: a) all businesses are required by law to establish consumer complaint departments, b) business must legally respond to complaints, c) government rules and policies should consider consumers' interests, d) none of the above.

10. The right of recourse means a purchaser: a) can return a purchase if he finds a cheaper supplier, b) has a right to a fair settlement of proven claims, c) is entitled to free legal advice from government appointed lawyers if the product does not meet his expectations, d) none of the above.

11. The suggested right to quality environment means: a) the environment should be such that it enhances life, b) concerns ecologists not consumers since it is too complex, c) recent technological innovations are responsible for much of the pollution existing today.

12. Consumer "Action Groups": a) have been outlawed by recent legislation, b) do have a positive impact on business practices, c) have not been effective on business practices, d) none of the above.

13. The Better Business Bureau: a) is in favor of increased government involvement in business, b) advises consumers to shop carefully, c) is concerned primarily with in-

creasing profits of businessmen,   d) all of the above,   e) none of the above.

14. With regard to warranties: a) they are all similar since the government requires producers to adhere to minimum standards,   b) they are not important in most normal household purchases,   c) they tend to vary,   d) none of the above.

15. Servicing of appliances: a) is uniform in similar industries,   b) may be inconsistent,   c) must be legally available in all parts of the USA,   d) none of the above.

16. A warranty is: a) sales receipt,   b) a sales contract,   c) a guarantee,   d) none of the above.

17. You may judge the value of a service warranty by: a) the written terms,   b) past performance of the dealer,   c) the condition of the repair facilities,   d) all of the above,   e) none of the above.

18. You should know the terms of a warranty: a) as soon as you receive delivery of the item,   b) before you mail back the warranty card,   c) before you make the purchase,   d) none of the above.

19. If a warranty is not in writing: a) do not make the purchase,   b) you can reasonably rely on the dealer's integrity,   c) you have no protection,   d) all of the above,   e) none of the above.

20. A limited warranty differs from a full warranty in that it: a) only covers parts,   b) only covers services,   c) only covers a specific geographic area,   d) all of the above,   e) none of the above.

21. Written warranties contain certain key points: a) most dealers will explain the restrictions to you before you make the purchase,   b) these restrictions are required by law in most states,   c) it is the duty of the buyer to find out if the conditions are suitable   d) none of the above.

22. While traveling out-of-state your car develops a malfunction within the warranty period: a) you must cancel the balance of your trip and return to the dealer for repairs,   b) you can pull in to the nearest station and have the car fixed,   c) you must generally have the car fixed at an "authorized" representative or dealer's facility,   d) all of the above,   e) none of the above.

23. If your car breaks down while under warranty, and you need a substitute in order to get to work, you will receive it: a) always,   b) never,   c) sometimes.

24. With regard to an owner's manual of instruction: a) it is too complex to be of much help,   b) it is wise to read and follow instructions and suggestions,   c) it is usually unnecessary since all products are made to allow successful use by normal consumers.

25. The best method to register a complaint is: a) write a letter,   b) telephone,   c) return the item in person,   d) none of the above.

26. When complaining about an allergic reaction to cosmetics, a copy of the letter should be sent to the _____.

27. Which of these is not a federal agency: a) U.S. Postal Inspection Services,   b) Better Business Bureau,   c) Consumer Product Safety Commission,   d) none of the above.

28. Complaints filed with the Better Business Bureau: a) must be submitted by a legal representative,   b) will not be relayed to the offending dealer unless requested,   c) are an indicator of problem areas,   d) none of the above.

29. If you make a complaint and receive no response: a) forget about it, take the loss, but

do not buy that item again, b) contact the BBB or the district attorney, c) your complaint is unjustified, d) all of the above.

30. If the eyeliner you used causes your eyes to become red: a) throw the rest of it away and do not buy that brand again, b) stop using it for a while and then try it again, c) complain to the FDA, d) none of the above.

31. The FDA watches over: a) drug abuse, b) cosmetic marketing, c) ecological hazards, d) all of the above, e) none of the above.

32. Consumer complaints regarding fradulent sales letters should be directed to: a) the Postal Service, b) the FDA, c) the FBI, d) none of the above.

33. The agency responsible for overseeing the marketing of food, drugs, cosmetics, and medical devices is: a) Consumer Product Safety Commission, b) Federal Trade Commission, c) Office of Consumer Affairs, d) Better Business Bureau, e) none of the above.

34. The federal agency which conducts extensive public information programs, investigations, surveys, and holds conferences on consumer issues is: a) Office of Consumer Affairs, b) Federal Trade Commission, c) Food and Drug Administration, d) none of the above.

35. The agencies that deal with consumer complaints at the state and local levels are: a) Better Business Bureau, b) media trouble shooters, c) Office of the Attorney General, d) all of the above, e) none of the above.

Matching: Place the letter from column II into the appropriate space.

I	II
36. local media assisting in resolving consumer complaints	A. Sherman Anti-Trust Act
	B. right to recourse
37. assures service everywhere in the U.S.	C. limited warranty
	D. Office of Consumer Affairs
38. oldest law enforcement agency in the U.S.	E. Consumer Federation of America
39. enacted to breakup monopolies	F. full warranty
40. reporters who assist and report on a wide range of consumer problems	G. Action Line
	H. Trouble Shooter
41. seize and ban hazardous products from market	I. U.S. Postal Inspection Service
	J. Consumer Product Safety Commission
42. responds to inquires and complaints on a local level	K. Food and Drug Administration
43. coordinates federal activities in the area of consumer protection	L. Federal Trade Commission
44. covers a specific geographic area	M. Magnuson-Moss Warranty Act
45. defines recourse procedures available to buyer	N. Better Business Bureau
46. responsible for overseeing the marketing of cosmetics	
47. national organization for the consumer movement	
48. administers the Truth-in-Lending Act	
49. fair settlement of just claims	

UNIT 6

SOME SCIENCE BASICS

The previous units of the text look at science from the consumer's point of view. This unit deals with the theory behind consumer science.

If you are curious about the underlying reasons as to why some of the lab experiences work, then this unit will answer those questions.

There is a body of knowledge, including physics and chemistry, which make up the fundamentals of science. Keeping mathematics as simple as possible, let us look at the necessary physics and chemistry to explain why "things happen".

Physics is a science which deals with matter and energy and the way they change. *Chemistry* is a science which deals with the building blocks of matter and the way matter is put together.

MATTER

What is matter? *Matter* is anything which occupies space and has mass. Matter could be solid, such as wood, iron, gold; or liquid, such as water, gasoline, alcohol; or gas, such as carbon dioxide, hydrogen, oxygen.

The general *properties of matter* include mass, inertia, volume, density, weight, impenetrability, porosity, cohesion, and adhesion.

- *Mass* describes the amount of matter that goes to make up the object.
- The *inertia* of an object is the same as the mass of the object. Since inertia is an object's resistance to its change in position or motion, then the greater an object's mass, the greater is its inertia. You'd notice this inertia if you ever kicked a pebble and then, with

the same amount of force, kicked a boulder. Ouch!!!
- *Volume* is the amount of space an object takes up.
- The *density* of an object is the relationship of its mass to its volume.
- *Weight* depends on the mass of the object, but also depends on the gravitational force acting upon the object.
- The property of *impenetrability* keeps two objects from occupying the same space at the same time.
- The property of *porosity* describes the number of small openings, or spaces in an object, such as is found in a sponge.
- The property of *cohesion* is the force of attraction that holds similar molecules together. To tear or break an object apart would require the separation of these molecules from each other.
- The property of *adhesion* is the force of attraction between unlike molecules. An example would be glue sticking to wood or chewing gum to the leather soles of shoes.

STATES OF MATTER

Matter can be either a solid, a liquid, or a gas. Since matter may exist in several forms, or states, let us look at the properties of matter as it is found.

PROPERTIES OF SOLIDS

A *solid,* such as a block of ice, would have a measurable volume and a definite shape.

The *density* of an object is the relationship of its mass to its volume.

The *hardness* of a substance is measured by its ability to scratch other substances. Hardness is measured on a scale of 1 to 10. Number 1 is talc, the stuff that is ground up to make talcum powder, and number 10 is the diamond, which is considered to be the hardest of all naturally occurring materials.

Malleability is the ability of a substance to be beaten or rolled into thin sheets and remain intact. Gold is one of the most malleable of materials. It can be hammered into a sheet with a thickness of 1/300000 of an inch. Iron, copper, tin, and aluminum are other malleable substances.

Ductility is the ability of a material to be drawn into fine wire. Platinum, gold, silver, iron and copper are substances which possess ductility. Because of the ductility of copper and aluminum, wire for electrical purposes can readily be made from these materials.

Elasticity is the ability of an object, such as a spring, to return to its original form after being stretched.

Tensile strength is the ability of a material to resist being pulled apart. It takes a force of about 35 tons to pull apart a rod of steel 1 square inch in cross section. Other materials of high tensile strength are wrought iron and bronze.

Conductivity is the ability of substances to transfer heat from one place to another. Metals are good conductors of heat. This explains why such devices as cooking utensils, stoves, irons, and radiators are made of metal. Metals are also excellent conductors of electricity. Some metals conduct heat and electricity better than others with platinum, gold, silver, and copper being among the best. For example, a teacher demonstration of conductivity is as follows:

Fasten four rods of identical dimensions to a common metal center: one should be of silver, one of copper, one of aluminum, and one of iron. At the end and at the middle of each rod, hang a wax ring. Now place a Bunsen burner under their common center. Each rod will conduct heat from the end in the flame toward the other end. The more rapidly the conduction takes place, the sooner the wax rings will melt and drop off. In this way, it is seen that silver is the best conductor of the four metals, with copper, aluminum, and iron following in that order.

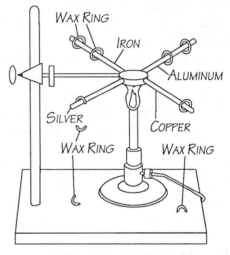

Figure 6.1   Conductivity

Specific gravity is the density of a substance as compared to the density of water. Water is the standard against which all other materials are compared. For example, the specific gravity of sulfur is 2. This means that sulfur is twice as heavy as an equal volume of water. Since 1 cubic centimeter (cm^3) of water has a mass of 1 gram (g), then 1 cm^3 of sulfur has a mass of 2g.

The relationship of mass (g) to volume (cm^3) is called density.

$$\text{Specific gravity} = \frac{\text{Density of substance}}{\text{Density of water}}$$

PROPERTIES OF LIQUIDS

If a block of ice were sufficiently heated it would melt or become a *liquid,* water. The water would have a measurably definite volume and its shape would be the shape of the container.

Cohesion is the attraction between similar molecules. It may be demonstrated when water is poured from one container to another. The continuous stream of water demonstrates cohesion.

Adhesion may be demonstrated by putting your finger into a jar of molasses, pulling it out, and then licking your finger. You realize that it takes a certain amount of force to lick the molecules of molasses from the molecules of your finger. Adhesion occurs between liquids and solids.

Surface tension demonstrates the property that makes every liquid act as though a strong elastic film were stretched over its surface. It is this surface tension which supports insects when they run over the surface of a pond.

Another property of the surface tension of a liquid is its tendency to shrink into the smallest possible area. Soap bubbles and drops of water assume a round shape for this reason.

Capillary action occurs when a liquid wets (adheres to) a tube. The adhesion between the liquid and the tube causes many of the surface liquid molecules to "pile up" on the walls of the tube thus forming a concave surface. Surface tension then causes this surface to contract until it is nearly flat. In contracting, the curved surface moves upward, pulling the liquid on its under side up along with it as shown in Figure 6.2, Type 1.

When the liquid does not wet the tube, as in Type 2, the cohesion within the liquid pulls the liquid molecules away from the walls of the tube, thus forming a convex surface. Again, surface tension tends to flatten out the surface, but in doing so, it now pushes the liquid down, thus lowering its level in the tube. In each type, the liquid is read at its lowest level.

Emulsion is a mixture of two liquids that

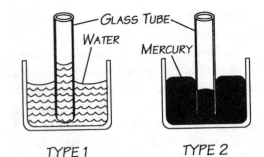

TYPE 1   TYPE 2

Figure 6.2   Capillary Action

usually do not mix. For example, the oil and vinegar in some salad dressings require a thorough shaking before using the dressing.

Viscosity is the internal friction in a liquid which keeps it from being moved or poured quickly. Cold causes lubricating oils to stiffen while heat causes them to thin. Lubricating oils are therefore selected so that they will react, as needed, to changes in temperature.

Buoyancy is the ability of an object to float. When an object floats, the water exerts an upward force. *Buoyant force* is the upward force which a liquid exerts on an object placed in it.

Archimedes' principle describes what happens when an object is placed in a liquid. The body displaces some of the liquid to make room for itself. The body is buoyed up by the liquid and seems to weigh less than it does in air. Using Archimedes' principle, it is possible to determine the density of an irregularly-shaped object.

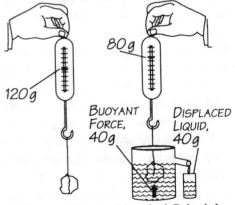

Figure 6.3   Archimedes' Principle

$$\text{Specific gravity} = \frac{\text{Density of liquid}}{\text{Density of water}}$$

See definition under Properties of Solids.

Solution is the dissolving of one substance in another so that the properties are the same throughout the mixture. To make a cup of instant coffee, add hot water to the coffee powder, stir, and you have hot coffee. As the coffee particles dissolve in the water, they spread evenly throughout the water. The *solute* is the substance that becomes dissolved; the *solvent* does the dissolving; the resulting product is called the *solution*. In our example, the coffee is the solute, the water is the solvent, and the resulting drink is the solution.

Suspension is a mixture of substances that separate upon standing. Sand mixed with water would be such an example.

Distillation is a purification process whereby a liquid is heated, vaporizing to form a gas, which is then cooled and changed back to a liquid. The impurities in the liquid are left behind when the liquid vaporizes. This is one of the methods used to purify water and alcohol.

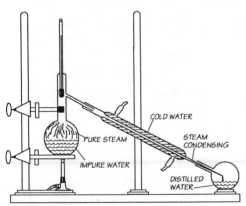

Figure 6.4   Distillation Apparatus

Diffusion is the mixing of the molecules of one substance in between the molecules of another substance. For example, if you place some sugar crystals into a beaker of water without stirring, some of the sugar molecules will diffuse into the water. This will occur without causing a rise in the water level.

PROPERTIES OF GASES

Gases have neither a definite volume nor a definite shape but expand to fill their containers. If you were to heat water till it boils, the resulting steam is matter as a gas. Steam will completely fill a container, even a room-sized container. The *expansion of gases* takes place when they are heated.

Diffusion is the mixing of the molecules of one gas in between the molecules of another gas, such as in a room deodorant spray. A few minutes after the spray is used in one corner of the room, the smell or fragrance is noticed throughout the entire room. This shows how rapidly gas molecules move.

Buoyant force is the upward force a gas exerts on an object placed in it. Archimedes' principle applies to bodies immersed in air, just as it does to bodies immersed in liquids. The apparent loss of weight of the body when in air is exactly equal to the weight of the air displaced by it.

Pressure occurs when a gas is confined. At a constant temperature, when the pressure exerted on a gas is doubled, then the gas will be compressed to half its original volume. This is known as *Boyle's law:*

$$P_1V_1 = P_2V_2,$$

where P_1 and V_1 are the original pressure and volume of a gas before pressure is exerted on it. P_2 and V_2 are the final pressure and volume after pressure is exerted on the gas.

Sample problem:

What volume of air, at an atmospheric pressure of 15 lb/in², must be pumped into an automobile tire having a volume of 2 ft³ in order to raise the pressure inside the tire to 45 lb/in²? Assume that the temperature is kept constant.

$P_1 = 15 \dfrac{lb}{in^2}, P_2 = 45 \dfrac{lb}{in^2},$

$V_2 = 2 \ ft^3, V_1 = ?$

Applying Boyle's law:

$P_1 V_1 = P_2 V_2$

$15 \ (V1) = (45) \ (2)$

$V_1 = 6 \ ft^3$

Sample problem:

We measure 500 cm³ (volume) of a gas at a pressure of 750 mm of mercury. What volume will this gas occupy if the pressure is increased to 800 mm? (cm³ = cubic centimeters; mm = millimeters) Answer: 469 cm³

MEASUREMENT

It is important to be able to measure objects, and in physics these measurements are expressed in terms of length (meter), mass (kilogram), time (second), temperature (degrees Celsius), and electric charge (coulomb).

Metric measurements and their English equivalencies are discussed in Unit 1, Page 13. Metric measurement applications are to be found throughout the text.

When we talk about quantities such as length, area, volume, mass, density, and time, they can be described by a number with an appropriate unit. For example, a table may be described as being 3 meters (m) long or a lead block having a mass of 40 kilograms (kg). The number is called a *scalar quantity* and tells the magnitude of each of the quantities; magnitude means "how much". A quantity, which requires both magnitude and direction to describe it, is known as a *vector quantity*.

TABLE 6.1
MEASUREMENT SYSTEMS

	Length (l)	Area (A)	Volume (V)	Capacity (V)	Mass (m)	Force (F)	Time (t)
MKS	meter (m)	square meter (m²)	cubic meter (m³)	liter (l)	kilo‑gram (kg)	newton (nt)	second (sec)
CGS	centi‑meter (cm)	square centi‑meter (cm²)	cubic centi‑meter (cm³)	milli‑liter (ml)	gram (g)	dyne	second (sec)
FPS	foot (ft)	square foot (ft²)	cubic foot (ft³)	quart (qt)	slug	pound (lb)	second (sec)

Legend:
MKS = meter-kilogram-second
CGS = centimeter-gram-second
FPS = foot-pound-second

FORCES AND VECTORS

FORCES

Weight depends on the gravitational force acting on an object. To describe a force completely, we need to tell both its magnitude as well as the direction in which the force acts. Weight is a *force* acting toward the center of the earth.

Displacement is a change of position. Displacement requires both distance and direction for its complete description. Displacement is a vector quantity. For example, let us say an airplane flies 200 kilometers (km) on a bearing of 090 degrees (°), and then turns and flies 100 km on a bearing of 000°. We are saying that the plane flies due east for 200 km, and then turns, and flies due north 100 km. This is known as displacement and can be used to determine the airplane's distance and direction from beginning to end points.

Forces produce or prevent motion. Forces are vector quantities since they have both magnitude and direction. Some different kinds of forces are defined as follows:

- *Parallel forces* are forces acting in the same or opposite directions.
- *Friction* is a force which opposes motion.
- A *resultant* force is the single force which has the same outcome as two or more forces acting together. It may be substituted for these forces.
- An *equilibrant* force is the force which produces equilibrium. Equilibrium is the condition of a body in which there is no change in its motion. The equilibrant force is equal in magnitude, but acts in the opposite direction, to the resultant force.
- The *resolution of forces* is the separation of a single force into two component forces which act in definite directions on the same point.

For example, if one person pulls eastward on a rope with a force of 40 lb and another person joins in and pulls on the rope in the same direction with a force of 60 lb. The resultant force is 100 lb acting eastward on the rope. One stronger person taking their place could produce the same effect by pulling eastward on the rope with a force of 100 lb. This is shown in the vector diagram Figure 6.5.

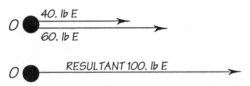

Figure 6.5   Two Forces in Same Direction

Now one person pulls eastward with a force of 40 lb and another person pulls westward on the same point with a force of 60 lb. The resultant force is 20 lb pulling westward on the point.

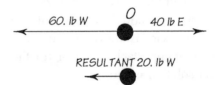

Figure 6.6   Two Forces in Opposite Directions

GRAPHICAL VECTOR ANALYSIS

The *graphical method of vector analysis* is done with pencil and paper, a ruler, and a protractor. An arrow is used to represent a vector. The direction of the arrow represents the direction of the vector, and the length of the arrow is proportional to the magnitude of the vector. Using a ruler and protractor, one can add and subtract vectors. The vector produced by adding or subtracting two or more vectors is called the resultant.

To add vectors graphically see Figure 6.7. In (a) two forces F_1 and F_2 are applied to the same point. Arrows are drawn to represent the forces; their lengths are proportional to the magnitude of the force. In (b)

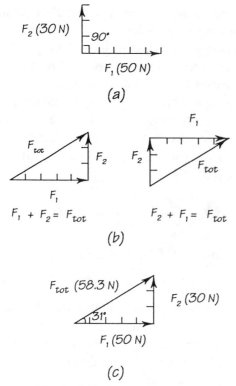

Figure 6.7   Vector Analysis

the arrows are moved head to tail and the total force vector is drawn. The order of addition is unimportant. Then in (c) the numerical solution is shown.

Magnitude and direction may also be determined using both algebra and trigonometry. These methods are not discussed here.

MOTION

In presenting a very brief discussion of motion, we will define motion, velocity, acceleration, Newton's laws of motion and his law of universal gravitation.

Motion is a continuing change of place or position. *Average speed* is the rate of motion or the distance an object moves divided by the time it takes to make this move, such as 4 m/sec. *Velocity* is the rate of displacement, or the speed with which an object moves in a particular direction, for example, 6 mi/hr, 090°. *Acceleration* is the rate of change of velocity, or how long (time) it takes the object to change its speed in a particular direction.

tion, for example, 7 m/sec/sec (7 m/sec²). Speed is a scalar quantity; velocity is a vector quantity.

NEWTON'S LAWS OF MOTION

Every year automobile accidents claim thousands of victims. Many of these accidents might have been avoided if the drivers had paid more attention to the three basic laws which govern the motion of all bodies. These laws are known as *Newton's laws of motion* which are (1) the law of inertia, (2) the law of acceleration, (3) the law of action and reaction.

Newton's first law, the *law of inertia*, is a nonmathematical statement which says that force is needed to change the motion of any body, whether it is moving or at rest: A body at rest stays at rest while a body in motion remains in motion unless acted on by an outside force. The mass, or inertia, of a body determines the amount of force which must be applied to change what the body is doing.

When a train starts suddenly, the people in it are thrown backward. Since the passengers were originally at rest, they tend to remain at rest even when the train moves forward. If the moving train stops suddenly, the people in it are thrown forward. Since the passengers were moving forward with the train, they tend to continue to move forward even though the train has stopped.

Newton's second law, the *law of acceleration*, says that the acceleration of a body is directly proportional to the force exerted on the body, that the acceleration is inversely proportional to the mass of the body, and that the acceleration will be in the same direction as the applied force. This law makes sense when we realize that the larger the object, the more force would be necessary to move it. The larger the object the slower it will move, and finally, the object will move in the direction in which the force was applied.

The law of acceleration give us the famous formula:

Force = mass x acceleration (F = ma),

or $a = \dfrac{F}{m}$

Sample problem:

What force in newtons (which is the metric unit of force) is required to accelerate a small cart having a mass of 10 kg at the rate of 5.0 m/sec² in an eastward direction?

F = ma

F = 10 kg x 5.0 m/sec²

F = 50 nt, eastward

Newton's third law, the *law of action and reaction,* states that for every action there is an equal and opposite reaction. The third law has many everyday applications. On a slippery road, the wheels of an automobile often spin rapidly without giving the car any forward motion. The slippery condition of the road prevents it from reacting to the backward push of the car wheels. This uncertain reaction between the road and the car wheels causes the automobile to skid. When we row a boat, the oars exert a force against the water and the water exerts an opposite force against the oars. In a jet propelled airplane the reaction of the hot gases, which are driven backward from the jet of the engine, is what drives the plane forward.

Figure 6.8   Law of Action and Reaction

NEWTON'S LAW OF UNIVERSAL GRAVITATION

Newton's law of universal gravitation describes the force of attraction between the earth and everything on or near it. A statement of the law of universal gravitation says that the force of attraction between any two bodies is proportional to each of their masses, and that the force of attraction is inversely proportional to the square of the distance between them. It also says that every object in the universe attracts every other object. We do not notice this attraction between ordinary objects, such as books, chairs, and tables, because the force between them is extremely small.

However, when one or both of the bodies involved has a large mass like the sun, the earth, or another planet, this attraction shows itself very clearly. It is the attraction between the sun and the earth that keeps the earth moving about the sun in an almost circular path. Also, the tides are due to the force of attraction between the moon and our oceans.

WORK

The word *work* in everyday language describes any mental or physical activity. In science, work means that a force has actually succeeded in moving a body. For instance, doing homework is not work in a scientific sense. However, if you lift up or push a carton of books across the floor you have done work by exerting a force on the carton of books.

Work is measured by the unit called the *joule.*

Work = Force x Distance (W = F x s)
Distance is represented by the symbol "s".

One joule of work is accomplished when a force of one newton (nt) acts through a distance of one meter (m).

Sample problem:

A woman weighing 750 nt climbs a

flight of stairs that is 5 m high. What work does she do?

$$W = F \times s$$
$$W = 750 \text{ nt} \times 5 \text{ m}$$
$$W = 3750 \text{ joules}$$

Work is also measured in foot-pounds (ft-lb).

Sample problem:

A man exerts a 40 lb force to push his stalled car forward a distance of 20 ft. How much work does he do?

$$W = F \times s$$
$$W = 40 \text{ lb} \times 20 \text{ ft}$$
$$W = 800 \text{ ft-lb}$$

POWER

Power is work divided by time. The power of a machine tells us how much work that machine can do in a unit of time.

$$\text{Power} = \frac{\text{Work}}{\text{time}}$$

since Work = Force x Distance,

$$\text{then, Power} = \frac{\text{Force x Distance}}{\text{time}}$$

$$\text{Power (watts)} = \frac{\text{Force (nt) x Distance (m)}}{\text{time (sec)}}$$

Sample problem:

An individual exerts a force of 740 nt walking up a flight of stairs 12 m high in 30 sec. What power has the individual used?

$$\text{Power} = \frac{\text{Force x Distance}}{\text{time}}$$

$$\text{Power (watts)} = \frac{740 \text{ nt} \times 12 \text{ m}}{30 \text{ sec}}$$

Power = 296 watts

The power of most machinery is measured in a unit called *horsepower* (hp). This unit is supposed to be the rate at which a strong horse can work. One horsepower is equal to 550 foot-pounds (ft-lb) per second, or 33000 ft-lb per minute. Actually, the av-

erage horse can work at the rate of about 3/4 hp, but it is close enough for our purposes to call it 1 hp.

When we say that the power of a machine is 1 hp, we mean that it can do 550 ft-lb of work during every second that it is in operation. A 2 hp machine can work twice as fast as a 1 hp machine — that is, it does 2 x 550, or 1100 ft-lb of work per second.

$$\text{Horsepower} = \frac{\text{Work (ft-lb)}}{\text{time (sec)}} \times 550 \text{ ft-lb}$$

Sample problem:

A steam shovel raises a load of 6600 lb of gravel a distance of 10 ft in 4 sec.

a) How much work is done by the shovel?

$$\text{Work} = \text{Force x Distance}$$
$$W = 6600 \text{ lb} \times 10 \text{ ft}$$
$$W = 66000 \text{ ft-lb}$$

b) What is its horsepower?

$$\text{hp} = \frac{\text{Work}}{\text{time}} \times 550 \text{ ft-lb}$$

$$\text{hp} = \frac{66000 \text{ ft-lb}}{4 \text{ sec}} \times 550 \text{ ft-lb}$$

$$\text{hp} = 30$$

ENERGY

Matter acquires *energy* when work is done against gravity in raising an object to an elevated position. Matter also acquires energy when work is done to set it in motion. The water trapped behind a dam has energy and can be used to turn a water wheel. Winds possess energy, too, and can drive windmills or push sailboats.

Energy is the ability to do work. This work can appear as heat, electricity, light, sound, mechanical and nuclear energy. The amount of energy a body possesses is shown by how much work that body could do if all its energy were used. For example, a body that can do 20 ft-lb of work is said to have 20 ft-lb of energy.

The units that describe work, the joule and the foot-pound, are the units to describe energy.

Potential energy and *kinetic energy* are discussed in Unit 3, Page 113. Read that material now so that we can add some information to it.

POTENTIAL ENERGY

Potential energy is the energy a body has because of its condition, its position, or its chemical state. The water at the top of a dam, or a waterfall, possesses potential energy because of its high position. This energy may be used by having the water turn water wheels as it falls. The potential energy of gasoline is due to its chemical state.

Since any raised weight has potential energy because of its position, we can calculate the potential energy of such a weight by finding the work done in raising it to this position.

Potential Energy = Weight x Height
P.E. = w x h

Sample problem:

What is the potential energy of a 50 lb stone block which is on the top of a skyscraper 700 ft high?

P.E. = w x h
P.E. = 50 lb x 700 ft
P.E. = 35000 ft-lb

Since energy and work use the same units, the joule and the foot-pound, and we know that Work = Force (F) x Distance (s) then, P.E. = Work = F x s.

In lifting an object, its weight (F), is equal to mass (m) times gravity (g). In lifting the object, the distance (s) becomes the vertical distance or height (h) to which it is lifted. (The value for gravity is 9.8 m/sec^2 or 32 ft/sec^2).

Then, P.E. = mass x gravity x height (mgh)

Sample problem:

What potential energy in joules is acquired by a block of steel whose mass is 50 kg when it is raised 5 m?

P.E. = mgh
P.E. = 50 kg x 9.8 m/sec^2 x 5 m
P.E. = 24500 joules

KINETIC ENERGY

Every object in motion can do work. Until the object is stopped, it can force other objects to move. Moving objects therefore possess energy. The energy that a body has because of its motion is called kinetic energy. Moving water and moving air have *kinetic energy* which may be harnessed, as in water and wind mills.

The greater the speed of a body and the greater its weight, the greater will be its kinetic energy.

K.E. = 1/2 mass x velocity^2
K.E. = 1/2 mv^2

Sample problem:

A baseball has a mass of 0.14 kg. If it is thrown with a velocity of 7.5 m/sec, what is its kinetic energy in joules?

K.E. = 1/2 mv^2
K.E. = 1/2 x 0.14 kg x (7.5 m/sec)^2
K.E. = 3.93 joules

To calculate the kinetic energy of a body in foot-pounds, the equation is:

$$K.E. = \frac{wv^2}{2\,g,}$$

where w (weight), v (velocity),
g (gravity, 32 ft/sec^2)

Sample problem:

What is the kinetic energy of a 6400 lb truck moving at the rate of 20 ft/sec?

$$K.E. = \frac{wv^2}{2\,g,}$$

where w = 6400 lb, v = 20 ft/sec,
g = 32 ft/sec^2

$$K.E. = \frac{6400 \times (20)^2}{2 \times 32}$$

K.E. = 40000 ft-lb

HEAT ENERGY AND WORK

Since heat is a form of energy, it may be converted into work. This is what happens when we use steam and gasoline engines. On the other hand, work and other forms of energy may be transformed into heat. James Joule, an English physicist of the 19th century, measured the quantity of work that is equivalent to a single unit of heat. He found that 1 calorie = 4.19 joules of work. Also, 1 BTU = 778 ft-lb of work.

The law of conservation of matter and energy may be restated as follows: Energy and matter can be transformed into other forms of energy, or matter, or both, but the sum total of energy and matter in the universe remains the same. Some energy transformations are:

Transformation	Application
Chemical to electrical	Storage battery
Mechanical to electrical	Generator
Electrical to mechanical	Motor
Sound to electrical	Microphone
Electrical to sound	Speaker
Light to electrical	Solar cell
Electrical to light	Electric lamp
Light to heat	Solar heater
Heat to light	Electric lamp
Light to chemical	Photography
Mechanical to heat	Friction
Heat to mechanical	Steam engine
Nuclear (atomic to heat)	Nuclear reactor

While some energy may be lost as heat and friction, engineers in their design of products try to maximize energy transfer and minimize energy losses.

MACHINES

MECHANICAL ADVANTAGE

In every machine, we deal with two forces, the effort and the resistance. The effort is the force exerted by the person who is using the machine. The resistance is the weight or object the person is trying to lift or overcome. The ratio of the resistance overcome by a machine to the effort applied to it is called the *mechanical advantage* of the machine. Thus,

$$\text{Mechanical advantage} = \frac{\text{Resistance}}{\text{Effort}}$$

$$\text{M.A.} = \frac{R}{E}$$

We can divide machines into two main types:

- Those that *multiply force at the expense of distance.*
- Those that *multiply distance at the expense of force.*

An example of a machine that multiplies force would be an automobile jack and a barber's chair. An example of a machine that multiplies distance is a bicycle. In the bicycle example, the effort applied to a pedal is transmitted to the wheel through a gear-and-chain arrangement which multiplies distance. When the rider pushes the pedal a certain distance, this machine causes the bicycle to move forward a much greater distance.

Machines make it possible for us to do tasks which otherwise would be extremely difficult, or even impossible, without some assistance. The five purposes for which machines are used are:

- To *transform energy.* A steam turbine transforms heat energy into mechanical energy. A generator transforms mechanical energy into electrical energy.
- To *transfer energy* from one place to another. The connecting rods, crankshaft, drive shaft, and rear axle transfer energy from the combustion in the cylinders of an automobile to the rear wheels.

- To *multiply force.* A mechanic uses a system of pulleys to lift an engine out of an automobile. The pulley system enables the mechanic to raise the engine by exerting a force which is less than the weight of the engine. The engine moves more slowly than the chain on which the mechanic pulls. A machine enables us to gain force, but only at the expense of speed or distance.

- To *multiply speed.* A bicycle is used to gain speed, but only by exerting a greater force. No machine can be used to gain both force and speed at the same time.

- To *change the direction* of a force. The single pulley at the top of a flag pole enables one end of the rope to exert an upward force on the flag as a downward force is exerted on the other end by the person raising the flag.

SIMPLE MACHINES

There are six simple machines: the lever, the pulley, the wheel & axle, the inclined plane, the screw, and the wedge. The pulley and the wheel & axle are basically levers, while the screw and the wedge are modified inclined planes. All other machines, even the largest and most complex, are combinations of two or more of these simple machines.

A *lever* consists of a bar which is free to turn about a fulcrum or pivot point. When a force is applied to such a bar, it causes the bar to turn. In doing so, the lever moves a resistance or weight acting at some other point of the bar. For example, when we row a boat we use the oars as levers. The oarlocks are the fulcrums, the effort-forces are exerted on the handles, and the resistance-forces are exerted on the blades. Many common levers consist of two bars pivoted at the

same fulcrum, i.e. scissors, pliers, and nutcrackers.

Levers are divided into three classes, depending on the position of the fulcrum (F), resistance (R), and effort (E).

- In *first class lever,* the fulcrum lies between the effort and the resistance. Examples are the see-saw and the crow-bar. The mechanical advantage of a first class lever may be equal to 1, greater than 1, or less than 1.

- The *second class lever,* places the resistance between the effort and the fulcrum. Examples are the wheelbarrow and the nutcracker. Since the resistance arm is always smaller than the effort arm, the mechanical advantage of a second class lever is always greater than one.

- In *third class levers,* the effort acts between the resistance and the fulcrum. Thus the effort arm is always smaller than the resistance arm, and the mechanical advantage is necessarily less than 1. Third class levers enable us to multiply distance at the expense of force. Examples are tweezers and the human forearm.

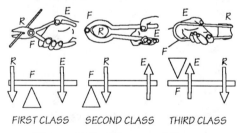

FIRST CLASS   SECOND CLASS   THIRD CLASS

Figure 6.9   Classes of Levers

A *pulley* is a grooved wheel supported in a frame. It can be fastened by a hook to a fixed beam or a ceiling, or it may be fastened to the resistance to be overcome. If fastened to a beam, the pulley does not move, and is called a fixed pulley. When fastened to the resistance, the pulley moves with the resistance, and is called a movable pulley.

Pulleys in various combinations are very widely used to lift heavy objects by applying relatively small forces.

For example, suppose that a piano mover is able to raise a 400 lb piano by applying a force of 100 lb to the rope of a set of pulleys. The piano mover's effort is 100 lb, and resistance overcome by the mover is 400 lb. The M.A. of these pulleys is R/E or 400 lb/100 lb = 4.

The ideal mechanical advantage of a set of pulleys is equal to the number of strands holding up the resistance. A pulley system multiplies the effort applied to it, but does so at the expense of distance.

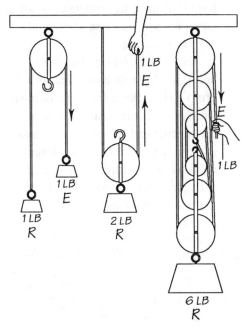

Figure 6.10   Pulley Systems

In its simplest form, a *wheel & axle* consists of a large wheel which is rigidly attached to a smaller wheel (axle). Both wheels, therefore, turn together. By applying an effort to the large wheel, a large resistance can be overcome on the small wheel. In the door knob, for example, we apply a small force to the knob (large wheel), and the shaft (axle) turns the latch. The steering wheels of automobiles, boats, and the windlass are other examples of this machine.

In some wheels & axles, the effort is applied to the small wheel in order to gain speed. An example is the back wheel and sprocket wheel of a bicycle. In this combination, the effort is applied to the sprocket or small wheel to turn the large wheel.

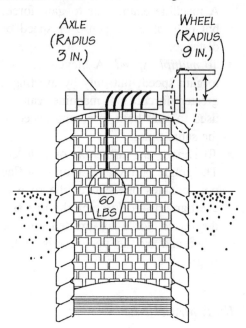

Figure 6.11   Wheel & Axle

Hills, stairways, gangplanks, chutes, and ramps are examples of the simple machine called the *inclined plane*. Inclined planes are used to raise objects that are too heavy to lift directly. For example, a safe must be lifted 3 feet before it can be placed on a truck. To lift the safe vertically would require the effort of four people. Although the safe weighs 200 pounds, an individual person would need to exert a force of only 50 pounds to push it up an inclined plane. The individual pays for the advantage by having to move the safe a greater distance.

The *screw* is an inclined plane wound around a cylinder. The jackscrew, commonly used in lifting automobiles, is an example of this machine. Suppose an ordinary

327

FOUR PEOPLE NEEDED TO
LIFT SAFE ONTO TRUCK

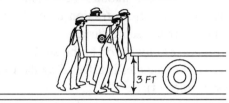

ONE PERSON DOING
THE SAME JOB

Figure 6.12   Inclined Plane

screw is being turned into a piece of wood.
When the screw turns through one complete
revolution, it advances a distance equal to
the space between two successive threads.
This distance is called the *pitch* of the screw.

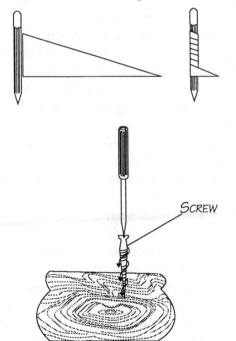

Figure 6.13   The Screw

The *wedge* may be considered to be a
combination of two similar inclined planes
placed back to back, or base to base. Axes,
chisels, knives, nails, and pins are common
examples. As the sharp edge of each of these
machines is pushed or hammered into an
object, the sides of the wedge exert great
force upon the object, tending to split or
push it apart. The longer and thinner a
wedge is, the more effective it will be.

Many complicated machines are combinations of simple machines. The crank of a
food chopper works on the principle of the
wheel & axle. The crank turns a screw
which forces the food through small holes,
where it is chopped off by the wedge action
of a cutting disk. Such a combination of two
or more simple machines is called a *compound machine.*

FORCE vs. DISTANCE

The fact that a machine multiplies distance at the expense of force or force at the
expense of distance can be expressed by a
law of work. This law describes an ideal machine where the effort multiplied by the distance it moves is exactly equal to the
resistance multiplied by the distance it is
moved.

The effort times the effort-distance represents the amount of work put into the machine by the individual using it; this is called
the work input. The resistance times the
resistance-distance it moves is called the
work output.

Effort x Effort-distance = Resistance x
Resistance-distance

or Work input = Work output

The *ideal mechanical advantage* (IMA)
of a machine is the ratio of the distance the
effort force moves to the distance the resistance force moves.

The *actual mechanical advantage* (AMA)
is the ratio of the resistance force to the effort force.

EFFICIENCY

Since some of the work put into an actual machine is always wasted in overcoming friction, the work done (output) will always be less than the work put into it (input). The *efficiency* of a machine is the ratio of the work done by the machine to the work put into it.

$$\text{Efficiency} = \frac{\text{Work output}}{\text{Work input}}$$

$$\text{Efficiency} = \frac{\text{R x R-distance}}{\text{E x E-distance}} = \frac{\text{AMA}}{\text{IMA}}$$

Efficiency is usually expressed as a percent. It tells what part of the work put into a machine actually does useful work, and what part is used up by friction. Efficiency is always less than 100%.

Sample problem:

To lift a 150 lb barrel 20 ft, a man applies a 50 lb force to a set of pulleys and pulls in 100 ft of rope. What is the efficiency of the pulley system?

$$\text{Efficiency} = \frac{\text{R x R-distance}}{\text{E x E-distance}}$$

$$\text{Efficiency} = \frac{150 \text{ lb x } 20 \text{ ft}}{50 \text{ lb x } 100 \text{ ft}}$$

$$\text{Efficiency} = \frac{3}{5} \text{ or } 0.6$$

Efficiency = 0.6 x 100% = 60%

Sample problem:

A machine has an ideal mechanical advantage of 5, but an actual mechanical advantage of 4. What is its efficiency?

$$\text{Efficiency} = \frac{\text{AMA}}{\text{IMA}} \text{ x } 100\%$$

$$\text{Efficiency} = \frac{4}{5} \text{ x } 100\% = 80\%$$

FRICTION

Friction is the force which opposes the movement of one body over another. Rolling friction is less than sliding friction. A body which rolls over another body encounters less opposition from friction than if it were sliding over the same surface.

Frictional opposition to the sliding of one surface over another is affected by the roughness of the surfaces.

- The rougher the surfaces, the greater the friction between them. Small irregularities on the surfaces of bodies are the primary cause of friction.
- Friction is usually greater when the surfaces are just starting to slide over one another than when they are already in motion.

The *disadvantages of friction* are that some of the work put into every machine is used in overcoming friction. This decreases the efficiency of the machine. This wasted energy, moreover, usually turns into heat and may result in the intense heating and even burning out of some of the parts of the machine.

The *advantages of friction* are that although friction is the cause of considerable losses of energy, it also performs some indispensable services for people. Without friction, we would not be able to walk. Our feet would not "grip" the ground. Friction makes it possible to get vehicles going or, once started, to bring them to a halt by applying the brakes.

The following methods are commonly used *to reduce friction:*

- Make the rubbing surfaces as smooth as possible.
- Place ball bearings and rollers between the surfaces in contact, thus causing them to roll, rather than to slide, over each other.
- Spread a lubricant, such as oil or grease, between the rubbing surfaces. The lubricant forms a film between the two surfaces so that their irregularities do not stop the sliding motion.

HEAT ENERGY

In Unit 3, Page 114, the text introduces the concept of *heat energy.* Read that material now. Here are some additional concepts of heat energy.

Quantities of heat are measured by the effects they produce. For example, the amount of heat given off when a fuel burns may be measured by the temperature change in a known quantity of water.

The *heat capacity* of a substance is the quantity of heat needed to raise the temperature of the substance one degree.

Two heat measurement units are the *calorie* (cal) and the *British thermal unit* (BTU). The calorie is the amount of heat needed to raise the temperature of one gram of water one Celsius degree. The BTU is the amount of heat needed to raise the temperature of one pound of water one Fahrenheit degree.

SPECIFIC HEAT

Specific heat (c) is the ratio of the heat capacity of a body to its mass or weight. The specific heat of a substance tells us how much heat each gram of substance must receive for each degree that its temperature rises. For example, water has a specific heat of 1 cal/g°C, which is high when compared to most substances. Copper, for example, has a specific heat of 0.093. This means you would have to add about 0.093 of a calorie to raise the temperature of one gram of copper from 10°C to 11°C.

A benefit of the high specific heat of water is that regions bordering on large bodies of water generally have cooler summers and warmer winters than inland regions at the same latitude. In summer, the water absorbs large quantities of heat from the surrounding warmer air and land, thus keeping them cool. In winter, the water slowly gives off its heat thereby warming its surroundings.

The total number of calories, or the quantity of heat (Q) gained or lost by a body when heated, may be calculated as follows:

Heat gained = Mass x Specific heat x Change in temperature

$$Q = m \times c \times \Delta T$$

Sample problem:

How much heat (Q) is needed to raise the temperature of 500 grams of iron from 50°C to 250°C? (c for iron is 0.11 cal/gC°)

The change in temperature (ΔT) is 200°

Heat gained = Mass x Specific heat x Change in temperature

$$Q = m \times c \times \Delta T$$
$$Q = 500 \text{ g} \times 0.11 \times 200°$$

Heat gained,

$$Q = 11000 \text{ calories}$$

Sample problem:

An aluminum cylinder weighing 3 lb is heated to 300°F. How many BTU are given off as the cylinder cools to 50°F? (c for aluminum is 0.22 BTU/lbF°)

$$Q = m \times c \times \Delta T$$
$$Q = 3 \text{ lb} \times 0.22 \text{ BTU/lbF}° \times (300° \text{ F} - 50° \text{ F})$$
$$Q = 165 \text{ BTU}$$

Most measurements of specific heat are made by the *method of mixtures.* In this method, a mass of water at a known temperature is mixed with a given mass of another substance at some other temperature. Since heat is a form of energy and therefore cannot be created or destroyed, it follows that the heat gained (or lost) by the water and its container must be equal to the heat lost (or gained) by the other substance. The mixing is generally done in a special container called a calorimeter.

To illustrate the method of mixtures, suppose that we have 420 g of pure lead in small pieces, and that we wish to determine the specific heat of this lead. We would do the following:

1. Heat the lead until its temperature is 100°C.

2. Determine the weight of the copper calorimeter, say 110 g. (c for copper is 0.09 cal/gC°)
3. Pour 100 g of cold water into the calorimeter, and measure the temperature of the water, say 10°C.
4. Now pour the hot lead into the calorimeter, and mix with the water. Measure the temperature of the mixture, say 19.3°C.

From the above data, we can calculate the specific heat of lead. Note that temperature of the lead fell 80.7° (from 100°C to 19.3°C), while that of the water and the calorimeter rose 9.3° (from 10°C to 19.3°C.

Let "X" be the specific heat of the lead. The quantity of heat lost is equal to the quantity of heat gained.

Using the formula,
$$Q = m \times c \times \Delta T,$$
Heat lost by lead = 420 g x X x 80.7° = 33894 X cal.

Heat gained by calorimeter = 110 g x 0.09 cal/gC° x 9.3° = 92.07 cal.

Heat gained by water = 100 g x 1 cal/gC° x 9.3° = 930 cal.

Since the water was contained in the calorimeter, they must both be at the same temperature. Therefore, the total heat gained must be equal to the total heat lost.

Heat lost by lead = Heat gained by water + Heat gained by calorimeter

33894 X cal = 930 cal + 92.07 cal

X = 0.03 cal, the specific heat of lead

LAB EXPERIENCE 6.1
SPECIFIC HEAT

Purpose: To determine the specific heat of one or more metals.

Materials:

Calorimeter

Thermometer

Stirring rod

Steam boiler

Tripod for steam boiler

Bunsen burner and
   rubber tubing

Hot mitts

Set of masses

Double pan balance

Metal cylinders: lead,
   aluminum, brass,
   copper

Magnifier

Strong twine

Goggles

Note: Water will be brought to boiling temperature in this experiment.
      BE CAREFUL!!!

Procedure:

1. Determine the mass of the metal cylinder.
2. Fill the boiler half full with water and place over Bunsen burner.
3. Attach a piece of twine, about 30 cm long, to the metal cylinder and lower it into the steam boiler.
4. While the water is heating to boiling, determine the mass of the empty calorimeter.
5. Fill the calorimeter about two-thirds full with water which has been chilled so that it is several degrees cooler than room temperature.
6. Determine the mass of the calorimeter and water. Keep the calorimeter away from the Bunsen burner so that it doesn't get warm.
7. Measure the temperature of the boiling water with the thermometer. Since the metal cylinder is being heated in the boiling water, its original temperature will be the temperature of the boiling water.
8. Stir the water in the calorimeter and measure its temperature. Make sure the thermometer bulb is completely submerged in the liquid. Put your eye at a level where you can easily read the thermometer and if necessary, use the magnifier to read the thermometer.
9. Lift the cylinder by means of the twine and quickly transfer the solids to the calorimeter of cold water.
10. Gently move the cylinder in the water and then stir the water with the stirring rod.
11. Read the temperature of the mixture of water and heated cylinder.
12. Complete the chart below.
13. Repeat the procedure with a second metal.

LAB EXPERIENCE 6.1 (Continued)
SPECIFIC HEAT

DATA ITEMS	TRIAL 1	TRIAL 2
1. Kind of metal	_____	_____
2. Mass of metal	_____ g	_____ g
3. Mass of calorimeter	_____ g	_____ g
4. Mass of calorimeter and water	_____ g	_____ g
5. Mass of water	_____ g	_____ g
6. Specific heat of calorimeter	_____ cal/gC°	_____ cal/gC°
7. Temperature of solid initial (temperature of boiling water)	_____ °C	_____ °C
8. Temperature of water and calorimeter, initial	_____ °C	_____ °C
9. Temperature of solid, water, and calorimeter, final	_____ °C	_____ °C
10. Temperature change of water and calorimeter	_____ C°	_____ C°
11. Calories gained by calorimeter	_____ cal	_____ cal
12. Calories gained by water	_____ cal	_____ cal
13. Total calories gained	_____ cal	_____ cal
14. Calories lost by solid	_____ cal	_____ cal
15. Temperature change of solid	_____ C°	_____ C°
16. Specific heat of solid	_____ cal/gC°	_____ cal/gC°
17. Accepted value for specific heat of solid	_____ cal/gC°	_____ cal/gC°
18. Error	_____ cal/gC°	_____ cal/gC°
19. Percentage error	_____ %	_____ %

Questions:

1. Why is it desirable to have the water a few degrees colder than room temperature when the intial temperature is taken?

2. What is the method for determining the specific heat of substances?

CHANGES OF STATE

We have seen that a substance may exist in either the solid, liquid, or gaseous state. We say a substance has undergone a *change of state* when it goes from one state to another.

The change from the solid to the liquid state is called melting or *fusion.* Crystalline solids, such as ice, salt, copper and tin, melt at definite temperatures called their melting points. Thus copper melts at 1083 °C, tin at 232 °C.

To melt a solid, heat must be added to it. During the time a crystalline solid is melting, its temperature remains the same. For example, when ice at 0 °C (its *melting point*) is heated, it begins to melt, but remains at 0 °C until all of the ice has melted. Only then, on further heating, does the temperature rise.

The change from the liquid to the solid state is called freezing or *solidification.* The liquids of crystalline substances freeze at definite temperatures called their freezing points. Thus, water freezes at 0 °C, liquid tin at 232 °C.

To freeze a liquid, heat must be removed from it. While the liquid is solidifying, its temperature remains the same. Thus, when water at 0 °C (its *freezing point*) is cooled, it begins to solidify, but remains at 0 °C until all of the water has frozen. Only then, on further cooling, does the temperature fall.

In crystalline substances, melting and freezing occur at the same temperature. Thus, the melting point of ice and freezing point of water is 0 °C. The melting and freezing points of tin are 232 °C. Other substances, such as paraffin, glass, tar and butter, have no sharply defined melting or freezing points. On heating, such substances become soft at first and then gradually turn to liquids.

Most substances contract on freezing, but there are some exceptions. Water, for example, expands on freezing. Another substance that expands on solidification is cast iron. This property makes it suitable for producing accurate castings.

When a substance is dissolved in water, the freezing point, and therefore the melting point, is lowered. In winter we add antifreeze products to the water in automobile radiators to prevent it from freezing. This is also the reason we use rock salt to melt ice on the roads.

HEAT OF FUSION

If a mixture of water and ice is gently heated, some of the ice will melt, but the temperature of the mixture will remain at 0 °C. The heat that was added must, therefore, have been absorbed by the ice when it melted.

The number of calories needed to melt one gram of any substance at its normal melting point, without any temperature change, is called its *heat of fusion.* For example, the heat of fusion of ice is 80 calories. This means that one gram of ice at 0 °C must absorb 80 calories of heat as it changes into one gram of water at 0 °C.

The method of mixtures is used to determine the heat of fusion of ice and other solids.

In the following lab experience, the drop in the temperature reading will be measured when a given quantity of very hot water in a calorimeter is cooled by a given quantity of ice which is added to the calorimeter. The heat given off by the water will first melt the ice and then warm the water.

LAB EXPERIENCE 6.2
HEAT OF FUSION

Purpose: To determine the heat of fusion of ice.

Materials:

Calorimeter	Pan for ice
Balance	Paper towels
Set of masses	Ice cubes
Thermometer	Magnifier
Stirring rod	Goggles

Procedure:

1. Determine the mass of the calorimeter.

2. Fill the calorimeter about half full of water having a temperature of about 35° C.

3. Determine the mass of the calorimeter and water.

4. Stir the water in the calorimeter with the stirring rod and read the temperature, using the magnifier if necessary.

5. Wipe two ice cubes, or an equal amount of ice lumps, with a towel to remove any water clinging to them. Then put them in the calorimeter carefully so that there is no splashing.

6. Stir rapidly until all the ice is melted, and read the temperature again.

7. Determine the combined mass of the calorimeter and its liquid contents.

8. Complete the chart below.

9. If time permits, repeat the experiment.

LAB EXPERIENCE 6.2 (Continued)
HEAT OF FUSION

DATA ITEMS	TRIAL 1	TRIAL 2
1. Mass of calorimeter	———— g	———— g
2. Mass of calorimeter and water	———— g	———— g
3. Mass of water	———— g	———— g
4. Mass of calorimeter and water (after ice is melted)	———— g	———— g
5. Mass of ice	———— g	———— g
6. Specific heat of calorimeter	———— cal/gC°	———— cal/gC°
7. Temperature of water and calorimeter, initial	———— °C	———— °C
8. Temperature of water and calorimeter, final	———— °C	———— °C
9. Temperature change of water and calorimeter	———— °C	———— °C
10. Calories lost by calorimeter	———— cal	———— cal
11. Calories lost by water	———— cal	———— cal
12. Total calories lost	———— cal	———— cal
13. Calories used to warm water formed by melted ice	———— cal	———— cal
14. Calories used to melt ice	———— cal	———— cal
15. Heat of fusion of ice	———— cal/g	———— cal/g
16. Accepted value for heat of fusion of ice	———— cal/g	———— cal/g
17. Error	———— cal/g	———— cal/g
18. Percentage error	———— %	———— %

Questions:

1. What is the heat of fusion of a solid?

2. What practical use do we make of the heat of fusion of ice?

BOILING

When a liquid is heated, its molecules move faster and faster. More molecules are able to leave the surface and escape into the air. With continued heating and depending on atmospheric pressure, a temperature is reached at which not only molecules at the surface of the liquid, but also those within the liquid, will have enough kinetic energy to escape as vapor. Bubbles of vapor will then form throughout the liquid. The liquid will boil. The temperature at which this occurs is called the *boiling point* of the liquid. At sea level for example, water boils at 100 °C, ether boils at 35 °C, and mercury boils at 357 °C. At high altitudes because of the decrease in pressure, it takes a long time for water to come to a boil.

When the pressure upon a liquid is increased, its boiling point is raised. When the pressure upon a liquid is decreased, its boiling point is lowered. When a substance such as salt (NaCl) is dissolved in water, the boiling point is raised, therefore, it takes longer for the water to come to a boil.

Some facts about boiling liquids:

- While a liquid is boiling, its temperature remains at the boiling point.
- It takes a definite additional amount of heat to change a liquid to its gaseous or vapor state.
- Additives elevate the boiling point of substances.

HEAT OF VAPORIZATION

The quantity of heat needed to change 1 gram of a liquid at its boiling point into a gas is called the *heat of vaporization* of that liquid. The heat of vaporizaton of water is 540 calories. This means that 540 calories of heat must be added to change 1 gram of water at 100 °C into 1 gram of steam at 100 °C.

The change from the vapor back to the liquid state is called *condensation*. When 1 gram of a vapor condenses, it loses the heat it absorbed when it evaporated. This heat, which is called the *heat of condensation,* is exactly equal to the heat of vaporization. Thus, when 1 gram of steam at 100 °C changes to water, it gives off 540 calories of heat to its surroundings. This fact is utilized in steam heating. When steam in the radiators of a room condenses, each gram of the steam gives up 540 calories of heat to the room thereby warming the room. The heat of condensation of steam may be measured by the method of mixtures.

WAVE MOTION

TYPES OF WAVES

A *wave* is a disturbance that travels through matter or space. As a wave travels, energy is carried from one place to another. Energy may be transferred by the movement of matter as in wind and water waves. Energy may also be transferred by the motion of particles. As an example, electricity and heat are both conducted through metals by the motion of electrons.

To produce *mechanical waves,* we need a source which produces a disturbance, and an elastic medium to transmit the disturbance. A medium is any material—solid, liquid, gas—in which waves travel.

There are two kinds of wave motion through matter. A *transverse wave* is one that moves at right angles to the moving particles of the medium. Each wave consists of a *crest* (high point) and a *trough* (low point). Rope and water waves are examples of transverse waves. These waves move forward horizontally, but they cause the medium over which they pass to vibrate vertically.

The second kind of wave is a *longitudinal wave.* This kind is a series of compressions

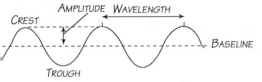

Figure 6.14 Transverse Wave

and rarefactions, one following the other. The *compression* is the squeezing together of the particles of the medium. The *rarefaction* is the spreading apart of the particles of the medium. A spring would be a good medium in which to show a longitudinal wave.

As the coils of the spring vibrate, they move back and forth in the same line of motion as the wave. They do not move up and down as in a transverse wave. It is the energy, not the matter, that is carried along with the wave.

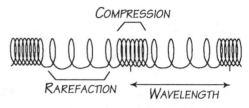

Figure 6.15 Longitudinal Wave

TABLE 6.2
TRANSVERSE AND LONGITUDINAL WAVES

TYPE OF WAVE	DIRECTION OF WAVE	DIRECTION OF MOTION OF MEDIUM	WAVES
TRANSVERSE	⟹	↕	
LONGITUDINAL	⟹	⟺	

PROPERTIES OF WAVES

As shown in Table 6.2, transverse waves are made of crests and troughs. Each wave has a certain wavelength. A *wavelength* is the distance from one crest to the next crest or from one trough to another. Longitudinal waves are made of compressions and rarefactions. The wavelength of a longitudinal wave is the distance between two compressions or two rarefactions.

You can make big waves and small waves in a rope. The size of a wave is measured by its amplitude. *Amplitude* is the distance

from the crest or trough of a wave to the base line of the medium.

The faster you vibrate a rope or spring, the more waves you make each second. The number of waves produced each second is the frequency. The *frequency* of a wave can be thought of as the number of vibrations per second. Frequency is measured in a unit called the hertz. One *hertz* (Hz) is one wave per second. Frequency and wavelength are related. As the frequency of a wave increases, its wavelength decreases (see Figure 6.16).

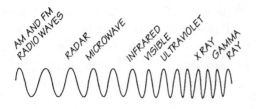

LOW FREQUENCY   HIGH FREQUENCY
LONG WAVELENGTH   SHORT WAVELENGTH

Figure 6.16   Electromagnetic Spectrum

An *electromagnetic wave* is a disturbance that moves through space. An example would be radio, microwave, visible light and x-rays.

Once a wave is produced, it moves through the medium at a certain speed. The *speed* of a wave is related to its wavelength and frequency. You can find the speed of a wave by using the equation:

Speed = Frequency (Hz) x

Wavelength (cm)

This equation works for both transverse and longitudinal waves.

Sample problem:

Suppose you generate rope waves with a frequency of 2 Hz. You find the wavelength of the rope waves to be 3 cm. What is the speed of the waves as they travel along the rope?

Speed = Frequency x Wavelength

Speed = 2 Hz x 3 cm

Speed = 6 cm/sec

The crest of this wave moves forward at the rate of 6 cm/sec.

Common properties of waves include *rectilinear propagation* which is the movement through a uniform medium in a straight line. *Reflection* is the turning back at the boundary of the transmitting medium, as in radar and sonar tracking. *Refraction* is the change in direction as the wave passes from one medium to another of a different density. *Interference* is combining the disturbances of two wave motions. *Diffraction* is the bending of a wave around obstacles in its path. *Super-*

position occurs when two or more wave disturbances move through a medium at the same time.

SOUND

All *sounds* are produced by the *vibrations* of objects. In pianos and violins, the sound is given off by vibrating strings. In the saxophone, it is a reed that vibrates. The human voice is the result of the vibration of the vocal cords. The number of vibrations an object makes per second is called its frequency. The human ear can normally hear sounds made by vibrating objects whose frequency is between 20 and 20000 vibrations per second (Hz).

PROPERTIES OF SOUND

Most sounds are transmitted to our ears through the air. However, any elastic substance whether solid, liquid, or gas, can transmit sound. For example, you may hear a neighbor's TV through the floors, walls, and windows of the house. For sound to be heard, there must be a source, a medium, and a receiver. Sound cannot pass through a vacuum.

You know that although you can hear sound, a longitudinal wave, you cannot see it. However, scientists have a device that displays sound waves. This device is called an oscilloscope. The picture of the sound wave is caused by the energy of the wave. As the sound wave moves, it carries energy with it. When the wave hits the receiver, the sound energy is converted to electrical energy. The electrical energy appears on the screen as a transverse wave. For example, connect an oscilloscope to a microphone and let the students "see themselves talk" or connect the output from a radio or stereo to the oscilloscope instead of a speaker. Most sounds consist of more than one frequency and thus appear very jagged on the oscilloscope, but all of them are built up from single frequencies.

The speed of sound in air at 32 °F is found to be about 1090 feet per second. For each one Fahrenheit degree rise in temperature beyond 32°, there is an increase in the speed of sound of 1.1 ft/sec. The speed of sound in air is about 330 m/sec at 0 °C. As the temperature of the air rises, the speed of sound increases at the rate of about 0.6 m/sec for each one Celsius degree. The decreased density of the air as the temperature rises allows the sound to travel faster.

In water, sound travels about four times as fast as it does in air. In steel, the speed of sound is about fifteen times as great as in air. The speed of sound in liquids and solids is very moderately affected by changes in temperature.

In a large auditorium, sounds are reflected from the floor, walls, and ceiling many times. This process of multiple reflection is known as reverberation. To eliminate reverberation, as well as echoes, the walls of a hall are often hung with draperies or covered with some soft material which will absorb the sounds that fall upon it.

The physical properties of sound waves are *intensity* and *frequency.* The effects of these two properties on the ear are called loudness and pitch. The *loudness* or volume of a sound depends on the *amplitude* of sound waves. The greater the amplitude, the louder the sound. The highness or lowness of a sound is called *pitch.* Pitch depends on the frequency of sound waves.

Tone or *quality* is the property which distinguishes one sound from another sound where both have the same pitch and loudness. Quality depends on the manner in which the object is vibrating and the shape of the sound waves that are produced. For example, different musical instruments produce their own characteristic tones.

For ordinary sounds, the decibel (dB) is the practical measure of intensity. On this scale, the intensity of a whisper is about 40 dB, while that of ordinary speech is about 65 dB. For each 10 dB, the intensity of sound increases ten times. Sounds above 90 dB can cause temporary hearing loss. People who work near loud noises must wear protective devices over their ears.

TABLE 6.3
FAMILIAR SOUNDS

Source of Sound	Loudness in Decibels
Jet engine	160
Nearby rock band	115
Subway	100
Vacuum cleaner	85
Busy street	75
Normal talking	65
Whisper	40
Rustling of leaves	15

THE DOPPLER EFFECT

If you ever had a car blow its horn as it passed you, you might have heard a change in pitch. As the car approaches you, its sound waves crowd together. The wavelength decreases, the frequency increases, producing a higher pitch. As the car moves away, the waves spread apart. The wavelength increases, the frequency decreases, and the pitch gets lower. The change in the frequency of waves from a moving source is called the *Doppler effect.* You can listen for this effect when trains and trucks pass you.

Speeds faster than sound would include supersonic speeds and shock waves. Supersonic speeds are faster than the speed of sound. Scientists use the term Mach number to compare the speed of sound with the speed of a moving body. Thus, an airplane flying at the speed of sound is traveling at

SOUND WAVES

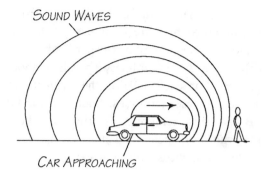

CAR APPROACHING

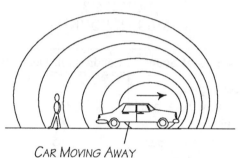

CAR MOVING AWAY

Figure 6.17   The Doppler Effect

Mach 1. Current supersonic jets can fly at speeds as high as Mach 5.

A shock wave is a moving area of crowded molecules produced when the source is traveling faster than sound. When the shock wave reaches the ground, this region of crowded air molecules produces a thunderlike sound called a sonic boom which is strong enough to rattle windows and shake dishes. A sonic boom transfers a great deal of energy to the ground.

LIGHT

Light is made up of particles, called photons, which travel as waves. The speed with which light travels in outer space or in a vacuum is about 186000 miles per second, or about 300000 kilometers per second.

An object can be seen only when sufficient light from it falls upon the receiver. On this basis, substances may be divided into two groups.

Luminous objects are those which emit light of their own. Examples of luminous substances are the sun, incandescent solids, and burning fuels, such as candles or kerosene lamps.

Illuminated objects are those which are seen by the light they reflect. Illuminated objects receive light from luminous sources. Some examples are the moon, the pages of this book, the floor, walls, and furniture of the room.

An *opaque* substance is one through which light cannot pass. The floor and walls of the room in which you are now seated are opaque.

A *translucent* substance is one that lets light pass through, but distorts the light in such a way that objects on the other side cannot be seen clearly. Some examples are wax paper, frosted glass, and some window shades.

A *transparent* substance is one through which light passes so that objects on the other side can be seen clearly. Plastic wrap, cellophane, plate glass, and air are examples.

Light can travel through thin fibers of glass or plastic without escaping out the sides. Light inside these fibers is reflected so that it stays in the fiber until it reaches the fiber's other end. Such optical fibers are being used to carry telephone messages. Sound waves are first converted to electric signals. The signals are coded into a series of light pulses. These pulses move through the fibers at the speed of light and are then converted back to sound.

Light travels in straight lines which explains our inability to see around corners. Since light travels in straight lines, it leads to the formation of shadows. When light from a luminous source is intercepted by an opaque body, a dark space called a *shadow,* is formed behind the body. A point source of light, such as an arc light, produces a sharply defined shadow called an *umbra*.

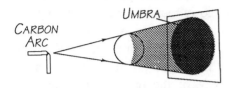

Figure 6.18   Point Source of Light

When the source of light is larger than a point, it will cast a shadow consisting of two parts, an umbra and a *penumbra*. The umbra is the totally dark, central portion of the shadow which receives no light from any part of the light source. The penumbra is a lighter shadow surrounding the umbra; it receives light from some, but not all, parts of the light source.

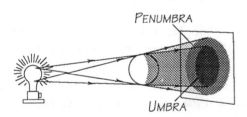

Figure 6.19   Large Source of Light

ECLIPSES

Eclipses of the sun and the moon are the result of shadows. An eclipse of the sun (solar eclipse) occurs when the moon passes between the sun and the earth. The shadow of the moon then falls upon the earth. Those parts of the earth that are located within the umbra of this shadow will be in total darkness during the period of the eclipse. People living in this area will not be able to see the sun until the umbra of the moon's shadow has passed over them. In these localities, the eclipse is said to be total. People living in regions where the penumbra of the moon's shadow falls will see a partial eclipse. That is, they can see part of the sun throughout the period of the eclipse.

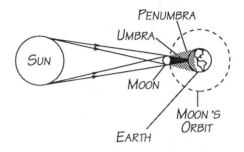

Figure 6.20   Eclipse of the Sun

During an eclipse of the moon (lunar eclipse), the earth is between the sun and the moon. The moon is, therefore, in the umbra of the earth's shadow. The solar rays passing through the earth's atmosphere are diffused and refracted so that the moon is seen in a reddish light.

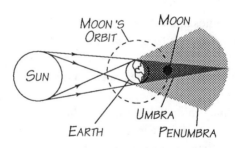

Figure 6.21   Eclipse of the Moon

REFLECTION

Another basic property of light is *reflection*. Reflected light follows a simple law. The *law of reflection* states that the angle of incidence equals the angle of reflection, or that the angle at which the light ray (incident ray) strikes a surface such as a flat mirror is equal to the angle at which the light ray (reflected ray) is reflected from the surface.

The same law of reflection applies to all

surfaces. Yet different surfaces reflect light differently. Rough surfaces scatter light in many directions. Smooth surfaces reflect light in one direction.

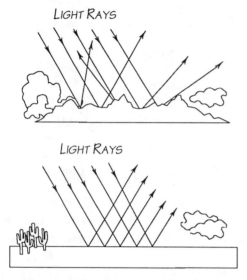

Figure 6.22   Types of Reflection

REFRACTION

Pebbles and other objects at the bottom of a pond appear to be nearer the surface than they actually are. Sticks or branches that are only partly submerged seem to be broken at the point where they enter the water. These familiar optical illusions are due to the *refraction* of light. Since light travels slower in water than it does in air, the ray of light coming from the air at an angle is slowed down as it enters the water. This results in a change in path of the ray, and thus gives the

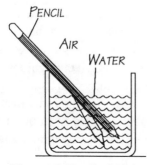

Figure 6.23   Refraction

illusion that the stick or branch is bent or broken.

If a narrow beam of light is allowed to pass through a triangular glass *prism,* it will undergo refraction both on entering and on leaving the prism. A prism is a piece of solid glass shaped in the form of a triangle. Light entering a prism always bends toward the base of the prism. Since light travels more slowly in glass than it does in air, light is refracted when it passes through the prism.

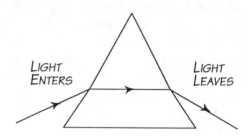

Figure 6.24   Refraction in a Prism

White light, such as sunlight, when passing through a glass prism, comes out of the prism and separates into the colors of the *spectrum* from red to violet. The spreading out of white light into its component colors is known as *dispersion*. Dispersion occurs because each color travels through the prism at a different speed and bends at a different angle. The rainbow of beautiful colors that we sometimes see after a rainfall is caused by dispersion. Each raindrop appears to behave like a prism separating the sunlight into the colors of the spectrum.

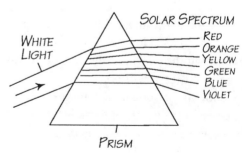

Figure 6.25   Separation of White Light

POLARIZATION OF LIGHT

Polarized light is light in which the vibrations are confined to a single plane. The plane is at right angles to the direction of the ray of light. Light behaves like a transverse rope as seen in Figure 6.26. At first, the waves are vibrating in many directions. As the waves pass through the screens, some vibrations are blocked so that the waves may pass in only one direction. These are waves that vibrate along a single plane and are called polarized waves.

Polarized light is used by engineers to study the strains in mechanical structures such as bridges. Polarized sunglasses cut down glare by blocking out all but one path of vibration.

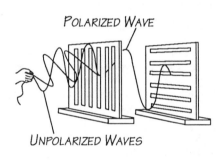

Figure 6.26   Polarized Light

LENSES

An optical device used to bend light is a *lens*. A lens is a piece of glass or plastic that is not uniform in thickness, and has polished curved surfaces. By refracting the light that passes through them, lenses can either magnify the size of objects or make them appear smaller. A *convex* lens magnifies objects, while a *concave* lens always makes objects appear smaller.

A lens that is thicker in the center than at the edges is called a convex (converging) lens. Convex lenses bring light rays to a point or focus. Visual farsightedness causes the image to fall behind the retina. The con-

dition can be corrected by using a convex lens which bends the light rays together before they enter the eye. This causes the image to be formed on the retina.

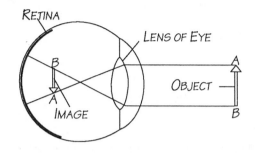

UNCORRECTED

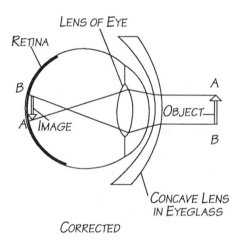

CORRECTED

Figure 6.27   Convex Lens

A lens that is thinner in the center than at the edges is called a concave (diverging) lens. A concave lens spreads light rays. Visual nearsightedness causes the image to fall in front of the retina of the eye. The condition is corrected by using a concave lens which spreads the rays of light apart before they enter the eye. This causes the image to be formed on the retina.

By refracting the light that passes through them, lenses can either magnify the size of objects or make them appear smaller. A convex lens magnifies nearby objects, while

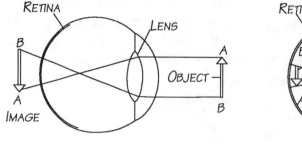

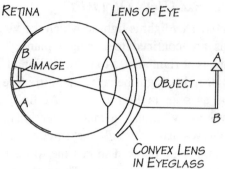

UNCORRECTED   CORRECTED

Figure 6.28   Concave Lens

a concave lens always makes objects appear smaller. Lenses are used in eyeglasses, microscopes, cameras, movie projectors, and telescopes. There is great similarity between the human eye and the camera. A comparison between the two is shown in Table 6.4.

TABLE 6.4
COMPARISON OF A CAMERA AND AN EYE

Camera	Eye
Is enclosed in a lightproof box.	Is enclosed in a lightproof eyeball.
Light enters through the lens and produces an image on photographic film.	Light enters through the lens and produces an image on the retina.
Light is focused by means of a convex lens.	Light is focused by means of a convex lens and by the cornea.
The amount of light admitted is controlled by the diaphragm.	The amount of light admitted is controlled by the iris and the pupil.
The image is focused by moving the lens nearer to or farther from the film.	The image is focused by the lens. The muscles of the eye automatically change the thickness (convexity) of the lens, allowing the lens to focus properly.
The image on the film must be developed and fixed to be seen.	The image on the retina causes an impulse to be sent to the brain along the optic nerve. The brain interprets the image.

MAGNETISM AND ELECTROMAGNETIC INDUCTION

MAGNETISM

A *magnet* is generally recognized by its ability to attract and hold pieces of iron. Cobalt, nickel, iron, and alloys of these materials are strongly attracted by magnets.

If a bar magnet is suspended at its midpoint so that it can turn freely, it will come to rest with one end pointing in a general northerly direction, and the other end pointing southward. The end of the magnet which shows this tendency to point north when the magnet is freely suspended is called the *north pole* of the magnet. The opposite end is called the *south pole* of the magnet. Every magnet, no matter what its shape, has both a north seeking and a south seeking pole. The strength of the magnet is concentrated at these poles.

The *law of magnetic poles* states that like magnetic poles repel each other, while unlike poles attract each other. The force between two magnetic poles is directly proportional to the strength of the poles and inversely proportional to the square of the distance between them.

Research indicates that the individual molecules of a magnetic substance do not act independently but combine their magnetic effects to form groups called *domains*. Each domain is a tiny magnet having a north and south pole. When an object is magnetized, these domains line up so that their magnetic poles combine to produce a strong north pole at one end of the object and a south pole at the other end. In an unmagnetized object, the domains are arranged haphazardly, so that they have no net magnetic effect.

The space around a magnet in which its influence is felt is called the *field* of the magnet. A "map" of the field of a bar magnet can be made as follows: put a large piece of paper over a bar magnet and sprinkle iron filings over the paper. The lines formed by the iron filings are called *lines of force*. All of them together make up the magnetic field of the magnet. Lines of force have the following properties:

- They never cross each other.
- They form closed curves. Lines of force leave the north pole of the magnet, enter the south pole, and complete their path through the magnet.
- The concentration of the lines of force at any part of a magnetic field determines the strength of the field at that point.
- Lines of force repel each other, and thus tend to spread farther and farther apart as they leave the north pole of a magnet.

There are three ways to turn a magnetic substance into a magnet.

- The first way, by contact, where the substance is stroked with a magnet. The stroking must be done in only one direction so that the magnets in the domains line up properly.
- The second way, by induction, is to place a magnetic substance in the magnetic field of a magnet, and the substance will become temporarily magnetized. When the substance is removed from the magnetic field, it loses its magnetism.
- The third way is to pass an electric current through a wire. This sets up a magnetic field around the wire. As long as the electricity flows, the wire behaves like a magnet. This is demonstrated by putting some iron filings close to a wire and noticing the attraction of the filings to the wire when it is carrying an electric current.

The magnetic field around a wire carrying an electric current may not be very strong. There are several ways to increase the strength of the field.

- The first way is to put an iron core inside the coil of wire. The core concentrates the lines of force. This is called an electromagnet.
- The second way is to put more turns of wire in the coil. The greater the number of turns, the stronger the electromagnet becomes.
- The third way is to increase the amount of current thereby producing a very strong magnet.

Electromagnets are used in the electric bell, the telegraph sounder, the telephone receiver, the motor, the generator, and electrical measuring instruments such as the galvanometer, the ammeter, and the voltmeter. Huge lifting electromagnets are also used in foundries, railroad yards, and mills for loading and unloading scrap iron, steel rails, and other iron objects.

THE ELECTRIC MOTOR

An *electric motor* converts electrical energy into mechanical work. A simple motor consists of four main parts:

- Two stationary magnetic poles, called *field poles.*
- A rotating part, called the *armature (loop).*
- A *commutator,* which is a metal ring composed of two segments that are mounted on the axle of the motor and are insulated from each other.
- Two metal or carbon strips, called *brushes,* which are mounted in such a way that each is always in contact with one half of the commutator.

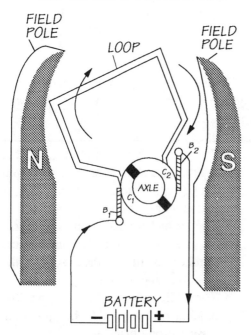

Figure 6.29   The Electric Motor

The motor in Figure 6.29 consists of a metal loop mounted on an axle. One end of the loop is connected to one half of the commutator (C_1) and the other end of the loop is connected to the other half (C_2). As current from the battery flows through the loop, one side of the loop becomes a north pole and the other side a south pole. Since the loop is inside a stationary magnet (field poles), the side of the loop which has become a north pole will be repelled by the north-field pole, and turn away from it. As the loop's north pole approaches the south-field pole, the commutator (C_1) has turned and is now touching the positive-side brush (B_2). Commutator (C_2) has turned and is now in contact with negative-side brush (B_1). The reversing of poles causes the loop to spin. As long as the current flows, the loop will continue to reverse polarity causing the axle to spin. The spinning motion of the axle in a motor can be used to move things, such as wheels, pulleys, and fan blades.

ELECTROMAGNETIC INDUCTION

Placing a coil of wire next to a strong magnet and moving the coil back and forth across the magnetic field, produces a current. This is called *electromagnetic induction.* The current that is produced is called an induced current. Electromagnetic induction is the key to another important device, the generator.

THE GENERATOR

While a motor changes electric energy into the mechanical energy of motion, a *generator* is a device that uses the energy of motion to produce electricity. The generator is exactly opposite to the electric motor. A generator is a coil with many loops of wire rotated in a very strong magnetic field. The coil is mounted on a shaft. High pressure steam, wind, or falling water sets the shaft spinning within the field. Magnetic forces act on the electrons in the moving wire. The electrons gain energy and begin to flow in the coil. This flow of electrons is electricity. Large generators usually produce electricity with voltages ranging from 12500 volts to 25000 volts while small generators can produce 12–24 volts of electricity such as may be found in an automobile battery.

ATOMIC STRUCTURE

COMPOSITION OF MATTER

All substances are believed to be made up of units called *molecules*. A molecule is defined as the smallest part of a substance which has the properties of that substance. For example, a molecule of water is the smallest quantity of water that has the physical and chemical properties of water.

Molecules, though very small themselves, are composed of still smaller particles called *atoms*. A molecule of water, for example, may be split into two atoms of hydrogen and one atom of oxygen.

Atoms, in turn, are composed of at least three types of smaller particles known as *protons, electrons,* and *neutrons.* Every atom contains a positively charged area called its *nucleus,* around which are distributed a number of negatively charged bodies called *electrons.* There is an attraction that holds electrons around the positively charged nucleus. The electrons are not standing still nor do they have a definite location. Electrons are located somewhere in a cloud around the nucleus. These electron areas are called levels, shells, or orbits. The level or shell closest to the nucleus, the K shell, will not experience any molecular change when it contains two electrons. The outer shells of most atoms are stable when they contain eight electrons.

The nucleus of an atom is composed of two types of particles, called protons and neutrons. The only exception is the common form of hydrogen, which has no neutrons. *Protons* are tiny, positively charged bodies. A proton has a mass about 2000 times greater than the electron, but carries an amount of positive charge which is equal to the negative charge of the electron. *Neutrons* are bodies having approximately the same mass as protons, but possessing no electrical charge. Since these relatively heavy particles, protons and neutrons, are all contained in the nucleus of an atom, almost the entire mass of the atom is concentrated in its nucleus. The *mass number* is equal to the number of protons and the number of neutrons located within the nucleus.

The number of protons in the nucleus of an atom is the *atomic number* of that atom. The mass number minus the atomic number is equal to the number of neutrons located in the nucleus.

THE ELECTRON THEORY AND CHARGED BODIES

An electrically neutral atom has exactly as many electrons surrounding its nucleus as it has protons within its nucleus. Therefore, the atom has an equal quantity of positive and negative charges and is *electrically neutral.*

An object, as a whole, generally retains all of its protons but may either gain or lose electrons. The ready transferability of electrons helps us to understand how a neutral body can acquire a positive or a negative charge.

IONIZATION

Ionization is the process where electrons are stripped off the outer shell of the atom forming an ion. An *ion* is an atom that has an unequal number of electrons and protons, and therefore, has an electrical charge. Energy is emitted in the process of electron transfer. The resulting ions are more stable than the original atoms.

When atoms combine to form molecules, the atoms are held together by forces of attraction, called chemical bonds. *Valence electrons* are the electrons that take part in a chemical bond. These electrons are found in the outermost energy level, or "valence shell". Since they are involved in bonding, valence electrons determine the properties of an element.

IONIC BONDING

Ionic bonding occurs when one or more electrons are shared by the outer shell of one atom and the outer shell of a second atom. By this process, both atoms usually attain outer shells with a very stable configuration. For example, when a sodium atom shares an electron with a chlorine atom the sodium now has 11 protons and 10 electrons, and is a sodium ion. Similarly, the chlorine atom has 17 protons and 18 electrons, and is a chlorine ion. The sodium ion has one less electron and is said to have a charge of $1+$. In the same way, the chlorine ion has one more electron and is said to have a charge of $1-$. The oppositely charged particles, by attracting one another, form a chemical bond, resulting in the compound common salt (NaCl).

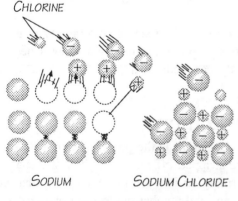

CHLORINE

SODIUM   SODIUM CHLORIDE

Figure 6.30   Ionic Bonding

COVALENT BONDING

In *covalent bonding,* atoms may share outer shell electrons in an attempt to attain stability. For example, each hydrogen atom has an unfilled valence shell. Atoms of this gas do not exist as single atoms in nature. They occur in pairs held together by covalent bonds. Thus the two hydrogen atoms each share an electron in forming a hydrogen molecule. *Diatomic* molecules contain two of the same kind of atoms joined by a covalent bond. Some examples of diatomic molecules are hydrogen (H_2), nitrogen (N_2), oxygen (O_2), and chlorine (Cl_2). Figure 6.31 shows the diatomic molecules of hydrogen and oxygen and how they combine to form water molecules.

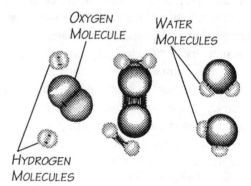

OXYGEN MOLECULE   WATER MOLECULES

HYDROGEN MOLECULES

Figure 6.31   Covalent Bonding

METALLIC BONDING

Metallic bonding occurs in solid metals. The atoms are packed closely together so that each atom has 12 other atoms surrounding it. The outer shell electrons of all these atoms are loosely held and are continually exchanged. The atoms bonded together in a solid are more stable than the independent atoms which exist in the vapor of a metal.

ELEMENTS

A substance which is made up of atoms with the same atomic number is called an

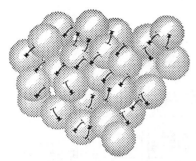

Figure 6.32   Metallic Bonding

element. An element is considered to be the simplest type of matter. It is made up of only one kind of material. Elements are the basic units from which all other matter is built.

Elements can be distinguished by their individual properties, that is, by their appearance and behavior. Elements may exist in any of three phases of matter. Most elements are solids, some are gases, and a very few are liquids. Scientists have identified elements with atomic numbers ranging from 1 to 109. Number 1 is hydrogen, number 2 is helium, number 3 is lithium, and so forth. Several elements do not occur in nature but are made in the laboratory.

Elements, as they occur naturally, are mixtures of *isotopes* in definite proportions. Isotopes are atoms whose nuclei contain the same number of protons but different numbers of neutrons. Therefore, the isotopes would have different mass numbers. The *atomic weight* of an element is the average of the atomic masses of all its isotopes based on their relative abundance.

Chemists have given each element a symbol of one or two letters. The symbols come from the Latin or English names for the elements. The natural and laboratory-made elements are arranged on a chart called the *Periodic Table of the Elements* and is shown in Table 6.5.

The period arrangement of elements is strictly on the basis of atomic number and similarities of properties. They are arranged horizontally by increasing the electron number, by one, as you go from left to right across the Table. The elements are arranged vertically, by family, with each element in the family having the same number of electrons in the outermost shell of the atom.

Some common elements are: iron (Fe), which is a grayish metal; mercury (Hg), which is a silvery metallic liquid; and radon (Rn), which is a colorless, odorless, toxic gas.

COMPOUNDS

A *compound* is made of two or more elements that have been chemically combined in a definite proportion by weight. When this occurs, their atoms have joined together and the resulting compound has properties different from the properties of the elements. A molecule represents a compound, and is the smallest part of a compound. For example, water is a compound consisting of molecules made up of atoms of hydrogen and atoms of oxygen. Since all samples of a given compound have the same composition, compounds are said to be homogeneous. The major properties are listed in Table 6.6.

A *chemical formula* is a convenient shorthand showing the composition of the compound. The formula is made up of symbols and subscripts. The symbols show what elements are in the compound. The subscripts tell how many atoms of each element are present.

Some common compounds are: water (H_2O), which is a colorless, odorless liquid; salt (NaCl), which is a white crystalline

Periodic Table of The Elements

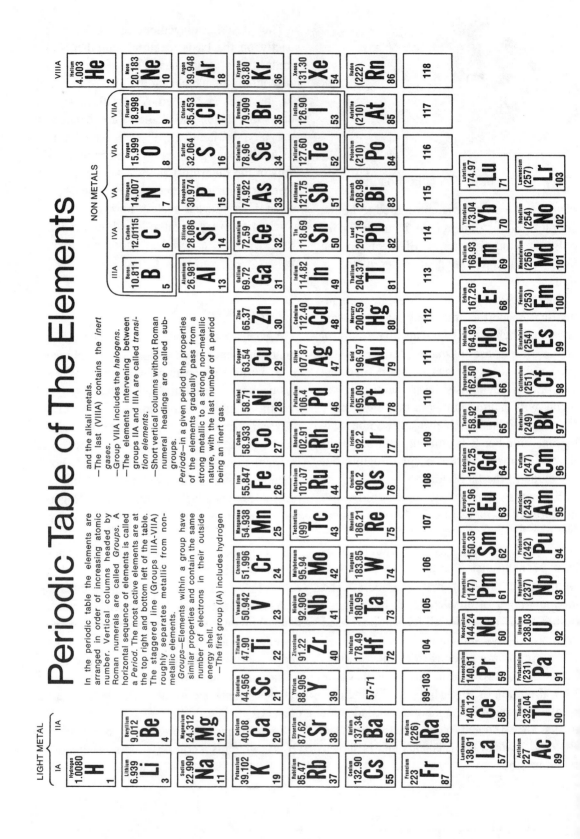

In the periodic table the elements are arranged in order of increasing atomic number. Vertical columns headed by Roman numerals are called *Groups.* A horizontal sequence of elements is called a *Period.* The most active elements are at the top right and bottom left of the table. The staggered line (Groups IIIA-VIIA) roughly separates metallic from non-metallic elements.

Groups—Elements within a group have similar properties and contain the same number of electrons in their outside energy shell.

—The first group (IA) includes hydrogen and the alkali metals.

—The last (VIIIA) contains the *inert gases.*

—Group VIIA includes the *halogens.*

—The elements intervening between groups IIA and IIIA are called *transition elements.*

—Short vertical columns without Roman numeral headings are called subgroups.

Periods—In a given period the properties of the elements gradually pass from a strong metallic to a strong non-metallic nature, with the last number of a period being an inert gas.

solid; and carbon dioxide (CO_2), which is a colorless, odorless gas.

MIXTURES

When elements or compounds combine physically, another kind of matter called a *mixture,* forms. A mixture has a variable composition and can be separated by physical means. The matter in the mixture remains unchanged and retains its original properties. For example, when a mixture of iron filings (black metal) and powdered sulfur (yellow) is assembled, the mixture is magnetic because the iron is unchanged, and dark yellow because the sulfur is unchanged. However, when the mixture is heated a black nonmagnetic compound, iron sulfide, results. These new properties indicate that the new substance has been formed. The major properties of mixtures are listed in Table 6.6.

TABLE 6.6
PROPERTIES OF COMPOUNDS AND MIXTURES

Compounds	Mixtures
Made up of only one kind of particle	Made up of two or more different kinds of particles
Formed during a chemical change	Not formed in a chemical change
Can be broken down only by chemical changes	Can be separated by physical changes
Has properties different from those of its ingredients	Has same properties as its ingredients
Has definite amount of each ingredient	Does not have definite amount of each ingredient

SOLUTIONS AND SUSPENSIONS

Solutions are examples of mixtures. A solution contains particles the size of molecules, evenly distributed throughout another substance. The dissolved particles are so small that you cannot see them. Grinding, stirring, and heating increase the rate of dissolving by helping mix molecules of solute and solvent. The *solute* is the substance to be dissolved. The *solvent* is the material doing the dissolving. A *solution* is the end product of mixing together a solute and a solvent. The particles do not settle soon after they have been dissolved. The parts of a solution can be separated by physical means.

A *dilute* solution has only a small amount of solute compared with the amount of solvent. A *concentrated* solution has a relatively large amount of solute compared with the amount of solvent. A solution is said to be *unsaturated* as long as more solute can be dissolved. In a *saturated* solution at any one temperature, no more solute can be dissolved. The *solubility* is the amount of solute that can be dissolved in a given amount of solvent at any one temperature. It is the amount of solute that makes a solution saturated. An increase in temperature increases the solubility of a solute. A *supersaturated* solution contains more solute than it normally has at a given temperature.

A *suspension* is a mixture made of parts that separate upon standing. The particles mixed into a suspension are larger than molecules or ions. An example would be coarse sand and water.

COLLOIDS

Colloids are much like solutions. A colloid consists of undissolved particles or droplets that stay mixed in another substance. An example of a colloid is fog which is a mixture of fine water droplets in air. Both solutions and colloids contain small particles that do not settle. Colloids scatter a beam of light passing through the mixture. Colloid particles suspended in a fluid can be used to demonstrate the property that molecules are constantly moving. The random zigzag movement of molecules is called *Brownian motion.*

EMULSIONS

An *emulsion* is a suspension of two liquids that usually do not mix together. An example would be oil and water. Any substance that keeps the parts of an emulsion mixed together is called an *emulsifier.* A few drops of liquid soap added to the oil and water, then shaking the solution, would break the oil into droplets that would stay mixed for a longer time. The liquid soap acts as an emulsifier.

CHANGES IN MATTER

Iron rusts, water freezes, sugar dissolves in water, milk sours, radium disintegrates and eventually produces lead. These are just some of the changes which occur frequently.

Changes in matter are of three kinds: physical, chemical, and nuclear.

- In a *physical change* the composition of the substance is not lost. The substance consists of the same molecules, or atoms, or ions as it did

before the change occurred. Some examples of physical changes are tearing, breaking, grinding, and turning wood into sawdust. When water freezes and forms ice, its composition remains the same. If we heat the ice, it changes back into water. When sugar dissolves in water it undergoes a physical change. If the water evaporates, the sugar remains behind.

- In a *chemical change* the composition of the substance is changed, and a new substance with new properties is produced. We still have the same number of atoms or ions, but they are rearranged to form new substances. The rusting of iron produces a new material, iron oxide. Sour milk certainly has different properties from the sweet milk it was originally.

- A *nuclear change* is like a chemical change because new substances with new properties are formed. However, in nuclear change the new materials are formed by changes in the identity of atoms themselves. Some of these changes take place naturally and spontaneously. An example is the change of radium atoms into lead atoms.

Chemical changes may occur slowly or rapidly. depending on the substances involved. Most often a *catalyst* is used to help a reaction. A catalyst is a substance which can change the speed of a chemical reaction without itself being permanently changed. For example, the element nickel, in a finely divided form, is present in the production of margarine. Margarine is made by adding hydrogen to liquid oils such as soybean oil. The hydrogen and oil react to form solid margarine. The nickel remains unchanged and can be reused.

Chemical changes involve energy changes. Every chemical reaction involves some form of energy, such as light, heat, or electrical energy. A reaction which releases energy is *exothermic*. For example, when coal burns, stored chemical energy in the coal changes to light and heat energy. This is an exothermic reaction. A reaction which absorbs energy is *endothermic*. Baking powder contains chemical compounds that react in dough and make it rise. However, the chemical reaction does not happen until you put the dough into a hot oven. The dough absorbs heat and tiny bubbles of carbon dioxide gas form. The gas causes the dough to rise. This is an endothermic reaction.

CHEMICAL EQUATIONS

A *chemical equation* represents a chemical reaction and indicates the substances which interact, called the reactants, and the new substances, or products, that are formed. For the equation to be completely correct it must be balanced. Equations are balanced to show that atoms are not created or destroyed in a reaction. For example, when iron (Fe) rusts it combines with oxygen (O_2) to form a new compound which is mostly iron oxide (Fe_2O_3). The chemical equation for this reaction would be:

$$(4Fe + 3O_2) \rightarrow (2Fe_2O_3)$$
(Reactants) yield (Products)

The large numbers in the equation are called *coefficients*. They are used to balance the amount of material used in the reaction and the resulting products according to the law of conservation of mass. The total number of atoms of each element on the left-hand side of the equation is exactly equal to the total number of atoms of each element on the right-hand side of the equation.

The number of atoms it takes to make up an element's atomic mass in grams is described by *Avogadro's number*. This quantity is also called a *mole* and is equal to 6.023×10^{23} units. The units could be atoms, molecules, ions, or whatever is being considered.

Let us look at another example of a chemical reaction, the combination of magnesium with oxygen to yield magnesium oxide.

$$2Mg + O_2 \rightarrow 2MgO$$

The 2 in front of the Mg refers to the amount of magnesium entering the reaction. It means two moles of magnesium are used. The subscript 2, as in O_2, represents the fact that the element oxygen ordinarily does not exist in the form of individual atoms, but rather as pairs of atoms. Such diatomic units are called molecules of the element. The entire reaction can be read as follows, "two moles of magnesium react with one mole of oxygen to yield two moles of magnesium oxide".

PROPERTIES OF MATTER

Matter can be classified in different ways using physical and chemical properties. Some *physical properties* are color, odor, density, hardness, solubility, melting point, and boiling point. A chemical property is a description of the chemical characteristics of a substance. *Chemical properties* are determined by the reaction of a substance with other substances. Examples of chemical properties are how a substance reacts with acids, reacts with oxygen in air, decomposes on heating, and is acidic or basic.

NUCLEAR ENERGY

RADIOACTIVITY

Radioactivity is the spontaneous breakdown of the nuclei of atoms with the emission of particles and gamma rays. Radioactivity is a property of all elements with atomic numbers greater than 83.

Radioactive elements give off invisible radiation from their nuclei. The forms of this radiation are *alpha particles* (helium nuclei), *beta particles* (electrons), and *gamma rays* (high energy electromagnetic waves). Alpha particles may be stopped by a sheet of paper. Beta particles may be stopped by 1 cm of aluminum. Gamma rays may be stopped by 60 cm of concrete or 30 cm of lead.

The process in which an element emits a particle from its nucleus to form a new element is called *transmutation*. Alpha decay and beta decay are two types of transmutations.

Isotopes are nuclides of an element. The *nuclide* is an atom with a specific amount of energy and with a set number of protons and a set number of neutrons in its nucleus. Each type of radioactive nuclide decays at a fixed rate called a half-life. The half-life of a nuclide is the length of time necessary for one-half of the radioactive material that is present to disintegrate. Radiation may be detected by Geiger counters, cloud chambers, and photographic methods.

FISSION AND FUSION

Fission and fusion are two types of nuclear reactions that release energy. *Fission* occurs when a large unstable nucleus breaks into smaller, usually more stable nuclei. *Fusion* occurs when two small nuclei are combined to form a larger, stable nucleus. Nuclear reactors are used to produce radioactive isotopes, test materials, breed new fissionable materials, and serve as sources of heat energy in nuclear power plants.

PROBLEMS

A. Forces and Vectors

1. What is a resultant force?
2. a. What is equilibrium?
   b. What is an equilibrant force?
   c. How does it compare with its corresponding resultant force?
3. A force of 2 nt on a bearing of 045° acts on a point. Determine the magnitudes of the northward and eastward components of this force.
4. A force of 15 lb on a bearing of 210° acts on a point. What are the magnitudes of its westward and southward components?
5. A single force that has the same effect as all the forces acting on an object is the _____.
6. If two objects are brought closer together, the pull of gravity between them becomes _____.
7. The upward force that water and other fluids exert on objects is called a _____ force.
8. An object whose mass is 20 g has a volume of 25 cm³. Will the object float in water?

B. Speed, Velocity, and Motion

1. The distance traveled each second is called _____.
2. A change of velocity per unit of time is called _____.
3. The tendency of an object to oppose a change in its motion is called _____.
4. a. What is speed?
   b. How is speed measured?
5. a. What is velocity?
   b. Distinguish between speed and velocity.
6. Why is speed a scalar quantity but velocity a vector quantity?
7. How can the magnitude and bearing of the resultant of two velocities which act in the same or in opposite directions be determined?
8. The highway distance from Indianapolis to Denver is 1720 km.
   a. If the driving time is 30 hr, what is the average speed of the trip?
   b. What is the direction of this displacement?
9. Minneapolis and Des Moines are 260 miles apart.
   a. If a man makes the trip to Des Moines in 8 hr, what is his average speed?
   b. In which direction does he travel?
10. A motorboat travels 20 km/hr in still water.
    a. What will be the velocity of the boat if it is directed upstream on a river which flows at the rate of 4 km/hr?
    b. In which direction will the boat go?
11. What is acceleration?
12. Why is acceleration a vector quantity?
13. An automobile can be accelerated from 45 mi/hr to 65 mi/hr in 8 sec. What is the acceleration of the automobile?
14. When a direction is given to an object's speed, you know the object's _____.

15. Two different objects cannot a) be made of the same substance, b) occupy the same space, c) have the same mass, d) be liquids.

C. Work and Power

1. The units of work are the
    a. _____ and
    b. _____.
2. The units of power are
    a. _____ and
    b. _____.
3. One horsepower equals
    a. _____ ft-lb/sec or
    b. _____ ft-lb/min.
4. A girl weighing 700 nt ran up the stairs from the first floor to the third floor in her school building, a vertical distance of 10 m.
    a. How much work did she do?
    b. Her science teacher times her with a stop watch and finds that she requires 10 sec running time. What was the girl's power?
5. a. How much work is done in raising 2000 lb of coal from a mine 150 ft deep?
    b. What horsepower is required to raise the coal in 150 sec?
6. What is the power of a machine that can do 5000 ft-lb of work in 4 minutes?
7. An electric motor lifts a 50 lb weight 60 ft in 20 sec.
    a. Compute the work done.
    b. What is the power of the motor in ft-lb/sec?
8. An electric hoisting machine raises a load of 8000 lb a distance of 55 ft in 20 sec.
    a. How much work does it do?
    b. What horsepower does it develop?
9. How much work can a 10 hp engine do in 5 min?
10. How long would it take a 2 hp motor to raise 9900 lb a distance of 100 ft?
11. How much work is done in lifting a 60 nt box 4 m?
12. A 120 lb girl climbs a ladder 12 ft high. How much work has she done?
13. A force of 50 nt is used to push a loaded wheelbarrow 175 m along a horizontal walk. How much work is done?
14. The rate at which work is done is known as _____.
15. The watt is a unit of _____.
16. One horsepower is equal to _____ watts.
17. How much work must be done to raise a block weighing 980 lb to a height of 35 ft?
18. In everyday language, work is done a) in studying a science lesson, b) in sleeping, c) in solving problems, d) in playing football.
19. In a scientific sense, work is done a) in lifting an object from the floor to the table, b) in supporting an object on your shoulder, c) in preparing a lesson in science, d) as an object is pushed along the floor.
20. The two factors which determine the amount of work done are a) force and weight, b) distance and time, c) force and distance, d) force and time.

21. In everyday language, power may mean a) work, b) physical strength, c) energy, d) authority.
22. In a scientific sense, power is a) the ability to work, b) the time it takes to do work, c) the product of force and distance, d) Fs/t.

D. Energy

1. In raising the hammer of a pile driver, _____ must be exerted over a given distance.
2. When the hammer has been raised to its elevated position,
    a. _____ has been done on the hammer.
    b. In this elevated position, the _____ of the hammer is increased.
3. As the hammer in Question 2 is released and falls, its
    a. _____ is converted to
    b. _____.
4. The rate at which the pile driver works is its _____.
5. To measure the kinetic energy of an object, the mass and _____ of the object must be known.
6. The higher up an object is, the _____ potential energy it has.
7. Energy is a) the ability to do work, b) acquired by an object whenever its position is changed, c) acquired by an object when it is set in motion, d) measured in work units.
8. Kinetic energy is a) energy due to the position of a mass, b) energy due to the motion of a mass, c) a form of mechanical energy, d) proportional to the mass of the object concerned.
9. Potential energy is a) energy due to the position of a mass, b) energy due to the motion of a mass, c) a form of mechanical energy, d) proportional to the mass of the object concerned.
10. Matter and energy are a) different aspects of the same basic entity, b) unrelated, c) interchangeable, d) indestructible.
11. A man lifts a 60 lb box and puts it on a shelf 5 ft above the floor. What potential energy is stored in the box?
12. How high must a 400 lb weight be above the ground to have 6000 ft-lb of potential energy?
13. What potential energy is acquired by a hammer which has a mass of 1 kg when it is raised 1 m?
14. A woman lifts a mass of 2 kg from the floor to a table 0.80 m high. What potential energy, in joules, does the mass have because of this change in position?
15. A man lifts a 160 lb box and puts it on a shelf 15 feet above the floor. What potential energy is stored in the box?
16. If a ball has a mass of 1 kg and a velocity of 10 m/sec, what is its kinetic energy?
17. How much energy does a ball weighing 0.25 lb have when it is moving at the rate of 32 ft/sec?
18. What is the kinetic energy of a 4000 lb automobile moving at the rate of 8 ft/sec?
19. Find the kinetic energy of a bullet weighing 0.10 lb if its speed is 20000 ft/sec?
20. A meteorite weighing 500 lb strikes the earth with a velocity of 150 ft/sec. What is its kinetic energy?

21. How much kinetic energy does a 2 kg bowling ball have if it moves at a speed of 3 m/sec?

E. Machines

1. A machine can multiply either
   a. _____ or
   b. _____, but not both at the same time.
2. In an ideal machine,
   a. the work _____
   b. and the work _____ are equal.
3. In an actual machine,
   a. the work _____ is always greater than
   b. the work _____.
4. Three household utensils that are examples of wedges are
   a. _____,
   b. _____, and
   c. _____.
5. The see-saw is an example of a lever of the _____ class. In levers of this class, the mechanical advantage may be equal to 1, greater than 1, or less than 1.
6. When the moving parts of a machine are oiled, the effort needed to operate the machine a) increases, b) decreases, c) remains the same.
7. List five purposes for which machines are used:
   a. _____
   b. _____
   c. _____
   d. _____
   e. _____
8. Name the six forms of simple machines:
   a. _____
   b. _____
   c. _____
   d. _____
   e. _____
   f. _____
9. What is meant by
   a. machine input?
   b. machine output?
10. Why can the ideal mechanical advantage of a machine never be equal to the actual mechanical advantage of a machine?
11. Which of the simple machines may be thought of as modifications of the lever?
12. Which of the simple machines may be thought of as modifications of the inclined plane?
13. Why are sloping ramps easier to climb than flights of stairs?

14. a. In what way is friction an advantage in the use of an ordinary screw?
    b. In what way is friction a disadvantage in the use of an ordinary screw?
15. A device, such as a screwdriver or a lever, is a _____.
16. The point about which a lever rotates is known as the _____.
17. The force applied to a machine is called a(n) _____ force.
18. The amount of work done by a machine is known as the _____.
19. The usefulness of a machine is indicated by its _____.
20. Machines are less than 100% efficient because of _____.
21. In all machines, some of the work put into a machine is used to overcome _____.
22. A screw and a wedge are both examples of _____.
23. A simple machine that is actually a kind of inclined plane is a a) pulley, b) gear, c) wedge, d) balance.
24. A first-class lever helps do work by a) multiplying effort, b) changing the direction of the effort, c) both of the above, d) none of the above.

Match: Place the number from column I in the appropriate space. Use a number only once.

I		II
25. efficiency	_____	A. A rigid object that can rotate around a fulcrum.
26. effort	_____	B. The force you apply to a machine.
27. fulcrum	_____	C. Work output divided by work input x 100%.
28. gear	_____	D. A simple machine with no movable parts.
29. inclined plane		E. The amount of useful work obtained by using a
30. lever		machine.
31. mechanical advantage	_____	F. Grooved wheel with a rope running through it.
32. pulley	_____	G. A balanced point on a lever.
33. simple machine	_____	H. Any device that makes work easier.
34. wheel & axle	_____	I. A wheel with teeth.
35. work input	_____	J. Output force divided by effort.
36. work output		

F. Heat

1. In what units is heat measured?
2. What is the heat capacity of a body?
3. What change of state is called fusion?
4. What name is given to the temperature at which fusion occurs?
5. What is solidification?
6. What name is given to the temperature at which solidification occurs?
7. What is meant by the term specific heat of a substance?
8. Define the terms:
   a. fusion
   b. heat of fusion
   c. heat of vaporization
   d. heat of condensation

9. How does the melting of ice cubes in a drink cool the drink?
10. Why does the land and air around a lake gain heat when the lake freezes?
11. If salt is dissolved in water, the freezing point of the solution will be a) above 0 °C, b) 0 °C, c) below 0 °C?
12. When 1 g of water at 0 °C freezes, it _____ 80 calories.
13. When 1 g of steam in a steam radiator condenses, it liberates _____ calories of heat to the room.
14. How much heat must be absorbed by 100 g of water to raise its temperature from 10 °C to 50 °C?
15. How much heat will 2 lb of water lose when it cools 8 Fahrenheit degrees?
16. The specific heat of aluminum is 0.22 cal/gC °. If 440 calories of heat are added to an aluminum pan weighing 500 g, how many degrees will its temperature rise?
17. How many calories are needed to raise the temperature of 300 g of aluminum 50 °C? (c of aluminum is 0.22 cal/gC °)
18. A cube of iron weighs 4 lb. How many BTU will be needed to raise its temperature from 70 °F to 500 °F? (c for iron is 0.11 BTU/lbF °)
19. How many calories will be needed to change the temperature of 500 g of water from 20 °C to 100 °C? (c for water is 1 cal/gC °)
20 How much heat is given off when 85 g of lead cool from 200 °C to 10 °C? (c for lead is 0.03 cal/gC °)
21. How much heat is lost by a copper bar weighing 2000 g when it cools from 100 °C to 40 °C? (c of copper is 0.09 cal/gC °)

G. Wave Motion, Sound, and Light

1. What is the term used for the material through which a wave travels?
2. Through which states of matter can waves travel?
3. What kind of wave moves at right angles to the disturbance?
4. What kind of wave moves in the same direction as the disturbance?
5. What does a wave carry?
6. Draw a transverse wave and label a crest and a trough.
7. Waves carry _____ from place to place.
8. The speed of a wave is different in different _____.
9. As the amplitude of a wave increases, its energy _____.
10. Frequency is measured in a unit called a _____.
11. The energy of a wave is measured by its a) wavelength, b) frequency, c) amplitude, d) direction.
12. The low point on a wave is its a) trough, b) crest, c) wavelength, d) frequency.
13. A series of compressions and rarefactions is a a) water wave, b) longitudinal wave, c) transverse wave, d) longitudinal or transverse wave.
14. The speed of a wave depends on its a) frequency, b) wavelength, c) neither a nor b, d) both a and b.
15. A water wave has a frequency of 2 Hz and a wavelength of 7 cm. The speed of the wave is a) 14 cm/sec, b) 9 cm/sec, c) 5 cm/sec, d) 3.5 cm/sec.
16. As the wavelength of a wave increases, its frequency will a) increase, b) decrease, c) remain the same, d) decrease, then increase.

Match: Place the number from column I in the appropriate space. Use a number only once.

I		II

I

17. amplitude
18. compression
19. crest
20. frequency
21. hertz
22. medium
23. rarefaction
24. speed
25. trough
26. vibration
27. wave
28. wavelength

II

_____ A. A disturbance moving through matter.
_____ B. A low point on a wave.
_____ C. A material that carries a wave.
_____ D. The number of waves each second.
_____ E. The height of a wave.
_____ F. Region where particles are close together.
_____ G. The distance between two crests.
_____ H. A unit used to measure frequency.
_____ I. Frequency times wavelength.
_____ J. A high point on a wave.

29. The characteristic of a sound that depends on the energy of the vibrating body is
_____.

30. When matter is moving back and forth rapidly, it is said to be _____.
31. Sound travels a) faster, b) slower, in air than it does in solids.
32. The characteristic of a sound that depends on its frequency is called _____.
33. What is the range of frequencies heard by the human ear?
34. What unit is used to measure the intensity of sound?
35. What are sounds from reflected sound waves called?
36. List 5 properties of light:
    a. _____
    b. _____
    c. _____
    d. _____
    e. _____
37. What property of light do shadows illustrate?
38. What is the speed of light in air?
39. How can light be polarized?
40. Matter that is vibrating produces a) sound, b) heat, c) magnetism, d) light.
41. When an object is producing sound, the vibrations travel through space as a) matter, b) molecules, c) sound waves, d) light waves.
42. The sound waves that leave a vibrating body travel a) only downward, b) only upward, c) only in straight lines, d) in all directions.
43. Your sister is on the other side of the fence. You cannot see her but you can hear her moving around in the grass. You can therefore conclude that a) sound travels only in straight lines, b) sound can travel around corners, c) sound travels faster than light, d) light travels faster than sound.
44. The speed of sound in air at 32 °F is about a) 25000 miles per second, b) 186000 miles per second, c) 1090 feet per second, d) 1000 feet per minute.

45. The speed of sound in air at 0 °C is about a) 2500 meters per second, b) 186000 feet per second, c) 330 meters per second, d) 1000 meters per minute.
46. With an increase in air temperature, the speed of sound through air a) remains the same, b) first increases then decreases, c) decreases, d) increases.
47. At the same temperature, sound travels fastest through a) air, b) steel, c) water, d) wood.
48. The number of vibrations per second of a sound is known as its a) tone, b) pitch, c) frequency, d) loudness.

H. Magnetism, Electromagnetic Induction, and Generator

1. a. What is meant by a magnetic substance?
   b. Name three common magnetic substances.
2. a. What forces do magnetic poles exert upon each other?
   b. What two factors determine how great the force between two magnetic poles will be?
3. What is meant by magnetic induction?
4. Name three methods of producing magnetic induction:
   a. _____
   b. _____
   c. _____
5. a. What is meant by the field of a magnet?
   b. State one method of showing a magnetic field around a bar magnet.
6. State four properties of the lines of force of a magnetic field:
   a. _____
   b. _____
   c. _____
   d. _____
7. Using eight lines of force in each drawing, show the appearance of the magnetic field in the following cases:
   a. The field around a bar magnet.
   b. The field between a north pole and a nearby south pole.
   c. The field between two south poles.
8. A magnet whose magnetism is caused by a current in a wire is a(n) _____.
9. A device that changes electrical energy into mechanical energy is a _____.
10. To increase the strength of an electromagnet, a) increase the current in the coil, b) add an iron center to the coil, c) increase the number of loops of wire in the coil, d) all of the above.
11. If a magnet is brought near a magnet suspended on a string, the a) north poles attract each other, b) north poles attract the south poles, c) south poles attract each other, d) north poles repel the south poles.
12. Which one of the following substances will not be attracted by a magnet? a) brass, b) iron, c) cobalt, d) steel.
13. A bar magnet usually has a) one pole, b) two poles, c) three poles, d) four poles.
14. If the south pole of a bar magnet is brought near the north pole of another bar magnet,

the magnets will a) repel each other, b) lose their magnetism, c) attract each other, d) produce an electric spark.

15. Magnetic lines of force can be mapped with a magnet and a) aluminum filings, b) iron filings, c) sand, d) shredded paper.
16. An iron core will a) increase, b) decrease, c) not affect, the strength of the magnetic field of a coil of wire carrying a current.
17. A device that does not contain an electromagnet is the a) electric doorbell, b) electric motor, c) electric stove, d) telephone receiver.

Match: Place the number from column I in the appropriate space. Use a number only once.

I		II
18. alternating current	_____	A. A small region in a piece of iron where atomic magnetic fields line up in the same direction.
19. armature (loop)		
20. commutator		
21. electromagnetic induction	_____	B. The rotation coil in an electric motor.
22. generator	_____	C. A device that converts mechanical energy into electrical energy.
23. magnetic domain		
24. magnetic field	_____	D. The production of current in a wire that is moving across a magnetic field.
	_____	E. A device that reverses the direction of current in a motor.
	_____	F. The space surrounding a magnet that can be affected by it.

I. Atomic State and Chemistry

1. Matter is anything that has
   a. _____ and
   b. _____.
2. Matter with no definite shape or volume is a _____.
3. The amount of matter in a body is called its _____.
4. At extremely high temperatures, matter is usually in the _____ phase.
5. A catalyst always _____ the speed of a chemical reaction.
6. When atoms unite to form molecules, _____ are transferred or shared.
7. An uncharged particle in the nucleus of an atom is the _____.
8. In molecules, atoms are held together by chemical _____.
9. When atoms gain or lose electrons, the atoms become _____.
10. Two atoms of the same element joined by a covalent bond form _____ molecules.
11. A water molecule is made of
    a. _____ atom(s) of hydrogen joined to
    b. _____ atom(s) of oxygen.
12. An ion is an atom in which the number of _____ does not equal the number of protons.
13. A chemical equation indicates the reactants and _____ in a chemical reaction.

14. The law that states that mass does not change in a chemical reaction is called the _____.

15. In the compound CO_2, the number 2 below the letter O stands for the number of oxygen atoms in each _____.

16. In the equation $2Hg + O_2 \rightarrow HgO$, the number that must be placed in front of HgO to balance the equation is _____.

17. A solution in which the solute comes out of solution is _____.

18. A solution is saturated when _____.

19. As long as more solute can dissolve, a solution is _____.

20. The two parts of a solution are
    a. the _____ and
    b. the _____.

21. Three ways of increasing the rate of dissolving a solute are:
    a. _____
    b. _____
    c. _____.

22. Suspensions and solutions differ because, upon standing, particles mixed in a suspension gradually _____.

23. Water is described as odorless, colorless, and has a density of 1 g/cm³. What kind of properties are these?

24. Burning and rusting are examples of _____ properties.

25. When you compress a spring or twist a rubber band, you are producing a _____ change.

26. A substance that cannot be broken down into other substances is a(n) _____.

27. When the elements H_2 and O_2 combine chemically, the _____ water can result.

28. When oil and water are mixed, they retain their own properties. This combination is called a(n) _____.

29. Two negatively charged particles will _____ each other.

30. The positively charged part of an atom is called the _____.

31. The negatively charged particles that move in a "cloud" around the nucleus are called _____.

32. Atoms can be identified by their number of _____.

33. The state of matter depends on the arrangement and rate of movement of very small particles called a) elements, b) compounds, c) mixtures, d) molecules.

34. The building blocks from which all elements are composed are known as a) atoms, b) molecules, c) gases, d) liquids.

35. Found in the nucleus of an atom are a) electrons and protons, b) electrons and neutrons, c) neutrons only, d) neutrons and protons.

36. Of the following, the one that is an element is a) water, b) hydrogen, c) carbon dioxide, d) salt.

37. A metal that is liquid at room temperature is a) copper, b) lead, c) mercury, d) zinc.

38. A compound results from the chemical union of a) an electron and a proton, b) two or more elements, c) a neutron and an atom, d) a neutron and a proton.

39. An example of a compound is a) nitrogen, b) oxygen, c) carbon dioxide, d) iodine.

40. The smallest part of a compound is a) an atom, b) a molecule, c) an electron, d) a proton.
41. An element that is naturally radioactive is a) radon, b) helium, c) magnesium, d) potassium.
42. When matter undergoes a change in size and appearance only, the change is called a) chemical, b) physical, c) radioactive, d) fission.
43. When matter is changed into new matter having different properties, the type of change is a) physical, b) chemical, c) electrical, d) atomic.
44. When an electron is removed from a neutral hydrogen atom, the remaining particle is a(n) a) proton, b) neutron, c) isotope.
45. The number of protons in the nucleus of an atom is the a) relative mass, b) atomic number, c) mass number.
46. Atoms of the same element with differing masses are called a) isotopes, b) neutrons, c) standard atoms.
47. The atomic particles with no charge and a mass equal to that of a proton is a(n) a) electron, b) neutron, c) isotope.
48. Aluminum has an atomic number of 13 and a mass number of 27. The number of neutrons in aluminum is a) 40, b) 27, c) 14, d) 13.
49. The maximum number of electrons in the outermost energy level of an atom is a) 2, b) 4, c) 6, d) 8.
50. An atom has the same number of electrons as its a) atomic number, b) atomic mass, c) mass number, d) isotopes.
51. Which of the following is not a solution? a) air, b) tea, c) soil and water, d) sugar and water.
52. Which of the following is a property of colloids? a) the particles settle out, b) the particles are large enough for you to see, c) the particles scatter light.
53. Oil and water will stay mixed together if you a) shake them, b) stir them, c) mix them with soap, d) strain them.
54. Fog is an example of a a) solution, b) solute, c) colloid.
55. All of the following are physical properties except a) density, b) mass, c) burning in air, d) color and shape.
56. Which of the following involves a chemical change? a) water freezing and becoming ice, b) baking powder making a cake rise, c) cutting a cake, d) using the brakes to stop a bicycle.
57. The nucleus of an atom contains a) only neutrons, b) only protons, c) protons and neutrons, d) electrons.
58. Which of the following is a unit of mass? a) centimeter, b) grams per cubic centimeter, c) cubic centimeter, d) gram.
59. The formula for water is a) H_2O, b) CO_2, c) H_2CO_3, d) HO_2.
60. Carbon, oxygen, and hydrogen are examples of a) mixtures, b) elements, c) compounds, d) chemical combinations.
61. When two or more elements are combined in a chemical reaction, they form a) a mixture, b) an element, c) a compound, d) an atom.
62. If a small stone had a volume of 15 cm³ and a mass of 60 g, its density would be a) 75 g/cm³, b) 0.25 cm³/g, c) 0.25 g/cm³, d) 4 g/cm³.

63. Which one of the following substances can be broken down into other substances?
a) oxygen, b) water, c) carbon, d) chlorine.

64. Draw a model of an electrically neutral atom that has 5 protons.

Match: Place the number from column I in the appropriate space. Use a number only once.

I		II
65. atom	_____	A. A property that can be observed without changing the identity of a substance.
66. chemical change		
67. chemical	_____	B. Two or more substances combined physically.
68. compound	_____	C. An uncharged particle in the nucleus.
69. electron	_____	D. The dense, central part of an atom.
70. mixture	_____	E. A change of a substance into one or more new substances.
71. molecule		
72. neutron	_____	F. Two or more elements combined in a chemical reaction.
73. nucleus		
74. physical change	_____	G. A negatively charged particle traveling around the nucleus.
75. physical property		
76. proton	_____	H. The smallest particle of any substance that can exist independently.
	_____	I. Particle in nucleus having a positive charge.
	_____	J. The smallest particle of an element that has the properties of that element.

APPENDIX A

SUGGESTED TOPICS FOR TERM PAPERS

Reports can be made with an emphasis on consumerism or on science. Most products have been discussed in consumer magazines and the student should find additional sources of information and/or do some original investigation.

1. Liquid Makeup
2. Contact Lenses
3. Consumer Fraud
4. Soft Drinks
5. Nutrition and Advertising
6. Health Spas
7. Caffeine
8. Photography
9. Consumer Credit and the Law
10. Medicine and Nutrition
11. Health and Beauty Aids—Private Labels vs National Labels
12. Microwave Ovens
13. Eyeglasses
14. Jewelry—Buying, Evaluating, Insuring
15. Baby Food
16. Premenstrual Syndrome and Nutrition
17. Breakfast Cereals
18. Electronic Funds Transfer
19. VCRs
20. Buying a Used Car/Buying a New Car
21. Fad Diets vs Good Nutrition
22. Supermarket Savings
23. The Fabrics We Wear
24. The Use of Lasers in Medicine
25. Air Pollution
26. Airline Fares
27. Anabolic Steroids and Their Use in Sports
28. Oil Refining
29. Rating Mineral Waters
30. Cameras
31. Drug Abuse
32. Fragrances
33. Vegetarianism
34. Insomnia and Sleeping Pills
35. Fluorides in Water
36. Junk Foods
37. Iodine and its Effect on the Body
38. Sodium Epidemic
39. Diet Pills
40. Nuclear Power

APPENDIX B

FILM LIST

Many utility companies, manufacturing organizations, and industries have speaker bureaus. These groups will arrange a program for presentation or lend films to a student group. Some films that are available are listed below.

1. The Metric Film
2. Food Labeling — Understanding What You Eat
3. Fad Diet Circus
4. Cholesterol — Eat Your Heart Out
5. Understanding Matter and Energy
6. Light — On the Subject of Light
7. Coal and Water
8. Look Before You Eat
9. Food — Surviving the Chemical Feast
10. Consumerism in Medicine — Whose Body Is It Anyway
11. Mineral Elements and Vitamins
12. Nutrition — Minerals and Vitamins
13. How Dangerous Is High Blood Pressure
14. Radiation and Public Health
15. X-rays — How Safe
16. Fuels — Their Nature and Use
17. Pure Water and Public Health
18. Soap
19. Foods and Drugs
20. Drugs, Drinking, and Driving
21. The Consumer's Role
22. The Water Series
23. Radiant Energy: More Than Meets the Eye
24. The Energy Picture
25. Clean Water, What's In It For You
26. Bill Smith's New Chemical

APPENDIX C

SOME TOPICS FOR FUTURE EDITIONS

Please forward any suggestions for material to be considered for future editions to the publisher. The following topics are under consideration for future editions.

1. Eyeglasses — A Study of Light and Lenses
2. Art and Photography — A Study of Color and Light
3. The Automobile — Gears, The Internal Combustion Engine, and Energy Use of Gasoline vs. Other Fuels
4. Television and Radio — A Survey of Electronics
5. Computers — Some Basics
6. First Aid, Home Remedies, Hospital Stays
7. Liquid Dishwashing Soap Evalulation

APPENDIX D

NUTRIENT SOURCES

What Foods Supply Protein?

Food (ready-to-eat)	% U.S. RDA per serving
35% U.S. RDA or more	
Beef, roast (3 oz. 85 g)	60
Ham, baked (3 oz. 85 g)	60
Tuna, canned in oil (3 oz. 85 g)	60
Beef patty (3 oz. 85 g)	50
Beef liver (3 oz. 85 g)	50
Chicken, broiled (3 oz. 85 g)	45
Cheese, cottage ($1/2$ c. 113 g)	35
15% U.S. RDA or more	
Milk, lowfat 2%+ (1 c. 246 g)	25
Milk, skim (1 c. 245 g)	20
Milk, whole (1 c. 244 g)	20
Beans, lima, dry ($1/2$ c. 95 g)	17[1]
Peanut butter (2 tbsp. 32 g)	16
Cheese, cheddar (1 oz. 28 g)	15
Peas, blackeye, dry ($1/2$ c. 125 g)	15
Egg (large, 50 g)	15
Frankfurter (2 oz. 56 g)	15
2% U.S. RDA or more	
Bagel (3" 55 g)	10
Cornbread, enriched, Southern-style ($2 1/2$" x $2 1/2$" x $1 1/2$" 83 g)	10
Peas, green ($1/2$ c. 80 g)	7[1]
Potato, baked (1 long, 202 g)	6
Noodles, egg, enriched ($1/2$ c. 80 g)	5
Oatmeal ($1/2$ c. 120 g)	4
Bread, white or whole wheat, enriched (1 sl. 25–28 g)	4
Rice, white, enriched ($1/2$ c. 102 g)	3
Cornflakes ($3/4$ c. 19 g)	2
Tortilla, corn (6", 30 g)	2
Grits, enriched ($1/2$ c. 122 g)	2

What Foods Supply Carbohydrate?

Sugars and Starches
(No U.S. RDA for carbohydrate)

	Percentage by Weight
Sugar, granulated	99.5
Candy, hard	97.2
Sugar, brown	96.4
Rice, puffed	89.5
Cornflakes	85.3
Honey	82.5
Raisins	77.4
Popcorn	76.7
Flour	76.1
Fudge, chocolate	75.0
Cookie, sugar	68.0

What Foods Supply Carbohydrate? (Cont'd)

Sugars and Starches
(No U.S. RDA for carbohydrate)

	Percentage by Weight
Syrup, maple	65.0
Cake, angel food	60.2
Bread, white, enriched	50.5
Bread, whole wheat	47.7
Pie, apple	38.0
Rice, cooked	24.2
Banana	22.2
Potato, baked	21.1

Food Sources of Cholesterol

	Cholesterol (mg)
Meat, Fish, Poultry, Eggs	
(Average serving after cooking)	
Liver (3 oz. 85 g)	372
Egg (1 large, 50 g)	274
Shrimp, canned, solids (3 oz. 85 g)	128
Veal (3 oz. 85 g)	86
Lamb (3 oz. 85 g)	83
Beef (3 oz. 85 g)	80
Pork (3 oz. 85 g)	76
Lobster (3 oz. 85 g)	72
Chicken, breast ($1/2$ breast, 80 g)	63
Clams, canned, solids ($1/2$ c. 80 g)	50
Chicken, drumstick (1, 43 g)	39
Oysters, canned (3 oz. 85 g)	38
Fish, fillet (3 oz. 85 g)	34–75
Desserts	
(Average serving)	
Ladyfingers (4, 44 g)	157
Custard ($1/2$ c. 133 g)	139
Pie, apple ($1/8$ of 9" pie, 144 g)	120
Pie, custard ($1/8$ of 9" pie, 114 g)	120
Pie, lemon meringue ($1/8$ of 9" pie, 105 g)	98
Pudding, raisin bread ($1/2$ c. 133 g)	85
Pie, peach ($1/8$ of 9" pie, 114 g)	70
Pie, pumpkin ($1/8$ of 9" pie, 144 g)	70
Cake, yellow, from mix ($1/16$ of 9" cake, 75 g)	36
Cake, chocolate, from mix ($1/16$ of 9" cake, 69 g)	33
Brownie, homemade (1, 20 g)	17
Pudding, chocolate, made from mix ($1/2$ c. 130 g)	15
Pudding, raisin rice ($1/2$ c. 133 g)	15
Dairy Foods	
(Average serving)	
Milk, whole (1 c. 244 g)	33

APPENDIX D (Continued)

NUTRIENT SOURCES

Food Sources of Cholesterol (Cont'd)

	Cholesterol (mg)
Ice cream (1/2 c. 1/4 pt. 67 g)	29 1/2
Yogurt, plain or vanilla (1 c. 227 g)	29
Cheese, American process (1 oz. 28 g)	27
Cheese, Swiss (1 oz. 28 g)	26
Cream, whipping, heavy (1 tbsp. 15 g)	21
Milk, lowfat, 2% (1 c. 246 g)	18
Cheese, cream (1 tbsp. 14 g)	16
Butter (1 pat. 1 tsp. 5 g)	11
Buttermilk (1 c. 245 g)	9
Half-and-Half (1 tbsp. 15 g)	6
Cream, sour (1 tbsp. 12 g)	5
Cheese, cottage (1/2 c. 100 g)	5–15 1/2
Milk, skim (1 c. 245 g)	4

Protein Teams that Work Together

Team Animal Proteins—with Grains:

beef taco
milk breakfast cereal
cheese pizza
cheese sandwich
meat/Oriental vegetables rice
milk/rice pudding
tuna/rice casserole
cheese/macaroni

with Legumes:

cheese/bean stew
chili con carne with beans
meat/soy analogue
ham/split pea soup

with Seeds:

meat/Oriental vegetables/nuts

Team Plant Proteins—Legumes with Grains:

baked beans/brown bread
blackeye peas/rice
beans tortilla or cornbread
beans/barley soup
dahl (pureed lentil sauce)/East Indian rice
lima bean/corn (succotash)
beans/pasta
peanut butter sandwich
refried beans/rice
chickpea puree/Syrian bread
soy analogue/pasta
peas/rice Viennese

Legumes with Seeds:

green beans/almonds
peanuts/mixed nuts

Food with High-Nutrient Density

Milk, whole, fortified with vitamin D
1 cup (237 ml)
Percentage Contribution to Recommended Dietary
Allowances for Adult Women Aged 23–50

	0%	10%	20%	30%	40%
Calories	7.5%				
Protein		17%			
Vitamin A	7.7%				
Vitamin C	5%				
Thiamin	9%				
Riboflavin				33%	
Niacin	1.6%				
Calcium					36%
Iron	0.7%				

Food with Low-Nutrient Density

Soft Drink, cola
1 cup (237 ml)
Percentage Contribution to Recommended Dietary
Allowances for Adult Women Aged 23–50

	0%	10%	20%	30%	40%
Calories	4.8%				
Protein					
Vitamin A					
Vitamin C					
Thiamin					
Riboflavin					
Niacin					
Calcium					
Iron					

APPENDIX E

CALORIES PER SERVING

FOOD	CALORIES
Almonds, 12, shelled	100
Almonds, chocolate, 5	100
Almonds, chopped, 1 cup	550
Apple, 1 large	100
Apple, baked, 2 tablespoons sugar	200
Apple, baked, 1 tablespoon sugar	150
Apple brown Betty, 1/2 cup	250
Apple pie, 1/6 of 9-inch pie	300–350
Applesauce, 3/8 cup	100
Apple tapioca, 1/2 cup	205
Apricots, cooked, 3 large halves with 2 tablespoons juice	100
Apricots, dried, 9 halves	100
Apricots, fresh, 5	100
Artichoke, French, 1	158
Asparagus, 10 large stalks, no butter	50
Asparagus, 10 large stalks with butter	150
Asparagus, 10 large stalks with hollandaise sauce	240
Asparagus soup, cream of, 1/2 cup	100
Avocado, 1/2 fruit	120–300
Bacon, broiled, 4 small slices	100
Bacon fat, 1 tablespoon	100
Baking powder biscuits, 4 small biscuits	200
Bananas, average size	100
Beans, Lima, dried, 1/2 cup uncooked	273
Beans, Lima, fresh or canned, 1/2 cup	100
Beans, navy, canned baked, 1/3 cup	100
Beans, navy, dried, 1/2 cup uncooked	342
Beans, soy, dried, 3 1/2 tablespoons	200
Beans, string, 1/2 cup	22
Beef, corned, boiled, lean, 3 ounces	100
Beef, dried, 4 thin slices	100
Beef, Hamburg steak, broiled, cake 2 1/2 inches diameter, 7/8 inch	100
Beef loaf, slice, 4x6x1/8 inches	100
Beef rib, roasted, lean, slice, 5 x 2 1/2 x 1/4 inches	100
Beef, round steak, lean, 4-ounces	170–220
Beef steak, lean, broiled, slice 2 x 1 1/2 x 3/4 inches	100
Beef stew, 1 cup	250
Beet greens, 1/2 cup	22
Beets, 2, 2 inches in diameter	50
Blackberries, fresh, 25	50
Blackberries, cooked, with sugar, 1/2 cup	200
Blueberries, fresh, 1/2 cup	50
Bluefish, broiled, small serving	100
Bologna sausage, slice 2 1/8 inches diameter, 1/2 inch thick	100
Bouillon, 1 cup	25
Brazil nuts, 2	100
Bread, Boston brown, slice 1/2 inch thick	52
Bread, rye, slice 1/2 inch thick	70
Bread, white, slice 1/2 inch thick	50

FOOD	CALORIES
Bread, 50% whole-wheat, slice 1/2 inch thick	75
Bread crumbs, dry, 1 cup	400
Bread crumbs, soft, 1 cup	150
Broccoli, 1 cup	45
Brussels sprouts, 6	50
Butter, 1 tablespoon	100
Buttermilk, 1 cup	84
Cabbage, cooked, 1/2 cup	32
Cabbage, raw, shredded, 1/2 cup	13
Cake, 2 egg, 1 3/4-inch cube	100
Cantaloupe, 1/2	50
Carrots, cooked, 1/2 cup	30–40
Cauliflower, 1/2 cup	25
Celery, 2/3 cup	15
Celery soup, cream of, per cup	200
Chard, cooked, 1/2 cup	36
Cheese, American, grated, 1 tablespoon	33
Cheese, 1-inch cube	70
Cheese, cottage, 5 tablespoons	100
Cheese, full cream, 2 x 1 x 3/8 inch piece	100
Cheese soufflé, 1/2 cup	100
Cherries, 10 large	50
Chestnuts, 7 average	100
Chicken, roast, slice 4 x 2 1/2 x 1/4 inch slice	100
Chicken salad, 1/2 cup	200
Chocolate, bitter, 1 ounce	173
Chocolate, bitter, 1 tablespoon grated	29
Chocolate cake, 1 small piece	200
Chocolate cream candy, average piece	80–100
Chocolate cream mint, 1 1/2-inch diameter	100
Chocolate drop cookie, 2-inch diameter	60
Chocolate éclair	260–400
Chocolate fudge, 1-inch cube	80–90
Chocolate malted milk, large glass	465
Chocolate, milk, sweet, 2 1/2 x 1 x 1/8 inch slice	100
Chocolate nut caramel, 1 cube	100
Clams, 6	50
Cocoa, powder, 1 tablespoon	40
Coconut, shredded, 1 tablespoon	34
Codfish, creamed, 1/2 cup	100
Cod-liver oil, 1 tablespoon	100
Coleslaw, 1/2 cup	50
Collards, cooked, 1/2 cup	50
Consommé, 1 cup	25
Corn bread, average piece	120
Corn, canned, 1/3 cup	100
Corn flakes, 3/4 cup	100
Corn, fresh, on cob, 1 ear, 6 inches long	50
Corn meal, cooked, 1/3 cup	50
Corn meal, uncooked, 1/2 cup	252
Corn syrup, 1 tablespoon	75
Crackers, graham, 2 1/2	100

APPENDIX E (Continued)

CALORIES PER SERVING

FOOD	CALORIES
Crackers, soda, 2	50
Cream, heavy, 40%, 1 tablespoon	60
Cream, whipped, 1 tablespoon	35
Cream, thin, 18%, 1 tablespoon	30
Cucumber, 10 inches long	50
Cup custard, 1/2 cup	100
Currants, dry, 1/4 cup	126
Currants, fresh, 1/2 cup	34
Dates, 3 or 4	100
Doughnut	200
Duck, 4 ounces	234
Egg	70–75
Eggs, scrambled, 1/4 cup	100
Eggnog, 1 cup	200
Farina, cooked, 3/4 cup	100
Figs, dried, 1 1/2	100
Filberts, 8 to 10	100
Frankfurters, 1	100
French dressing, 1 tablespoon	67
Fruitcake, 1 (7/8 x 1 7/8 x 3/8 inch) slice	100
Ginger ale, 1 cup	72
Grapefruit, 1/2, average size	100
Grapefruit, 1/2, average size with 2 teaspoons sugar	134
Grapefruit juice, 1 cup	100
Grape juice, 1/2 cup	100
Grapes, large bunch	100
Grapes, Malaga, 20 to 25	100
Griddlecake, 1 (4 to 5 inch) cake	100
Halibut, cooked, 3 ounces	85–110
Ham, 1/4 pound	270–400
Hard sauce, 1 tablespoon	100
Hickory nuts, chopped, 1/2 cup	607
Hominy grits, cooked, 1/2 cup	62
Honey, 1 teaspoon	25
Ice cream, commercial, vanilla, 3/8 cup	100
Kale, cooked without fat, 1/2 cup	20
Kohlrabi, creamed, 1/2 cup	100
Lamb chops, broiled, 1 (2 inches thick)	100
Lamb, roast leg, 4 ounces	225
Leeks, 3 (5 inches long)	45
Lemon, 1	30
Lemon juice, 1 tablespoon	5
Lemon meringue pie, 1/6 of 9-inch pie	450
Lettuce, 1/4 head	12
Lettuce, 1/4 head with salad dressing	100–150
Liver, 1/4 pound	145–220
Macaroni, cooked, 1/2 cup	67
Macaroni with cheese, 2/3 cup	200
Macaroons, each	50
Mackerel, 1/4 pound	85–100
Maple syrup, 1 tablespoon	67
Marshmallows, 5	100
Mayonnaise, 1 tablespoon	100

FOOD	CALORIES
Milk, irradiated evaporated, 1/2 cup undiluted	175
Milk, skim, 1 cup	88
Milk, whole, 1 cup	170
Mince pie, 1/6 of 9-inch pie	450
Muffin, 1	125–150
Mutton, 1/4 pound	225–500
Napoleon, average size	453
Oats, rolled, cooked, 1/2 to 3/4 cup	100
Olives, each	15
Onions, cooked, 3 to 4, small	50–60
Orange, large	100
Orange juice, 1 cup	133
Oysters, according to size, each	6–16
Parsnips, 1 (7 inches long)	100
Peaches, canned, 1 large half with 1 1/2 tablespoons juice	50
Peaches, fresh, 1 small	35
Peanuts, 1/4 pound, shelled	620
Peanut butter, 1 tablespoon	100
Pears, canned, 1 half with 1 tablespoon juice	34
Pears, fresh, 1 medium	50
Peas, dried, 1/4 pound	400
Peas, fresh, cooked, 3/8 cup	50
Pea soup, cream of, 1 cup	150
Pecans, 6 nuts, shelled	100
Peppers green average size	20
Pineapple, canned, 1 slice, 3 tablespoons juice	100
Pineapple, canned, shredded, 1/4 cup	100
Pineapple, fresh, 1 slice, 3/4 inch thick	50
Pineapple juice, 1 cup	150
Plums, 3 or 4 large, fresh	100
Popcorn, popped, 1 1/2 cups	100
Popover, 1	100
Pork 1/4 pound	300–620
Pork chops, broiled, 1, fat not included	200
Pork sausage, cooked, 2 sausages 3 inches long, 1/2 inch in diameter	100
Potato, 1, average size, white	100
Potato chips, 8 to 10	100
Potato salad, 1/2 cup	210
Prunes, average size, 1	25
Pumpkin, cooked, 1/2 cup	35
Pumpkin pie, 1/6 of 9-inch pie	225
Radish, average size, 1	3
Raisin pie, 1/6 of 9-inch pie	450
Raisins, 1/4 cup	100
Raspberries, fresh, 1/2 cup	45
Rhubarb, stewed and sweetened, 1/2 cup	100
Rhubarb pie, 1/6 of 9-inch pie	280
Rice, steamed, 1/2 cup	70
Rice pudding, plain, 1/2	200
Rice pudding, with egg, 1/2 cup	133
Salmon, canned, 1/2 cup	100
Sardines, canned, 2 (3 inches long)	50

APPENDIX E (Continued)

CALORIES PER SERVING

FOOD	CALORIES
Sauerkraut, $^3/_4$ cup	25
Shrimp, without oil, each	5
Soda, chocolate	400
Spinach, $^3/_4$ cup	25
Spinach soup, cream of, 1 cup	150
Spongecake, hot water, 2 x $2^3/_4$ x $^7/_8$ inches	100
Squash, Hubbard, cooked, $^1/_2$ cup	50
Squash pie, $^1/_6$ of 9-inch pie	225
Strawberries, fresh, $^1/_2$ cup	50
Strawberry shortcake	480
Strawberry shortcake with whipped cream	530
Sugar, 1 teaspoon	17
Sundae, chocolate	350
Sweetpotato, 1 medium	140
Tapioca cream, $^1/_2$ cup	100

FOOD	CALORIES
Tomatoes, canned, $^1/_2$ cup	25
Tomatoes, fresh, 1 large	50
Tomato juice, 1 cup	50
Tomato soup, cream of	225
Tuna, canned with oil, $^1/_4$ pound	315
Tuna, canned, without oil, $^1/_4$ pound	140
Turnips, $^1/_2$ cup	25
Turnip greens, $^1/_2$ cup	35
Veal, $^1/_4$ pound	115–200
Waffles, 1 (6 inches in diameter)	250
Walnuts, English, 16 halves	100
Watercress, $^1/_2$ bunch	10
Watermelon, $^3/_4$-inch slice, 6 inches in diameter	100
Wheat breakfast food, dry, 1 ounce	100

INDEX